TEN LESSONS BANKERS NEVER LEARN

How Banks Operate and Why Bankers Screw Up

COURTNEY DUFRIES

iUniverse, Inc.
Bloomington

Ten Lessons Bankers Never Learn
How Banks Operate and Why Bankers Screw Up

iUniverse books may be ordered through booksellers or by contacting:

iUniverse
1663 Liberty Drive
Bloomington, IN 47403
www.iuniverse.com
1-800-Authors (1-800-288-4677)

ISBN: 978-1-4620-3324-9 (sc)
ISBN: 978-1-4620-3325-6 (hc)
ISBN: 978-1-4620-3326-3 (e)

Library of Congress Control Number: 2011912045

Printed in the United States of America

iUniverse rev. date: 09/15/2011

To Cynthia and Ron,
and to the many friends who joined me on
this extraordinary adventure.

Warning

Not all reading materials are suitable for everyone, so please consult your physician before beginning this or any other book. You should always warm up for a few minutes before starting, and you should never read beyond the level at which you feel comfortable. If you are pregnant, please consult your doctor before reading. If at any time you feel you are reading beyond your current abilities or you should feel discomfort, please discontinue reading immediately and look at the pictures instead.

Table of Contents

Prologue

Part I – In the Beginning

Table of Contents

Part II – In the Middle

Table of Contents

Table of Contents

Prologue

Acknowledgments

I am extremely grateful for the generous support provided by a team of professionals, an incredible number of family and friends, and a few village idiots.

First on the list is my dear friend and wonderful editor Neva Corbin, without whom this book would have never made it to print, at least not in a readable form. Before I wrote the first word, I knew Neva would be the perfect editor. The book is a more enjoyable read because she insisted I make it less dense and more interesting, but with fewer cuss words. To the extent there are errors or omissions, you can't blame her. To the extent you enjoy it, you can credit her. Thank you, Neva, for getting my sense of humor.

Special thanks to Bill Wells and Maribeth Hnatyk for helping me prevent some factual errors from appearing in the book. Any errors in the book are entirely my own, and not theirs. Thanks also to my friend Kent Hudson, who has written a very good book on the Community Reinvestment Act and who provided excellent suggestions and a great perspective for me on this project.

Professionally, a sincere thanks to my friends at the Federal Reserve System, the Federal Home Loan Bank System, US Banking Alliance, and all the kind folks who allowed me to meet and learn from them over the past thirty years. Thanks also to the folks at SNL Financial for their invaluable research assistance, and to the kind people who allowed me to use their photographs and images.

It's impossible to list everybody, although it looks like I am trying. Here's a round of thanks and eternal gratitude to the people who encouraged me and offered great ideas and insight on this project. They are (in no particular order): Kevin Soden; Rob, Kurt, Toby, and Sam (my fellow Bonnaroo travelers); my brothers and sisters, who patiently listened as I tested material on them; Barrett and Catherine; Mike and Trisha; the Lonesome Traveler Band (Colorado); Richard; Sean; Sheri; Alli; Jack and Joey; Kim and Stephen; Johnny Griffin; Jessica; Hugh and Brittany; Paulie; and Anita and Jim (who inspire me all the time).

Finally, I'd like to acknowledge two women who amaze me with their courage and kindness: my incredible sister Maureen and my wonderful niece Kaitlin.

Introduction

My friend Barrett is a very talented banker and a fine gentleman.

I can't imagine why we're friends.

You can blame him for this book. When I hung up my traveling shoes as a bank consultant, he suggested I write a book on banking and even suggested the title *What Bankers Won't Tell You.* I told him he was crazy, and yet here I am, writing. After all, he was right when he argued that I was in a unique position. I had worked in the industry and traveled the country for over twenty-five years as a banker, a regulator, and a consultant. I had covered all aspects of banking: backroom operations, deposit products and pricing, all types of lending, bank ownership, bank boards of directors, and all points in-between. And the remarkable (some might even say radical) changes that occurred during this time make for a pretty exciting eyewitness story.

I didn't want to write an academic book. That's not me. My goal is to have a conversation with you about money, why banks even exist, how they operate, who regulates them, and why they fail. I want to give you a different perspective than you might get from others—an eyewitness account from the front line.

My viewpoint is not an unbiased viewpoint because I happen to think that commercial and thrift bankers are great. They have earned my respect and appreciation, and I enjoyed a long career working side by side with some of the finest people imaginable. They catch more grief than they deserve, but they usually manage to take it in stride, and most strive consistently to do the right thing. I'm proud to be a part of the industry and to associate myself with them.

Unfortunately, the good folks in this business are all too often overshadowed by bad bankers, those high-profile leaders or greedy executives who do foolish things. It's not right that so few people can damage the reputation of the several million people working hard in this industry to do the right thing for their families, their communities, and their shareholders. But it happens when people do things for the wrong reasons. In the recent debacle, some bankers were unethical, some immoral, some outright criminal. Some were driven by greed; others just made foolish mistakes that caused serious losses or outright failures. We can and must learn from what they did, and this book is designed to call them out for their stupid behavior. The point is always to learn from mistakes and find ways to prevent them from happening again.

I hope you will appreciate my sense of humor because banks are filled with people from all walks of life, and let's face it: people are pretty damn funny. Of course you have every right to expect factual and accurate information, and I have done extensive research to combine with practical experience. That's why you will see so many footnotes and a bibliography at the end. There's some great stuff out there about money and banking, and if you want it, this information can be helpful.

So the book is as factual as I can make it while keeping it entertaining. C'mon, man. If you want to cover every single nuance about banking you have to read twice as much material, and I'm bored to tears just thinking about it. So every chapter will have some entertaining stories, a few quips along the way, some food for thought, and a structure so that you can follow along.

After introducing readers to the ten lessons, we'll start with "In the Beginning" to cover the evolution of money. This journey begins from around 2000 BC through the 1600s. Then we'll go on to issues in the 1700s, including money problems in the Colonial States and during the American Revolutionary War. We'll continue with "wildcat banking," counterfeiting, the Civil War, greenbacks, gold and silver standards, and our national currency. Along the way we'll discover pirates, Dixie, the Irish, God, Patty Hearst, FDR, Flavor Flav, and drugs. I'm as surprised as you are.

"In the Middle" we'll discuss a lot of things bankers never told you, in part because they sometimes didn't know themselves. And who can blame them? Banking is such a specialized industry now. Consumer lending is very different from business lending, and deposit product design and pricing is an expertise all its own. More often than not, your banker may be very knowledgeable and talented in one area of the industry but much less so in another. In a sense, it's sort of like your own job. How much do we really know about other parts of our own companies: the areas or divisions where we don't work?

Banks are very diverse, and the term itself is very broad. "In the Middle," will explain the differences between commercial banks, investment banks, and savings banks. Unfortunately, we won't get to talk about credit unions and insurance companies. They are important too, but if they were included you'd be yelling, "Too much information!" Those important institutions will have to wait for another day.

What can't wait is a review of our confusing regulatory structure. Changing it is difficult, and although we hear a lot about changing it, I'd be really surprised if even the boldest proposals cause radical changes. Understanding the origin and culture of these institutions will help you understand why changing the structure is so difficult.

Ours is a uniquely American way of doing business. We have a wide variety of financial institutions competing with each other. Our regulators serve distinct roles, but many of these roles overlap. To make it even more unique, we have a variety of government-sponsored enterprises (GSEs) that are private companies with a government charter to serve a specific public purpose. This somewhat bizarre system includes companies whose names sound like your country cousins: Farmer Mac, Fannie Mae, Freddie Mac, and Ginnie Mae. These GSEs also include very large institutions such as the Federal Home Loan Bank System and the Farm Credit System. All provide some benefits, all pose huge risks, and all interact or compete with banks and thrifts in a way that you need to know. Two of them, Fannie and Freddie, screwed up so bad that they are now government-owned institutions. You'll read how they managed to become so big and so bad.

"In the End" will review the Panic of 2008 because there is simply no way to avoid talking about that big ol' elephant in the room. This book won't overanalyze the debacle and failures of our financial system—the meltdown that occurred with high-risk mortgage lending in particular. But every institution mentioned in this book suffered from the modern-day banking panic, and every one of them helped cause it. When you understand the institutions involved, you will better understand the dynamics of this debacle and be able to judge the domestic and international responses.

It's hard to know how much you know about banking and finance. Over the years, I have *never* been surprised to discover the gaps in our understanding of money and finance.

Money and banking shouldn't be a mystery, and it doesn't need to be overly complex. If some of what I present is simplistic, then good! I want to give you a lot of in-depth information in a simple way. If you think I'm "talking down" to you, please don't get ticked off. Just assume that I'm speaking to the person next to you who isn't as smart. You would be amazed at the lack of understanding *that person* has to overcome! This book is not written for intellectuals. It is written for Everyman.

Anytime you use a cut-to-the-chase approach you leave out some of the details that help you understand the issues; so sometimes I may drone on with too much information. Don't throw tomatoes at me if I include too many numbers, ratios, and dates. I'm trying to provide a good book, but I sure don't want to bore my friends like Britney, who was attending college in southern Maine. When I told her about this book she expressed some excitement about reading it but asked if I could cut out the "banker stuff" and just send the funny parts.

That's impossible, of course. Bankers aren't funny.

Chapter 1
The Lessons

I remember talking to my friend John, who was working in marketing for Popeye's Restaurants (delicious fast-food, Cajun-style chicken), when he lamented that all he does is "sell chicken." Well, we could have argued, as I did, that there was more to it than that: he worked in an industry that created jobs which fed families and supported our economy and tax base. It was good for everybody except maybe the chickens. Even I had to admit it was a stretch. In contrast, I think of the young Arkansas banker who, in response to my question, "Why do you enjoy banking?" responded without hesitation. "I make dreams come true." She went on to describe some of her customers and how she helped guide them through the process and lend them the money to accomplish their goals. I don't mean to sound sappy, and I mean no disrespect to people who work in marketing, but I think her job beats the hell out of selling chicken.

Banking is meaningful work. Besides, most of the people are pretty cool, and it pays reasonably well. This book is about lessons the bankers never learned, but the truth is, most bankers I have met know these lessons already. It's just that too many of the industry leaders forgot them or failed to act accordingly.

The lessons are good for everybody to know and appreciate. You could list the ten lessons in any order you want and, undoubtedly, you could add many more. Throughout the book, you will see these lessons italicized after an event or story to help illustrate the point. The lessons aren't listed every time though. That would be too distracting.

I hope that you will read a story and have that "Aha!" moment, when you recognize a lesson even though it isn't specifically listed. Great! That's part of the fun. You may even discover other lessons not covered in the book as you go along. Hey, when I began writing, I started with over twenty lessons! But fortunately for everybody, I have whittled it down to these ten. I've also included some personal stories in this chapter to help introduce these lessons.

1. **We got this way for a reason.**
2. **Good government is necessary.**

3. **Don't sleep with each other.**
4. **Greed has a price.**
5. **Accounting is not a game.**
6. **Bigger is not always better.**
7. **It's almost always bad loans.**
8. **We should have seen it coming.**
9. **People matter.**
10. **It's easy to misplace blame.**

Lesson Number 1: We got this way for a reason.

It was January 13, 1982, when one of my coworkers at the Federal Reserve Bank in Atlanta, Arland Williams, boarded a Boeing 737 after leaving a meeting at the Federal Reserve Board in Washington DC. It was a miserable day to fly. The temperature was a freezing 24 degrees with unexpected ice and snow, causing long delays at the airport.

The runway had been closed for over an hour, and now the passengers and five crew members had to wait another forty-nine minutes on the taxiway before takeoff. When the plane was cleared to depart, it struggled to get airborne, exceeding the normal takeoff point by about two thousand feet. The pilots had limited experience flying in inclement weather and made several unforgiving mistakes, most notably not properly deicing the plane. Thirty seconds after takeoff the plane crashed into the barrier wall of the crowded Fourteenth Street Bridge, hitting six cars and a truck before breaking into four large pieces and plunging into the ice-covered Potomac River. Seventy airline passengers, four crew members, and four car passengers died that day.

Arland was *not* like the other passengers boarding Air Florida Flight 90. He was one of only six stunned people who escaped from the crash, holding onto pieces of the floating wreckage in the frigid 34-degree water topped with so much ice it prevented rescue boats from arriving.

Twenty-one agonizing minutes after the crash, a US Park Police helicopter arrived and, although it wasn't equipped for emergency water rescues, aggressively lowered ropes with loops and life rings to rescue five of the six survivors, who were dragged across the icy water to shore. When they dropped a lifeline to Arland, he passed it to a flight attendant, who was then rescued. When they returned with two lifelines, he passed his line again to another passenger, who would then survive. When they returned a third and final time to pull Arland from the water, it was too late. The plane's tail section had dragged forty-six-year-old Arland Williams down as it sank. Twice he passed on a chance to save his own life, choosing to save others instead. He died a true hero.

He was posthumously awarded the US Coast Guard's Gold Lifesaving Medal and has an elementary school named after him. That Fourteenth Street Bridge is now named in his honor, and he has memorials and tributes at both the Citadel (his alma mater) and the Federal Reserve Bank. They even made a movie about it.

After the crash, a lot of airline safety measures had to change, and they did. The harnesses used to retrieve victims from accidents were changed. Pilots got better training. Air traffic controllers got better training. Airport safety measures were changed. Most people who flew after that crash never knew how much things had changed, or why.

These changes were implemented in response to a crisis, and of course the changes were imperfect but good. And the same holds true for banking. As we uncover the history of money and banking in the next several chapters, it will become clear that the system we have today was not developed with an evil intent, but was done so in response to a crisis or to specific problems. The changes were imperfect but good. And unless we find a better way to solve those problems, going back would be worse. *We got this way for a reason.*

Lesson Number 2: Good government is necessary.

Over the past few years, the banking industry has a gotten a well-deserved bloody nose. Many bankers put the country on the verge of a complete financial collapse. People blame everything under the sun for the debacle, often pointing their fingers at anything that doesn't meet their ideological views. Far too many people believe the country is run by Wall Street and our government is in bed with them, throwing bailout money to their cronies. For many taxpayers, their jobs were at risk, their homes were at risk, and they believe the system was designed to let these crooks get away with murder. They don't trust the regulators, and they don't trust the government.

They have a right to expect more from our government and industry. After all, while it is true that government intervention has side effects, it is also true that intervention can be worth it and that some government programs actually pay their own way (and make profits too). It's another important lesson never learned: *good government is necessary*. Good government is ... well, good!

Several years ago I remember hearing Bill Estes, senior vice president of the Atlanta Federal Reserve Bank, respond to the question from one of his board members about what concerned him as head of the Division of Supervision and Regulation. His response as the head honcho over the Atlanta Fed's bank examiners (one of his many duties) was right on the mark: "What keeps me up at night," he said, "is figuring out how to supervise a $1 trillion institution."

You're darn straight that would keep you up at night. But that's what regulators do, and in spite of all the criticism, until now they've done it pretty well. Bank supervision and regulation is far from perfect. In fact, it is flawed. But although it is an imperfect system, and a complex system, and an expensive system, it's also true that it is absolutely necessary too. Outside of anarchists, everybody agrees that at least some government oversight is important. While the issue of how much oversight is debated, one thing remains certain: *good government is necessary.*

Lesson Number 3: Don't sleep with each other.

It is true that somewhere along the line, our regulators got too cozy with the industry and allowed it to take on high-risk activities. We operated under the notion that the industry could self-regulate, and we argued that less regulation was better for everybody. That argument has some merit, but there should have been limits, and our regulators should have known better. Just the perception that the regulators are sleeping with the regulated will force our elected officials to act. It should.

One of the more painful maladies to affect our nation's financial health was the savings and loan (S&L) debacle in the 1980s. Debacle is the perfect word. According to the *Cambridge International Dictionary of English,* it means "a complete failure, especially because of bad planning and organization." And a complete failure it was, as in a taxpayer bailout to the tune of $153 billion spread out over several years. The industry itself had to cover almost 20 percent of the losses caused by the weaker and failed institutions.[1]

There are plenty of good books out there covering the S&L debacle, and I can't do it justice here. The short version of a long story is that the industry was allowed to enter new markets where they had limited or no experience. They operated with too little capital (investors' money). They were making long-term loans using short-term deposits. They were investing in higher risk products. Too many had weak management teams. Some were paying excessive salaries to their executive officers. Some were making outrageous purchases of art, airplanes, boats, buildings, and homes. They were regulated terribly. Many people thought they were in bed with their federal thrift regulator, the Federal Home Loan Bank Board.

People were not happy about the nation's thrifts, the government bailout, and, in some cases, restrictions on withdrawing their deposits. The public wanted action, and their elected officials responded.

The Federal Home Loan Bank Board was stripped of its responsibility for regulating thrifts and was put out of business. A new agency, the Office of Thrift Supervision (OTS), was created to supervise the thrift industry. And a new government-owned company, the Resolution Trust Corporation (RTC), was formed to sell the assets of failed thrifts. So it was left to the OTS and RTC to clean up the mess. It wasn't easy, but they were successful.

Sadly, the OTS later fell into the same trap as the Federal Home Loan Bank Board. They failed to learn. They began sleeping with the thrifts they were charged with supervising. Chapter 6 covers how they got too close to the industry, again. They loosened regulations, reduced examination staff, allowed higher risk products, and promoted themselves as a more tolerant, less restrictive regulator. The result was large-scale, expensive thrift failures, the abolition of new federal thrift charters, and the elimination of the OTS as a regulator.

The Federal Home Loan Bank Board and the OTS are two good examples of this important lesson. Sadly, throughout the book you will encounter even more stories like these. It's another lesson never learned. *Don't sleep with each other.*

Lesson Number 4: Greed has a price.

Bankers have reason to be concerned about proposed statutory and regulatory changes to their business. They need to pay attention. Some voters still want revenge—a lot of revenge—and some of our elected officials are anxious to give them what they want. People have been angry following the deep recession that officially began in December 2007. People want heads to roll. Frankly, we all do. There should be a price to pay for causing financial harm to others. The question is, what price?

My friend George is a great guy and an honest capitalist. In a funny conversation over cocktails with friends, somebody asked him if there was anything he wouldn't do for a million dollars, after tax, and assuming nobody was harmed. After all, a lot of people would work most of their life for that kind of money, but if he had a chance to earn it for a few hours of work and without causing any harm, is there anything he wouldn't do?

Would he, for example, cheat on his wife? At that point his wife interjected, "For a million dollars, he better!" Then it got even funnier. Assuming the other party was willing, would he sleep with Hillary Clinton? Yes. Rosie O'Donnell? Unlikely to happen, but yes again. How about a man? Probably. What if it was actor and comedian Danny DeVito?

It was at this point in the conversation that he decided a million dollars might not be enough. We call it the **DeVito Line.** *Where is that line in the sand where the money you make isn't worth the actions you take?*

Cynics would say that executives who engaged in high-risk, unethical, or even fraudulent investment banking activities would have to lose a helluva lot of money and serve a long prison sentence before crossing the DeVito Line. That kind of punishment rarely occurs.

Sure, many people get called before Congress to testify about their bad business practices, but more often than not, that's it. One good public berating, and you can keep the money. The recent collapse of our financial system was caused in large part by greed. Companies like AIG, Bear Stearns, Lehman Brothers, and many others engaged in higher and higher risk activities for one simple reason: more money. They got greedy. They paid themselves handsomely. So far, the executives of these companies have come nowhere close to the DeVito Line.

Even so, that story is not yet over, and history has shown that bankers and their industry have frequently paid a high price for their actions. It isn't always quick, and it doesn't include everybody, but there is always a price when financial panics occur. Sometimes it's individuals who pay the price. Sometimes it's the industry itself. But there is always a cost. *Greed has a price.*

Lesson Number 5: Accounting is not a game.

I suppose nobody should be surprised that some people lie. But it's still a surprise when we discover executives of large public companies who have lied about their company's finances. It happens more often than we think. For example, executives of Freddie Mac, Fannie Mae, AIG, and others all lied about their finances. We'll talk about the details later, but it's shameful that so many investors lost money because of lies. Sure, the chief executive officers (and others) lost their jobs. Good. They deserved to be fired. Perhaps even jailed. This is not a game.

In the case of Freddie Mac, its 2000 reported profit was *understated* by a *billion* dollars, and the 2001 profit was *overstated* by a *billion* dollars![2] Freddie Mac later disclosed that it had misstated earnings by some $4.4 billion over three years!

Fannie Mae was even worse. Their regulator claimed they overstated earnings in order to pay the maximum executive bonuses. They created a "cookie jar" of cash reserves that executives could draw from in bad years to cover up weak performance and meet bonus goals. They installed software to produce favorable financial reports regardless of whether the reports were accurate or not. Worst of all, Fannie Mae classified a huge number of transactions (derivatives) improperly to report over $12.2 billion of losses on its income statement.

But AIG takes the cake. Because of sloppy and inaccurate financial disclosures, they had to resubmit five years of financial statements (2000–05) with the SEC. The government even sued them for intentionally misleading analysts and investors, and AIG paid $825 million to settle the claims. AIG was accused of cheating on their taxes and paid $818 million to settle those claims. They advised a client to illegally hide bad loans, and paid $126 million in penalties and fines for it. Their systems were so rotten they even lost control of $4.3 billion of AIG stock that was held in trust for AIG employees!

Those mistakes were costly all right, but the worst accounting mistake was in its derivatives activities (covered in detail later). Buried in small print on page 166 of their 2006 SEC annual report was a reference to derivatives activities by their financial products division (AIGFP). AIG claimed that "the likelihood of any payment obligation by AIGFP under each transaction is remote, even in severe recessionary market scenarios." There was nothing remote about it! It was exactly these activities that caused AIG to collapse.[3] *Accounting is not a game.*

Lesson Number 6: Bigger is not always better.

Some of you might remember when banks could not do business across state lines, or in many cases, even across county lines. Until a Supreme Court ruling in 1985 cleared the remaining obstacles, banks or the companies that owned them couldn't set up branches across state lines.[4] There were ways around this rule, such as opening a "loan production office" (called LPO) that could make loans but not accept deposits, but basically, banks couldn't do business outside their own state.

Interstate banking was eventually legalized, but only after a transition period that allowed banks in some states to get big enough to compete with the larger banks, especially those in New York and California. Community banks were afraid they would be dominated by larger banks. California was of some concern especially to West Coast states, but there were still a lot of small banks opening shop there in the 1980s in spite of competition from large banks like Wells Fargo. The bigger fear was the large New York banks. People were legitimately worried that because of their size, the New York banks would rule the country.

So, for a limited time, regional "reciprocal banking" laws were enacted where banks in one state could merge with banks in certain other states if both states passed laws to that effect. New York was initially left out of any regional reciprocal banking agreements. Even New York's neighbors, Connecticut and Massachusetts, initially excluded New York. They joined with Maine, New Hampshire, Rhode Island, and Vermont to form a bank region. Other states quickly formed banking groups around the country in the West, Midwest, Southeast, Southwest, and Midcentral regions.

These banking regional compacts allowed smaller banks a chance to grow significantly before nationwide banking was allowed. All of this helps explain how a little ol' bank in Charlotte, called North Carolina National Bank (NCNB), could grow up to become Bank of America, at one time the largest banking company in the country with total assets exceeding $1.2 trillion. Two other North Carolina banks (First Union and Wachovia) also grew and merged to become Wachovia Bank, once the fourth-largest commercial bank in the country.[5] Ironically, Wells Fargo acquired Wachovia in a fire sale in 2009, proving that regional pacts were helpful but not foolproof. Wachovia is a great example of management growing too fast and too large to manage. It led to their failure.

There is no question the size of the largest banks continues to get bigger, while the number of commercial banks has been dropping. At its peak in 1921, the United States had about thirty-one thousand banks. There was a dramatic decline in the number of banks during the Great Depression in the early 1930s, but even more recently we have seen an unprecedented number of mergers, acquisitions, and failures. As a result, the number of commercial banks has declined from over 14,800 in 1980 to fewer than 8,100 in late 2009.[6]

Yet, people say they hate the big banks. Then how did these banks get so damn big? And how do they stay so big? It's not like the customers are so mad they yank their deposits out as soon as a bank hits a certain size. Banks and other companies get big and stay large because we let them.

Growth is normally a very good thing for banks. As a shareholder of a bank, or any company really, if the size of the pie keeps getting bigger, your slice will too. Grow your institution, and your wealth grows with it. But we sometimes forget the risk of growing too fast or too large. It can lead to failures.

Have we allowed banks to get too big? So far in this decade, the number of banks has declined over 18 percent while the assets they manage have grown 78 percent. By the end of 2008, the top two commercial banks alone (Bank of America and JPMorgan Chase Bank) held over 20 percent of all banking assets, over $1 trillion each.[7] Clearly, large banks pose a lot of risk because they become so tangled up with other banks and businesses. As this book will explain, experience has shown that allowing such mammoth banks to fail could bring the entire economy to its knees.

The problem with companies becoming too big to fail is one of *moral hazard*: people take a lot risk of if they don't have much to lose. For example, moral hazard exists when people with fire insurance become less committed to putting fire prevention programs in place. People tend to be less careful if they have insurance. Similarly, if people think the government will bail out a large troubled company to protect the public interests, the company may be less careful and take higher risks.

Analysts, politicians, and other commentators speak out against government bailouts because they fear it will increase moral hazard. Their voices fall on deaf ears because governments everywhere have a long history of bailouts, and even with the opposition chatter, that's not likely to change.

We too have a long history of bailouts. For example, President Hoover's Reconstruction Finance Corporation in 1932 loaned money to troubled banks, railroads, savings and loans, and life insurance companies. Loan guarantees were given to Lee Iacocca's Chrysler auto company in 1979. The savings and loan industry got the same deal in 1989 and so did the airline industry after September 11, 2001. It's usually a bipartisan affair; both Democrats and Republicans have traditionally supported bailouts. When the airline industry's $15 billion bailout was approved eleven days after the September 11 attack on the World Trade Center, the House vote was 356–54 and the Senate vote was 96–1 to approve the bailout. President George W. Bush signed it into law immediately.[8]

In reality, bailouts are a fact of life for large companies and industries. As we have learned, the problem with these bailouts is the incredible cost to taxpayers. Sure, size has advantages, but when banks grow too fast or too large, they present big risks to their investors and to the economy. And if they fail, that's an even bigger risk. *Bigger is not always better.*

Lesson Number 7: It's almost always bad loans.

There are many things that can kill a bank. Bad investments, fraud, or high-cost deposits can all lead to trouble. But most failures occur because the bank had too many bad loans. And that issue is more personal.

The Farm Crisis in the early 1980s still sticks with me. I was one of the examiners reviewing bad farm loans in the early and mid-1980s while listening to the radio as John Mellencamp sang his hit song "Rain on the Scarecrow" and as the first "Farm Aid" benefit concert, organized by Mellencamp, Willie Nelson, and Neil Young was taking place in Champaign, Illinois.

It was a hard time for family farmers and for the bankers who loaned them money. Examiners had the unenviable task of requiring the banks to write off the bad farm loans, knowing full well that the banker would probably have to repossess farm equipment or even foreclose on the farm. Not to oversimplify such an emotional likelihood, but after reworking the loans several times over a couple of years and still not getting any real reduction on the principal (and in many cases, interest payments either) it was gut-check time for some of these banks and their regulators. How long could they allow the family farms to operate at a loss and not pay back their loans? At some point, the risk of having to close the local bank became very real.

It was terrible. You can only imagine how hard it must have been on the farmers and bankers. They clearly faced difficult choices. I wouldn't pretend to know how hard it was on them personally, but being there did give bank examiners like me at least some sense of the hardships these folks faced.

Bank examiners would drive to these rural communities, some of which had only one or two banks, few decent hotels, and a whole bunch of farmers. In one case when our crew came into a Tennessee town in the middle of the farm crisis, the hotel had posted a sign on their marquee that read "Welcome, Federal Reserve Bank Examiners." Nice. Talk about feeling a bit "at risk."

Later, I remember overhearing a conversation between two clerks as my coworkers were leaving a drugstore. "That one's Marion; the shorter one is Dennis; the other one must be Jack." The locals knew why we were there, and the bankers made it very clear to their past-due borrowers that we were forcing their hand (and we were). I suspect some of those family farmers would have liked to kick our asses.

In hindsight, it had to be one of the most interesting times in a banker's career and in a regulator's career too. It challenged our morals, our sense of fairness, our business sense, even our courage to make tough calls. Classifying a loan as uncollectible was not done carelessly or callously, because the repercussions were very real. I will say from firsthand experience that the bankers and the examiners had a high level of sensitivity and compassion as they honestly tried to do the right thing.

These bankers knew the farmers well. Their kids went to school together and played sports together. They lived near each other and attended church together. John Mellencamp would sing, "Hey, calling it your job, ol' hoss, sure don't make it right. But if you want me to, I'll say a prayer for your soul tonight." The truth is that it sucked for everybody, so thanks for the prayers, John.

Scandals, fraud, and corruption grab our attention and make the headlines. But banks don't usually fail because of those reasons. Sure, some banks fail because of fraudulent loans made by crooked bankers, or obtained by crooked borrowers, or both. But a lot of times it's because honest lenders made loans to honest borrowers who encountered circumstances beyond their control. They couldn't repay the loans, and the bank failed. That's why banks absolutely must be diligent in approving loan requests. They should never forget that while lending drives profits, it also causes failures. *It's almost always bad loans.*

Lesson Number 8: We should have seen it coming.

Institutions usually fail because they do not adequately prepare for the risks. They forget that bad things happen fast and that panics still happen. The red flags are always there and become very clear in hindsight.

Sometimes, if we just look for the red flags, we can prevent problems. For example, I served on the board of one particular nonprofit lending organization. Their mission was sound, and their staff and board members were first class. All of us were relatively new to the nonprofit, and a change in leadership was taking place. So shortly after signing up, I took it upon myself to go out and look at the houses we had as protection (collateral) on the housing renovation loans we had extended to various nonprofit community groups.

You can imagine my surprise when the collateral on one of our fully funded home renovation loans was missing. The collateral—a house—was completely gone! Apparently halfway through the project, somebody decided that the house was in such bad shape it would be less expensive to build a new one rather than repair the old one. Thanks to the help of a college fraternity, the nonprofit borrower was able to quickly remove the entire house and clear the lot.

It seems they failed to check with their lender about it first, and a new, larger loan was now necessary to rework the whole deal. Nobody acted in bad faith, but because the lender failed to monitor the loan more carefully (they should have funded the loan more slowly, only allowing the borrower to "draw" more funds after they inspected the renovation progress) and because the nonprofit borrower failed to understand the loan terms, a lot of well-meaning people learned a lot of lessons that day. The house was in very bad shape to start with. The nonprofit had limited renovation experience. The red flags were there. The problems occurred. We should have seen it coming and prevented it from happening.

As you venture through the book, you will discover this really isn't much different from the problems that have occurred with financial panics throughout history. Yes, our country has had a long history of financial panics but has a short memory. In far too many cases, had we been more cautious and paid attention to the warning signs, we could have prevented panics from happening. The loss caused by the small nonprofit occurred because their lender ignored the red flags. The losses the large financial institutions had that we cover in this book occurred for the same reason. In all cases, the red flags were there. We just chose to ignore them. *We should have seen it coming.*

Lesson Number 9: People matter.

As a bank examiner in 1985, I went to Cincinnati and to Cleveland during the savings and loan crisis when their state-chartered financial institutions were overwhelmed by "runs." A run happens when so many depositors want to withdraw their cash from the bank that the banks don't have enough money in their vaults to pay them, and the depositors panic. Banks have to begin selling or borrowing against their loans and investments to generate cash for their depositors, and a liquidity crisis develops. You can watch Jimmy Stewart in *It's a Wonderful Life* for more details. That's what happened to his building and loan association.

The Ohio crisis happened when Cincinnati's Home State Savings Bank was about to fail and depositors rushed to this and other savings and loans (also called thrifts) for their money. When the state's thrifts could not convert assets to cash fast enough to meet the demand, the Ohio governor had to declare a statewide "bank holiday," and depositors couldn't get to their money until later. I was there to help get collateral from these institutions so they could borrow money from the Federal Reserve (to pay depositors) and to monitor any other "runs" that could cause even more panic.[9]

I knew this was a big deal, and it made a lasting impression on this twenty-five-year-old examiner. It seems a little silly to say, but at the time I felt important, like a cop on the streets after a crime had occurred trying to bring calm and security to the community. You could sense the tension everywhere. I didn't completely understand it all, but I wanted to do my part, whatever it was, to be sure that people could get their money back. I wasn't alone. Bank examiners from around the country were brought in as a show of force to restore confidence. We didn't speak directly to bank customers, but we hoped our collective presence would assure people that we were trying to help them recover their money.

We take it for granted now, but imagine going to your bank to withdraw money only to discover that not only is the bank closed, but you have no idea when it will open again. The Ohio deposits were insured by a private company, the Ohio Deposit Guarantee Fund, which had failed. It was as if there was no bank, there was no insurance, and there was no cash. Depositors at some Ohio thrifts could only withdraw up to $1,000 a month from their account until their thrift obtained new *federal deposit insurance.* (A similar problem happened in Maryland, and the state eventually put up $185 million of taxpayer money to cover the losses.)

It was quite serious, and people were in a bind. For a while, some small businesses couldn't meet their payrolls, and some people couldn't pay their mortgages and rents. Clearly, this was not acceptable. The public would not stand for it. The Ohio crisis serves as just one example in the book where the public demanded action.

I discovered a number of things during the Ohio crisis. The local Skyline chili (three-way) was every bit as delicious as Atlanta's Varsity hot dogs. Cincinnati could get incredibly cold in March. Banks really do have hidden buttons under their desks that activate alarms (oops). But more importantly, I discovered that *people matter.*

Lesson Number 10: It's easy to misplace blame.

Following the Ohio thrift crisis, a series of (Pulitzer Prize–winning) articles by investigative reporter Bill Dedman was published in the *Atlanta Journal Constitution* in May 1988 that drew national attention. The articles showed that African Americans in Atlanta were being denied loans two and a half times more frequently than whites, even when incomes were the same. An analysis of the data by Federal Reserve officials confirmed that the lending disparities were true. Dedman shared the methodology he had used to analyze loan data with reporters around the country, and newspapers everywhere began publishing articles showing similar disparities.

Bankers, community groups, government agencies, and regulators were all compelled to respond aggressively because regardless of the reasons behind the lending disparities, people were angry. In Atlanta alone, there was a series of protests culminating when about fifteen hundred people marched outside the Atlanta Fed just before the Democratic National Convention in July 1988 to complain about the regulators' indifference to unfair lending practices. The Atlanta Federal Reserve Bank rarely had protestors outside, so this was a very big deal.

When it happened, the senior officers at the Atlanta Fed locked down the building for security. After all, the Federal Reserve Banks store a ton of cash in their basement vaults to distribute to banks when they need it. It was smart to be safe. They gave my boss, Ron Zimmerman, a statement to read to the protestors and media promising to address their concerns (which were legitimate). It's funny now, but I'm sure Ron didn't appreciate the humor as much when told he had to face the protestors because he was the most "expendable" of the senior officers. They then hustled him outside and locked the doors behind him.

1915 Warranty Deed

To Have and to Hold the above described property unto the said purchaser and assigns forever, subject, however, to the conditions and stipulations following, which are hereby consented to by the said purchaser, viz.:

(1) That at no time shall the premises sold be occupied by negroes other than as domestic servants, nor shall the said property be sold in whole or in part to any negro or person of African descent.

(2) The house or other improvements to be constructed upon the premises shall not be less than **Eight (8) Feet** from the property line.

That these conditions shall be contained in each and every subsequent sale or transfer of said property.

Naturally, bankers were offended by the discrimination accusation in no small part because there was absolutely no sign of illegal *overt* discrimination. As a nation, we had moved so far beyond the days of banks openly discriminating against African Americans that even the implication that bankers might be doing it was shocking.

No longer was it legal for homebuyers to have restrictions on their warranty deeds that specifically prevented African Americans from ever owning the property, such as the one reprinted here from 1915. No longer was it permissible to "redline communities," a practice of drawing red lines on a map delineating areas where lenders would never lend because it was too "black" and thus high risk.

In fact, a large number of bankers were actively involved in charity programs, such as those supporting minority neighborhoods and schools. They were rightfully upset. But the lending disparities were a fact. The accusations of wrongdoing were out there. Banks and thrifts were accused of discrimination; they were being blamed for the disparities.

For many years, I was the Atlanta Federal Reserve Bank's community affairs officer. Our team was responsible for promoting community development finance in low- and moderate-income communities in the southeastern United States (Florida, Georgia, Alabama, and parts of Tennessee, Mississippi, and Louisiana). We were also charged with addressing issues of poverty and discrimination in the South. For the record, we were against both.

We knew the lending disparities had not occurred because banks were run by racist groups or individuals. We had never found any evidence of overt lending discrimination, and we looked hard for it too. What we found was that lending disparities arose from a multitude of less sensational issues. They include differences in personal savings, net worth, and credit reports caused by historic discrimination in employment and education. There were problems with property appraisals and the lack of banking relationships. There were problems with the amount of debt borrowers had *relative to their income.* There were some things bankers could and did change to improve their lending records. But blaming them solely for problems caused by historic discrimination is not honest, or fair. *It's easy to misplace blame.*

This book contains a large number of people who blame others for their company's failures or for the country's financial collapse. For example, later you will read how the CEO of failed investment bank Lehman Brothers blamed the Federal Reserve System, the media, investors, and the SEC for their bankruptcy. And how the CEO of Freddie Mac blamed investors, home buyers, Congress, and the poor.

Sometimes the blame game occurs as people try to justify a particular political view or ideology. Some conservative commentators, for example, blamed a thirty-year-old law, the Community Reinvestment Act (CRA), as causing the 2008 financial crisis. CRA is a law designed to encourage depository institutions to help meet the credit needs of all the communities in which they operated, including low- and moderate-income neighborhoods, consistent with safe and sound banking practices.

The idea behind the law was that in return for limiting competition (by not approving applications to open banks in markets where there was already a lot of competition), for federal deposit insurance (that gives the bank or thrift a tremendous edge in attracting money), and for access to the Federal Reserve Banks' Discount Window (another advantage in attracting low-cost money) banks and thrifts should *at least try* to provide credit in the areas where they take the deposits. The law does not require institutions to make high-risk loans that jeopardize their safety. On the contrary, it specifically requires that these activities be done in a *safe and sound manner.*

Regardless, a *Wall Street Journal* editorial incorrectly claimed that "this 1977 law compels banks to make loans to poor borrowers who often cannot repay them."[10] The *National Review* made this absurd allegation: "the CRA empowers the FDIC and other banking regulators to punish those banks which do not lend to the poor and minorities at the level that [President] Obama's fellow community organizers would like."[11] And an editorial in the *Investor's Business Daily* (IBD) presented an equally absurd and insulting perspective, claiming that the act "triggered the subprime crisis by relaxing lending standards across both the primary and secondary mortgage markets."[12]

These editorials reflect an ideological perspective that ignores the fact that the secondary mortgage markets at the heart of the 2007 financial meltdown *were not subject to CRA.* The CRA applies only to insured depository institutions that, as noted before, are provided with limited competition, federal deposit insurance, and access to the Federal Reserve Discount Window in return for an *affirmative obligation to help* meet local credit needs. Not Fannie Mae, not Freddie Mac, not Ginnie Mae, and not any of the other private-label securities dealers such as Bear Stearns or Lehman Brothers were subject to CRA. *It's easy to misplace blame.*

Parting Shots

It's easy to misplace blame, and directing it at the regulators may be fine, but taking cheap shots at programs for minorities or the poor is offensive. I saw firsthand how CRA and other laws were being implemented. I know CRA is an unpopular law with many bankers, but I also know there are a lot of good bankers doing an exceptional job, routinely, to meet local credit needs that just so happen to also comply with the CRA. They make money, they don't fail, and they don't mind doing the right thing.

In fact, I tip my hat to community affairs professionals at all the banks and regulatory agencies. They work hard to improve loan underwriting standards so that thousands of families can qualify to buy a home and get other loans *safely and fairly*. You probably don't know these dedicated people, but they are among an army of folks fighting to improve lending practices and ensure that working-class families, minorities, and women have equal opportunities. It's a constant battle to fight predatory and unethical subprime lending, but we should all take comfort in knowing there are plenty of financial experts willing to do the work. There really are people in this industry who give a damn and give it their all.

When I was working with these community-development professionals, we hosted hundreds of well-attended and highly rated conferences and events on CRA and community development topics. These were good conferences, but that isn't to say they weren't occasionally challenging. Not everybody likes the idea of bank regulators enforcing unpopular laws. When explaining the laws, I'll admit that my people skills were not always the best either. As you may notice in this book, even though I sincerely have the highest respect for the folks in this industry, I don't always come across that way.

One time, I was standing at the podium in a conference for bank directors and senior executives when an especially frustrated Louisiana banker challenged me in the Q&A portion of the general session. We were in a luxury hotel banquet room, and there were about 150 conservatively dressed bank presidents and directors in the audience.

"You mean to tell me," he bellowed in his strong Cajun accent, "we're gonna have a bunch of these bank examiners comin' down from *New York City* to tell me how to run my bank in *this here parish*!"

"Yeah! Yeah!" the audience of bankers grumbled in support of the question.

"Of course not," I replied honestly. "They're from Atlanta."

Fortunately, even they thought that was funny.

Part I
In the Beginning

Chapter 2
Money

Academics say money was invented by mankind to facilitate trade. Without money, we would be bartering for our goods and services, and I don't know about you, but I'd rather get money for my work instead of some live animal or a bushel of corn. That's not to say bartering isn't good, but I prefer to save it for visits to the flea markets on weekends. And really, it's not especially convenient to barter when it comes time to pay my American Express bill. Although, the thought of sending Am X a truckload of chickens each month is appealing.

Bartering became a lot easier when we could find a common object, such as gold or silver or cattle, to use in the exchange. Every tribe or village or town or country did it a little differently, but basically we found a common means of exchange suitable to everybody.

"I'll give you six buckets of corn for one bow and three arrows" eventually became "I'll give you this small piece of gold for one bow and three arrows," which eventually became "I'll give you $2.2 billion for thirty Apache Longbow attack helicopters."

The exact origin of money is impossible to determine, but evidence of some form of its existence can be traced as far back as 3000 BC in Sumer, a region in southern Mesopotamia that is today part of Iraq. The first signs of coinage also appeared separately in China around that same time.[13] These objects, initially made from bronze or copper metals because they were portable and durable, served as a common tool for transactions.

Over time, people recognized that carrying coins like this could be unsafe, so, just like today, they hid it somewhere in their homes or, for a small fee, would store it with somebody they trusted who would keep it in a safe, centralized location. The person storing it, either an individual, a group of individuals, or in some cases a government entity, would give a receipt indicating the quantity and quality of the deposit.[14] Eventually, people began trading the receipts rather than having to go fetch the coins from storage, a bit like checks that are exchanged today.

Somewhere along the way, the guy holding the coins figured out that he was storing a lot more than he had to deliver when the receipts were presented. He had to keep some coins on reserve in case anybody came looking for them, but he also figured he could lend the rest of the coins to others for a fee, or for interest, or for both. Admittedly, this seems a bit screwball. The guy who is paid good money to protect the coins is actually taking a bit of it and "lending" it to others. What a thief!

This person, we will call him a banker for convenience, told his depositors that if they ever wanted their coins, he would have them available and, in fact, as it turns out, he did deliver them as agreed. Seeing they could get their coins back, people gained confidence and ended up leaving more coins with him. As long as everybody had confidence that they could get their coins, the system worked.

The word bank is derived from the Italian word "banco," meaning a bench. Banco refers to the practice of setting up benches in marketplaces to exchange money and facilitate trade, a common practice around 800 AD. Some coins were less valuable than others because they were worn and contained less gold or silver than newer coins, and the bankers would help set a value for these coins at the marketplace. Other coins were from distant places, and the bankers would trade these for local coins or other bills to allow exchange with the local merchants.

Bankers charged a fee for this service, and occasionally the locals would turn against them either because the bankers were unable to honor their commitment to exchange receipts for coins or because the bankers had "sweated" some of the coins, by unscrupulously removing a small amount of gold from the coins or by clipping some silver off the edges. When locals or soldiers turned against the bankers, this "antibanking" contingent would destroy the bankers' benches and put them out of business, a practice called "bancorroto" meaning "broken bank" and from which the word bankruptcy comes.[15]

For the most part though, people trusted the bankers back then, and in the twentieth and twenty-first centuries, we, like the customers of 800, have come to terms with the fact that as long as *everybody* doesn't go *at the same time* to get *all* of their currency, everything will be just fine. To make it even better, these early bankers agreed to reduce or even eliminate the fee they charged to store the coins, and they agreed to lend any excess coins if needed.

Technically, it's called a "fractional reserve banking" system. The banker needs to keep only a fraction of money in reserve because *so few* people want *all of their deposits* at the same time. Today, the Federal Reserve System determines how much "reserve" is required, and the banks file weekly reports that auditors confirm and examiners review to make sure they aren't lying about it. There are formulas based on different account types and all, but roughly speaking, bankers keep enough cash on hand to cover about 10 percent of the deposits their customers ask them to store. They keep it in their own vaults, at other banks, or with the Federal Reserve Bank. It's called a Federal *Reserve* Bank for a reason!

That's a little scary, isn't it? There is only enough cash on hand for about 10 percent of our checking account balances! But it seems to work out fine as long as we have confidence in the system. And banking is all about confidence. The industry and the government understand this, which is why they both go to great lengths to ensure that "we the people" have confidence in the banking system. It's frequently about perceptions, about being viewed favorably by the community.

Just look at the bank buildings. They often present an air of respectability, of accumulated and protected wealth. Vaults are often in public view so everybody can see the lengths banks will go to protect your money. The buildings themselves are often the anchors of many communities and are well maintained, distinguished structures that can help to bring life to a downtown area or central business district.

Adding to the perception of security, our state and federal governments all have banking departments with examiners and regulators who monitor the industry. We also have federal deposit insurance that basically guarantees if the bank loses up to $250,000 of your deposits, you'll get them back. Hey, until the end of 2012, they would guarantee *any amount* you had on deposit if it was in certain accounts that didn't pay interest, like checking accounts. Feel better now? Actually, we should. It's not just smoke and mirrors. It's a carefully refined program developed over hundreds of years that works very well and helps our economy grow and create jobs, wealth, and prosperity.

We got this way for a reason.

The 1600s

Consider what it was like to live in the 1600s in what is now the USA. Given the shortage of gold, silver, and other valuable metals to make coins, we used a variety of things for our currency. One of the important currencies at the time was wampum, which were beads of polished shells strung together. It seems weird, and frankly it wasn't the best currency, as noted by Margaret G. Myers in her book *A Financial History of the United States*.

> According to the account of Governor Bradford of Plymouth colony [*sic*], the Dutch settlers were the first to adopt this wampum or "Wampampeake" money. The black beads were made of the inside shell of clams or mussels and were rarer and therefore more valuable than the white beads from conch shells. The beads were strung on leather thongs and were sometimes worked into belts to be exchanged as tokens of friendship when treaties were signed. Both Indians and Europeans accused each other of dyeing the white wampum to make it pass for the more valuable black. The ratio of black to white shell was usually two to one, but it varied considerably, as did the prices quoted in wampum. New Netherland merchants complained to the "High and Mighty Lords States General of the United Netherlands" in 1649 that "Wampum, which is the currency here, has never been placed on a sure footing."[16]

Cheating and counterfeiting were not uncommon, and folks would dye the white wampum to make it pass for the more valuable black! Sometimes we forget that there was plenty of crime in the old days too. Fortunately, wampum wasn't the only currency. People were using other things, such as bullets, nails, live animals, beaver skins, and, quite commonly, tobacco. Perhaps tobacco was especially popular because it didn't stink when dead. It was lightweight, it was durable, and, hey, it could even be smoked in times of stress or celebration.

In official warehouses in Virginia and Maryland, folks who stored tobacco for safekeeping got a receipt that certified the quantity and, even more importantly, the quality of the tobacco. This receipt became a form of paper currency that people exchanged, similar to the way the US dollar is today. The official receipts became legal currency in Virginia and Maryland around 1730, and the value of the currency depended simply on the value of tobacco at the time.

At this point in the 1600s and early 1700s, there is still no "national" currency because we are colonies, and other than an occasional attempt at making government-authorized coins, we simply improvised.

So we made it to the mid-1700s this way, and although we had fits and starts with coins, the colonies still had no currency of their own. It was no big deal because Spain had some excellent coins made from silver and gold, and we used those along with similar coins from other foreign countries. The system worked reasonably well, and the Spanish coins were so popular that they even opened some production mills to make coins in Mexico City (1732), Lima,

Peru (1751), Santiago, Chile (1751), Guatemala City (1754), Bogota, Colombia (1759), Potosi, Bolivia (1767), and Popayan, Colombia (1769).

For now, let's just ignore any issues associated with worker exploitation or concerns that Spain was pillaging these countries of their precious commodities because, in spite of our opinion that the locals likely got a bum deal, it's hard to know with certainty how all this played out. Suffice it to say it worked out really well for the Colonial States, except perhaps for the problems with pirates stealing the coins en route to the colonies.

After all, it was coins like these that pirates such as Henry Morgan (1688), Blackbeard (1718), Black Bart (1722), and Laffite (1820s) tried to get.

It's not surprising when you think about history, about pirates, about the artistry and so forth, that there is an entire world of coin collectors who appreciate the metals from this era. You can find all of these coins for sale or trade on the Internet or at coin collection stores. Call me a nerd if you want, but it is easy to get hooked on collecting these old and valuable coins. The coins really are cool even if wannabe collectors like me are not.

Pirates Wish List

Take a look at what Americans were using for business and pirates were seeking as booty in the 1700s and early 1800s, and how their influence is still noted today.

Gold and silver escudo coins from Central and South America that were made in the early 1700s can be quite valuable today, with some auctions selling them for around $4,300. It takes eight escudos to equal one gold doubloon. At one time, they were quite the rage for pirates in the Caribbean! If you are not a pirate and can't afford gold doubloons, you can still try your luck catching similar plastic doubloons frequently tossed from floats at Mardi Gras parades.

Silver pillar dollars could literally be broken in half to make two bits, and those broken in half to make four bits, and those broken to make eight bits. Thus the coin was also known as "pieces of eight," with each of the smallest pieces equal to 12.5 cents. These coins still influence American culture, having become famous in musical couplets with the line "shave and a haircut—two bits" (which would have been one crummy haircut!). You might remember its use as a musical cue before commercial breaks on the TV show *The Beverly Hillbillies*, or as part of the plot in the animated film *Who Framed Roger Rabbit*. Two bits are also used in the school cheer, "Two bits, four bits, six bits, a dollar. All for the home team stand up and holler!"

Not all coins in the colonies were from Spain. Similar to the pillar dollar was the Dutch silver coin, called a lion dollar, made in Gelderland, Netherlands, in 1643. It was in circulation in the early 1700s, especially in the northeastern United States, Lion dollars would become so worn over time that the lion began to resemble a dog. Thus they were also called "dog dollars." The inscriptions around the edges of coins like these were to keep dishonest people from clipping silver from the edges. If you hear the sympathetic expression "You've been clipped!" it comes from this practice of clipping coins.

The Revolution

It's 1776 and the Declaration of Independence has been … well, declared, but we still haven't got a national currency. That's not necessarily a problem given that the thirteen colonies wanted a decentralized government. It becomes a problem only if you need money to finance a war, and the states haven't been forthcoming with the cash. The Continental Congress, our government at the time, developed some Articles of Confederation allowing it the right to set "quotas" for the amount of money the colonies should each contribute to the war, but the colonies seldom met the quotas. So the Continental Congress did the same thing the colonies were doing. It issued its own paper money, called the **Continental currency,** and borrowed extensively. After all, you had to do something to raise money for a war.

Wars are expensive, and for a number of reasons, including competition from the states that were issuing their own weak paper money in large quantities, inflation kicked in. By 1782, the Continental currency was pretty much worthless. The declining currency made financing the war a terrible problem because so many troops were paid in this currency. They couldn't spend their pay anywhere, and they would sometimes get mad about it and desert. You don't hear it so much anymore, but the old expression "not worth a Continental" came from these bills being worthless.

As noted, states also each issued their own currency, some of which was in dollars, others in (British) pounds. They suffered the same problems with inflation as the Continental currency.

The government tried valiantly to prop up the Continental paper with laws *requiring* merchants to accept it as payment. And they tried to control inflation and bring back value to the currency by passing some mandatory price controls on select goods. That didn't work because merchants just stopped carrying so many of the unprofitable supplies subject to those controls. Some say these price controls contributed to the problems George Washington's twelve thousand troops experienced in Valley Forge, PA, during that miserable winter of 1777 where they all froze their butts off because there was a shortage of blankets, shoes, and food, which were subject to price controls.

Fortunately, the war effectively ended in 1781 when the British troops surrendered in Yorktown, and officially ended with the Treaty of Paris in 1783. The national paper currency, the Continental, had no real value, and the appetite for a new national currency was pretty slim too. As a result, Congress got out of the currency business and left it to the states.

Something else interesting happened after the Revolutionary War. Congress chartered the **first official bank** on December 31, 1781, in Philadelphia. It was called "The President, Directors, and Company of the Bank of North America," or as we say today, "Wells Fargo." No, really. The bank was eventually acquired by Wachovia Bank, which is now owned by Wells Fargo. It was technically chartered by the state of Pennsylvania (we had no nationally chartered banks yet) and, like many state banks, was established for a specific business purpose. That purpose was to receive federal government deposits and to manage repaying debts from the Revolutionary War. The original depositors and stockholders were some of the big shots of the times: Thomas Jefferson, Alexander Hamilton, Benjamin Franklin, John Paul Jones, James Monroe, John Jay, and Stephen Decatur.[17]

The bank was organized by a wealthy guy named Robert Morris, who was a major fund-raiser for the war and afterward the first "superintendent of finance" for the United States, a position similar to the secretary of the Treasury today. Bankers reading this might wonder if the large Robert Morris Associates Company, now called RMA, is related to him, and the answer would be yes but in name only. RMA, founded in 1914, is headquartered in Philadelphia and, according to their website, has three thousand members that include banks of all sizes. They seem to do a very nice job providing to their members products and services related to managing risks.

Ironically, they named this company after a guy who ended up in debtors' prison. Apparently, Robert Morris, the former banker and "superintendent of finance," got into real estate development along the East Coast. It went sour, he went broke, and there you have it: debtors' prison. He may not have been the first, but he certainly joins a long list of political appointees who wound up in jail. That's a pretty crappy way to end his career because without his help in raising money to finance the Revolutionary War, we might all be talking with a peculiar British accent today. (Debtors' prison is a stupid idea under any circumstances.)

When the war ended, we had a real dilemma about the direction of the country. Should we pursue a strong federal government with a common currency or a decentralized federation of state governments with separate currencies? Chapter 6 reviews this dilemma in more detail because this epic Hamilton-versus-Jefferson battle took place over many years and resulted in the financial and regulatory system we have today. For now, suffice it to say the governments couldn't agree on a course of action for a long time. In the 1780s, each bank was issuing its own currency, and each state was issuing its own currency, and we had the relatively worthless Continental currency. The value of these currencies varied considerably. For example, in 1781, you would have had to cough-up $7,500 of the Continental currencies to buy $100 of Spanish-American silver dollars (a 75 to 1 ratio).[18]

The 1800s

Things changed in 1791 when Alexander Hamilton helped push through Congress a federal charter for our very first "national" bank called **"The First Bank of the United States (First Bank)."** One of its goals was to help stabilize currency. To its credit, the First Bank did a great job helping to stabilize currencies when it imposed a strong gold (and silver) standard.

The bank charter had a twenty-year life, and when that charter expired in 1811, Congress did not renew it. While it was alive, this bank received all federal deposit accounts and was very dominant. However, it became quite unpopular because it imposed a very high standard on everybody who issued currency. For state governments, bankers, or their customers, doing business with the federal government usually required using the services of the First Bank, and that meant everybody's currency had to be backed by silver or gold. This certainly wasn't what people wanted to hear, especially those who favored less restrictive standards to facilitate expansion out west and in rural areas. Proponents of states' rights especially disliked it because it was a federal-government-supported bank that was imposing its will on state banks.

If you eliminate whatever constraints you have on currency, you get rapid growth, and we did. The number of commercial banks rose from eighty-eight when the First Bank of the United States closed to 246 just five years later, and the volume of state bank notes in circulation is believed to have tripled![19]

Question: What happens when you combine weak oversight with fast economic growth? Answer: Bank mismanagement, increased counterfeiting, and inflation. Toss in the War of 1812, and you have some serious strain on the economy.

So Congress established another national bank in 1816 called, cleverly enough, "**The Second Bank of the United States,**" with a similar twenty-year charter. The bank was poorly managed by political appointees before Nicholas Biddle became its president in 1823. It didn't take Biddle and the newly elected president, Andrew Jackson, long to butt heads, so, although the bank had a lot of success in stabilizing currency by reinforcing the gold and silver standards, its charter was not renewed in 1836. Question: What happens when you combine weak oversight with fast economic growth? Answer: Bank mismanagement, increased counterfeiting, and inflation. Sound familiar?

The period after the Second Bank of the United States lost its charter has been described as one of "financial chaos," with "unsound loans" and "illegal loans to stockholders."[20] You could argue that at this point the banking industry began what was pretty much the financial equivalent of an out-of-control Grateful Dead rock and roll concert in the 1960s, but, in fairness, fewer people have ever been hurt at a Dead show.

Wildcat Banking (1837 to 1863)

People will often refer to this period as the "wildcat banking" era, which refers to the practice of opening banks in remote, rural areas, especially in the West where, at the time, only the "wildcats roam." Because the banks were located in faraway places, it was awfully hard for anybody to actually come out to the bank and redeem its paper currency for gold or silver. A wildcat bank was usually owned by unscrupulous bankers whose only purpose was to steal land, products, services, or other sound currencies by issuing their own notes backed by little or nothing.

The terms "wildcat banking" and "free banking" are sometimes used interchangeably and incorrectly to refer to this period of minimal regulation and lots of corruption. Academics prefer to define this era as "free banking" when banks were free of *federal* regulations and constraints although state regulations, which varied, were still in effect. Academics would distinguish the definition of the free banking era as one with no federal regulation, from wildcat banking, the practice of opening in remote areas so the banks could make exchanging notes for gold or silver problematic. Although those distinctions are far more accurate, they're boring, so most people just call this whole era wildcat banking!

The big advantage of this era was that states that adopted free banking laws could allow individuals to form a bank without a state legislative act if certain conditions were met. Some of these conditions were selling a set amount of stock, buying specific amounts of bonds from the state government, and having silver and gold on hand to back their currency. Starting a bank meant that you didn't have to lobby the politicians for a charter. New York pioneered the practice, and because the bank was required to buy state bonds as part of the deal, starting a bank helped finance the state government. If you wanted to open a bank, you had to buy some of the state's bonds.

It worked so well that free banking laws were passed in Michigan (1837); Georgia (1838); Alabama (1849); New Jersey (1850); Illinois, Massachusetts, Ohio, and Vermont (1850); Connecticut, Indiana, Tennessee, and Wisconsin (1852); Florida and Louisiana (1853); Michigan again (1857); Iowa and Minnesota (1858); and Pennsylvania (1860).[21]

Not surprisingly, US banks were often formed before and after the free banking era with a specific business purpose in mind, and some states would allow just about anybody—private companies too—to open a bank if they had enough money and, in the early years, enough political connections. Sometimes individuals would form banks without the benefit of a state charter but with the intent of issuing their own currency anyway. Other banks were formed by successful businesspeople who saw a bank as an outgrowth of their current business, and whose sound reputation helped establish credibility for the bank. Here are some examples:

- The Manhattan Company (often called the Manhattan Bank) was chartered in 1799 to supply New York City with drinking water.
- The Chemical National Bank in New York was chartered in 1824 by the owners of a drug manufacturing company.
- The New Orleans Gas-light & Banking Company was chartered in 1835 to develop gaslights in New Orleans and Lafayette, Louisiana.
- The Manual Labor Bank was formed in 1836 in Philadelphia without a charter to be a safe depository for laborers.
- The Cotton Planters Bank was chartered in Thomasville, Georgia, in 1861 to serve the interests of cotton planters (which included the right to build ships to transport cotton).

Counterfeiting

The banking system was certainly interesting and definitely flawed because we had crooks who would counterfeit currency on a large scale. During this wildcat-banking period, about thirty thousand different notes were in circulation, and about one-third of those notes were probably counterfeit![22]

Picture this: It's 1850, and you walk into the local store to buy some groceries. You hand the grocer a ten-dollar bill from your bank. Your grocer then pulls out the weekly edition of "Thompson's Bank Note Reporter," or one of over seventy similar publications, to determine if the currency is authentic.[23] They actually published newspapers describing counterfeit bills!

The grocer would also have to determine if the bank was still viable. Many times, it was worse to accept currency from a bank whose reputation was bad than to accept a counterfeit bill. A well-made counterfeit could be passed on to some other unsuspecting fool, but a troubled bank's currency was worth less because too many people knew that the bank could fail. In any event, if people thought that the currency was questionable because it was from a distant area, or that the currency might be counterfeit, or that a bank might be in financial trouble, grocers and others might accept it anyway but at less than the face value. A one-dollar bill might only be worth seventy cents or so.

At the time, counterfeiters weren't the only currency crooks. Some banks would issue more currency than they had gold or silver to support it, making the currency worth less when people found out. So who was worse: the banker issuing excess and in effect fraudulent currency, or the counterfeiter issuing fraudulent currency? As disturbing as it may sound, some counterfeiters were simply accepted as good people just trying to make a living, while the banker was held to a much higher standard.

Take this fellow named Stephen Burroughs, for example. Here's a guy living in Canada and manufacturing counterfeit notes of banks in New Hampshire, Maine, Connecticut, and Rhode Island.[24] You would think the Canadians would have been uncomfortable with a guy considered one of the most notorious counterfeiters at the time living in their community, but he was actually a popular, likeable guy. Apparently nonviolent, he genuinely cared about his neighbors in Stanstead, Canada, a community along the US border near Newport, Vermont. He not only helped build a twenty-mile-long road to help farmers sell their produce, but he also cared for several residents during a smallpox epidemic.[25]

Bankers didn't see him that way, and many wanted him executed, which was permitted by law. The Canadian government, however, did little to stop his activities for many years until it finally conceded to pressure from the Vermont government. Eventually, this legendary and prolific counterfeiter was caught, tried, convicted, and then—surprise!—pardoned by the head honcho of Canada at the time, Governor James Henry Craig. He was never deported to the United States.

Dixie

The word Dixie has been around to describe the southern United States for over one hundred years. Its exact origin is unknown although there are a couple of theories. Some say it came from a New York Plantation owner named Dixy, or that it came from the Mason-Dixon Line defining the boundary between Maryland and Pennsylvania. I doubt it. The most likely explanation is that the word came from a well-known Louisiana bank, the Citizens Bank and Trust Co., that issued ten-dollar currency printed in both English and French. The two languages accommodated sailors arriving in New Orleans and locals working in either the American or the French quarters of the city.

A 1919 article published in the *New Orleans American* newspaper explained that on the back of the currency, beginning in the 1830s, instead of the number 10, there was the French word Dix. "It became so common when you were going down the great [Mississippi] river to trade at the Southern metropolis for you to say that you were going south to acquire some Dixies. Thus it became known as the land of the Dixies, or 'Dixieland.'"[26]

The New Orleans Canal Banking Company

All banks have their own stories, and they are normally quite interesting. Here is a short story of a large, generally successful bank that, frankly, is disturbing. Like many banks at the time, Canal Bank was formed in 1831 for a specific purpose, to build a canal from Lake Pontchartrain to the American sector of New Orleans, close to the French Quarter. Canal Bank became one of the two largest banks in Louisiana before the Civil War and was dominant right up until the Great Depression. Banks did not have restrictions on their investments like we have now, and these bankers used their investors' and depositors' money to buy the land, hire the labor, and construct the "New Basin Canal."

Historians say the bank's canal builders "preferred to hire Irishmen to do the hard labor because the work was dangerous, and they did not want their more expensive slaves injured or killed. Laboring in water up to their hips, canal diggers were very susceptible to yellow fever, malaria, and cholera."[27] It has been reported that as many as thirty thousand Irishmen died building the canal. The canal itself, however, was considered a financial success. By comparison, the Panama Canal, started by the French (1880 to 1889) and finished by the United States (1904 to 1914), had a similar number of total deaths reported as well, around twenty-eight thousand, mostly Frenchmen.

The bank failed just over one hundred years later (1933) and its remaining assets were acquired by the National Bank of Commerce in New Orleans, a new bank but with the same owners as before. That bank changed its name to First National Bank of Commerce (1971), was acquired by Bank One (1998), and was acquired again by JPMorgan Chase Bank (2004).

Isn't it disturbing that so many people died building a canal owned by the bank? We all complain when the bank charges three bucks or so for an ATM withdrawal, but in the 1830s as many as thirty thousand bank employees were killed on the job, and all they got was a small statue in New Orleans. It was erected in 1997 and is maintained by the Irish Cultural Society of New Orleans. Those deaths, by the way, are in addition to the plantation loans made, where Canal Bank and its competitor, Citizens Bank, together accepted about thirteen thousand slaves as collateral between 1831 and 1865, and eventually "owned" approximately 1,250 slaves as the result of loan defaults.[28]

Today, the canal entrance is in a prosperous part of New Orleans and serves as the entrance to the Municipal Yacht Harbor. The canal originally extended from Lake Pontchartrain along present-day West End Boulevard and Pontchartrain Boulevard, turning toward the business district along what is now part of I-10, and ending in a turning basin close to the Superdome. The canal has since been filled with dirt and was used as a dumping ground during the cleanup of Hurricane Katrina.

The Civil War and Confederate Money

The Civil War breaks out in 1861, and as you know, wars are expensive, so in the South the Confederate States of America, individual states, private banks, and others all issued their own currencies to finance the war. The notes were backed by a wide variety of things, from cotton, for example, to interest-bearing bonds paying around 8 percent. They became worthless when the war ended, but if you take a quick look on the Internet you'll find plenty of people selling the currencies. Just be aware that there were plenty of counterfeit Confederate bills back then, including some that were produced by the North to disrupt the southern economy, but, then again, there are collectors looking for them too.

Isn't it odd that President Lincoln himself had a five-dollar Confederate bill in his wallet that (April 1865) night he was killed by John Wilkes Booth at Ford's Theatre in Washington DC? It's true.

In the North, things were slightly different. Initially, to finance the war the federal government issued 6 percent "interest-bearing notes" that could be redeemed in sixty days. Soon after, the government issued more of these for one year, two years, or at 7.3 percent for three years. Their value was pretty risky during the Civil War, but today, bankers like these interest-bearing notes (called Treasury bonds) because they pay well, can be sold if necessary, and are considered very creditworthy.

Greenbacks and Legal Tender Notes

In 1861 and 1862, the US Treasury began to issue federal "demand notes" that were redeemable in gold coins. Produced by the American Bank Note Company (New York), these Treasury demand notes served as a form of currency. They had green ink on the back and were popularly known as "greenbacks." Given that it was backed by gold, it was initially well received. It seems like there should be a better story to the "greenback" nickname, but no. That's the deal.

Congress was fully aware of the problems of the state bank currencies (including counterfeiting, weak regulations, and high failure rates) and needed to figure out a better way to finance the Civil War. Perhaps more importantly, because people were worried about the war, they began to hoard gold coins so much that the state banks were facing a crisis as their gold reserves declined. In fact, things got so bad that while they continued to exchange gold for the federal demand notes, some New York City banks stopped exchanging it for their state bank currencies altogether.

To make the situation even worse and, frankly, because they needed money to finance the Civil War, the federal government also issued "Legal Tender Notes" (1862) that were backed by, well … umm, nothing really. Correction: they were backed by the "full faith of the federal government," and were also commonly called greenbacks. This marked a big change for the United States because in the past the government had issued paper notes that paid a set interest rate and could be used as a form of currency. Now, for the first time, these greenbacks did not pay interest and were not backed by gold or silver, but instead were fiat money backed by faith in the government. For the record, fiat is a word used to describe an "authoritative order" such as a government decree. Fiat money, then, is something not backed by a physical commodity, such as gold, but by a government decree that it is "good for all debts, public and private." Fiat was also an Italian auto manufacturing company, but that's beside the point.

Unfortunately, during the Civil War, the first greenbacks in circulation that were "fiat money" didn't pan out so well, and their value fluctuated considerably, especially when the North lost a few battles. People began to worry about fiat money's value should the South win the war.

National Bank Currency

At the start of the Civil War, we had a mess: state bank currency, Confederate currency, federal greenbacks backed by gold, federal greenbacks backed by faith, Spanish coins, and plenty of counterfeit money. So how do you fix a situation like this? Well, under the direction of Treasury Secretary Salmon P. Chase, Congress established a new "national" banking system to function along with state banks by passing the cleverly named National Banking Acts of 1863 and 1864.

Like most banks chartered by state governments for a specific purpose, national banks were also chartered by the federal government for a specific purpose. In this case, the purpose was to issue stable paper currency and to purchase government securities that would finance the war for the North. This odd and uniquely American system of state banks and national banks, called a "dual banking system," started in large part because of the Civil War and continues today. *We got this way for a reason.*

Now you have a choice of where to get a bank charter—from the state where the bank is based or from the federal government through the US Treasury's newly formed Office of the Comptroller of the Currency (OCC). It's strange that the national banks were initially chartered for only twenty years, but today they have no expiration date. Shown on the left is a guy from Indiana named Hugh McCulloch, the first comptroller of the currency and, in effect, our nation's first national bank examiner. Until the 1990s, it seems that bank examiners still looked and dressed as he did in this photo from around 1860.[29]

Hugh McCulloch, left, courtesy of US Library of Congress. Courtney Dufries, right, courtesy of himself.

National banks were allowed to issue currency, but with a twist. Unlike state banks, national banks couldn't actually "print" their own bills. First, they were required to buy US Securities from the Treasury Department, and then the Treasury would have the paper currency printed on the bank's behalf. The advantage was that bankers wouldn't be able to produce more currency than they had securities, which kept bankers honest, and it made counterfeiting more difficult. Also, all national banks had to honor these notes regardless of which national bank issued them. This was good because unlike some other currency, you could get face value for the note at any national bank in the North, and eventually after the war, the country. *Good government is necessary.*

It really did help business and commerce because the national currency was accepted just about everywhere. But the dominance of these national banks was very strong, and the number of state-chartered banks declined considerably, especially as the Civil War came to an end. Many of those Southern banks with Confederate bonds and Confederate currencies went out of business. A lot of northern state banks went away too. Just before the national banks were chartered in 1863, there were 1,466 state banks in the northern states. Two years later, there were only 349.[30]

Even so, the problem with some state banks floating more currency than they had reserves did not stop. Here is a very good excerpt of what happened next, according to the March 2008 OCC website:

> It was the job of the bank examiner to visit the bank and certify that it had enough cash on hand to redeem its outstanding currency. Because this was not always done, many bank note holders found themselves stuck with worthless paper. It was sometimes difficult or impossible to detect which notes were sound and which were not, because of their staggering variety.
>
> By 1860 more than 10,000 different bank notes circulated throughout the country. Commerce suffered as a result. Counterfeiting was epidemic. Hundreds of banks failed. Throughout the country there was an insistent demand for a uniform national currency acceptable anywhere without risk.[31]

It may be an exaggeration to say that there was an "insistent demand" for a uniform national currency in 1860. After all, the Civil War was about to start in part because of the South's insistence that the federal government stay out of its affairs. Even so, it would really stink if the merchant you were doing business with in another community would not accept your currency, or when the state currency you held was suddenly worth less, or even worthless.

There was merit to having only one secure national currency, and an effective way to do that was to just tax the state currency out of existence. In 1866, Congress did exactly that, to the tune of a 10 percent annual tax on all state bank note issues in circulation. If you had $1 million of notes passing through your bank and into circulation, you paid the feds $100 grand a year. Ouch. Not surprising, it only took a couple of years for the lawsuits to be settled, to eliminate all state bank notes, and to see large numbers of state banks convert their charters to national banks.[32]

Checking Accounts

Not all banks converted to a national charter because state regulations were more lenient, and state banks could make real estate loans while national banks were prevented by law from doing so. Also, while virtually all state currency was being taxed out of existence, a new form of doing business was taking place. Remember that several hundred years earlier, people passed around receipts for gold they had in storage. Well now, instead of passing the currency into circulation, bankers allowed their customers to pass around receipts that their currency was on deposit at the bank, and all they had to do was bring the receipt by, and the bank would "check" to see if the currency was available. It was, quite simply, a checking account, or as bankers call it a *demand deposit account* because it was an account where somebody could "demand" a payment from the bank with this check. Currency was now becoming a little less important because checking accounts were becoming more popular. Bankers promoted these checking accounts to get out of paying those 10 percent taxes![33]

For a long time, bankers liked offering checks because having their company name and logo on them served as good advertising. That's why they sometimes offered discounts to governments that used their bank checks to do business. At some point though, people stopped paying as much attention to the bank name on the check, and the advertising became less effective. People probably pay less attention to the bank name because we're all too busy looking at the nature scenes, sports teams, cartoon characters, playful kittens, or other cutesy clutter that was being printed on the checks instead. But I could be wrong about that.

In any event, the policies enacted because of the Civil War resulted in a dual banking system (state and national banks), a new set of bank examiners, a new national currency, and our modern-day checking accounts. It would appear that checking account overdraft fees came along around the time of the Civil War too. Yes, war is hell.

From 1862 to 1923, we had (1) Legal Tender Notes (also called United States Notes), which were issued directly by the US Treasury and backed by "the full faith of the government." We also had (2) national bank notes issued by banks themselves and showing their names on the currency, such as the 1886 Crocker Woolworth National Bank in San Francisco (see sidebar). These were backed by the bank's assets, which included US Treasury securities. And we had (3) both Gold Certificates (the last series for public use was issued in 1928) and (4) Silver Certificates (the last series was issued in 1957), backed by whiskey and water. I'm kidding. They were backed by gold and silver. But wouldn't that be something? Imagine bank vaults filled with barrels of whiskey rather than stacks of bills and piles of coins. Larger bills could be backed by the better booze; smaller bills by the cheap stuff. Robbing a bank would be more like throwing a party! But I digress ...

If your goal was to reduce the number of paper currencies, this was exceptional progress. The number of paper currencies in the country dropped from over ten thousand to just these four in only a few years.

The Greenback Party

An era of rapid railroad growth followed the Civil War, and of particular interest was the Northern Pacific Railway, which received a lot of its funding from a well-known entrepreneur, Jay Cooke. Jay owned a large and highly respected investment company in Philadelphia and was very fond of this railroad and its ties to Minnesota, especially the city of Duluth. By the way, Duluth was not only the inspiration for the 2008 movie *Leatherheads* (George Clooney, Renee Zellweger), but was legendary musician Bob Dylan's birthplace. Minnesota is a great state, no matter what Wisconsin tells you, and the railroad business was huge in the early 1870s.

Cooke believed so strongly in Northern Pacific and the importance of a northern transcontinental railway from Seattle to Duluth and the Great Lakes region that he apparently sold a substantial number of bonds to fund the railroad that he couldn't repay. Worse yet, his investment company, Jay Cooke & Co., purchased $4.1 million of the bonds themselves, some of which was financed with over $1.5 million in loans. A concentration of railroad bonds combined with the loss of income from selling federal bonds for the US government led to his company going bankrupt. It also contributed significantly to "the Panic of 1873" followed by a very long recession, which lasted about sixty-five months.

It's unfair to lay the blame completely on Cooke for causing the deep, long recession, but it certainly didn't help things when his large well-known company, like others at that time, couldn't pay their bonds when they came due. His was a $7.9 million company in September 1873 (about $140 million today), but its high profile caused everybody to start selling their bonds; panic ensued and the recession kicked into full gear.[34] In a sense, it would be similar to the repercussions we might see today when major investment firms like Lehman Brothers go bankrupt. *Panics happen.*

Complicating the panic was the lack of currency. The Legal Tender Notes and greenbacks were originally intended to be a temporary currency to finance the war, and eventually the federal government began to remove them from circulation. But this lack of currency made matters worse, and a lot of people thought that going back to the gold standard, which made currency harder to come by, contributed to the bad economy. So many of these people thought this was the case, especially farmers who made up over half of the working Americans at the time, that they formed a new political party in late 1874, called the Greenback Party.[35] The Greenback Party favored women's right to vote, an eight-hour workday, and more greenbacks that were not tied to gold or other commodities.

Patty Hearst and the Crocker National Bank

When the US Treasury began chartering national banks, they also printed their currency. For example, on bills such as those printed in 1886 for the Crocker Woolworth National Bank in San Francisco, it would read "National Currency" right across the top. All national currencies were identical in every way except for the obvious stuff like bank name, charter number, serial numbers, and, of course, the two bank officer signatures.

Crocker National Bank (Woolworth had died) became legendary on April 21, 1975, when its branch office in Carmichael, California, was robbed of fifteen thousand dollars by a group calling itself the Symbionese Liberation Army (SLA). It was their second robbery, having held up a branch of Hibernia Bank in San Francisco for ten thousand dollars on April 3, 1974, two months after kidnapping nineteen-year-old Patty Hearst, daughter of wealthy media mogul Randolph Hearst. The SLA demanded the release of jailed SLA members as ransom (it was denied) and then demanded that her father publish some of their propaganda and distribute food to the poor, which he did, but not to their satisfaction.

Two months after her kidnapping, Ms. Hearst announced that she had joined the organization and changed her name to "Tania." She had participated in both bank robberies, and this photo of her holding a sawed-off M1 Carbine firearm was distributed by the SLA during her captivity. Ms. Hearst was found and arrested in September 1975, and after a thirty-nine-day trial six months later, she was convicted of robbery.

Her awful defense was led by prominent attorney F. Lee Bailey, who was later accused of being drunk at the closing. She served almost two years of her seven-year sentence before it was commuted in 1979 by President Jimmy Carter. The president believed that she was a victim of Stockholm's Syndrome and was only sympathizing with her captors after suffering from their mental, physical, and sexual abuse. She received a full pardon by President Bill Clinton in 2001.

Ms. Hearst was not the only victim. Myrna Lee Opsahl, mother of four and only forty-two years old, had come to the bank to deposit the collections from her church and was killed by SLA member Emily (Harris) Montague during the Crocker National Bank robbery. Emily Montague was sentenced to eight years in prison for second-degree murder. She was paroled in 2009. The bank was acquired by Wells Fargo Bank in 1986.

In God We Trust

Did you know that printing "In God We Trust" on our coins required an act of Congress? It was April 22, 1864, when Congress passed a law allowing the US Mint to print the phrase on both the one-cent and the two-cent coins. Yes, we had two-cent coins from 1864 to 1873.

The inscription was initially limited to these two coins, but Congress kept voting to expand it and the Coinage Act of February 12, 1873 eventually allowed it on all coins but not on paper currency.

It's not often that US politicians vote against things involving God, but some, like President Teddy Roosevelt in 1907, were opposed to printing this phrase on currency because they thought it would cheapen the meaning by using it on money, on postage stamps, or in advertisements.

In July 1956, Congress passed and President Eisenhower approved a joint resolution declaring "In God We Trust" as our national motto. The national motto would complement the national bird (bald eagle in 1782), anthem (the "Star Spangled Banner" in 1931), and flower (rose in 1986). In spite of over thirty attempts since 1965, the square dance has failed to achieve national dance status.

The national motto was primarily a congressional response to the rise of communism and its apparent promotion of atheism. The next year (1957), the national motto began appearing on printed currency.

Because it is such a large part of the national culture, the Supreme Court has on at least three occasions shot down any challenges to use of the motto on the grounds that it reflects more of a historical reference than a religious promotion that would conflict with the "separation of church and state" required by the Constitution.

Gold and Silver

It's true that the return to an exclusive gold and silver standard was tremendously controversial, and that, in part, is why it remains a topic of interest today. Some people are still advocating its return. It's not as simple as you might think and not especially desirable. The gold and silver standard has significant limitations, which is why we got away from it in the first place. *We got this way for a reason.*

The gold standard is a system whereby the folks issuing paper currency guarantee to redeem the paper upon demand for a set amount of gold. It's the same thing with a silver standard—paper currency is exchanged for silver. Currency tied to both gold and silver is called bimetalisim. One of the problems with bimetalism is determining the value of the metals. If you let the "markets decide," then every day your currency could have a different value. If gold or silver is in short supply, the currency value would be higher; if there is a large supply, the value would be lower. Imagine the chore of buying groceries and discovering the cost changing frequently simply because the currency value is changing.

To solve that problem, the government would officially peg the value of the dollar to an ounce of gold or silver, but that solution too had problems. Perhaps you've heard of **Gresham's law**, which claims "bad money chases out good." Sir Thomas Gresham (1519–1579) was a banker who explained that if you have two coins in circulation, the more valuable coin is often stored in a safe place while the weaker currency is circulated. That makes sense. It's in our own best interest to unload the less valuable coin when possible and hold onto the good coins for ourselves. So bad money keeps circulating, and good money is taken out of circulation: bad money chases out good.

Our country tried supporting both silver- and gold-backed paper currency, but Gresham's law got in the way: bad money kept on chasing out good. When Congress set the value of gold backing the dollar too high, everybody wanted to trade their paper currency for real gold and circulated the less valuable silver-backed currency instead. When the value of silver backing the dollar was too high, the reverse was true. The government tried time and again to get it right, but to no avail. Some argue that we could have made it work, but for a variety of reasons the United States gave up silver currency in 1873, which was quite controversial and became known as the "**Crime of 1873.**"

Not to overstate their role, but the Greenback Party was partly successful in helping ease this "crime" when they convinced Congress to pass a new law, the Resumption Act, in 1875. Miners in the western United States (yeah, we had special interest groups back then too) were especially concerned about the abundance of silver they were mining and wanted to ensure that there was a sound market for it. The Resumption Act eliminated fractional currency (oddly, we had paper bills for ten, twenty-five, and fifty cents) and replaced them with silver coins while also keeping greenbacks in circulation. In effect, we had a gold paper standard, silver coins, and fiat money (greenbacks).

Protecting the silver mining interest continued over the years. Congress passed silver purchase acts beginning five years after the "crime" that authorized the Treasury to buy silver and issue silver coins and silver certificates. Congress passed silver purchase acts eight times before it repealed them in 1963., and the Federal Reserve replaced silver certificates with Federal Reserve Notes.[36] You can still find an occasional silver certificate in circulation, and you will know what it is because it says on the front "SILVER CERTIFICATE." Up until 1968, they could be redeemed for silver at the US Treasury, but not anymore. In 2008, a quality one-dollar silver certificate was worth about $2.50 to a collector.

Gold certificates are much harder to find because they were typically used to transfer money between banks and were not used much in general circulation. They were printed in $20, $100, $500, $1,000, $5,000, and a very cool $10,000 bill. A $100,000 bill was also issued for use by the Federal Reserve Bank and the US Treasury but not for the public. The United States stopped issuing new gold certificates in 1928.[37]

Flavor Flav (left) courtesy of PNP/WENN. FDR (right) courtesy of the Franklin D. Roosevelt Presidential Library and Museum, Hyde Park, New York.

During the Great Depression, more and more people began demanding gold for their currency. Fearing an outright run on banks, President Franklin D. Roosevelt issued an executive order in 1933 that made possessing gold or gold certificates illegal, and his order lasted until 1964. Seriously, owning gold was illegal from 1933 until 1964! It appears Flavor Flav and others would have been okay if they had lived in the 1930s because the order made exceptions for jewelry, industrial uses, and small-scale coin collecting. While the gold "grillz" on their teeth might have violated the spirit of the law, they would have probably met the legal exceptions for jewelry *or industrial uses.*

Although gold was not available for domestic use, it was still used to back

US currency in international trade. In 1934, the government set the price of one ounce of gold at $35, and we used this value as our exchange rate with foreign governments. But inflation hit the United States hard in 1971, and President Richard Nixon ended the formal practice of trading gold for $35 an ounce, which effectively removed us from the gold standard completely. In 1972, Congress "devalued the dollar" by setting the price of an ounce of gold at $38, and then again at $42.22, but beginning in 1973, we stopped using gold in foreign trade completely.

Every now and again, you hear people calling for a return to the "gold standard," arguing that having a gold standard keeps governments from printing excess currency, and this keeps inflation low, especially in the long run. It also restricts the role of central banks, which they do not trust or consider competent to manage economies. They believe that budget deficits would be hard to finance under a gold standard, which would reduce the size and scope of government. There is a certain nostalgia for the simpler times that a gold standard would seem to provide, but we sometimes forget there is an important downside to the gold standard.

Some people distrust the Federal Reserve System and believe, among other things, that its policies contribute to excessive economic swings, such as the housing "bubble" that burst in 2007. If the Federal Reserve System hadn't been able to expand the money supply, some would argue, fewer housing loans would have been available, and the market crash would have been less likely to happen.

It may very well be the case that fewer housing loans would have been made if the nation's money supply had been limited. But in fact, fewer loans of any type would have been made, and that was precisely the reason so many people wanted off the gold standard in the first place. It's why the Greenback Party was formed in 1874. In their view, restricting the supply of money and restricting loans reduced economic growth, individual opportunity, and family wealth, especially for people in the southern and western United States. When currency was restricted to a set amount, people contended, only the elite living in large cities (along the East Coast) could easily get it. The limited amount of gold-backed currency available in the southern and western states and territories was expensive. Naturally, people were unhappy that they couldn't get affordable business loans. They demanded change. *People matter.*

The boom-and-bust economic cycles we see today wouldn't go away even if we had a gold standard and did away with the monetary policy role of the Fed. After all, while our elected government officials manage government tax and spending programs, our *fiscal policy*, it's primarily the Federal Reserve System, through its influence on bank deposits, that manages the currency supply, our *monetary policy*. This influence, especially with its impact on short-term interest rates, is almost always much more immediate and frequently far more helpful than fiscal policies.

Outside of the Great Depression, the boom-and-bust cycles were far worse before the Federal Reserve System came along, and the longer the Federal Reserve has been in existence, the better it has become at controlling inflation and deflation. In fact, the fifteen recessions or depressions that occurred over the sixty years before the Federal Reserve was established lasted an average 22.5 months. In contrast, the most recent fifteen recessions over the past eighty-six years have lasted an average of only thirteen months (and that includes the forty-three-month-long Great Depression).[38] More importantly, the severity and length of all recessions and depressions were far worse when the Federal Reserve restricted the money supply or the government failed to stimulate the economy with spending programs (an expansive *fiscal* policy). Although it's possible to reduce the impact of economic downturns with fiscal policy alone, the time lag from when the federal government passes spending bills until the money actually hits the street makes this approach alone highly ineffective and sometimes futile.

Ironically, the Great Depression was more severe than it had to be precisely because the Federal Reserve System restricted the money supply and kept the gold standard longer than most industrialized countries in the world. As University of California at Berkeley economist Dr. Brad DeLong has reported, while we were on the gold standard during the Great Depression, it was far more disastrous for us than for countries that were not, or who abandoned the standard sooner:[39]

> "... attachment to the gold standard played a major part in keeping governments from fighting the Great Depression, and was a major factor turning the recession of 1929–1931 into the Great Depression of 1931–1941.
>
> - Countries that were not on the gold standard in 1929—or that quickly abandoned the gold standard—by and large escaped the Great Depression
> - Countries that abandoned the gold standard in 1930 and 1931 suffered from the Great Depression, but escaped its worst ravages

- Countries that held to the gold standard through 1933 (like the United States) or 1936 (like France) suffered the worst from the Great Depression"

Gold standard advocates argue passionately about returning to the gold standard, but it isn't clear that they fully recognize how much families and businesses suffer when the government doesn't use pro-growth monetary and fiscal policy during recessions. Because the government and the Federal Reserve System have become so effective at reducing the severity of economic downturns, until recently most Americans had not seen the full extent of how bad it can get. The dark side of severe recessions contains increased levels of hunger, homelessness, poverty, and suicide. *People matter.*

In the end, many advocates for the gold standard distrust the government and thus prefer hard commodities over fiat currency. Unfortunately, advocates of the gold standard might tolerate individual suffering for what they perceive as longer-term stability and individual freedom from government intervention, but this would not be just a little suffering. It could be tremendous, and there is no such thing as long-term stability under these conditions. We tried that approach for a long time and found we could do better.

Printing Currency, Minting Coins, and Storing Gold

Since 1877, all national currency printing is done by the US Treasury's Bureau of Engraving and Printing (BEP), in Washington DC, and more recently in Fort Worth, Texas. The BEP also produced hand-engraved US postage stamps for 111 years, until private printers won the business away with more competitive pricing using cheaper, lithographed stamps in 2005.

Coins, on the other hand, are produced by the United States Mint, with offices in Washington DC; Philadelphia, PA; West Point, NY; Fort Knox, KY; Denver, CO.; and San Francisco, CA.

While the US government owns more gold than any other country and stores large amounts of it at Fort Knox and West Point, the largest stockpile of gold anywhere in the world (well over $200 billion) is at the Federal Reserve Bank of New York, which stores gold on behalf of the United States and most other countries. The Federal Reserve Bank of New York's stockpile has about 540,000 gold bars, weighing about twenty-eight pounds each.

I haven't counted them to be sure they were all there, but I did see them once while working at the Federal Reserve Bank. I was even allowed to hold a gold brick stored in the New York vault, and yes, seeing all that gold and holding a brick was awesome!

Our Money Supply

The Federal Reserve doesn't print any money at all, and they don't mint any coins, but they do distribute the currency and coins. Later we will see how the Federal Reserve System can influence the economy to reduce inflation or promote employment or provide confidence in the banking system. We will review the many roles it plays in things such as clearing checks between banks, lending money to banks (for short periods), regulating banks, et al. Until then, it might surprise you to discover who decides how much currency should be in circulation. You do!

In casual conversations, paper currency and coins are sometimes grouped together and called money. For example, when your momma told you to *never talk about money* in public, she meant both currency and coins. On the other hand, when she told you she needed money for rent or you would have to move out of the house, she didn't mean coins! In this book, we'll keep it more casual and use money to refer to both currency and coins.

When you need money, you go to the bank and ask for it. If it is money that the bank is holding for you from a previous deposit, they give it back. If you don't have enough money on deposit, you might ask them to loan some to you or your business. The bank reviews your ability to repay the loan, and if they agree to your request, they lend you some of the excess money they have from other depositors.

If they don't have enough money in their vaults from other depositors, they can call the District Federal Reserve Bank and ask for a shipment from any reserves they've kept in the Fed's vaults. If they don't have enough on reserve, they can borrow some from the Fed. The Federal Reserve Banks do a pretty good job of lending money to banks (they have never had a loss), and they always require the bank to provide something of value the Fed can sell to repay the loan (collateral) if necessary.

There are several kinds of acceptable collateral. It is usually government securities, but it can also be consumer or business loans, including your own loan. That's right! In effect, the currency your bank received may have been available because they borrowed it from the Fed using loans like yours as collateral. That way, if business is booming, the economy is expanding, and people need more loans, money will be available for them.

We're all in this together. As long as most of us repay our loans, and as long as our federal, state, and local governments pay back their debts, the currency is sound. As a backstop and in the very rare event that real problems come up, the government can also tax its citizens to support the currency.

So where does the Federal Reserve get its currency? Well, just like your bank has deposits from other customers who they might use to make loans, the Fed has deposits from other banks (called reserves) that they can lend. And if the Fed runs short on currency, they can put up some collateral (typically government securities and loans they made to banks like yours) and borrow some from the Treasury.

At one time, the Treasury printed a national currency with the specific bank's name on it. The bank got the currency when it put up government securities as collateral. That way, the government knew it wasn't just printing money without any gold backing it. The local bank had to produce collateral!

Now, the Treasury prints a national currency with the Federal Reserve's name on it, called a Federal Reserve Note. The Federal Reserve Banks only get currency from the Treasury when they put up collateral, typically government securities and other good assets such as loans they made to local banks. A "Note" is a legal written agreement promising to pay a debt. No problem—the Federal Reserve Note has lots of collateral backing it, primarily government securities backed by taxpayers (public debt), or loans made to banks that are backed by collateral they provided (private debt). The Federal Reserve Note is legal tender for all debts, public and private. Don't believe me? Look at the currency in your wallet. It says exactly that!

It's not that astonishing really. At one point, we used gold owned by the bank to back its individually printed currency. Now, instead of gold, we use other items of value that the bank owns to back the national currency it distributes. This includes, for example, a bank's investments in government securities and consumer and business loans. It does not include every bank asset, such as the bank building, its computers, its tables and chairs, or that little out-of-ink pen chained to the counter in the lobby.

Look at it this way: As long as the government pays its debts and people honor their loan agreements, our currency is sound. We have created a system whereby we all support each other. Your loan supports my currency which allows me to conduct trade with your company, which allows you to pay back your loan.

If enough people screw up and default on their loans, our economy gets in trouble, and people begin to worry that their currency is not worth much. They begin to get rid of dollars and buy other foreign currencies or gold or silver or real estate or something else that they believe is safer. So the government is very much interested in making sure that banks are carefully regulated and that they don't make a lot of bad loans. And that, my friend, is why God invented bank examiners. Wow! That's the first time anybody has ever used "God" and "examiners" in the same sentence without the word "damn."

There are hundreds if not thousands of websites, articles, and videos warning people about the perils of our banking and currency system. Their complaint seems to be that this system is all based on trust, and some of those authors have little or no trust in bankers, governments, or agencies. It's interesting that these websites do not complain that the system is an unknown mystery. In fact, some folks profess concern that the system is widely known but not enough people care about the risks. Fair enough.

Our system evolved from the school of hard knocks, and, while imperfect, it does work pretty darn well for most of us. There is a reason our currency is still the most widely traded currency in the world, and that's probably because our system is pretty good, warts and all. Oh, there will always be problems. But we should all have confidence we can fix them. Overthrowing the government or eliminating the Federal Reserve's role in monetary policy may satisfy people's lust for revenge from a bad economy, but it is shortsighted just the same.

Drug Money

A study from the University of Massachusetts in Dartmouth presented to the National Meeting of the American Chemical Society in August 2009 by Yuegang Zuo found that 90 percent of paper currency in the United States has traces of cocaine on it. Currency can become contaminated with cocaine during drug deals and by snorting the product through rolled bills. The coke spreads to other bills when it touches them, and that can happen in ATM machines, cash registers, currency counting machines, etc.

The amount of cocaine residue is too small to get you high, so there is no point in sniffing or licking the bills before you spend them. However, you may still choose to kiss your cash good-bye when walking into casinos.

Part II
In the Middle

Chapter 3
Commercial Banks

There are plenty of reasons to like banks, although people don't talk about that much. If you typed into your Internet search engine the phrase "reasons to like banks" you would get about 13.6 million hits, but they would include reasons to like gold, "Five More Reasons Why Tyra Banks Has to Go," and 1,000 reasons to like the old television show *MacGyver*. Those would have been the favorable hits. The others are far more negative except for the obvious advertisements posted by the institutions themselves.

You can track the negative responses to the recent crisis that became painfully evident to most people in 2007. It might surprise you that in one of the worst economies in our lifetime, when the worst of the subprime and other high-risk real estate loans seems to have hit the banks the hardest, the banking industry still reported a $10.2 billion profit in 2008.[40] Granted, it is a pitiful profit compared to normal times and was the smallest profit in nineteen years, but it was a profit nonetheless. Less than two hundred of the eighty-three hundred commercial banks and thrifts in the country failed from 2007 to 2009. The death toll began winding down over the next few years, and a government bailout prevented it from being catastrophic, but the banking system itself survived yet another disaster.

Surviving that disaster is a good thing too, because without a strong, vibrant commercial banking industry, we would all be a lot less well off. Small businesses in particular rely heavily on loans to finance their businesses. A recent survey reports that 89 percent of small-business owners used some form of credit to run their business. Commercial banks supplied nearly half of all small businesses (46 percent) with most of their credit. Small companies' access to business loans is critical for the economy because these small companies (fewer than five hundred employees) provide most of the jobs in the United States, measuring 50.2 percent of all nonfarm jobs in 2006.[41] Commercial banks play a huge role in helping these employers provide good jobs.

Given that these jobs represent a significant national interest, it's important to monitor the level, trend, and cost of credit from banks to small businesses and others. It's awfully frustrating for bankers to be so heavily regulated and to have such extensive reporting requirements, but the interaction of banks and small businesses is so important that our government tracks relationships like this closely.

The Great Depression

Much of this tracking and bank regulation can be traced back to lessons we learned after the stock market crash on October 29, 1929 ("Black Tuesday"), and the Great Depression. Before that, banks were opening rapidly with not much regulation or even shareholder money (capital). They did things like invest directly in stocks of companies, including those to whom they had also loaned money, and they invested in speculative real-estate gambles that might or might not pay off. Sometimes it worked, but sometimes it didn't, and they ended up failing, costing the depositors and shareholders their money.

Following Black Tuesday, things really got bad. Imagine living in the United States in 1933. Unemployment had reached 25 percent, and runs on banks were common. About four thousand commercial banks and seventeen hundred savings and loan associations failed in that *one year.* There was no government protection for depositors, and in the five years following Black Tuesday, depositors had lost about $1.3 billion.[42] Wow! Can you imagine putting your hard-earned money into a checking account and then waking up to discover that the bank has failed and some or all of your money is gone? It was as if you were being robbed at gunpoint.

Actually, that happened to me once in the mid-1990s. My friend Mitchell and I were robbed at gunpoint while walking back to my house in Grant Park following an Atlanta Braves baseball game. It happened in the middle of a well-lit street not far from the stadium and close to my home. The three young guys had a pistol (and a knife) and got less than one hundred dollars. Mitchell was not happy that I was negotiating terms. "Yes, you can have our cash." "No, we're not stepping into the woods." "No, you can't have my shoes." (That last demand seemed absurd!)

They had a gun pointed at us and took our money. When banks failed following Black Tuesday, no gun was pointed at the depositors, but they too were robbed of their money. Some bankers went to jail for it, and some committed suicide. Even one of the most prestigious banks at the time, the nearly 150-year-old Bank of the United States in Philadelphia (established in 1791), could not honor its customers' checks and had the distinction at the time of being the largest US bank ever to fail. Nobody was exempt from the repercussions. Check out these excerpts on three different banks from *Time* magazine on March 27, 1933:[43]

> … the conviction of Bernard K. Marcus, president, and Saul Singer, vice president, of the **Bank of U. S.** was affirmed by the New York Court of Appeals. Banksters Marcus & Singer were notified to get ready to serve their three-to-six-year terms in Sing Sing (the conviction of Herbert Singer, young son of Saul Singer, was reversed). The Bank of U. S. (with 59 branches and $160,000,000 of deposits) still remains far the biggest U. S. bank failure.

> Robert S. Stunz, executive vice president of **Park Savings Bank** at **Washington, D. C.**, told friends that there was less than a half million shortage in his bank's books, then put two bullets through his head. It was feared the shortage might be three times as great.

> Despite the fact that suicide is a crime in Church & some States, another kind of banking morality was evident last week: Howell Getty, cashier of **First National Bank of Wilmington, Pa.**, left a directors' meeting, drove two miles out on a country road and shot himself through the head. In the automobile, atop his hat and glasses, was found a note: 'The $50,000 insurance policy which the bank holds on my life will pay the depreciation on the bond account and allow the bank to re-open.'

You can see why, in return for a government bailout, bankers at the time (and today too) were willing to put up with some regulations to protect their careers. It beats prison or suicide.

After the stock market crashed, it seemed to make sense that the banks might be less inclined to lose your deposits if they were not engaged in so many diverse activities. If they had a very narrow business focus, primarily raising money from shareholders and depositors and then making loans, they and their depositors would be better off. So Congress passed, and President Franklin D. Roosevelt signed, the Glass-Steagall Act in 1933. Thanks to Glass-Steagall, banks now had specific and strict restrictions on their ability to engage in "nonbanking" activities. For instance, they couldn't own real estate unless it was for bank premises.

When the famous Glass-Steagall Act was passed, not all existing investments had to be sold because they were "grandfathered-in." Not all investments were bad, and some still remained on the banks' books, such as the ownership of Coca-Cola stock by SunTrust Banks in Atlanta.

Perhaps the most important change of all in 1933 was the formation of the Federal Deposit Insurance Corporation (FDIC) and in 1934 the Federal Savings and Loan Insurance Corporation (FSLIC). These government-backed deposit insurance companies were formed to give every depositor confidence that their money (up to $2,500 when it started in 1934) was safe. In the 1980s, a severe savings and loan crisis caused FSLIC to become insolvent. We, the taxpayers, bailed it out, and it eventually became part of the FDIC in 1989.

Like any insurance company, the FDIC charges premiums. The banks have to pay those premiums based on the types and amount of deposits. In rough times, the insurance premiums are high. For example, in 1991 they averaged about 27 cents per $100 in deposits. In good times, when the fund appears to have enough money to cover the risks, the bank might have to pay a flat annual fee, such as a modest $2,000. You can always tell whether your bank has federal government deposit insurance to protect you. If they do, you'll see an FDIC sign or sticker at every teller station.

One of the tasks of a bank examiner is to review all "nonbank" activities to ensure that they comply with the government rules. In most cases, it's very clear cut. For example, a bank can't own a skyscraper in Chicago unless it uses most of the space for bank offices or document storage. But in other cases, exceptions are allowed if the investment meets a "public benefit" test. For example, a bank can purchase an ownership interest in a company whose sole purpose is to invest in developing low-income housing in a specific, distressed neighborhood (usually by purchasing tax credits).[44] A lot of bankers use the permissible opportunities in the public benefit exceptions to do some very good projects.

Coca-Cola

In the early 1960s, Coca-Cola had this terrific advertising slogan: "Things Go Better with Coca-Cola." It turns out that banking goes better with Coca-Cola too!

Back in 1919, Trust Company of Georgia, now called SunTrust Banks and one of the largest banks in the United States, helped underwrite the initial public offering of Coca-Cola stock. That's a fancy way to say they helped put together the legal paperwork and then market the sale of Coca-Cola (Coke) stock on the New York Stock Exchange. Trust Company was very good at deals like these thanks to the leadership of their president, Ernest Woodruff.

Coca-Cola was created by an Atlanta pharmacist named John Pemberton in 1886, reportedly using extract from coca leaves and kola nuts (thus the name), among other ingredients. When it was mixed with carbonated water at Jacobs Pharmacy a few doors from Pemberton's office, it became somewhat popular, but not just for the cocaine in its formula, which has since been removed, but because it tasted great.

Following Pemberton's death two years later, entrepreneur Asa Candler purchased the rights to the business for about $2,300 (that's roughly $54,000 in 2010). Candler was an exceptional salesman and entrepreneur and expanded Coca-Cola's distribution around the country and some parts of the world. (He gave generously to charity too.) After his death in 1919, banker Ernest Woodruff helped put together some investors to buy the Coca-Cola Company from Asa's children for about $25 million.

After Woodruff's group got control, Trust Company of Georgia helped underwrite the sale of 500,000 shares of Coke stock, which went for $40 a pop, by the way, and took some of the stock as part of their fee. By the end of 2006, they owned 48.3 million shares (3.58 percent of all Coke stock), worth over $2 billion!

SunTrust Banks is sometimes called the "Coca-Cola Bank" because of this deal, and because the "secret Coke formula" is kept in its vault. The partnership between company and bank has always been strong. In fact, Ernest Woodruff's son, Robert Woodruff, was appointed president of the Coca-Cola Company in 1923. He was exceptional at the job, and he served as Coke's president for thirty-one years. In 2007, two Coca-Cola executives sat on SunTrust's board of directors.

So it goes like this—pharmacist gets $2,300; rich guy's kids get $25 million; bank gets over $2 billion; bank president gets filthy rich, and his son becomes Coke president. The only guy not getting rich was the pharmacist, which just proves once again that dealing drugs does not pay.

SunTrust has recently begun selling its Coca-Cola stock, beginning with a 2007 sale of 4.5 million shares and another 10 million in 2008. It announced plans to gradually sell another 30 million shares over seven years.

What's in a Name?

Thus far, the book has used the word "bank" somewhat generically, but we need to clarify that word a little. There are many people and organizations out there that use the word "bank" in their title. For example, we have commercial banks, savings banks, central banks, food banks, and sperm banks. There are commercial bankers, mortgage bankers, investment bankers, community bankers, and state bankers. There are probably sperm bankers out there too, but let's not go there.

After the famous stock market crash in 1929 and the start of the Great Depression, Congress passed the Glass-Steagall Act in 1933, and commercial banks had to separate themselves from investment banking activities. It was an interesting choice because you had to declare yourself either a commercial bank or an investment bank.

A good example is J. P. Morgan & Company in New York, which was a powerful institution and helped establish giants such as General Electric, U.S. Steel, and International Harvester.[45] When the Glass-Steagall Act passed, they remained a commercial bank while several individuals from the company, including Henry S. Morgan and Harold Stanley, left in 1935 to form what later became one of the largest brokerage firms in the United States of America, Morgan Stanley.

Others also left J. P. Morgan & Company (in 1940) to form Drexel and Company, which eventually merged into Drexel Burnham Lambert, a firm best known for its junk bond trading in the 1980s. Michael Milken, who was known at the time as the "junk bond king," led Drexel Burnham Lambert. Milken eventually pled guilty to security fraud charges brought against him by Rudy Giuliani, the United States attorney for the Southern District of New York. Giuliani later became the state governor and was a US presidential candidate. Not long after the Milken ordeal, Drexel's reputation was so damaged that they ended up selling out to Smith Barney. *Greed has a price.*

At one time both commercial banks and investment banks were in the same business—lending and investing—and were called the same thing: *bank.* There is no law that prevents folks from calling themselves a bank, so for purposes of this book, a bank is simply a company that makes loans and that accepts deposits insured by the FDIC. You can withdraw your deposits by writing a check or using an ATM. The key word here is "deposits."

A lot of people thought separating investment banking, commercial banking, and insurance activities back in 1933 was overkill. Eventually, they convinced the federal government to ease these restrictions, so Congress passed the Gramm-Leach-Bliley Act (GLBA, pronounced "Glib-uh"). The act was named after its three sponsors, Senator Phil Gramm (R-TX), Representative Jim Leach (R-IA), and Representative Thomas Bliley (R-VA). It was signed into law by President Bill Clinton in 1998. It allowed investment companies, insurance companies, and banks to merge, which meant that these three distinctive personalities were now all in the same family. And you thought your family Thanksgivings were awkward! These lines of business can now be part of the same parent company, which is known as a financial holding company.

These financial holding companies are similar to the kind of structure that banks had back in the 1920s, but with a few important differences:

1. The bank is a separate entity that is typically wholly owned by the financial holding company. That way, if something goes wrong with the investment or insurance businesses, it has less effect on the bank.
2. The holding company is supposed to serve as a source of strength to the bank. The holding company cannot charge excessive fees to the bank for services, such as computer processing, accounting, management, etc., and it could have limits on the amount of dividends it can receive if the bank regulators note problems at the bank.
3. You, the bank depositor, have FDIC insurance on your deposits so you won't have panic attacks if there are problems at the holding company.

The recent financial crisis has had some leaders calling for the complete or partial repeal of the Gramm-Leach-Bliley Act so that commercial banking (where you have your deposits), investment companies, and insurance companies would be separate like they were before the GLBA was passed. Former Bank of America CEO Ken Lewis even suggested as much on his way to a meeting with President Obama by saying, "Commercial banks are the fabric of any community in which they operate, and we probably need to separate the commercial banks from the investment banking activities."

He later backed off from the comment, but on December 16, 2009, Senators Maria Cantwell (D-WA) and John McCain (R-AZ) went even further by introducing a bill to that effect. It was called the Banking Integrity Act of 2009, and, outside of its catchy name, it never caught on with members of the Senate Committee on Banking, Housing, and Urban Affairs, where it was sent to die. It is especially noteworthy that "maverick" Senator McCain cosponsored the bill because his key economic advisor during his failed presidential campaign the year before was former Senator Phil Gramm, for whom the original bill (GLBA) was named.

Typically, all banks are delighted to do business with consumers who have decent credit. The larger banks have a lot of different products; the smaller banks (but definitely not all of them) might limit their products to the ones they do best. For example, some small or rural banks might choose not to make loans for mortgages or home construction because they don't have the staff or expertise to make it worthwhile. And most Internet-only banks limit their loans and other offerings because they don't have the staff to manage them.

You can still get some clues about a bank's specialty by the way they have historically described themselves. A bank that has the word "commercial" or "business" in its title, such as Commercial Bank of California in Costa Mesa, California, or Community Business Bank in West Sacramento, California, might specialize in business loans and deposit products. If the word "consumer" is in the title, such as Consumers National Bank of Minerva, Ohio, the bank is likely to specialize in consumer needs. A Farmers Bank might focus on agricultural lending.

People also talk about "thrift institutions," or "thrifts" for short. The phrase is still commonly used for a lot of different kinds of "thrift institutions": savings banks, federal savings banks, savings and loan associations, mutual savings banks, cooperative banks (co-ops), and even credit unions. That's because people usually see a thrift institution as being formed to focus on serving consumers. These thrift institutions offer products such as personal savings accounts and mortgage loans. A commercial bank, on the other hand, focuses on business products such as commercial loans. In fairness, a lot of commercial banks are every bit as focused on consumers as some thrifts, and the differences among all of these institutions are beginning to blur.

Thrifts and commercial banks do have their own unique histories and some important differences. One big distinction is that thrifts have restrictions on the amount of business loans they can make. After all, their main purpose is to serve consumers, not businesses. This sometimes means that a thrift may have more expertise in mortgage lending than a commercial bank, which may have more expertise in business lending. Another obvious difference is that mutual savings banks, co-ops, and credit unions are owned by their members (depositors) and are treated as nonprofit organizations. Because they are nonprofit organizations, they are exempt from certain state and federal taxes.

Banks really do come in all shapes and sizes. Some are small, family-owned banks. Others are huge, multinational companies with hundreds of shareholders. Some institutions, such as mutual savings banks and credit unions, are even established with a public purpose, for example, to serve a specific community or trade union. Suffice it to say that these financial institutions all have three things in common: (1) they take deposits, (2) they make loans, and (3) they are regulated by the government.

The Three-Legged Stool

Imagine a three-legged stool. The shareholders, one leg of the stool, want management to provide a fair return on their money. Employees, the second leg, want a good salary and benefits. Customers, the third leg, want a good return on their deposits and a reasonable rate on any loans. Everybody wants a commitment that the bank will operate safely so that shareholders don't lose their investments, employees don't lose their jobs, and customers don't lose their deposits. For senior management of the bank especially, it is sometimes a daunting task to balance all three legs. Cut one leg short, and the stool falls over.

Let's say that you are a bank shareholder with five thousand dollars invested in common stock. You could open an insured-deposit account at the bank, and probably earn a reasonable rate of return along with the government guarantee that your five grand is safe. Or you can buy stock in the bank and take a higher risk with no guarantees, expecting instead to get dividend payments or stock appreciation or both. If you can't earn more by buying stock than you can in a government-guaranteed deposit, you would be crazy to buy the stock.

Management knows this, which is why they work hard to be sure that shareholders (one leg of the stool) earn more over time than the depositors (the second leg of the stool). But good employees (the third leg) don't come cheap, and they don't work for free. They also demand a return. The more we pay employees, the less we can pay shareholders and depositors. It's a tough job keeping the stool balanced.

Corporate culture, employee personalities, community pressure, competitors, and shareholder demands all interact in a truly fascinating way. You can probably imagine the struggle bankers have finding the right balance. For a lot of people working at the bank who make these calls, the dilemma becomes very personal. For example, consider the conflicting agendas at a small town bank of a consumer lender making car loans and a customer service representative promoting deposit products.

The consumer lender who makes car loans typically knows the borrowers very well. The borrower is often a regular guy or gal working to make ends meet and support their family. The car is critical to drop the kids off at school, get to work, pick up the kids after school, get the groceries, make it to the soccer game on weekends, etc. In most places public transportation isn't an option, and having a car is just a necessary part of life. Money is tight for this working-class borrower, and every penny counts. Their friends might tell them to work with this particular consumer lender because he/she is honest and will say yes to their loan request.

The consumer lender understands what it takes to make the deal work. "Yes, you can have the loan. Yes, we can arrange an affordable monthly payment. Yes, you can have the money right away." Consumer lenders are quite popular, by the way. They know just about everybody in town and could even be elected mayor (and many have been). The consumer lender might argue for the lowest interest rate possible for their hardworking borrowers.

On the other hand, the bank tellers or customer service representatives who sell deposit products such as certificates of deposit (CDs), know their customer equally well. CDs are a type of deposit product that pays higher interest rates if the customer agrees to leave the deposit untouched for a certain amount of time, such as six months or a year. The CD customer is often a senior citizen living on their Social Security income and the interest they earn on their CDs at the bank. All the tellers know about the person's rheumatoid arthritis and the grandkids in Denver. They come into the bank every Wednesday whether they need anything or not because it's part of their social network. This super likable senior wants the highest interest rate possible on their CD, and we don't blame them because they need it to pay for groceries and medicines. The tellers and customer service reps would like to get the highest possible interest rate for their depositors.

It's hard to offer low rates on loans and high rates on deposits without sacrificing somewhere else, such as salaries or shareholder returns. It's even more challenging when you have employees paid on commissions, like some mortgage lenders whose annual bonus might be based on how much they loan. Raising interest rates on mortgage loans could impact their own paychecks! Naturally, they will be reluctant to support higher mortgage loan rates, even if it means a better deal for the senior citizen CD customer and the shareholders, or even the other employees.

Get the idea? The dynamics really are interesting, and reflect the bankers' personalities, their jobs, and their perspectives. Senior management must successfully balance these competing interests, and some are better at doing it than others. There are many scorecards used to measure their success, such as community awards and recognition, regulator examination ratings for operating safely, the board of directors approving great pay packages, etc. But the most widely viewed scorecard of a bankers' success is contained in their published financial statements.

Income and Expenses

Every bank is different, but some things are very consistent: Most of a bank's income (71 percent) comes from the interest and fees they charge on their loans.[46] They try their best to generate income any way they can. They might rent space in their buildings to other companies or charge fees for safe-deposit boxes, for example. They charge fees on their deposit products or expand into selling insurance products. That's all fine and good. But it's still interest on money they lend to consumers, businesses, governments, and others that generate the most income. As a result, bankers devote a lot of resources to making quality loans. It is both an art and a science to analyze the loan requests. This includes loans they make to governments, which are in the form of government securities they buy.

Lots of folks moan and groan about the fees they have to pay on checking accounts, especially for overdrafts or for ATM machines, and who can blame them? We all feel like we are being nickeled and dimed to death sometimes. Even so, although these fees might be significant to consumers, they are still a relatively small percentage of a bank's income, only 5 percent. It's all those loans that generate the income, and in particular the loans to consumers and businesses (54 percent of income) and government securities (10 percent) that bring in the most money. As long as they can continue to originate quality loans and investments, this interest income can help the bank grow and prosper. The financial scorecard clearly shows their success in doing so.

Unfortunately, loans and securities can go bad, and they do. Bankers try to grow too fast, buying and originating many marginal loans and investments in the process. They can't keep up, or they get sloppy. *Bigger is not always better.* Sometimes they loosen their credit standards too much, figuring the economy is strong, the borrower is creditworthy, and the loan is properly secured. *It's almost always bad loans.*

Most of a bank's expenses, about 41 percent, are for the interest they pay to a variety of customers for money that they can lend or invest. In fact, about 21 percent of their expenses are just for the interest paid to their consumer and business depositors.

In 2006, the cost of salaries and benefits for bank officers and employees was also about 21 percent of total expenses. That's not to say the salaries and benefits were equally distributed. Commercial lenders, for example, are some of the highest paid people at a bank while tellers are paid more like school teachers—poorly. So be nice to the tellers at your bank. They aren't paid enough for you to yell at them! Anyhow, under the three-legged stool analogy, it appears that the bankers are balancing the money paid to their consumer and business depositors and to their employees fairly well, with each group comprising about 21 percent of total expenses.

And finally, let's not forget that some people won't be able (or willing) to repay their loans. Bankers must set aside part of their earnings to cover the losses on bad loans. After all, the bank was using their depositors' money to make loans. It's not like they can just tell depositors, "Sorry, we can't honor your check because Fat Albert's Restaurant didn't repay their loan." In 2006, money set aside to help cover bad loans was 4 percent of the average bank's total expenses. Not surprisingly, it was a whole lot higher for the next few years because so many loans defaulted during the recession. When a bank has so much at stake with its lending activities, any mistake can be costly.

Profits

You can measure a bank's profitability in a lot of ways, but the two most common measuring sticks are return on average assets (ROA) and return on equity (ROE). ROA looks at how much profit a bank earned given the size of the bank. It is calculated by dividing a bank's profit (net income) by the bank's size (average assets).[47] A typical bank in a typical year would probably have an ROA of a little over 1 percent. That means the bank earns one cent for every dollar of assets. That's why they like to get big—more assets mean more profits!

ROE, on the other hand, looks at how much profit was generated given the amount of shareholder money. It is calculated by dividing a bank's profit (net income) by the average amount of the shareholders money at risk (equity). Once again, a typical bank in a typical year would probably have an ROE of a little over 10 percent. That means the bank earns ten cents for one dollar of equity. That's why they like to keep their shareholders money to a minimum. More shareholder money means those profits have to be shared more too!

Regulators and analysts both look at tons of data, and they don't use any particular ratio without also considering a lot of other information. But for a "quick and dirty" look at bank profits, bank examiners frequently use ROA. The ROA is a nice snapshot of the bank's performance given its size and without any bias toward the shareholders' return. It isn't meant to be disrespectful to shareholders or to sound too simplistic, but the bank examiner is much less interested in an appropriate return for the shareholders and, instead, is looking to make sure that the privately owned bank has enough profit to prevent risks to the depositors. After all, a regulator's goal is to protect your government-insured deposit. They don't have a mandate to protect your stock investments.

Investors are obviously more concerned about their investment, and the ROE is a great way to evaluate it because the ratio allows an "apple-to-apple comparison" with other companies and industries.

Profits at all US Commercial Banks

	ROA	ROE
2003	1.05	10.53
2004	1.06	10.63
2005	1.09	10.92
2006	1.05	10.44
2007	0.90	8.82

To evaluate the bank profits, you not only want to know its level of profits but also its trend, as shown here for all banks in the United States.[48] The ROA in 2003 was 1.05 percent, meaning that the banking industry averaged $1.05 profit on every $100 of stuff they owned (average assets). The ROE that year was 10.53 percent, meaning the industry averaged $10.53 profit on every $100 of shareholders investment (average equity).

As you can see, earnings were very good and consistent until 2007 when the problems with real estate lending and the weakening economy hit. Whether you're a regulator or an investor, you want to look for big changes, either good or bad. For example, the banking industry profits spiked a little bit upward in 2005, which doesn't mean anything by itself but does serve as a red flag. What was happening to cause profits to go up compared to previous years? Well, a closer look would have shown that the banks were charging more for their loans than they were paying on their deposits compared to two years earlier, and therefore their "net interest margin" increased. That's normally a good thing for shareholders. Unfortunately, some of those loans were more risky, and two years later, banks paid the price because it cost more to collect these loans, and the banks had to pay more into their "loan loss reserve" accounts. *We should have seen it coming. It's almost always bad loans.*

Did you know that banks earned about one cent for every dollar of assets they own? Or that they earned about a 10.25 percent return for their shareholders? For comparison, the average five-year ROE (ending in 2006) for automobile manufacturers was 17.9 percent; distillers and vintners, 16 percent; oil and gas companies, 21.6 percent; pharmaceuticals, 35.6 percent; and railroads; 8.9 percent.[49]

Hmm, banks had better profits than the railroads but have not done as well as the drug and alcohol businesses. Surely there is a country song in this somewhere.

Assets and Liabilities

Banks make money off of the things they own, such as loans to their borrowers; bonds they buy from federal, state, and local governments; or even income they get from their extra office space. They work hard to ensure that almost everything they own can be used to generate earnings, and it is very important that analysts track the level of "earning assets." At a typical bank, over 92 percent of the bank's assets are considered earning assets, and the higher this level is, the better chance these assets have at generating profits.

Assets are things the bank *owns*; liabilities are things they *owe* to others. For example, they owe you the money you deposited with them; it's a liability. We know banks pay most of their expenses to raise money and earn most of their income from loans. So it makes sense that for all US commercial banks, their biggest asset is loans (65 percent of average assets) and biggest liability is deposits (83 percent). It might surprise you that the fancy buildings owned by the bank are less than 2 percent of their average assets and that, until recently, the foreclosed properties, called other real estate owned, or OREO (yes, just like the cookie) was only about seven-tenths of 1 percent.

Capital Standards

Banks decide how much down payment or equity you should have in a deal before they lend you money, so who decides how much money they should have in the deal to start or run a bank? You guessed it: the regulators. *Good government is necessary.*

This makes sense because even though the banks themselves must purchase insurance to protect your deposit accounts, the government will still step in if necessary and bail out the industry in bad times. The repercussions if the government didn't step in could be severe, for example, a prolonged depression.

Regardless of your type of business, if you have some government backing, it's only fair that you should also have some minimal level of shareholder money (capital) at risk too. The shareholders can help ensure that bankers are not taking too much risk because the shareholders would lose most or all of their money before taxpayers were asked to step up to the plate. The idea is to force bankers to answer to both shareholders and regulators. The question is, how much shareholder money should the bank have at any time?

It doesn't make sense for the United States to have one set of really tough capital standards while banks from other countries who are competing with us have much looser standards, or vice versa. That's why the Basel Committee on Banking Supervision was formed in 1974 by the central banks or similar agencies from ten countries, including the United States. Eventually, in 1988, the Basel Accord (because the conference was held in Basel, Switzerland) required all banks at the conference to have similar minimum international capital standards. An updated set of capital standards, known as Basel II, has also been adopted and implemented in most countries, but to varying degrees. Basel III is now being promoted but has not yet been fully implemented.

On average, investors put about 10 percent of the money (capital) into a bank, and the bankers borrow about 90 percent of the money (liabilities). It's very similar to a loan you might get from the bank. You have to make a 10 percent down payment before the bank lends you the other 90 percent.

You might think this was an easy task for regulators. But because different countries had different definitions of "capital," they had to first figure out how to *define* capital before they could set any standards! It gets quite complex, and, come to think of it, the whole topic might seem boring, but hang in there. It's not as bad as it sounds.

Banks are subject to two main minimum standards. The first required its total capital to equal 8 percent of its risky assets. Total capital includes a lot of stuff, such as money from the shareholders when they purchased bank stock, any profits the bank earned but had not paid to shareholders (called undivided profits), and money the bank has set aside in a reserve for bad loans.

The second standard is called the Tier 1 capital ratio and only looks at the pretty solid stuff, the core capital. This ratio doesn't include things that are less solid, like the bank's loan loss reserve because that account could be wiped out real fast if too many loans go bad. Regulators required the Tier 1 capital ratio to equal at least 4 percent of risky assets.

Both capital ratios refer to risky assets (technically called "risk-weighted assets"). That's because some assets are riskier than others and should be weighted as such. For example, federal government securities have little risk because they are backed by taxpayers. They don't need to be counted as risky assets. State and local securities, however, even though they are often backed directly by taxpayers (called general obligation bonds) still have some risk, so we should count at least 20 percent of them as risky assets. At the time, the banking authorities at the Basel conference also agreed that generally speaking, mortgage lending is not too risky, so we count only 50 percent of the "performing" mortgage loans when adding up the risky assets.

But what about things that are risky but are not shown on the bank's books? For example, what if I have a business line of credit from the bank but haven't used it yet? The bank has some risk, not the least of which is that I might draw on my line of credit and then not pay it back. It's not on the bank's books as a loan because I haven't actually borrowed the money yet, so it's considered an off-balance-sheet risk. That's why the regulators have a fancy formula to review "off-balance-sheet" risks that they incorporate into calculating risk-weighted assets.

Whew! That's a lot to think about, and it is not a bad approach. But it still misses some important stuff, such as really weak earnings or management that stinks or liquidity problems when the bank has too many loans and not enough cash or concentrations of loans to one industry that could have a downturn, etc.

As you can see, just deciding how much money the shareholder should put up to operate a bank can get rather complex, which is why there are things bankers don't tell you because they probably don't know themselves. They depend on the chief financial officer to specialize in things like this, and they complain about the overly complex regulations they must deal with. The regulators are in the same boat too!

In reality, bankers try hard to ensure that their capital never gets to the point of regulatory scrutiny, and they prefer to keep extra capital on hand to take advantage of future growth opportunities. At year-end 2007, the Tier 1 capital ratio was at the highest level in five years: 10.6 percent. Given the bad economy, the capital cushion was not for growth as much it was for protection from the recession and higher levels of loan losses.

You could argue that the safety and soundness of your bank, of the banking industry, of the national economy ... hell! ... even our national security depends a lot on meaningful capital standards. And there is a natural conflict between bankers obviously wanting less regulation and smaller amounts of *required* capital while our national economic interests would want far more capital. And it's not just the United States. It's the same conflict for bankers around the world.

That's why the central bankers and their counterparts continue to tinker with these standards. Basel II goes beyond bad loans and investments (the credit risks). What if rising or falling interest rates spell trouble (a type of market risk)? What if there are internal problems at a bank, such as fraud or computer screwups (operational risks)? Newer, more complex and comprehensive standards to address those issues were put into effect in the United States beginning in 2009. There is even a Basel III standard under consideration now.

Whatever the standard regulators impose, it can't be too rigid because it could lead to some serious problems in an economic downturn, such as the one the United States had beginning in 2007. If loans and investments begin to go bad, you want to be sure that banks have enough capital to weather the storm. But if you base solutions on a rigid formula, you don't have flexibility, and you could make bad problems worse.

Let's assume we have a bad economy. Real estate values are declining, and the number of problem loans at the bank is increasing. That's what happened in 2008. To survive a serious recession, a bank might have to sell more stock (raise capital), or reduce the number of total loans it has booked (reduce their size), or both. That means the bank either cuts off lending, which can make the economy worse, or the bank tries to raise capital at a time when selling bank stock is awfully hard.

If you repeat this scenario at enough banks, the problems get even worse. Fewer loans get made, less capital gets raised, and bank failures rise, and it leads to a huge economic recession or worse! Sound familiar? That's one reason why the taxpayer money was used to buy stock in 2008 as part of the industry bailout (it was called the Capital Purchase Program). Bankers couldn't find enough investors to buy their common stock!

You may be thinking that there has got to be a better way! Everybody wants clear, simple standards, and this is nothing new. Some folks have even suggested a system that eliminates all the details and has a simple standard requiring 20 percent or more total capital to cover risk-weighted assets. Talk about scaring bankers! If the regulators required 20 percent capital, the shareholders wouldn't get much return on their investment. A lot of shareholders would sell their bank stock and invest somewhere else that paid better. The banks might then begin making riskier loans to get better returns and keep their shareholders content. It wouldn't be any fun for the regulators either. Higher capital standards would require much more oversight to prevent bankers from taking extra risk.

One thing is certainly clear. Banking is complex, and most people have a hard time understanding the minutiae. *Good government is necessary* to understand these complexities and protect the taxpayers. The terrible economy we faced beginning in 2007 and the huge shakeout in the banking, insurance, and investment industries will surely force changes in the way we protect against risks. Perhaps we can cover the results in another book entitled *What the Regulators Don't Tell You Because They Are Still Trying to Figure It Out!*

Shareholder Return

If you buy stock in a company, what do you expect in return? Most of us buy stock to get a good financial return. We may also want their products and services to be consistent with our own values.

For example, some of us believe in a strong national defense and find that buying stock in companies that support our military infrastructure is consistent with those values. Others of us might want to buy stocks of socially responsible companies such as those that promote a healthy environment. We might avoid companies that manufacture unhealthy products such as tobacco. Some of us might buy stock simply to influence the direction of the company by attending shareholder meetings and challenging the board about what it pays its executives or what its international investments are. And some of us could care less about all that stuff as long as our stocks make enough money for us to retire comfortably.

Whatever the motivation, virtually anybody who invests should expect a fair financial return on their money because if that isn't a priority, they could just give their money to these companies or to nonprofit organizations or to political activists.

When people buy stocks, they are looking for different returns. Some folks want investments to generate income every month because they plan to live on that money. Others want the value of their stocks to increase a lot over time, and they seek out "growth" stocks that they can cash out and retire on the profits. Others want a balance of both current income and growth stocks. And, fortunately, a lot of stocks that pay good dividends provide both. In fact, some studies have shown that higher-yielding stocks (those paying high dividends) have outperformed lower-yielding stocks (or those paying no dividends) over the long term.[50]

There was a time when people bought bank stocks mostly because they paid steady, predictable dividends and had a modest increase in value. From 1966 to 1983, about 95 percent of commercial banks paid consistent dividends to their shareholders, but that level dropped to about 85 percent in 2003.[51] Even at this lower level, bank stocks typically paid pretty good dividends. That's not the case anymore.

There is no guarantee that bank stock will appreciate or that a high dividend payout will continue. Buying bank stock can be risky, and some people prefer the comfort of a government-guaranteed deposit product instead. But others see real benefit in owning bank stock. They buy bank stock because the dividends paid are sometimes higher than interest they would get paid on that bank's deposit accounts. And of course, adding to its appeal, bank stock values can increase over time. People also buy bank stocks because they perceive them as an average or even lower risk when compared to other industries.

How has that worked out? Not especially well recently.

I'm not offering any advice here, and if you tracked my own investment portfolio, you wouldn't want to listen to me anyway. It hasn't performed that well! But with banks, one way to follow the industry's stock performance is by tracking an index fund such as those from the investment firm of Keefe, Bruyette & Woods. (Please note that these folks did not pay to have their name mentioned in this book, but if they had, Keefe, Bruyette & Woods would have been the names of my first three children.) KBW has two well-known bank index funds (a type of investment comprised of bank stocks). One lists two dozen large banks, and the other lists fifty regional banks. Over a five-year period ending December 2007, the large-bank index fund generated a modest 2.93 percent total return, and the regional-bank index generated a slightly smaller 2.40 percent return.

Both bank index funds show the real estate problems that began in late 2006. Generally speaking, both the large and small banks performance stunk compared with the overall stock market! In fact, the S&P 500 Index (comprised of 500 companies) had generated a solid 10.40 percent return for investors while the banks' returns were under 3 percent!

Ownership

If you want to know who owns the banks, it's not as simple as you might think because most banks are owned by other companies. These companies are called bank holding companies (BHCs), and they are owned by a lot of different investors: people like you and me and also large institutions. Institutional investors are owned by even more investors, and it can be challenging to track down a lot of detail.

The bottom line is that *generally speaking*, large banks are owned by holding companies, and holding companies are owned by lots of individuals, some mutual funds, and some institutional investors.

Community banks, *generally speaking*, are owned by the same groups except that there are fewer shareholders, and more of these individual owners tend to live in the community where the bank does business.

Small banks, *generally speaking*, are often owned by a family or by a small number of shareholders. This family and the shareholders typically live in the community and frequently work at the bank too.

If you want to know if your bank is owned by a holding company, you can go to the National Information Center website (www.ffiec.gov/nic), click on Institution Search, enter the bank's name, and look at the organizational hierarchy. It's free and easy.

It's really just an evolutionary process that resulted in this complexity. Before the 1930s, banks were owned directly by individuals and investors, and their charter allowed them to gather deposits, make loans, and speculate in real estate and in stocks and bonds. In 1933, the banks were restricted to just gathering deposits and making loans. They had to get rid of their investment banking activities (such as selling stocks) and other nonbanking activities (such as real estate investing). But you know how entrepreneurial people can be, and one way around regulated industries, such as telephones, utilities, railroads, and banking, was to form holding companies.

Holding companies were originally designed to own enough stock to have a controlling interest in a company that was doing business in a heavily regulated industry. The regulated companies, such as railroads or banks, would meet government restrictions while the holding company, on the other hand, could do whatever the heck it wanted. A bank holding company, for example, could set up banks across state lines, which the banks themselves were typically restricted from doing so until much later (1985). Holding companies could go into new lines of business that banks were prevented from doing (such as owning title insurance companies). They could have higher debt levels, own different types of investments, and gain tax advantages, for example, by offsetting the bank profits with another subsidiary's losses.

At first, not all politicians and regulators were excited about BHCs because they were afraid these companies might drain the bank's profits and capital base to grow their other businesses. BHCs could harm the bank if they charged excessive management fees for services they provided to the bank or required high dividend payouts to finance other businesses. Even worse, if the BHC or one of its nonbank subsidiaries ever got into trouble, the owners might try to divert money (or management) from the bank to help the troubled parent company or subsidiary survive. Given that the regulators' mandate was to protect the depositors and ensure that the federal deposit insurance program stayed solvent, regulators firmly believed that bank holding companies should serve as a source of strength to the bank rather than the other way around.

That's why the Banking Act of 1935 was passed. It gave the Federal Reserve Board the right to issue permits for BHCs to own bank stock and the Fed the right to inspect BHCs. A BHC was defined as a company that owns or controls 25 percent or more of a bank's stock, but the Federal Reserve Board presumes that a controlling interest is 5 percent.

The Bank Holding Company Act of 1956 and the Bank Holding Company Act Amendments of 1970, along with a variety of other laws and regulations that followed, continued to strengthen the Fed's role in supervising BHCs. The regulators developed BHC minimum capital standards, and they devised a rating system to better communicate their view of the financial and managerial condition of the BHC. They reviewed:

the condition of the **B**ank,
the holding company's **O**perations,
the condition of the **P**arent company,
the holding company's **E**arnings,
and the adequacy of its **C**apital
before assigning a "**BOPEC**" rating.

BOPEC (pronounced "Bo-peck') was a good regulatory acronym to rate bank holding companies, and it might also have been a good name for somebody's pet or perhaps an ugly kid. The regulators occasionally update the rating systems, and in 2005 they developed an improved rating system known as—seriously, this is true: "RFI/C(D)."[52]

In November 1999, the Gramm-Leach-Bliley Act changed things considerably by allowing banks, insurance companies, and securities firms to affiliate with each other through a financial holding company (FHC) structure. Many of the BHCs can now declare themselves to be an FHC by notifying the Fed. They can change themselves from a BHC to an FHC if they are well-capitalized and well-managed, and if they have satisfactory or better rating under the Community Reinvestment Act. They don't ever stop being a bank holding company when they change to an FHC, and they are still subject to the same rules and regulations as BHCs, but they can also own securities firms and insurance companies, which is the point.

Because it is a two-way street, investment firms and insurance companies can also set up holding companies to purchase banks and become FHCs. They are subject to the same Fed rules and regulations. As of March 30, 2008, there were 621 FHCs and 5,030 BHCs in the United States.[53]

Who Owns the Banks?

The question of whether any particular religion, or race, or culture has control over banking is not new and not unreasonable, even if it is uncomfortable. In fact, given the high level of government and regulatory oversight, no one race, culture, or religion in the United States is allowed to control the banking industry if it harms others.

Fortunately, it doesn't really matter because in addition to these extensive laws and regulations to prevent discrimination, we also benefit from a great number of specialty banks.

There are specifically chartered banks to serve African Americans, Asian Americans, Hispanics, women, and others. We have banks chartered to specifically focus on low- and moderate-income communities, on agricultural communities, and on high-income communities. Some banks target specific occupations as well, including accountants, builders, doctors, lawyers, truckers, and other professions. There is something out there for just about everybody.

It is understandable and appropriate for people to want the companies they do business with to reflect their values and ideals. Fortunately, it's easy to track who's on the board by just going to their website and reviewing their annual report.

You can also ask for their Community Reinvestment Act compliance report (you usually don't have to pay a fee). This report gives you insight about the bank's activities in the community, especially in the low- and moderate-income areas.

If you want a list of minority-owned financial institutions in the United States, you can get it from the Federal Reserve Board (www.federalreserve.gov.). In 2007, it listed over 135 institutions, including 45 Asian American, 41 African American, 24 Hispanic, 16 Native American, and 8 Caucasian women-owned banks.

The chart below shows the top twenty BHCs in March 2008. Within six months of that date, Wachovia was acquired by Wells Fargo, Washington Mutual failed and what remained was sold by the FDIC to JPMorgan Chase & Co., and Goldman Sachs and Morgan Stanley converted to bank holding companies. The industry has been changing at a crazy pace, so charts like this are obsolete almost as soon as they are created.

Top 20 US Banking Companies

Bank holding companies ranked by total domestic assets as of March 31, 2008

1) CITIGROUP INC.	New York, NY	$2.2 Trillion
2) BANK OF AMERICA CORPORATION	Charlotte, NC	$1.7 Trillion
3) JPMORGAN CHASE & CO	New York, NY	$1.6 Trillion
4) WACHOVIA CORPORATION	Charlotte, NC	$808.6 Billion
5) DEUTSCHE BANK AG	Frankfurt, Germany	$750.3 Billion *
6) WELLS FARGO & COMPANY	San Francisco, CA	$595.2 Billion
7) METLIFE INC	New York, NY	$557.1 Billion
8) HSBC HOLDINGS INC	London, England	$493.0 Billion *
9) BARCLAYS PLC	London, England	$485.6 Billion *
10) WASHINGTON MUTUAL INC	Seattle, WA	$319.7 Billion
11) U.S. BANCORP	Minneapolis, MN	$241.8 Billion
12) THE BANK OF NEW YORK MELLON CORP	New York, NY	$205.2 Billion
13) SUNTRUST BANKS, INC	Atlanta, GA	$179.0 Billion
14) ROYAL BANK OF SCOTLAND GROUP PLC	Edinburgh, Scotland	$161.8 Billion *
15) NATIONAL CITY CORP	Cleveland, OH	$155.0 Billion
16) STATE STREET CORP	Boston, MA	$154.5 Billion
17) CAPITAL ONE FINANCIAL CORP	McLean, VA	$150.6 Billion
18) REGIONS FINANCIAL CORP	Birmingham, AL	$144.2 Billion
19) PNC FINANCIAL SERVICES GROUP INC	Pittsburgh, PA	$140.0 Billion
20) BB&T CORP	Winston-Salem, NC	$136.4 Billion

* Reflects US assets only

Sources: American Banker On-Line database, the Federal Financial Institutions Examination Council's National Information Center (NIC), FR Y-9C data, and the Securities Exchange Commission, Form 10-Q

Foreign Bank Owners

Four of the top 20 largest companies that own banks in the United States were owned by foreign companies. Deutsche Bank in Frankfurt, Germany, owns a subsidiary company called Taunus Corporation, NY, which purchased Bankers Trust Company, NY, in 2002 and renamed it Deutsche Bank and Trust Company. If you don't know this bank but are a golf fan, you might know them as the title sponsor of the PGA Tour event played on Labor Day at the Tournament Players Club of Boston in 2007. If you are from Germany, you know them as the largest bank in that country and one of the largest in Europe.

HSBC Holdings in London owns HSBC North America Holdings, which owns HSBC Bank USA, NA. Over the years, HSBC North America acquired many finance companies and banks, including, for example, the Beneficial Finance Companies, Marine Midland Banks in New York, and Republic Bank in California. Some readers might remember Beneficial's catchy and happy musical slogan, "At Beneficial (toot-toot), you're good for more." Remember the tune? Ha! Now it's stuck in your head for the rest of the day! I said it was catchy.

Barclays PLC, also from England, owns Barclays Group U.S. Inc., which owns Barclays Banks (previously called Juniper Bank) and had a large California presence before selling those Barclay Bank locations to Wells Fargo in 1988. In 2008, Barclays had the naming rights to England's "Premier League" football team (soccer) and to a new multibillion-dollar sports arena in Brooklyn, New York, where the New Jersey Nets are scheduled to play.

Royal Bank of Scotland Group (RBS Group) owned Citizens Financial Group, Providence, Rhode Island, which has acquired several banking companies over the years, including Charter One Financial that operates in the Northeast and Midwest. It is the largest banking company in Scotland, one of the largest in the world, and owns the Royal Bank of Scotland, which was chartered in 1727.

But wait a minute! Why would the United States allow a foreign bank, any foreign bank for that matter, to own one of our own banks? Isn't there some sort of national security risk? Wouldn't we be in trouble if the foreign government had a dispute with the United States and froze all US banking assets?

Everyone can appreciate these concerns, especially given that at year-end 2007, foreign banking companies owned 23.7 percent of all US banking assets. In contrast, back in 1973, foreign banking companies owned only 3.8 percent of assets and 1.7 percent of our deposits.[54] But it really is a global economy now, and our banks have been buying controlling interests in foreign banks too.

As just one example, in 2007, New York-based Citigroup bought fifty-four banking subsidiaries in El Salvador, Costa Rica, Panama, Honduras, and Guatemala for $1.5 billion from a company called Grupo Cuscatlan, which is a subsidiary of Corporacion UBC Internatcional, headquartered in Guatemala. Buying banks around the world has become a two-way street and can make doing business much easier for international businesses and travelers.

The US regulators pay close attention to the foreign banks. In fact, even without owning US banks directly, the branches and agencies of foreign-owned banks in the United States are examined on-site every year. And the Federal Reserve Board must not only approve foreign bank branches, agencies, commercial lending subsidiaries, and other offices in the United States, but the Fed can also end the operations of foreign banks if necessary.

Following the provisions of the International Banking Act of 1978, the rules for both foreign banks and domestic banks are the same. They both have to have the same capital levels and other safety and soundness standards. The Fed expects foreign banks to strengthen its banks in the United States and will prevent any bank holding company, whether domestic or foreign, from draining the bank to support its other ventures. It would be very difficult for a foreign government to seize the bank's assets because the bank itself still has to follow the same laws and regulations as any other US bank. The bank itself must still operate under a US charter even if its owner doesn't.

Tracking Owners

If you want to know the specific owners of any bank or bank holding company, you can always go to their website (an excellent starting point) or review any reports filed with the Securities and Exchange Commission (cumbersome) or try a number of free sources, such as the MSN Money website.[55]

> *... if the institutional investors are dumping their bank stock, the regulators need to haul over to the bank and find out why!*

Large banking companies are often partially owned by institutional investors, which are companies that specialize in helping other investors, such as foundations, endowments, corporate treasurers, pension fund managers, and so forth. These institutional investors develop programs that meet their clients' specific needs. For example, if the head of a large trade union is responsible for investing the money of members who have contributed to a particular retirement plan, they might choose to hire an institutional investor such as Barclays to help set up a plan to purchase stock in companies such as Citigroup.

These institutional investors are focused on companies doing what they promised, and they have voting rights just like any other shareholders. If the company is not performing as the institutional investors expected, they can always vote to replace board members or at least try to talk to the board members or senior officers to pressure them to shape up. They can also sell the stock if it doesn't perform well, and when they do, other analysts will surely notice. In fact, regulators now watch stock prices closely and keep an eye on what these institutional investors do. As a general rule, if the institutional investors are dumping their bank stock, the regulators need to haul over to the bank and find out why!

Tracking Performance

There was a time when regulators would simply *call* the bankers and ask for financial statements, or what is more specifically known today as their "Consolidated Reports of Condition and Income." These balance sheets and income statements had to be produced when the regulators called, thus the nickname: **Call Reports.**

The bank's chief financial officer or cashier carefully prepares the Call Reports, and two top banking executives sign them. Bank management has to have independent auditors review the bank's accounting procedures and these reports to make sure they are accurate. Bank examiners check not only the scope (what the report covers) of the auditors' work, but they even review the reports themselves to be sure they are accurate.

In fact, bankers understand how important these reports are and have internal controls to be sure that everything is accurate. They'd better because if they don't, they are up for serious scrutiny by the regulators and auditors. They might even have to pay penalties. Bank accounting is nothing to mess with, and you sure don't want to go astray. *Accounting is not a game.*

When the regulators get the quarterly Call Reports, they run them through a series of calculations and develop a Uniform Bank Performance Report (UBPR), which is a very good way to evaluate a bank. And it's free! There's no reason you can't be just as smart as the bank president who reviews this report. Just go to www.ffiec.gov, click on "UBPR," and then "Search" to get a five-year financial history on any commercial bank or savings bank.

If you work at a bank, having studied the UBPR is a great way to improve your value to the company. You will be held in much higher regard when you ask smart questions about company financial performance at the next Monday morning meeting instead of bragging about shooting par at the golf course last week after chugging a six-pack of beer the night before. Not that your feat isn't impressive.

Examinations

What bankers won't tell you is how the regulators rate them because that is against government regulations and is just not allowed. Bankers know how they rate because the regulators prepare a report of examination and share the results with the bank's senior management. But the bankers can't share these reports. For one, if people suspect a bank is in trouble because of something in the regulators' routine examination, they will rush to the bank to yank out their money. Whatever problem the regulators found would then become much larger and more difficult to resolve. More importantly, the regulators' reports will identify loans by customer name that they want the banker to address. Sometimes it's because the loan stinks, and the regulators want more bank profits set aside in a loan loss reserve to cover potential losses. Sometimes the bank screwed up on the documentation (it's missing a signature, or the collateral wasn't properly documented, for example). Customers' personal information is very personal and should never be publically disclosed by the bank.

To be sure they were all using the same standards when examining a bank, all the regulators agreed in 1979 to use the same rating system. They call these ratings standards CAMELS (like the animal). The rating shows the condition of the bank, and it helps decide how often a bank is examined and how thorough that examination will be. CAMELS is an acronym that lists the key ratings of the parts of a bank examination. It's used to assess the bank's

Capital,
Asset quality,
Management,
Earnings,
Liquidity,
and **S**ensitivity

to market risk, which means sensitivity to interest rate changes, foreign-exchange rates, commodity prices, or even stock prices.

Examiners assign a rating of 1 to 5 on each part. One is the highest rating, and 5 is the weakest. They then assign an overall rating using the same scale. It's a subjective rating, not a mathematical average of the other ratings, because some parts could be so bad that they count more.

Some bankers and consultants say they would never want to have a composite 1-rated institution because the cost to get it is too high. They contend that a 2 rating is just as good, and if bankers focus too much on regulatory matters, other things suffer, not the least of which is earning profits. Others contend that regulators cut you a lot of slack when you are well rated, and these ratings simply reflect the great job the bankers are doing at managing a well-run, profitable company.

Bank examinations are usually conducted once a year, although the time between examinations may be more frequent depending on the bank's size and condition. It makes sense that a smaller bank in great condition doesn't need to be examined as often as a large bank in trouble. With the Federal Reserve System, one of the twelve District Federal Reserve Banks does the examination for the Federal Reserve Board (in Washington DC), and the bank gets a copy of the report as "a courtesy."

That always seems a bit odd that the examination findings are not for the bank but for the regulators in Washington DC, but because the banks don't "pay" a specific fee for the Fed's examination reports like they would pay for an outside auditors' report, the issue rarely comes up.

Except once when I was examining a bank in Florida back in the 1980s and the owner/president got quite upset at me for citing about a million internal control deficiencies at the bank. The hot issue at the time was not terrorism but laundering drug money. The states and the federal government have a bunch of laws requiring banks to track large deposits (at the time, any $10,000 cash deposit was suspect) to ensure that it isn't drug dealers' money.

> *"if you @#%& with me on this, I will have your job!"*

The Federal Reserve and the state of Florida would take turns doing the annual bank examinations, and when I began my review, I simply checked to see if the bank had corrected the deficiencies that the state examination had noted the year before. Routine stuff really. I used a standard bank examiner checklist taken right out of the ol' bank examiner manual.

It probably wouldn't have mattered, but I didn't know until later that the president had gotten so mad at the state bank examiner(s) the year before, that he demanded they leave his bank before their work was complete. I didn't know that the examiners reciprocated by citing him for every violation of every law and regulation related to money laundering. My review said, quite accurately I believe, that bank management had not "corrected the deficiencies" cited previously.

Well, I'm trying to be polite here, but suffice it to say the president was not enamored with my point of view. You can imagine the meeting as our senior examiner Scott, the bank president, and I are all seated around the boardroom table as I was presenting some of the examination findings. When I said we were citing him again for the same deficiencies noted by the state, he exploded with an in-your-face, finger-pointing, profanity-laced verbal assault that blew me away. Seriously, I was twenty-six years old with about four years of examiner experience and had never been blasted by a banker like that before. It ended with him saying something along the lines of, "If you @#%& with me on this, I will have your job!"

Technically, when Fed examiners present preliminary findings to the president at the end of an on-site examination, it is done as a courtesy and is designed to allow examiners to correct any factual errors they've made before they complete the final report and to get any clarifications or additional insight from the bank president. It was never, ever, designed to get this kind of reaction!

Fortunately, Scott came to the rescue with a very simple, firm, and direct response. "No, sir," he declared. "We have the evidence, and the problems from last year have *not* been corrected. And I will remind you that we are here as a courtesy to you but will not have you speak to us this way."

Did I mention that Scott was my superhero? That day he was, and I thank him again. There are three things I learned that day. First, volatile people are … uhmm, volatile, and you should be cautious when presenting negative information to them. Second, it's good to have friends back you up. Third, being blasted in a boardroom meeting like that is every bit as uncomfortable as being held up at gunpoint after a baseball game.

In thirty years in the business, only two bankers ever openly ripped into me (this one from Florida when I was a bank examiner and one from the state of Washington when I was a consultant), but I suspect a lot, okay, most bankers reading this have a sly grin in appreciation of a bank president giving a rookie bank examiner a piece of his mind. Examinations can be hard on bankers, and much like the coach screaming his head off at the umpire at a sporting event, sometimes we have it coming, sometimes we don't, but it all seems to even out in the end. No hard feelings, guys.

Wachovia Bank
1908–2008

In their 2006 annual report, Wachovia Corporation reported serving 13 million customers through a network of 3,400 retail banking offices in 21 states and 750 brokerage firm offices in 47 states. Their mortgage lending products were in every state, and with 40 international offices they were known around the world. They had about $800 billion in assets and 108,000 employees, give or take a few.

Proudly and with truly exceptional customer service, they had become the fourth-largest banking company and the third-largest brokerage company in the United States, a remarkable accomplishment for a bank whose roots go back to its origin one hundred years earlier as Union National Bank, Charlotte, North Carolina.

In 2006, they announced another solid year of profitability, with earnings up 22 percent from the past two years and dividends up 60 percent since 2003. Chairman and CEO Ken Thompson's only disappointment was that the year-end stock price of $57 was not commensurate with the quality and strength of their financial results. It was true. The stock price did not reflect Wachovia's quality and strength. It overstated them.

By the end of 2008, the bank was sold under duress to Wells Fargo for $6.50 a share, and the chief credit officer, chief financial officer, and chief executive officer were all gone.

Wachovia's downfall occurred from a series of financial and reputational blunders, such as (1) allowing an illegal telemarketing campaign ($150 million mistake), (2) illegally avoiding taxes on lease transactions ($975 million mistake), and (3) misleading investors on their auction rate securities sales ($9 billion mistake).

Although these financial losses were sustainable, the reputational loss was not, and a bank's reputation is right up there with its bottom line. Investors are reluctant to buy stock in companies whose reputations are damaged!

In the first example, Wachovia permitted a Pennsylvania telemarketing company to illegally submit withdrawal requests from unsuspecting Wachovia bank accounts, many of whom were owned by senior citizens. Wachovia had such weak internal controls, it didn't prevent the telemarketing company withdrawals that occurred over a ten-month period. Wachovia had to cover those losses and issue checks totaling over $150 million to more than 740,000 customers.[56]

Second example: Evading taxes with leasing transactions between 1999 and 2003. Under these deals, the bank would either buy or lease assets from a nonprofit organization that they could then use to deduct or depreciate on their taxes.

For instance, they bought 570 subway cars from the New York Metropolitan Transportation Authority that they then leased back to the Authority. Because the bank never actually took possession of the subway cars (and why would they?), the

IRS considered it to be just a ploy to avoid paying taxes (which it was) and ruled it illegal. The courts agreed. Oops. In June 2008, their earnings took a $975 million hit because of it.[57]

And the third example, the auction rate securities deal, tarnished the bank's reputation and cost it a lot of money. These were long-term securities (IOUs) from local governments, hospitals, utilities, and others, whose interest rates were set every week to five weeks in a bidding process (auction) with investors who wanted to buy them.

Wachovia brokers were accused of misleading the investors into thinking the securities could be quickly sold if necessary when, in fact, they couldn't. They weren't the only ones misleading investors like this. Morgan Stanley, JPMorgan Chase, Citigroup, and others had done the same. Wachovia paid a $50 million fine, had to make interest-free loans to the investors who wanted them, and had to buy back $8.8 billion of these securities.[58]

Many of these problems happened because Wachovia grew too fast. Wachovia was apparently trying to reach the "trillion dollar club" and had grown from $341 billion in assets in 2002 to almost $800 billion in only five years. Investors were losing confidence in their ability to manage the growth. *Bigger is not always better.*

As bad as these errors may have been, the biggest whopper of a mistake was purchasing California-based Golden West Financial Corporation, owners of World Savings Bank, at the height of the real estate boom in May 2006.

Golden West Financial was a company whose roots go back to 1963 when husband and wife team Herb and Marion Sandler used family money and bank loans to purchase a $34 million Oakland California savings and loan association. By the time they sold the company to Wachovia for $25 billion in 2006, it had grown to over $125 billion in assets, and World Savings was the second largest thrift in the country. *Bigger is not always better.*

Analysts didn't think this was a good deal for Wachovia, mostly due to the high level of risky Option ARM loans on the thrift's books. An Option ARM loan is an adjustable-rate mortgage with options that in many cases allow the customer to make payments for less than the principal and interest due on the loan.

What they don't pay is then added to the loan amount (called negative amortization). They called it the Pick-A-Pay loan. The name alone should have been a clue that it was too risky. *We should have seen it coming.*

After the acquisition, Wachovia became the largest originator in the country of these high-risk, Option ARM loans.

Three months later, the bank's level of seriously past-due loans had climbed from .38 percent of the portfolio before the acquisition, to 2.58 percent, and its liquidity and capital position had deteriorated to unacceptable levels.

By June 2008, Wachovia Corporation reported a $9.8 billion loss caused partly by having to sink $4.4 billion into its loan loss reserve for the Option ARM product and other bad loans. *It's almost always bad loans.*

Bank regulators forced Wachovia to sell its bank operations to Citigroup in September 2008 for $1 a share. The bank had experienced what reporters were calling a "silent run." People were reducing their deposit accounts to no more than what was protected by FDIC insurance. There were no long customer lines outside the bank, but so much money was leaving that the FDIC decided the bank wouldn't be able to meet the demand and forced a sale.

The investment company subsidiary would remain unsold, and the FDIC agreed to absorb any bank losses of more than $42 billion. But the sweet deal the FDIC arranged for Citi was too sweet to swallow.

Wells Fargo saw an opportunity, jumped into the fray, and made a more generous offer of $6.50 a share for the entire company and without any specific FDIC guarantees. Wachovia's board of directors immediately accepted, and on October 3, 2008, a merger agreement was in place. After some legal maneuvering by all three banks, the deal with Wells Fargo closed at year-end 2008.

Besides the 89 percent drop in stock price from 2006 to 2008, Wachovia laid off 6,950 employees and eliminated forty-four hundred unfilled positions.

Not everybody lost money. Before their company's bad loans became obvious, Herb and Marion Sandler sold out and received $2.4 billion for Golden West. After the bad loans became obvious, Wachovia CEO Ken Thompson was forced out and received $1.45 million cash and $7.2 million of stock in severance pay.

Chapter 4

Savings Banks

Many of us are concerned about poverty and discrimination and some of us have even spent a lot of time and effort working on these causes. It isn't always easy, but it is the most personally rewarding thing I have ever done. I spent many years in this line of work, in particular, promoting mixed-income communities. In the late 1980s, I lived in a transitional low-income neighborhood in downtown Atlanta that was being revitalized. I understand the issues pretty well, and can say that changing attitudes as well as land and buildings isn't easy. In fact, when I was living downtown, I got stoned on three separate occasions. No, not that kind. Mine was with rocks and an empty beer bottle, not pot.

The first time was after the Rodney King verdict in 1992 when the officers who were filmed beating him were found not guilty of assault. I was an avid runner and bicyclist at the time and was riding my bike past an apartment building where a group of men had gathered when I heard a voice yell out, "There's one!" I remember thinking "One what?" when a baseball-sized rock suddenly bounced off the street, hitting my bike. *Oh @#$%,* I thought. *One of me!* Somehow, I forgot I was a white guy in a bad place. I set a personal best individual time trial that day.

A few months later I was running past the Martin Luther King Center when somebody threw a beer bottle at me, breaking it on the sidewalk and hitting my feet. No harm. Undeterred, I ran the same route two days later, and had a rock skip past me. Fool that I am, I refused to give in and continued this route all summer long—never having a problem again.

At the time, I was determined to run that same damn route regardless of the circumstances. It was a matter of principle. Mine was a story of perseverance, of never giving up no matter the risks. My friend Ron saw it differently.

"You're gonna get killed," he said somewhat angrily.

"Well, if it happens you can put 'He Gave a Damn' on my tombstone,'" I declared defiantly.

"Yeah," Ron said without hesitation, "and underneath we'll put 'But the Other Guy Didn't.'"

Ron was right. In hindsight, mine was not a story of perseverance or of morality or of determination. It was just about being young and dumb. Even so, there is something noble and rewarding about fighting discrimination and poverty. In spite of the dangers and obstacles, people who battle these social ills deserve our respect. It is often these people, after all, who develop programs and solutions that benefit us all. Such was the case with the founding of savings banks.

Origin

Their story is one of evolution, not revolution. England developed the first nationwide system of savings banks in the early 1800s, and that inspired the United States to adopt a similar system around the same time.[59] It all began with the idea of being thrifty and of developing a self-help program for the poor. Those two factors (thrift and self-help) gave birth to savings banks in the United States and elsewhere, and thrifts still have that as part of their social mission today. *We got this way for a reason.*

Some folks dispute the exact origin of savings banks, and it's even been said that twenty-eight-year-old Daniel Defoe (Robinson Crusoe's creator) promoted the idea of savings banks back in 1689. His idea was that all wage earners should contribute to a pool of money that earned interest, managed by the government. Wage earners could withdraw from this pool during an emergency. But his idea was more of an insurance program than a savings bank.

Others say that the first savings bank, the "Tottenham Benefit Bank," was organized in 1804 by "social reformer" Priscilla Wakefield. The phrase "social reformer" seems more polite than calling her a "community activist" even if it means the same thing. Anyway, Ms. Wakefield had started a Female Benefit Club in 1798 that provided a pension to subscribers when they got older, if they become disabled, or for other reasons. She also formed a Children's Bank that allowed children to bring their pennies to deposit with her and then withdraw later for apprenticeship fees, clothes for service work, and other similar items.[60] The Tottenham Bank required members to deposit money on a scheduled basis that was used to buy shares in the company. If the members didn't meet the scheduled deposit plan, they had to pay penalties. The deposits earned 5 percent interest, and when the shares matured, the money could be withdrawn without penalty.[61]

Ms. Wakefield deserves credit for opening the first **Kids' Accounts**, which are still commonly offered at banks over 210 years later! But although Ms. Wakefield may be considered the originator of savings banks, much of the credit for the spread of savings banks goes to Rev. Henry Duncan (1774–1846) from Ruthwell, Scotland. He created and promoted a savings bank model that could be adopted around the world.

Reverend Duncan had worked at a commercial bank in Liverpool (Heywoods Bank) before leaving to become a minister at the Ruthwell Church in Scotland. As pastor of that church, he combined his banking expertise with his efforts to promote pride and independence among his parish, most of whose members were extremely poor.

Reverend Duncan had good business sense and recognized that many practical barriers prevented his parishioners from taking advantage of commercial bank products and services. For example, in the early 1800s, the minimum deposit to open an account in Scotland or England was typically about 10 pounds (twenty-four hundred pence at the time, or roughly $20 today), which was more than many people earned in a year. By the way, minimum deposits needed to open an account and minimum loan amounts are still topics of contention at banks today.

At the newly formed Ruthwell Parish Bank (1810), depositors needed only six pence to open an account (compared to twenty-four hundred) if they agreed to save forty-eight pence a year for three years.[62] Reverend Duncan persuaded a commercial bank, the British Linen Bank, to accept the total sums as deposits and pay an annual interest rate of 5 percent. His depositors would receive 4 percent interest once they had saved one pound, rising to 5 percent after three years. Much to his credit, he had convinced a commercial bank to work closely with his savings bank to better serve an unbanked, low-income population. This strategy of using a third party to help commercial banks serve low- and moderate-income populations continues today. Credit unions, mutual savings banks, community development corporations, and other nonprofit organizations serve a role today similar to the role of the Ruthwell Parish Bank in 1810.

Types of Savings Banks

Although savings banks were originally formed as mutual companies, today there are also stock-owned savings banks. Stock-owned banks have shareholders and a board of directors, and they want to make a profit. Mutual savings banks, on the other hand, are nonprofit. Their owners are the depositors. After paying all expenses and setting aside enough reserves for any contingencies, mutual savings banks return the excess money to the depositors.

Previously, we compared banking to a three-legged stool. Management has to meet the needs of three groups, or legs: depositors, employees, and stockholders. Mutual savings banks do not have one leg of the stool, stockholders, but they do have "stakeholders," which are the depositors who are entitled to a return of excess earnings. By design, management has to serve the depositors just as if the depositors owned common stock. The difference is that depositors accept—and sometimes expect—that management will put some of the extra earnings either back into the community through charitable donations or give it back to the depositors themselves.

In practice, most stakeholders aren't aware of how much power they have because they only vote on major decisions, and management is given a great deal of latitude to operate without significant pressure from depositors. One of the criticisms occasionally aimed at mutual savings banks is that their managers are not more accountable to their members.

Poverty Origins

Mutual savings banks were originally formed with support from wealthy and philanthropic business leaders whose role was to provide savings and investment opportunities for the poor. That doesn't mean they intended to turn over control of the business to the poor. These institutions were typically managed by a board of trustees because they were prominent in the local community and would be sure that the institutions functioned properly. Mutual savings banks frequently reflected some of the prevailing attitudes in England and Scotland of self-help and laissez-faire (no government involvement) when addressing poverty issues.

We've always had outspoken proponents of self-help, who maintain that poor people should pull themselves up by their own boot straps rather than rely on help from charities. Daniel Defoe is an example of just such a "stern individualist." Defoe said in his popular book from 1697, *An Essay Upon Projects*, that the poor man who begs without need ought to be punished "with the correction due a dog" and if he begs for need because he is lazy, that is, for "slothfulness and idleness," then "he ought to be punished for the cause."[63]

Defoe had some rather harsh views of the poor, even claiming in his book *Giving Alms No Charity* that he could "produce above a thousand families in England, within my particular knowledge, who go in rags, and their children wanting bread" even though their fathers are capable of working but instead are lazy or selfish.[64]

To say you personally know a thousand poor families with lazy or selfish fathers is an absurd stretch, and the guy is a real ass, which is especially evident in his 1725 pamphlet *Everybody's Business Is Nobody's Business* in which he attacks the wages and character of shoe-shiners, maids, watermen (oarsmen on London's River Thames), and other low-income laborers. His disdain for the poor led him to offer a wide variety of solutions, many of which were obnoxious and punitive.

In fairness, which is hard in this case, the ideas that he advocated were not always original ideas, and they were not always bad ideas either. For example, he supported the Pension Office in 1697. The working class ("laboring people") was to contribute to a type of insurance program that would provide money in times of illness, accident, disability, or extreme poverty rather than those folks depending on charities or the government to provide these funds. Interestingly, mandatory contributions to a special government program is not entirely unlike some of the social programs in the United States and other countries today, including Medicare, Medicaid, and Social Security, which are funded with payroll taxes.

To say you personally know a thousand poor families with lazy or selfish fathers is an absurd stretch, and the guy is a real ass ...

About one hundred years later, Reverend Duncan was also a strong advocate for self-help programs, and although he was as equally outspoken as Defoe, he was never as hostile to the poor. In the early 1800s, about 11 percent of England's population was supported by public charity, and it was causing some resentment and fear that poverty problems (mainly in urban areas) would grow in Scotland.[65] For comparison, in 2007 the Census Bureau listed the official US poverty rate at 12.5 percent, which is higher than what was worrying England in the 1800s.

According to the Reverend, "It is distressing to think how much money is thrown away by young women on dress unsuitable to their station and by young men on the debauchery of the alehouse and in other extravagant and demoralizing practices for no other reason than that no safe place is open to them for laying up their superfluous earnings."[66]

The Reverend Duncan's proposal for managing his savings bank operations was quite complex. There were ordinary members, extraordinary members, honorary members, and a court of directors. This structure proved hard to duplicate, and the Edinburgh Bank for Savings (in Scotland) implemented a more practical system that was widely adopted in the United States and elsewhere. The focus on empowerment that Duncan advocated is still an important feature of savings banks even if today's savings banks are not as paternalistic.

Unlike the Reverend Duncan's bank, the Edinburgh Bank did not fine its customers who failed to make scheduled deposits, and it didn't require approval for any withdrawals. Instead, the Edinburgh Bank allowed unlimited deposits and withdrawals.

While it may seem inconsistent with an empowerment concept to have the wealthy businessmen in a community manage the affairs of a savings bank, it really was more practical. First, they put up the seed money to start the bank—typically about 10 to 15 percent of the expected deposit base. At the time and even today, these business leaders had the financial and managerial expertise to run a financial institution. When it comes to the intricacies of finance—from asset/liability management to risk mitigation to regulatory reporting—you need a particular skill set that may not be available in low-income communities. Oh, sometimes there was corruption, so nobody can pretend it was a perfect system. But for the most part it worked, and the intentions of mutual savings banks then and today are still quite noble.

Rest assured that mutual savings bank management gets an earful on how to better serve the needs of low- and moderate-income communities, sometimes from their customers but even more so from the savings banks' employees. After all, employees frequently live in these communities, are fully aware of the company's mission, and know their customers very well. *People matter.*

Mutual Savings Banks in the United States of America

The original savings banks had no stockholders and were designed to serve low-income households and individuals. The first ones in the United States were the Philadelphia Savings Fund Society (December 2, 1816), the Provident Institution for Savings of Boston (December 13, 1816), and the New York Bank for Savings (March 26, 1819).[67]

Mutual savings banks do have their problems, however. Other than merging with each other, it's hard for them to grow. Unlike a bank, they can't just sell common stock. They must operate very conservatively to survive. Traditional mutual savings banks were just that—a place to save. It's changed now, but originally they were not a place to get loans because they were restricted to taking deposits and only investing the money in state and federal government bonds.

These banks were (and still are) highly concentrated in the Northeast. In 1980, more than 95 percent of the mutual savings bank deposits were held by institutions in Connecticut, Maine, Massachusetts, New Hampshire, New Jersey, New York, Pennsylvania, Rhode Island, and Washington DC.[68]

Between 1820 and 1910, the number of mutual savings banks grew from ten to 637, and it didn't take long before states began to allow them to make investments not just in federal and government bonds, but also in railroad bonds, blue-chip stocks (you know, *really* good companies), first mortgage loans on real estate, and other short-term but well-secured loans. However, the large down payments of 33 percent or more made it very difficult for low-income members (customers) to buy homes.

Up until the late 1700s and even the early 1800s, land was free or relatively cheap, and there were plenty of raw materials available to construct a home.[69] But when the industrial revolution began (around 1760), people began to migrate to the cities, where they could get jobs, especially factory jobs. The revolution was not sudden, but it was, well, revolutionary. People were living longer because food was more plentiful, diets were better, and disease was less prevalent. Their migration to the cities and out of rural areas provided more consistent wages, and, not surprisingly, the increased population provided a greater choice of prospective marriage partners.[70]

> *... the changed outlook led to changed buying patterns and took our economy away from one dominated by savings to one driven by spending.*

These are not trivial matters because along about the same time we had a tremendous growth of newspapers and increased advertising. The cities contained greater diversity— including diversity of thought—that challenged a variety of existing social norms from clothing choices to lifestyle choices. For example, when Eli Whitney invented the cotton gin in 1794 and Elias Howe the first sewing machine in 1846, people could dress (and express) themselves differently.[71]

The combination of inventions and more consistent wages contributed to big changes in economic behavior. No longer did a lot of people make wholesale sacrifices and avoid material goods in order to earn their reward in the afterlife. Instead, they could afford to buy things now rather than later.

From clothing to food to housing to marriage partners, the changed outlook led to changed buying patterns and took our economy away from one dominated by savings to one driven by spending. These changes also caused savings banks to become more than just a place for working-class people to save money. With steady incomes, people began to want loans too, and this paved the way for the introduction of "building and loan associations" and "savings and loan associations." They weren't as big as commercial banks, and there weren't as many of them, but they served an important role just the same.

Building and Loan Associations and Savings and Loan Associations

Do you remember Henry Potter from the classic movie *It's a Wonderful Life*, starring Jimmy Stewart, in 1946? Stewart played George Bailey, the president of the Bailey Building and Loan Association, a company started by his father to compete with the evil, for-profit commercial bank run by Mr. Potter. The use of the term "building and loan association" had already been replaced around 1945 with the term "savings and loan association," but because both names, building and loan association and savings and loan association, had about the same purpose and structure, the movie scriptwriters apparently didn't care.

There were other names for nonprofit financial institutions that operated like a building and loan association, and some still exist today. You'll find mutual loan associations, homestead aid associations, savings fund and loan associations, co-operative banks, co-operative savings and loan associations, etc.

Traditional savings banks were formed as self-help companies—a not-for-profit organization to serve the working class. As such, they were seen more for their social mission than as a business. The classic movie portrayed Mr. Potter as a creepy banker and, by association, all commercial banks as evil, but it portrayed the building and loan association much more favorably, and that view is consistent with the way folks viewed the origin of savings banks. They were "clubby" institutions. Their customers knew each other as well as they knew the employees. Robert Eric Wright accurately compared savings banks with commercial banks in his book *The First Wall Street.*

> Early U.S. commercial banks were not elitist cliques, as some historians have claimed. But neither did they have much to do with what [some] would have called the "industrious poor." Savings banks, on the other

> hand, tried to cater to *only* the working poor. Depositors in early U.S. savings banks included "mechanics, tradesmen, laborers, servants, and others living upon wages or labor," like boot cleaners, coachmen, cartmen, chambermaids, nurses, students, waiters, draymen, painters, sash makers, bakers, shoemakers, clerks, bartenders, printers, ship carpenters, bricklayers, sailors, coach makers, turners, plasterers, joiners, millwrights, storekeepers, porters, farmers, schoolmasters, gardeners, stevedores, upholsters, and other members of the "frugal poor."[72]

When people, especially working-class people, began to move into the cities during the Industrial Revolution, these savings banks began to change with the times. Their social mission did not change, and their reputation of providing opportunities for the working class didn't change, but their products and organizational structure did change.

In particular, the cities were becoming more crowded, and quality housing was hard to get. As a result, and drawing on the experience of British building societies overseas, entrepreneurs in the United States began to develop building and loan associations that were not only a place to save money but also a place to get housing loans.

Unlike the mutual savings banks, which had less than half of their assets in home loans (with the rest in government and railroad securities), the newer building and loan associations invested almost everything in housing loans. Eventually though, the mutual savings banks became more like the building and loan associations.[73]

Before the 1830s, to buy a home you had to borrow from private individuals under their terms or from commercial banks, which wanted as much as a 60 percent down payment! When you borrowed from commercial banks, the loan matured in less than five years or on demand. Insurance companies weren't much different. These are clearly not the best terms for working-class people, who would have to struggle to meet the down payment and other requirements. Building and loan associations were formed to address these limitations and to make owning a home more affordable.

The first of these building and loan associations was formed when thirty-six men in Frankford, Pennsylvania (part of Philadelphia), subscribed to stock in The Oxford Provident Building Association in 1831.[74] Like other building and loan associations at the time, Oxford Provident was a terminating institution, which means it was designed to go out of business once all members had a chance to buy a home, and all loans had been repaid. That's what happened, in

1841. Another Oxford Provident was then formed, also lasting ten years, and then a third one was established in 1852.

All institutions change with the times, and the one biggie here is that these building and loan associations evolved to something called a serial association, which mean that members could join every quarter, and there was no termination date. The restrictions on using the loans just to purchase homes began to go away, and eventually members could join any day they wanted to rather than just quarterly.[75]

Initially, shareholders in the Oxford Provident Building Association all agreed to buy stock up to a maximum of five shares at $500 each, or $2,500 total. Most building and loan associations would even let you borrow the money to buy the stock.[76]

Folks who purchased at least one share (even though they hadn't finished paying for it under the monthly installment plan) were then members, who could borrow money using the stock as collateral. As a practical matter, the building and loan association would have to first accumulate at least $500 from its members before loans could be made. Then bidding for a loan would begin. The loan proceeds could only be used to build or buy a "dwelling house." The member who offered to pay the highest loan fee would win, and could borrow money, but only on the condition that the house they bought or built was in the county and no more than five miles away.

It seems that for some of the early associations, the longer a member waited to bid for their loan, the fewer members would be competing for the money and the lower the fee would be. Those who were most anxious to buy a home had to compete against more borrowers and pay a higher fee to win the loan. In any case, the winning bidders all paid 6 percent interest on the loan. There was a $3 fee to originate the loan, a twenty-five cent late fee on past-due loan payments, and another twenty-five cent late fee on past due stock purchase payments. Boy, those were the days. Can you imagine a twenty-five cent late fee? Today a housing loan late fee would be more like 5 percent of the payment amount.

Deposit Products

Not surprisingly, given the success of these institutions and their favorable reputation among working-class people, not everybody wanted to cash out when they repaid their loans. Some folks wanted to keep on saving money, and everybody wanted help in tracking their savings and dividends, which led to the development of *passbooks* in the late 1870s.

These nifty little books (yes, you actually had a little book that looked like a passport) were used to record deposits and withdrawals every time the customer went into the bank. The passbook account was the main deposit product at savings and loan associations right up until the mid-1960s. Every now and again you will find a bank that still offers passbook savings accounts. When you do, it's either a really old-fashioned bank or it's a clever marketing program. Regardless, they should probably have a 1907 hand-cranked Victrola playing "Sweet Adeline" in the lobby to complete the picture (which, frankly, would be really cool).

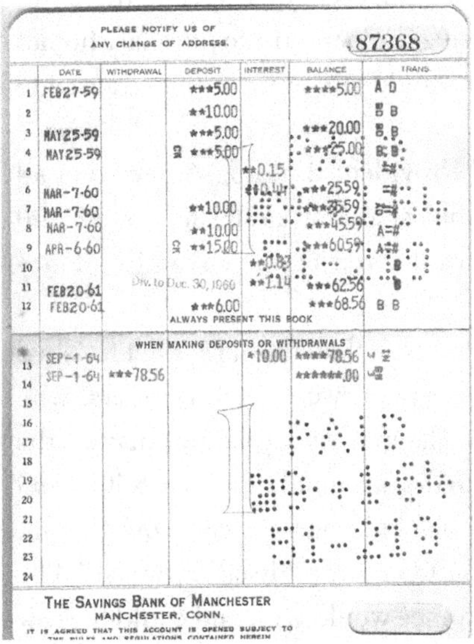

To be sure, not all building and loans were good companies. Much like drugs, where fools assume that if a little is good a lot must be better, some people assumed that if the local building and loan was a good idea, national ones would be even better. In the 1880s, national associations began to spring up around the country. They could operate on a larger scale by establishing a head office in places like Minneapolis and Chicago. They would raise a ton of money ($5 million or so) from wealthy investors, who would control the institution, and transfer this money from areas with larger depositors and less loan demand to areas with fewer deposits and greater loan demand, such as some rural areas.[77]

These nationals thought they could achieve economies of scale, where their larger size meant they could cover overhead expenses better and could pay higher dividends to their members. Their hype was very effective, and investors bought into the concept. It brings us back to one of the lessons never learned. *Bigger is not always better.*

By 1896, branches of these nationals could be found in every state. But unlike the locals, the nationals had much higher overhead expenses, especially with what they paid their employees, and to make the numbers work, they charged higher fees and had more restrictions about withdrawing your money.

The competition between local and national lending institutions is somewhat of an American tradition, and not only with building and loans. (State and national commercial banks compete with each other too.) Everybody began pressing their politicians for protective laws, claiming the other guy had unfair advantages and laws were needed to "level the playing field."

In the case of these building and loans, the locals were partly successful in restricting national expansion. New state laws were passed that capped officer salaries and that restricted the customer fees and fines that thrifts could charge. The nationals found it very challenging (and unprofitable) to comply with the different laws imposed by each state where they did business, especially those restricting its income.

Another Depressing Depression

The Depression of 1893 resulted from a lot of things: depressed real estate prices, overproduction of manufactured goods, and a decline in agricultural prices. Lower ag prices hit especially hard because farmers had a lot of debt, especially in Kansas, Nebraska, Indiana, and the Dakotas, where farms had hefty mortgages, and a lot of foreclosures occurred. This depression was harsh; unemployment was estimated at more than 10 percent for over five years running.[78] When you added the depression to those poorly structured and overhyped national building and loans, it resulted in huge losses for the members. Some of their deposits and shares were now worthless. By 1910, all national building and loans were out of business. A lot of hardworking people lost money.

The Depression of 1893 paled in comparison to the Great Depression that began with the stock market crash in 1929, and thrifts were not exempt from the pressure. In fact, out of 11,777 savings and loans at the start of the Great Depression in 1930, only 6,149 remained by 1945.[79] Only with World War II did employment begin to increase, and people began to save more. Increased employment and savings gave the thrifts that hadn't tanked when the Depression hit a chance to recover. They were able to unload foreclosed properties, replenish their reserves for loan losses, rebuild their capital base, and begin lending again.

The Great Depression also changed the savings and loan associations in other ways. For one, the Federal Home Loan Bank System was established in 1932. It could grant federal charters, and now, if thrift organizers had enough money, they could ask for a charter from either the federal government or the state government. By the way, you can tell if a thrift has a federal charter because it will have the word "federal" or the letters FSB for federal savings bank in its name. For example, the Savings Bank of Manchester in Connecticut (in 1959) didn't have "federal" or FSB in its name, so you could tell that it would have been regulated by the state. Far West Federal Savings Bank in Portland, Oregon (in 1979) was regulated by the Federal Home Loan Bank System.

The liquidity provided by the FHLB was important—and still is—because it allows its banks to borrow money at a low cost, much like commercial banks can borrow from the Federal Reserve. Having a federal charter was also good because it helped bring about more consistent thrift business practices around the country. Their regulator required similar "best practices" from all federal thrifts. It also placed more pressure on state regulators to strengthen their own oversight programs.

Unfair Thrift Taxes?

Commercial bankers often grumbled about an unlevel playing field because thrifts were tax exempt and could pay higher interest rates on deposits. It's a story that plays out time and again: bank or thrift trade associations and much of their membership claimed that the competition has unfair advantages. Today, thrifts and banks grumble about credit unions having unfair advantages.

What made commercial bankers really mad was when the FHLB began to loosen the federal thrift charter standards in 1949. Up until then, if you put money in a savings and loan, technically you were making an investment in the thrift, and the shares you purchased were held in a *share account*. When you took money out of the thrift, it counted as the thrift buying back your share. But the new FHLB rule allowed the thrifts to call these *savings accounts* instead of share accounts and *withdrawals* instead of share repurchases, which made the thrifts look very much like commercial banks.

Commercial bankers groused that if the thrifts were going to look and act like banks, they should have to follow the same rules as banks. What the banks had in mind was requiring thrifts to pay the same taxes they had to pay. Why should the thrifts be exempt?

The squeaky wheel gets results, and the politicians responded. President Truman signed the Tax Revenue Act of 1951 that helped level the playing field. Mutual savings banks and savings and loan associations had to pay federal corporate income taxes just like commercial banks except that the thrifts had generous deduction allowances if they met certain lending tests (called a qualified thrift lending test, or QTL).[80] Going forward, the penalty for failing to meet the test was harsh—the thrift would lose current and some of its past tax deductions, incurring a big tax penalty in the process.

It doesn't appear that the imposition of taxes was directly caused by the animosity between commercial banks and thrifts as much as it was caused by the animosity between the National Tax Equality Association and the National Associated Businessmen, who believed organizations like these thrifts were socialist structures that took advantage of the American free market. They led the charge for increased taxation.

In any event, none of this would have been such a big issue if we hadn't been fighting the Korean War. The Korean War forced taxes to go up to balance the budget and replenish the depleted military infrastructure. Once again, war is hell, and, in this case, it resulted in tighter constraints or higher taxes for thrifts.

Thrift Deposit Accounts

During the Great Depression, Congress passed a law that said regulators could set limits on the interest commercial banks paid on deposits. The idea behind the regulation (called Regulation Q because it came after Regulation P and before we had Regulation R), was that if banks didn't compete to pay high rates on deposits, they would not have to make riskier loans, where they charged high rates, to make a profit. But Regulation Q did not apply to savings and loan associations, and, not surprisingly, they were paying higher rates. Depositors' money flowed like wine, steadily pouring into the thrifts at the expense of the commercial banks.

That interest rate advantage changed in 1966. Congress allowed the FHLB to limit how much the thrifts could pay on savings accounts. Thrift savings accounts could now earn only 3/4 percent more and mutual savings bank accounts could earn only 1 percent more than the commercial banks could pay.[81] That probably seems really unfair to the banks, but until 1980, only commercial banks—not thrifts—could offer checking accounts. Besides, thrifts had a lot of limits on the types of loans they could offer, so there were reasonable, if imperfect, trade-offs.

Toasters and Other Giveaways

Not surprisingly, even at the higher interest rates, depositors began to take their money and loans out of both thrifts and commercial banks when inflation came into the picture. People wanted something that paid more interest, such as government and corporate bonds. So the banks and thrifts tried a different tactic to get deposits: they began giving stuff away.

It seems that bank giveaways have been around for as long as banks themselves, and one can only imagine what they used to attract deposits during the Bronze Age (swords, perhaps). Giveaways were and still are as diverse as the institutions themselves. In the 1920s, you could get wooden writing pens; in the '50s, you could get a toaster; in the '80s you could get everything from a microwave to golf clubs to power tools.

At least one rural bank even gave away guns. The 2002 Michael Moore movie *Bowling for Columbine* featured a Michigan bank that gave away Weatherby hunting rifles if you opened a deposit account (bullets were not included). Before you start thinking that these rural bankers were nutty, consider this: *Time* magazine reported in August 1980 that a New York bank was giving away an $84,000 Rolls-Royce Silver Shadow to anyone who would make an eight-year deposit for $160,000. They didn't get any takers. At least the gun giveaway generated some deposits.

Giving stuff away was an important strategy to generate deposits in the mid-1960s, especially when the government set maximum interest rates payable on the accounts. In fact, giving away freebies is still a popular strategy because bankers find that it doesn't cost as much money as they can earn from the deposits. These kinds of promotions are not likely to go away.

Expanding Product Offerings

Inflation hit the United States very hard in the early 1970s. It climbed from 3.2 percent annually at the end of 1972 to 11.3 percent annually in 1979.[82] Inflation was particularly hard on banks and thrifts, which by law were paying less on their deposits than the inflation rate. Simply put, deposit accounts were not keeping up with inflation, and people began to move their money to products that paid better. And who could blame them?

So how do you respond when money leaves your institution? You create something else that pays a higher rate. And that's exactly what happened when the FHLB allowed banks to issue certificates of deposits (CDs) where the customer agrees to leave the money for a specific time (or pay a penalty to withdraw it early). When a customer agrees to leave the money in the bank for a specific time, such as three months, six months, one year, etc., the bank pays the customer a bit more interest. CDs were very popular then and still are. In

1973, the FHLB even removed the interest rate ceilings on CDs over $100,000 (which are called "jumbo CDs" because one hundred grand is so large).

In 1978, the FHLB said that the banks and thrifts could also offer "money market certificates." These certificates helped keep depositors from putting their money in investment brokerage firms, which were promoting their own new money market product that paid higher rates and allowed some withdrawals. The interest on the thrift money market certificates could change every week depending on the interest paid on our national debt.[83]

Two years later, thrifts were allowed to offer a negotiable order of withdrawal account (called a NOW account). They operated just like checking accounts and were available to almost anybody or any organization (nonprofits, individuals, and government agencies) *except businesses*. The NOW product pays interest, and, unlike a checking account, which savings and loans couldn't legally offer, the NOW account allowed withdrawals subject to a fourteen-day or more notice requirement (which is rarely enforced). So a NOW account looks and acts like a checking account, pays interest, but doesn't have to be paid "on demand" like a checking account does.[84]

When the Depository Institutions Deregulation and Monetary Control Act (DIDMCA) was passed in 1980, it proved that politicians had hit rock bottom in coming up with names for their laws. DIDMCA sounds more like a rapper than a law. You can almost imagine a Kid Rock benefit concert for Waffle House employees featuring Run DMC and DIDMCA![85]

It's a lame name, but a really important law. DIDMCA finally ended controls on what interest rates the banks and thrifts could pay to depositors. It also allowed savings and loan associations to make consumer loans and offer credit cards. Two years later, the Garn-St. Germain Depository Institutions Act said that savings and loan associations could also offer checking accounts (and allow overdrafts). However, there was a catch. Although S&Ls could offer checking accounts, they also had to agree to the Federal Reserve's "legal reserve requirements," i.e., they had to keep on hand more money to pay depositor withdrawals.

These two laws (DIDMCA and the Garn-St. Germain Depository Institutions Act) went a long way toward ending the differences between commercial banks and savings and loan associations. It wouldn't be long until the last big differences were simply who regulated the two institutions and a few restrictions on what kinds of loans they could offer.

Loan Products

Deregulation in 1980 (DIDMCA) expanded S&L powers considerably, especially their ability to lend and invest. For the first time, federal savings and loan associations could issue credit cards. They could also make loans to consumers (initially up to 30 percent of assets), second mortgage loans, commercial loans (initially up to 10 percent of assets), commercial real estate loans (initially up to 40 percent of assets), and "out-of-territory" residential mortgage loans. This was a big change, and some bankers had no problem with the new powers while others were in over their heads.

Building and loan associations were originally focused on mortgage lending. And this remained true for about 150 years, right up until the 1980s. After World War II, the government passed the GI Bill of Rights. For the record, GI was originally an abbreviation for "Government Issue" during World War I, such as GI shoes, or a GI uniform. It soon became a slang term referring to the soldiers themselves.

Under the GI Bill of Rights, those serving in the military could get mortgage loans easier and at lower interest rates, which were set by the federal government through the Veterans Administration (VA). These VA loan guarantees meant that the bankers could lend money to veterans with no down payment required because the VA was guaranteeing that the loans would be repaid. Hey, it had been a hell of a second world war; over sixteen million US servicemen were involved, and over 405,000 died, so why wouldn't the country shower these folks and their families with benefits?[86]

At first, the guarantee generated a lot of loans for thrifts as they stepped up in a patriotic way to honor our servicemen and servicewomen. That declined a good bit over the next couple of years because the government set relatively low interest rates (which they adjusted periodically), and it reduced bank interest (pun intended) in the program. Besides, it was a hassle to deal with the government bureaucracy. Believe it or not, it's not so much of a hassle today. The government doesn't set the interest rates, and the bureaucracy is not an issue for astute lenders who know the rules.

The 1950s brought changes to two other very significant government programs. The Federal Housing Administration (FHA) mortgage insurance program and the Federal National Mortgage Association (FNMA, or Fannie Mae) secondary market also primed the lending pumps. Both institutions are covered later in this book, but it's worth noting now that all of these government programs had a huge impact on thrifts and on families. The nation's home ownership rose from 41 percent in 1940 to 57 percent in 1955.[87]

The phrase "conventional loans" was a common term in the 1940s to distinguish traditional, conservative underwriting from the more liberal, government-insured VA and FHA loans. Today, we have names to describe a wider variety of loans, including conventional, VA, FHA, subprime (higher risk), and predatory (unethical).

Charters

Technically, there are two distinct federal thrift charters: (1) a federal savings bank charter and (2) a federal savings and loan association charter. The two charters have the same powers. The industry suffered such terrible financial and reputational losses in the 1980s that many savings and loan associations changed their name to savings banks. By the late 1990s, only 60 percent of the thrifts had kept the term "savings and loan" in their titles.[88]

The thrift charter may be in jeopardy. The ongoing financial crisis that began in 2007 has raised important questions about their regulator's ability to supervise these institutions. There is no doubt that their ability to engage in some of the more risky ventures will be curtailed. The cost has been too high already. Consider these thrift problems in 2007–08:

- Washington Mutual Bank, the largest thrift in the country, failed. It was the largest financial institution in US history to fail.
- Countrywide Bank, FSB, the second largest thrift in the country in 2007, was sold under duress when its concentration of high-risk loans began to go bad and its senior debt was downgraded to "junk bond" status. (A junk bond has a weak credit rating and is considered very risky.)
- World Savings Bank, the second-largest thrift in the country in 2006 at $146 billion in assets, sold out to Wachovia Bank just months before its high-risk loans began to default big time. Wachovia got caught with the bad loans and suffered a loss that was so big that Wachovia had to sell out to Wells Fargo.
- IndyMac Bank, FSB, the tenth-largest thrift in the country in 2007, engaged in high levels of high-risk mortgage lending and failed in 2008. IndyMac's loss was so high that when the FDIC bailed it out, it cost the FDIC about 11 percent of its $53 billion insurance fund

Although thrifts have proven valuable to the nation, their failures have also been devastating to the country, both in the 1980s and again beginning in 2007. For one, it's risky to have such a high concentration of housing loans in your institution. When the housing industry gets in trouble, a large number of thrifts do too.

It also appears that some thrifts, such as Countrywide and IndyMac, had drifted far from the historic role of helping the poor and working class. Instead, they offered products that proved to be highly profitable to the institution's owners but unaffordable to the home buyers. *People matter.*

Many thrifts also made a strategic mistake in becoming too cozy with their regulator. They argued for less regulation, less oversight, and less intervention, and they got it. But when the thrift industry suffered massive losses beginning in 2007, some of which was attributed to weak oversight from their regulator, the Office of Thrift Supervision (OTS), Congress came down hard. Very hard. They eliminated the thrift regulator and, with it, new federal thrift charters. The roughly 750 existing thrift institutions would have a new regulator, the Office of the Comptroller of the Currency. These thrifts will be subject to more stringent federal rules and regulations. State charters will still be available, but they too will be subject to new consumer protection regulations.

It remains to be seen if the thrift charter proves to be a viable business model anymore.

IndyMac and Countrywide *1969–2008*

IndyMac and Countrywide were once part of the same company, Countrywide Mortgage Investments, which was incorporated in Maryland by David Loeb and Angelo Mozilo in 1985.

Countrywide was a real estate investment trust that also purchased, packaged, and resold loans, including higher risk "jumbo" and nonconforming mortgage loans through its subsidiaries and affiliates. Unfortunately, the parent company saw its earnings plummet 77 percent from 1991 to 1993, in large part because people paid back their loans early when interest rates declined and they found better deals elsewhere.

In an effort to regroup, the company owners formed the Independent National Mortgage Corporation, a subsidiary they dubbed IndyMac. IndyMac's purpose was to purchase, package, and sell mortgage loans, including a large number of loans to borrowers with shoddy credit, which they called "B through D" mortgages, as opposed to loans to their best "A" customers. They also made loans to borrowers who used lower-quality manufactured housing as collateral. Worse yet, the company kept a larger number of these loans in its own investment portfolios.

Not surprisingly, these higher-risk loans initially brought higher returns, and Countrywide Mortgage Investments saw its profits skyrocket from \$2.5 million in 1993 to \$50 million in 1996! But the profits were short-lived because so much higher-risk lending was ultimately too much. The company saw its own nonperforming loans (90 days or more delinquent) jump from a very high 2.4 percent in 1997 to an outrageously high 5.3 percent the next year. In contrast, a typical savings bank of that size and at that time had a past-due rate averaging only 0.97 percent!

These performance issues did not go unnoticed and credit agencies downgraded Countrywide Mortgage Investment's ratings (to BBB-). At the same time, the banks and others that were funding this company began placing significant restrictions on their activities. Management responded in several ways, most notably in 1997, by splitting up the company.

IndyMac and Countrywide were now separate entities. Founder David Loeb served as president and chairman of Countrywide until 2000, and as chairman of IndyMac until 2003. He died at the age of 79, shortly after retiring from the IndyMac board. Cofounder Angelo Mozilo was executive vice president of Countrywide, and he eventually assumed the role of its chairman and president. Michael W. Perry was the CEO of IndyMac and eventually assumed the role of its chairman too.

In a sense, these companies went from bad to worse because both IndyMac and Countrywide failed in 2008. Instead of being just one large failing company (Countrywide Mortgage Investments), they became two even larger, *government-insured*, failed companies.

IndyMac
1969–July 11, 2008

After the breakup with Countrywide, IndyMac was on its own under the original charter until 2000. That's when management saw an opportunity to expand by purchasing First Federal Savings and Loan Association of San Gabriel Valley, a southern California-based S&L with nine branches, \$490 million in assets, and twenty-seven thousand customers. It was just the beginning. By 2007, IndyMac had become the tenth-largest thrift in the country, with total assets of \$33 billion, 9,907 employees, and operations in all fifty states.[89] *Bigger is not always better.*

IndyMac was known for its portfolio of Alt-A loans, a higher risk loan that earned more interest for the bank because it didn't require borrowers with good credit to produce much documentation, such as records to verify their income or assets (called a "low-doc" loan). But when the real estate market took the inevitable downturn, IndyMac had too much of the high-risk Alt-A loans.

To make matters worse, IndyMac financed these loans with Option ARMS (26 percent of their portfolio) and interest-only loans (43 percent of their portfolio). The Option ARM loan was a higher risk adjustable rate loan with options that in many cases allow the customer to make payments for less than the principal and interest due on the loan. Some analysts thought that Alt-A, interest-only, and Option ARMs to good credit borrowers would perform better than subprime loans (which were considered the riskiest of loans). Perhaps, but these loans at IndyMac were rotten just the same. *It's almost always bad loans.*

The bank's level of past-due and nonaccrual loans (loans that aren't even paying the interest in the contract) measured an astonishing 7.64 percent by year-end 2007, even after charging off $56 million in bad loans. No other top-ten large thrift was even close to that level of bad loans except perhaps the second worst one of the group— their cousin Countrywide (3.56 percent).

IndyMac's share price tumbled from $50.11 in May 2006 to just twenty-eight cents when the FDIC shut it down on July 11, 2008.

Some people complained that IndyMac's failure was caused by a "run" on the bank when US Senator Charles Schumer (a member of the Senate Banking Committee) wrote a letter to the regulators that IndyMac "could face failure" if they didn't act quickly. He made the letter public, and eleven days later, the thrift had lost over $1.3 billion in deposits. Nobody disputes what the senator said or his right, perhaps even obligation, to say it to the regulators. But it's a terrible mistake for a member of the Senate Banking Committee to do so publicly. It's the equivalent of a fireman screaming "Fire!" in a movie theater.

But don't kid yourself: IndyMac failed because of bad lending practices and overly aggressive management, not a senator pointing out the obvious. And it would have surely failed much sooner if its regulator, the OTS, had not allowed the bank to "backdate" its capital—an unethical and illegal accounting maneuver that gave the appearance that IndyMac was in better financial condition than it was.

The FDIC reports that IndyMac's failure could cost the FDIC about $9 billion, and IndyMac is "honored" as the most expensive bank closing in FDIC history.[90]

The shareholders lost virtually all their money, and about ten thousand depositors lost up to $1 billion in all according to the FDIC.[91] Half the company employees lost their jobs. Most of the remaining assets were sold to OneWest Bank, FSB, a new thrift formed by a different group of investors.

Countrywide
1969–July 1, 2008

After Countrywide split from IndyMac, it was also on its own with a new charter as Countrywide Financial Corporation, a mortgage company that originated, purchased, serviced, and sold mortgage loans. Countrywide expanded very aggressively, growing from $8 billion in assets in 1997 to almost $200 billion in only ten years.[92] Countrywide Financial had become a huge holding company that owned several businesses, including a mortgage banking business that originated home loans, a savings bank that accepted deposits and made loans, a capital markets company that packaged and sold mortgage-backed securities, and an insurance company.

It was one of the largest mortgage loan originators in the country, and its bank subsidiary was responsible for funding most of the loans produced. The subsidiary bank had also become quite large, and when it converted from a commercial bank to a savings bank, it became the second-largest thrift in the country, behind only Washington Mutual (WaMu).

The bank's growth was astounding; it should have been alarming! It reached a crazy pace of 513 percent in 2002, 279 percent in 2003, 111 percent in 2004, 78 percent in 2005, and 27 percent in 2006 (compared to its peers, who averaged only 13 percent that year). While the bank was growing, the quality of the loan portfolio was falling. *Bigger is not always better. We should have seen it coming.*

Countrywide accomplished its rapid growth in part by becoming the largest subprime lender in the country, with $40.6 billion in subprime loans originated in 2006 alone, about 9 percent of their total production, vs. only 2 percent of loans ten years earlier. Subprime loans are among the riskiest, and engaging in higher risk lending usually means higher earnings at first. This was certainly the case, as profits climbed 1,267 percent (that's not a misprint!) over the ten years. But they were ignoring a very important lesson on why banks fail: *It's almost always bad loans.*

Everybody loves a winner, and Chairman/CEO and Founder Angelo R. Mozilo was richly rewarded. His 2006 compensation alone totaled an eye-popping *$51.8 million*, which included use of the company jet (at $90,000), a car, and annual country club dues. In 2003, Fannie Mae featured him with a two-page spread in its annual report; in 2004, the National Housing Conference (an affordable housing advocacy group) named him "Housing Person of the Year"; and in 2005, *Barron's* named him one of the thirty most-respected CEOs *in the world*. Stock prices climbed too, reaching $45 a share by February 2007.

But the real estate boom had peaked by then, and the poorly underwritten, high-risk, high-cost, and subprime loans were crashing down on the company. Not surprisingly, when the bad real estate loan problems were becoming evident in 2007 and the regulator began to apply pressure, Countrywide pulled a fast one. It converted from a national bank to a savings bank, which meant that it changed regulators.

It was shameful that the thrift regulators would allow the charter conversion. It didn't save Countrywide from failing; it only put the federal deposit insurance at higher risk. *Don't sleep with each other.*

Countrywide's delinquent loans had climbed to almost 7 percent by year-end, and the subprime loan portfolio was falling apart: 27.3 percent of the loans were past due, and 5.5 percent were in foreclosure! Wow! Standard & Poor's cut Countrywide's corporate debt rating to junk bond status in May, and the stock price crashed to $6.71 before Bank of America announced plans to buy the distressed company without government assistance.

The deal closed on July 1, 2008. Mozillo was paid an astounding $11.9 million for 2007, the year the company's problems caused it to collapse. Of course, although Mozillo is no longer involved, the process of foreclosing on single family homes will continue for some time.

Washington Mutual Bank (WaMu)
Sept. 25, 1889—Sept. 25, 2008

WaMu claimed it was "not like other banks." Its advertising campaigns even featured cutting-edge television commercials mocking stereotypical bankers (stodgy white men) who "just don't get WaMu's way of banking." WaMu had been around a long time—incorporated as Washington National Building Loan and Investment Association in 1889. It eventually converted from a nonprofit mutual and went public in 1983, changed names, expanded its scope, and grew to become the largest thrift and the tenth-largest financial institution in the country. With total assets of $320 billion, the company reported a *$3.5 billion profit* in 2006![93]

But sadly, and exactly 119 years *to the day* later, bank regulators decided that WaMu's claim was true. It was not like other banks. It was insolvent.

The FDIC seized WaMu and sold it to JPMorgan Chase Bank the same day. No depositors lost any money, and the FDIC insurance fund was untarnished. But shareholders of the holding company weren't so lucky. They had watched their stock climb to $46 a share in 2006, but they lost virtually their entire investment when the holding company declared bankruptcy. WaMu had become the largest financial institution in US history to fail.

Its demise can be attributed to two words: bad loans. Like others that failed or suffered tremendous financial pressure, WaMu had tried to grow the bank and increase its profits with high-risk, high-cost, subprime loans ($16 billion) and with poorly structured Option ARM loans ($58 billion). Like other institutions that sought fast growth and high profits, WaMu not only purchased a subprime lending company, Long Beach Financial in 1999, but it also pushed the Option ARM product to the point that it made up 47 percent of their home-loan portfolio in 2007. As if that wasn't bad enough, subprime loans were another 12.8 percent of the portfolio that year. To put it bluntly: bad idea. *It's almost always bad loans. Bigger is not always better.*

When these loans stopped paying, which happened on a large scale in 2007 and 2008, management was forced to set aside huge reserves ($12 billion from June '07 to June '08). WaMu suffered incredible losses ($7.5 billion for the first six months of 2008), cut its dividend by 75 percent, fired 3,150 people, and looked for new capital. JPMorgan Chase offered to buy them for $8 a share in March 2008, but WaMu's board turned it down.

Instead, it raised enough money to stay afloat by selling half the company to an investor group led by multibillionaire David Bonderman of TPG Investment Company for $8.75 a share. None of this was enough to stop the loan losses, and the credit agencies began downgrading their ratings, eventually reducing the bank's debt rating to junk bond status in early September 2008.

Alan H. Fishman, the former president and chief operating officer of Sovereign Bank, replaced CEO Kerry Killinger on September 8, but by then it was too late. Deposits poured out of the bank, including $16.7 billion in the ten days before the FDIC took over.

Killinger was paid $14.2 million in 2007, which included $144,000 for *personal use* of the corporate jet that year. Fishman received $20 million for seventeen days' work. A company press release issued by TPG stated "... obviously, we are dissatisfied with the loss to our partners from our investment in Washington Mutual."[94]

Obviously, they are not alone.

Chapter 5
Investment Banks

We all make mistakes. We all say dumb things sometimes.

I was setting up my computer and materials for a series of seminars I was conducting at a commercial bank in Salt Lake City, Utah, when a very kind banker asked if I needed anything. "Yes, thanks for asking," I replied. "Does your break room have any coffee made?"

"No," she said. "We don't serve coffee."

And that's when I said, "What? Is that some kind of religious thing?"

Actually, it was. Most Mormons don't drink caffeine, and, well, Salt Lake City has a lot of Mormons.

Another time I was speaking to an audience of about sixty-five bank examiners in a hot, crowded room when somebody in the middle seat was handed a note and got up to leave. It was rather distracting, as the people on his row had to stand up to let him pass, and everybody's attention was turned to the guy trying to exit. As he was leaving, I quipped:

"It's a note from his mother. She wants him to call her." A couple of people chuckled.

Apparently I was one of the few people in the room who didn't know his mother was in the hospital, seriously ill.

Yeah, I know. I'm an idiot. I apologized to the guy as soon as I found out, and he even laughed about it. I always try to make amends when I say or do dumb things.

We all make mistakes. We all say dumb things sometimes. If you acknowledge it and try to make amends, people are usually forgiving. Give us a reason to like you, and most of us will. That's why we love (cartoon character) Homer Simpson, who once said, "I never apologize … I'm sorry, but that's just the way I am."[95] At least he acknowledged his shortcomings.

It's not as funny when people use religion to excuse or justify their actions, like Goldman Sachs investment banker Lloyd Blankfein, who claimed he was "just doing God's work" when the financial meltdown occurred.[96] Being rich doesn't absolve you from sounding like a jerk. People weren't laughing when he said it.

People in the audience did laugh when investment banker Ivan Boesky said, "Greed is all right, by the way. I want you to know that. I think greed is healthy. You can be greedy and still feel good about yourself."[97] Boesky's famous quote was made during his commencement address at the University of California, Berkeley, in 1986. He wasn't laughing when soon after, he landed in jail for two years, paid a $100 million fine, and was barred for life from the securities industry. Getting convicted for insider trading is no laughing matter. *Greed has a price.*

To some people, wealthy investment bankers are the enemy. When people face losing their jobs and their homes because some hedge fund manager they never heard of screwed up, and bankers like Blankfein respond the way he did, the entire industry takes a reputational beating. Some of the disdain is deserved. But some of it isn't. There are over six thousand securities firms and investment banks, and the overwhelming majority are run by honest and ethical people. They do terrific things for their clients, families, and communities. This chapter isn't about them.

Instead, it is designed to help the reader understand the industry better by defining it, presenting its history, explaining how they make and spend money, and introducing their regulators. We identify a crook or two, and address controversial issues like executive compensation. In the process, we also explain derivatives, a unique product that caused havoc on the industry, and we introduce the credit rating agencies, a unique industry that really screwed up. We end the chapter with a recap of two huge investment banks that failed: Bear Stearns and Lehman Brothers. The chapter is designed to draw attention to lessons never learned. It is not intended as a blanket criticism of the industry. After all, *it's easy to misplace blame.*

Up to this point we've focused on commercial banks because among depository institutions, they are by far the biggest. In fact, in 2007 commercial banks held over 80 percent of the $13.8 trillion of insured *depository* assets, which explains why they are getting most of the ink in this book. But commercial banks and thrifts are not the only places to invest money and get loans. A lot of people use products and services from securities firms, investment companies, and investment banks too.

Securities firms (also called broker-dealers), are companies comprised of brokers who help investors buy and sell securities (stocks and bonds). **Invest-**

ment companies specialize in developing investment products, such as mutual funds. **Investment banks** not only help individuals buy and sell securities; they also specialize in many other activities, such as underwriting stocks and bonds, arranging mergers and acquisitions, providing industry and economic research services, and offering advice on restructuring companies. The largest investment banks are also called "market makers" that develop markets for certain products, such as mortgage- and asset-backed securities, preferred stocks, municipal securities, and bank loans.

Investment Companies

At year-end 2008, there were over sixteen thousand investment companies with total assets of $13 trillion, which was about $800 billion less than the combined assets of commercial banks, thrifts, and credit unions.[98]

It can be confusing, but investment *companies* are not the same as investment *banks.* An investment company forms and manages one of four types of investments: mutual funds, closed-end funds, exchange-traded funds (ETFs), and unit investment trusts (UITs). Unlike investment *banks* that help you buy and sell products such as mutual funds, investment *companies* are the ones that actually create the four products, especially the mutual funds. In fact, mutual funds comprised 93 percent of the combined investment company assets in 2008.[99]

Mutual funds are big business! According to the Investment Company Institute and the US Census Bureau, an estimated

Market makers are dealers who ***make sure there is always a market*** *for specific stocks, bonds, or other commodities. Market makers will agree to hold the specific investment in their own portfolio and then buy more of it or sell some of it at a publicly stated price. They do so on a very large scale and make a profit off the small difference between their stated purchase price (called the "****bid****") and their stated sell price (called the "****ask****").*

Mutual Funds, *also known as "open-end" funds, are set up by investment companies to allow a large number of people to pool their money in order to buy a more diversified portfolio of stocks, bonds, securities, etc. than they could do on their own. They are "open-ended" because buyers can purchase shares and sell them back to the fund at any time. The Vanguard Total Stock Market Index fund is an example of a popular, professionally managed mutual fund investing in over thirty-four hundred publicly traded US companies.*

Closed-end Funds *are similar to mutual funds except that a fixed number of shares are sold to start these funds, and then it is "closed" to new investors. However, the existing shares can later be sold or purchased on various stock exchanges. For example, the BlackRock High Yield Trust is a closed-end fund investing primarily in high-risk, high-yield company bonds.*

ninety-two million individual investors owned mutual funds in 2008. An overwhelming 95 percent of them were investing for retirement. Most mutual fund investors bought their funds through employer-sponsored plans, primarily 401(k) plans.[100]

Investment companies will most likely steer you toward their specific products, especially their "family of mutual funds." That's okay. You wouldn't expect a salesperson at Ford Motor Company to suggest you buy a Chevy, so why would you expect a representative of the Vanguard Group to suggest that you buy something from their competitor, American Funds? Both investment companies have good products and services, and both have their own interests at heart.

In 2008, about seven hundred financial firms around the world created and managed these mutual funds. Most were managed by independent fund advisors, like American Funds, BlackRock, Fidelity, and Vanguard. Others were managed by banks and thrifts, insurance companies, and investment *banks.*

Exchange-traded Funds (ETFs) *are a type of investment traded on stock exchanges like the NY Stock Exchange, or the London Stock Exchange— thus the name "exchange-traded." An ETF is often a fund comprised of the most common stocks sold on these exchanges. For example, the SPDR (called "spider") S&P 500 ETF is a fund that owns stocks from 500 large US companies traded on the NY Stock Exchange.*

Unit Investment Trusts (UITs) *are investment funds that promise to pay back all investors on a specific date. Folks buy "units" of the fund (like shares) and the money is invested in a relatively small number of places, such as twenty company stocks or bonds. UIT managers have a "buy-and-hold" philosophy, which gives people confidence that what they buy is what they get until the fund terminates. For example, the Greater China UIT was issued by First Trust Portfolios in late 2010, invested in thirty companies headquartered in China or Hong Kong, and terminates in late 2012.*

Investment Banks

Commercial banks accept government-insured deposits from customers and make loans directly to businesses and individuals. Investment banks, on the other hand, help their customers buy and trade stocks, bonds, mutual funds, and other similar investments; they help companies raise capital; they give advice on mergers and acquisitions; and they help manage investments, including mutual funds. As already noted, before1933, investment banks and commercial banks were frequently one and the same, but during the Great Depression they were separated. In 1999, however, the pendulum swung back, and depository institutions and investment banks are allowed to become affiliated again if a financial holding company owns both of them.

In other words, one company can now own both an investment bank subsidiary and a commercial bank (or thrift) subsidiary. But the two separate companies cannot be merged into one like happened before the Great Depression. The "firewall" separating the two is designed to prevent the failure of one subsidiary from causing other subsidiaries to fail. Examples of financial holding companies owning both investment bank and commercial bank subsidiaries include Citigroup, Bank of America, and JPMorgan Chase & Co.

Investment bankers have certainly screwed things up on more than one occasion, and let's face it: the debacle that began in 2007 will undoubtedly end as one of the worst periods in the history of the industry, our economy, and our own investment portfolios. But setting that aside, if possible, remember that we really need investment banks to help companies, governments, and others raise money to finance their growth.

Local governments use investment banks to help underwrite and sell bonds that are used to finance huge projects, such as roads and sewers or airports or schools. Businesses, universities, hospitals, and utilities all use investment banks' services to help them expand. Imagine where we would be without this financial expertise. Seriously, if investment banks did not exist, we would have to invent them. And while the headline-grabbing stories of greed and excess rightfully capture our attention, most investment bankers have done a commendable job that has served their clients well.

Investment banks underwrite and sell new issues of stocks, called initial public offerings (IPOs), or additional stock offerings from existing public companies. These securities can be sold privately to specific investors such as an insurance company, or they can be sold as public offerings to the general public. In 2006, companies such as Citigroup and J.P. Morgan Securities offered this area of expertise.

Besides underwriting and selling new issues of stocks, investment banks also play leading roles in arranging mergers and acquisitions, which not only includes helping companies find partners to merge with, but also helping them find the financing to complete the mergers. In 2006, the big players were companies such as Goldman Sachs and Morgan Stanley.

In 2007, the largest independent investment banks in the United States were Goldman Sachs Group, Inc., with total assets of $1.1 trillion, and Morgan Stanley, with total assets of $1.0 trillion. In September 2008, both of these companies found it necessary to convert their charters very quickly to bank holding companies. It was a highly unusual move, and the regulators approved the applications virtually overnight because of the financial crisis that was unfolding at the time. The companies had voluntarily subjected themselves to significantly increased government regulation by the Federal Reserve Board. In return, they got access to the Fed's Discount Window, where they could borrow money quickly and at low cost.

Wall Street History

If you enjoy history, then the story of investment banking and Wall Street is a good read that reflects both the best and worst of human nature. This book is primarily about commercial banking, but because commercial banking is so interrelated with investment banks, we must at least visit some of the many lessons never learned with investment banking too.

Courtesy of Jon Nail.

It all began with a twelve-foot-high wooden barricade built by a guy named Peter Stuyvesant. He built it in 1653 to protect the early Dutch settlers from attacks by Indians and the British. Years later, a street was built alongside this huge wall, and it was called, cleverly enough, Wall Street. It is here, literally, on this street in New York's lower Manhattan that merchants and traders gathered to buy and sell stocks and bonds.

Stock exchanges existed in Europe before they evolved in the United States. London and Antwerp, Belgium, had especially robust exchanges in the late 1700s. Although Philadelphia had the very first US stock exchange, other cities, especially Boston, Baltimore, and Charleston, were also selling government bonds. But it was outside on the curb of Wall Street where our nation developed "the first active market for the bonds and shares of emerging companies."[101] You can imagine how it must have looked in the late 1780s when large numbers of men gathered outdoors on the street twice a day to buy and sell stock. But it probably isn't surprising that this unregulated free trade was ripe with corruption too.

The First Insider Trading

One such case of corruption, or more specifically, insider trading, involved a man named William Duer. Now, you wouldn't have thought he would be a crook! He was a genuine patriot, a member of the Continental Congress, a signer of the Articles of Confederation (establishing the "United States of America" before the US Constitution was adopted), a respected New York judge, a Federalist who supported a strong national government, and our nation's first assistant secretary of the Treasury. He traded on Wall Street and lived an opulent lifestyle, throwing lavish parties for the rich and famous. Because of his position as secretary to the Board of the Treasury he knew a great deal about the inner workings of the Treasury and about international finance. He was admired and respected.

But, sadly, he was also a crook. Charles R. Geisst, in his book on the history of Wall Street, stated, "Duer had the distinction of being the first individual to use knowledge gained from his official position to become entangled in speculative trading; in effect, he was the first inside trader."[102] The Treasury Department brought charges against him in part because he had insider knowledge about the government's plans to repay government securities used to finance the Revolutionary War. The Dutch and French held large amounts of the securities, and they were rightfully concerned that they may not be repaid in full. Duer bought these securities cheaply on Wall Street knowing damn well what others had no way of knowing: the Treasury had decided to honor its commitment to pay for them, and that they would be worth much more later. Worse yet, he was reported to have leaked false rumors from the Treasury Department to drive down the price before he bought them. More rumors followed that would drive their price up, and then he would sell the securities at a profit.

He also secretly struck a deal that gave him the right to purchase from the US Congress, together with other unknown investors, an extensive amount of land in what is now part of Ohio.[103] The secret deal was simple. Duer would help convince Congress to allow the Treasury Department (where he held a senior position) to negotiate the price and terms of a very large land sale to a group of investors representing former soldiers and others who had organized themselves as the "Ohio Company." The soldiers had been paid in Continental currency, which wasn't worth very much, and would be better off if they could exchange these crummy currencies for land.

Once he had helped convince Congress to do the deal, Duer then "negotiated" on behalf of the Treasury some very good prices for the Ohio Company. The deal included buying outright one tract of land measuring about 1.5 million acres and an "option" to purchase another parcel of land that was bordered on the east by the Scioto River in central Ohio. In return for his lobbying skills and favorable purchase terms, the management of the Ohio Company would later transfer to the "Scioto Land Company" their option to purchase the second tract. Few people knew that Duer held the controlling interest in the Scioto Land Company.

The Treasury's wrongful conduct charge for this crooked deal never really mattered because Duer got in deep debt when he borrowed money to trade government securities on Wall Street. He had also been pumping a lot of his own money into the failed Scioto land venture, and when he could not come up with enough cash to cover his debts and honor his purchase commitments, he ended up in debtors' prison, where he eventually died. *Greed has a price.*

His sentence was especially harsh and was in no small part a payback for his opulent lifestyle and punishment for the Scioto land deal. He had originally planned to trade parcels of the Scioto land to the French (and Dutch) in return for their US government securities. In particular, he was working hard to get the French to trade him their deflated securities for actual land. What they didn't know was that Duer could then get full value for the securities by using them to pay Congress for the Scioto land—a clever nuance he incorporated into the deal he struck for the Ohio Company while at the Treasury. He would not only make money from selling the land at a profit, but also on the difference between the low market value he paid the French for their securities and the full face value he received for them from the government.

Unfortunately, a variety of problems plagued the venture. Corruption, fraud, theft, and his business partners' incompetence left him unable to pay for the land and honor his commitments to the hundreds of people who bought into the scheme. These citizens were mostly French, some of whom had undoubtedly spent their entire fortunes to travel long and difficult distances to Ohio in search of the American dream. They got screwed. It's one of the lessons never learned: *People matter*. Given his legacy of unpaid debts and human despair, prison may have been the safest place for Duer to live out his life.

Stock Exchanges

Following Duer's bankruptcy, everybody knew that the Wall Street "curb market" had to change, and the New York legislature passed a law to try to reign in the corrupt practices. As a result, in May 1792, twenty-four merchants and brokers met under a buttonwood tree at 68 Wall Street and signed the infamous "Buttonwood Agreement," to bring some order to their business. (If you read *The Economist* magazine, you might notice that it has a popular column each week called "Buttonwood." Now you know where the name came from!)

After the Buttonwood Agreement, the stock exchange moved indoors. Building on its success, in 1817 the New York Stock and Exchange Board was officially created. It later changed its name to the New York Stock Exchange (NYSE). In 2007, it merged with Euronext N.V. (a European stock exchange based in Amsterdam) to become, NYSE Euronext. That made it the largest exchange group in the world! It's really amazing to think it all began with a bunch of guys standing on a curb trying to make a few bucks. The next three largest are NASDAQ (another American firm), the Tokyo Stock Exchange, and the London Stock Exchange.[104]

But wait, there's more! On February 15, 2011, NYSE Euronext announced they had agreed to a merger with Deutsche Boerse AG, whose headquarters is in Eschborn, Germany (near Frankfurt). Others also began bidding to merge with NYSE Euronext. If approved by shareholders and regulators, Deutsche Boerse shareholders would own 60 percent of the combined group, and would designate nine of the fifteen board members.

Wow! The largest stock exchange in the world would get even bigger by selling out. The combined net revenues at the new German company were projected to exceed $5.4 billion annually, with approximately 37 percent of its total revenues coming from derivatives trading and clearing activities. Isn't that super? What could possibly go wrong? *Bigger is not always better. We should have seen it coming.*

How this or other proposed mergers pan out remains to be seen. But we do know that not all change is bad. When the NYSE moved to an indoor building, for example, members of this privately held company no longer had to stand on the curb to do business. They could literally sit in their own designated chair. They had a "seat" from which to do business. That's why membership on the NYSE was called a "seat" for 213 years. These memberships (seats) were very valuable, and the last seat on the NYSE sold for $4 million in 2005.[105] The

NYSE became a public company in 2006 and converted from permanent seats to annual trading licenses.

Doing business on the street curb added to the investment lingo too. The new exchange was indoors and had more structure; the securities in this new exchange had to meet higher standards. If a stock didn't meet the new standards, it wasn't allowed inside and had to be traded outside, on the "curb market." We still use that phrase to describe exchanges where the stocks don't meet high standards. In fact, at one time there was even a New York Curb Exchange, but you might remember them after they changed their name to the American Stock Exchange. The NYSE Euronext acquired the American Stock Exchange on October 1, 2008.

While none would come close to the size of the combined NYSE Euronext/ Deutsche Boerse merger, there are still over fifty other large exchanges or companies willing to facilitate the purchase and sale of securities, commodities, currencies, etc. For example, in the United States you can sell government bonds and other securities thru NASDAQ, the National Association of Securities Dealers Automated Quotation System. NASDAQ (pronounced "Naz-Dak") was the original electronic stock market allowing trades to be made online directly between two parties. They were called "over the counter" (or OTC) trades because they were done directly between two parties, as if exchanging money over a counter, rather than through a third party. While it originally featured a larger number of higher risk stocks, that isn't the case anymore.

You can also sell commodities (agricultural or mineral products, for example) on the Chicago Board of Trade, the Kansas City Board of Trade, the Minneapolis Grain Exchange, or the Philadelphia Board of Trade, just to name a few.

These exchanges provide a great service. Imagine you are a farmer wishing to sell a commodity, such as wheat. You can harvest the wheat and tote it to a big ol' town such as Chicago or Kansas City or Minneapolis, and try to sell it on the spot. But storing it is a problem, and if there is too much wheat already there, you may not get the price you want. It would be far better if you could strike a deal with a buyer for your wheat well in advance of the actual harvest. In fact, if you had a contract to deliver your wheat next year or some other future date, a "futures contract," both you and the buyer would know the price in advance and could plan accordingly. That's such a good idea, it became a common practice.

These futures contracts had real value. For example, sometimes farmers would decide they didn't want to grow wheat that year, so they would just sell the contracts to other farmers who did. Sometimes the buyers reconsidered too, and would sell their contracts to other buyers who wanted wheat. The price paid by buyers and sellers for the futures contracts fluctuated depending on things like the weather or production. But having these exchanges in business made buying and selling these futures contracts much easier because they placed minimum standards on the quality and quantity of the products being sold (called commodities) and helped standardize the practice.

So who regulates the exchanges that do commodities futures trading? Why, it's the Commodities Futures Trading Commission, of course.

Income and Expenses

Investment Bank Income

Like all companies, investment banks are in business to make a profit any way they can. Smaller securities firms get most of their income by charging fees (commissions) when they purchase or sell stocks, bonds, and other investments for their clients. On the other hand, investment banks are more diverse and complex than the smaller securities firms and often have several divisions that make money for the parent company.

Like smaller securities firms, they generate commissions from buying and selling stocks and bonds for their clients, and by offering financial planning services. But investment banks also make money by buying large amounts of stocks and bonds for themselves and then selling them later at a profit (trading activities). They earn income by underwriting and selling state and local government "general obligation bonds" and other government-sponsored debts such as industrial revenue bonds (IRBs). (The IRBs are repaid with *dedicated revenues* from a specific project, like a civic center, or a professional baseball stadium, rather than from the *general revenues* typically obtained from income taxes or residential property taxes.) Investment banks sometimes generate fee income from managing mutual funds or by advising and coordinating small and medium-sized company mergers and acquisitions. Some investment banks even own (through a financial holding company) banks or thrift institutions or insurance agencies.

Some securities firms (technically called broker-dealers) offer lower fees to their customers on Internet trading or investing, but they don't offer any specific investment recommendations. These "discount brokers" earn their money from commissions on large numbers of trades. Like everything else, they have evolved over the years to become more diversified as full-service broker/dealers. Examples of traditional discount brokers include ETrade, Fidelity, Charles Schwab, TD Ameritrade, and Scottrade.

The largest global investment banks use all of these ways to get income. They operate all over the world, and typically own (through their holding companies) insurance companies, commercial banks, thrifts, real estate, and other commercial businesses. They also earn a lot of income by taking risks in trading activities and by serving as a "market maker." They buy stocks and bonds, and other securities and commodities, for their own portfolio with the idea of selling them later at a profit. They buy and sell derivatives (see sidebar at the end of the chapter). Examples of large global investment banks include Bank of America, Merrill Lynch, Citigroup, Goldman Sachs, J.P. Morgan Securities, Morgan Stanley, and Wells Fargo Securities.

Derivatives generate modest income for investment banks and can provide excellent protection when used properly. The downside is they also generate serious risks, such as what happened to AIG (American International Group Inc.) insurance company. That nightmare is covered later.

By far, the investment bank making the most money in 2009 was Goldman Sachs, which reported a record high $45 *billion* in revenues, and an astounding $13.3 *billion* profit.

Investment Bank Expenses

Noncompensation expenses usually have to do with brokerage activities, such as the cost of clearing trades and paying fees to exchanges (such as NYSE Euronext). These expenses also include things like property depreciation expenses and taxes. Accountants, finance professionals, and company executives find these line items of great importance, but the public doesn't really care about these boring line items.

What grabs the headlines and infuriates the public are the compensation expenses. There's a reason for that. Compensation expenses comprise the largest percentage of all investment bank expenses. While they would typically run about 21 percent of expenses at your local commercial bank, they are substantially higher at global investment banks, running well over 30 percent. They even averaged an astounding 47 percent at Goldman Sachs from 1999 to 2008!

Compensation

Investment banks and companies provide a lot of well-paying jobs: about 841,770 jobs as reported in May 2007, and the annual average income per person was $80,130.[106] In contrast, the banking industry provides a hell of a lot more jobs (2,883,150), but those people make a lot less. A whole lot less. Their average annual income was $45,680.[107] These numbers are not 100 percent accurate due to some technical definitions with job classifications, but you get the idea. Investment banks and companies provide high-paying jobs.

Of course, the top executives get far, far more than that and a lot of people find it insulting to see the pay these folks have received, especially when their companies got in such bad shape they needed a taxpayer bailout. Yes, everybody in this industry benefitted from the bailout, even if they didn't take cash directly from the government. To make it more disturbing, while roughly 1.3 million homes faced foreclosure in 2007 (it climbed to 2.9 million homes in 2010), the investment bank executives were still raking in the dough. *Greed has a price.*

2007 Investment Banker COMPENSATION	**Bear Stearns CEO James E. "Jimmy" Cayne**	**Lehman Brothers CEO Richard S. "Dick" Fuld, Jr.**
Base Salary & Cash Bonus	$250,000	$750,000
Bonus	$17,070,746	$4,250,000
Stock Awards	$14,838,829	$26,968,528
Option Awards	$1,690,425	$2,238,600
TOTAL COMPENSATION	**$33,850,000**	**$34,207,128**

Bear Stearns was sold to JPMorgan in a "fire sale" that was arranged in March 2008 by the Federal Reserve, the day before the company planned to declare bankruptcy. Lehman Brothers filed for the largest bankruptcy in US history in September 2008.

Data for Bear Sterns and Lehman Brothers was obtained from their SEC 10-K filings and related proxy statements. Bear Sterns and Lehman Brothers fiscal year ended November 30, 2007.

According to the fourteenth annual CEO Compensation Survey prepared by the Institute for Policy Studies and United for a Fair Economy, two groups that focus on social justice issues, "top executives averaged $10.8 million in total compensation, over 364 times the pay of the average American worker, a calculation based on data from an Associated Press survey of 386 *Fortune* 500 companies" in 2007.[108]

Congress responded to the executive pay controversy by requiring companies to hold nonbinding shareholder votes at their annual meetings on executive pay packages. Although the vote is nonbinding, it is a start in allowing shareholders to express their displeasure about paychecks and may help to control what they see as excessive pay.

Capital

The Securities and Exchange Commission (SEC) sets the rules on how much capital a typical securities firm (called broker-dealer) must have. It's called "Rule 15C 3-1," and that might lead you to believe the SEC names their regulations after *Star Wars* movie characters, such as R2-D2. But, no. It was taken from the Code of Federal Regulations, Title 17, Chapter III, Part 240, Section 15c3-1. Boring, I know.

Generally speaking, Rule 15C 3-1 set the net worth to asset ratio at a minimum of 2 percent (and a $250,000 minimum). Yes, that seems really low, doesn't it? And if the securities firm doesn't maintain any customer accounts, they could operate with even less capital than that. The SEC figured a securities firm didn't need much capital if they were just making trades for customers.

For perspective, most securities firms are only engaged in securities trading, and they actually do need fewer assets to do the job than you might think. That's why when evaluating their size they are frequently measured by their capital, not their assets. So we are talking about an industry of over six thousand securities firms and investment banks in 2006. Their equity capital amounted to $164.1 billion, and total assets amounted to $5.22 trillion.[109] But most of the size is concentrated in the investment banks, not the smaller securities firms.

The SEC rule goes further and also limits the amount of *debt* a broker-dealer can have. If the securities firm borrows too heavily, it can put the company at too much risk.

The debt-to-net capital ratio is 15-to-1, meaning the firm may have fifteen dollars of debt for every dollar of capital. In theory, these firms would not want to go beyond that level because if they did, they could be required to stop all trading activity—a very stiff penalty. To be safe, they would normally run at less than a 12-to-1 maximum leverage.

To many people, these debt levels may seem outrageous. Would you want your household debt to measure fifteen dollars for every dollar of your wealth? After all, the average household debt measures less than fifty cents for every dollar of wealth, not fifteen dollars![110] But the securities firms are not households. They make a good chunk of their money with leverage, and they must answer to their lenders, their owners, and our regulators. The SEC developed these capital standards primarily to ensure securities firms could meet their customers' trade orders. Their interest was to protect these customers, not the securities firm themselves. But fifteen to one? Seriously? That's high.

Sweetheart Deal

One of the problems with the SEC capital rule was that the oversight did not extend in a meaningful way to the large investment companies. There was a similar issue in Europe, but they changed their laws to fix it. They not only required that these European investment bank companies be more tightly regulated, but that the laws also apply to any large US investment banks operating overseas too.

The US commercial and investment banks doing business in Europe would be regulated by the European Union unless they had an "umbrella regulator" in the United States that had authority over the securities firms and all of their affiliates. But who would be the US umbrella regulator of the investment bank holding companies? After all, these investment bank holding companies that would be subject to European Union oversight were huge! For instance, Goldman Sachs Group Inc. alone reported total assets of $885 *billion* in 2008, and that figure was *down* from $1.1 *trillion* in 2007!

If you manage a large investment bank, you probably wouldn't want European regulators overseeing your bank, and the thought of your own elected officials assigning a regulator to manage the task was hardly any better. Instead, you would prefer to choose your own regulator—one that already understood your business, would keep regulatory burden to a minimum, and would be less strict than the Europeans. Better yet, the ideal situation would be a *voluntary program* with *weak enforcement powers* and where you could *opt out anytime* you wanted by just announcing that you no longer wanted to be regulated by your regulator. Yeah, right! Like any regulator would go along with that!

Guess again. It isn't surprising that the largest US investment banks took matters into their own hands and asked the SEC to be their regulator under these incredibly lenient terms. What is surprising is that the SEC agreed to do so!

Previously, the SEC did not believe it had legal authority to subject the investment banks to their supervision and didn't appear to have much appetite for increasing their role as their regulator either. That is until the nation's largest investment banks lobbied them to do so.

The new capital program that the SEC adopted only applied to investment banks with capital over $5 billion, which just happened to be the five companies asking for special treatment: Bear Stearns, Lehman Brothers, Merrill Lynch, Goldman Sachs, and Morgan Stanley. Two other qualified investment banks, Citigroup and JPMorgan, were already subject to umbrella supervision by the Federal Reserve System and didn't need this special treatment from the SEC.

Under the new rules, these five companies would become part of the SEC's *voluntary* Consolidated Supervised Entity (CSE) program. In return for their voluntarily agreeing to SEC oversight, they could do business in Europe without answering to the foreign regulators, and they were allowed to create new capital standards that were different from other US securities firms. They would develop their own risk models to evaluate their capital needs. They could operate without those bothersome fifteen-to-one borrowing restrictions that were required of other securities firms. In return, they agreed to allow the SEC to review their entire operations.

The industry obviously supported the change. After all, they had requested it. But there was one dissenter who stands out. Leonard Bole, of L.D.B. Consulting in Valparaiso, Indiana, which specializes in computer risk modeling systems, wrote that using Value at Risk (VaR) models to compute capital was a *bad idea.* Using these models would actually lower the capital standards at investment banks, another *bad idea.* In particular, he reminded the SEC that VaR models would have failed miserably if they had been used in previous crises, such as "Black Monday" in 1987 when nearly 1,068 NYSE securities reached fifty-two-week lows. He pointed out that although these models provide good information, that information is certainly not good enough to determine capital adequacy at multibillion-dollar international investment banks. His comments included this thoughtful observation:

> The proposal offers a trade off: the Commission obtains greater oversight and the firms who opt for this structure are in compliance with the European mandate for consolidated supervision at the holding company level. This quid pro quo should provide adequate incentive to those firms seeking recognition as a CSE WITHOUT the added inducement of lowered capital requirements …

> Lowering capital charges for U.S. broker dealers in return for greater regulatory control could erode the system that has safeguarded U.S. investors. By all means, work with the large firms to facilitate a level playing field in Europe, but at the same time continue to protect market participants in this country by preserving the safety net afforded by the current capital requirements. [111]

He was absolutely right. The SEC politely acknowledged his comments and then ignored him.

On April 28, 2004, the five SEC commissioners unanimously voted to allow the five major American investment banks to compute their capital adequacy requirements according to this revised methodology.[112] The capital calculations they established for the investment banks were now based on international (Basel II) requirements, which meant the investment banks could evaluate their capital needs according to their own internal models.

This approach would require intense regulatory oversight. But that didn't happen. The SEC was seriously outgunned. For one, while the SEC was permitted to look at (limited) financial information on all of the other securities firms' parent and affiliate companies, they did little with the data they required these companies to submit.

One report indicated that as late as August 2008, over 86 percent of the firms required to submit financial statements were doing so *by paper.* The information was stored in old-fashioned filing cabinets. Only twenty companies (out of 146) filed electronically and even then the information was not stored in a database that could be efficiently and effectively analyzed.[113] Given that the SEC did so little with existing information, why would anyone think they would do significantly more with the big companies?

With *only three staff members* assigned to each of the five huge CSEs, there was no way the SEC could properly oversee these huge international organizations. The complex modeling systems the CSEs used placed unreasonably high values on the riskier mortgage-backed securities and other collateralized debt obligations (CDOs), which only helped convince their management to buy more of these securities and CDOs. In the end, three of the five CSEs didn't survive, and the other two, Goldman Sachs and Morgan Stanley, were forced to quickly convert their charters to bank holding companies.

The SEC was guilty of "regulatory capture," favoring special interests instead of the public interest. The SEC commissioners blew it when they agreed to do what its biggest customers wanted. In one example of being too close to the companies it was supposed to regulate, the SEC approved Bear Stearns as a CSE *before* even completing an inspection of the company! In another, the SEC approved the alternative capital methods at four of the five CSEs before it completed inspections of those investment banks! The list of SEC mistakes is extensive. For example, when the US Office of Inspector General conducted a review of the SEC's oversight of Bear Stearns, it identified eleven *serious deficiencies* and recommended another twenty-six corrective actions at that one investment bank alone. *Don't sleep with each other.*

Many of the biggest blunders seem very obvious now, and they should have been obvious at the time. In the past, investment banks had been limited to borrowing no more than fifteen dollars for every dollar of capital, but with the new program that disappeared completely. Bear Stearns and Lehman Brothers, for example, both exceeded 32-to-1 leverage ratios before they failed, and worst of all, they were borrowing the money to buy high-risk subprime and Alt-A mortgage-backed securities! The SEC was well aware of both the excessive leverage positions and the high mortgage concentrations but did nothing to stop it. *We should have seen it coming.*

> *... the SEC had allowed five of the largest investment banks in the country to more than double their debt levels, reduce their required capital, and invest heavily in higher-risk securities.*

Amazingly, under its new capital program and as the primary umbrella regulator, the SEC had allowed five of the largest investment banks in the country to more than double their debt levels, reduce their required capital, and invest heavily in higher-risk securities. This voluntary program of investment bank regulation would prove to be an abject failure. The SEC dissolved the program in September 2008. By then, it was way too late.

When SEC Chairman Christopher Cox announced the end of the CSE program following the 2008 financial meltdown, he said the experiences "... have made it abundantly clear that voluntary regulation does not work." He then went on to blame Congress because it had not given the SEC specific "...statutory authority for the Commission to require these investment bank holding companies to report their capital, maintain liquidity, or submit to leverage requirements."[114]

It's easy to misplace blame. Too easy.

Securities and Exchange Commission (SEC)

The SEC is not the main regulator of depository financial institutions or government-sponsored enterprises. Some might say they don't regulate anybody *at all*, but that's unkind. It's more polite to say they don't regulate anybody *very well*.

Perhaps that is by design. With the collapse of the stock market in 1929, public confidence in our financial system collapsed with it. As a result, Congress passed the Securities Act of 1933 that required certain fair and honest disclosures when companies offered securities for sale (a *prospectus*), and the next year, Congress established the SEC to oversee the securities markets and enforce federal securities laws. The SEC's philosophy is consistent with our free-enterprise system in that businesses should be allowed to fail or succeed on their own with minimal government intervention. Although the SEC has enforcement powers and works hard to fight white-collar crime, its main goal has been to ensure appropriate *disclosure* of investment opportunities, not to ensure profits for investors.

The SEC is supposed to interpret laws, issue rules and regulations, and then enforce the securities laws. The president appoints five commissioners to staggered five-year terms, and no more than three of the commissioners may belong to the same political party. Joseph P. Kennedy (President John F. Kennedy's father) was appointed the first chairman of the SEC in 1934.

The agency's functional responsibilities are organized into five divisions.

(1) **Corporation Finance** handles required company reporting and disclosures, such as their quarterly and annual reports to the SEC. The SEC has an exceptional, free online database of these reports, called EDGAR (Electronic Data-Gathering, Analysis, and Retrieval system).

(2) **Trading and Markets** oversees the securities exchanges, securities firms, self-regulatory organizations (SROs), credit rating agencies, and others. The SEC really dropped the ball when it was dealing with the rating agencies prior to the financial panic of 2007 and has since required more *disclosures* from them. This division also oversees the Securities Investor Protection Corporation (SIPC), a private, nonprofit corporation that insures the securities and cash in the customer accounts of member brokerage firms (firms that make transactions for a client) against the failure of those firms. (It doesn't cover investment losses.)

(3) **Investment Management** oversees activities related to mutual funds, exchange-traded funds, and similar organizations in this approximately $26 trillion industry.

A relatively new division, (4) **Risk, Strategy, and Financial Innovation** studies emerging trends and innovations to prevent potential problems.

(5) The **Enforcement Division** investigates securities law violations and pursues civil and administrative actions against people who violate securities laws and regulations. It is a herculean task under any circumstances to pursue

white-collar criminals. That's why the SEC relies heavily upon financially rewarding whistleblowers to identify and help prioritize their work. They have been under a great deal of scrutiny lately, when it became evident they blew it by ignoring many clear and convincing accusations that famed broker–dealer Bernie Madoff stole an estimated $50 billion of investors money in an illegal Ponzi scheme.

Regulating

At one time, the securities industry was regulated by states *and* the SEC, but the National Securities Market Improvement Act of 1996 restricted the states and made the SEC the chief regulator. Most importantly, the law meant that the states could no longer require these federally registered securities firms to also register in the states. Although the states could require certain fees and reports, they could not require the firms to register their stock offerings.

This would not be enough to stop the states from intervening, especially when the SEC was slow to act. In fact, state attorneys general have become much more active in pursuing allegations of misconduct. New York's Investor Protection Bureau has settled cases with dozens of broker/dealers and investment banks, including a $100 million settlement in 2002 with Merrill Lynch. Merrill Lynch had given misleading advice about the stock values of companies that did business with them. There was an even larger settlement that year of $400 million with Salomon Smith Barney for similar allegations. UBS Financial Services also had to pay $23.3 million in 2007 for steering people into unsuitable, overpriced accounts (including a ninety-one- year-old customer who was charged $35,000 for just four trades over two years!).

The New York state attorney general's office does not limit its cases to investment banks, securities firms, and investment companies. In December 2008, they reached an agreement with promoters for New Orleans rapper Lil Wayne after he cancelled his show for the third time in Rochester, New York. Fans who purchased tickets got their money back, which was good because his show hadn't been rescheduled before the multiplatinum artist ended up serving eight months in jail beginning February 2010 for illegal possession of a loaded 9mm handgun. This has little to do with investment banking, but it's a good story anyway.

In spite of their heavy workload, it isn't surprising that the states have stepped up pursuing criminal activity at investment banks and securities firms. The SEC just doesn't have enough manpower to respond to the high volume of complaints. They have to rely extensively on company public disclosures, state lawsuits, civil lawsuits, and the industry itself to keep things from getting out of control.

The largest independent securities firm regulator is FINRA, the Financial Industry Regulatory Authority, headquartered in Washington DC. It was established in July 2007 when the National Association of Securities Dealers and the regulation, enforcement, and arbitration function of the New York Stock Exchange merged. FINRA has twenty-two board members, including ten industry representatives. FINRA is responsible for overseeing 4,900 brokerage firms, about 172,000 branch offices, and approximately 665,000 registered securities representatives.

The organization can claim some success when it collected a modest $28 million in fines in 2008, and expelled nineteen firms from the industry, but at this point, it would be hard to claim that they are an aggressive or effective regulator. In fact, in 2008, 45 percent of broker-dealer firms that FINRA charged with wrongdoing had their cases dismissed. Even worse, the fines that FINRA wanted, a pitiful average of about $25,000, were reduced by the judges (hearing panel) in half of their cases to only $13,000.[115]

In January 2010, FINRA laid off five enforcement officers, including their chief counsel and chief litigation counsel. This followed a 10 percent reduction in staff from the year before.[116] Some of the changes happened because the regulatory divisions of NASD and NYSE merged, but it sure seemed odd that a regulator would reduce its enforcement staff to focus on "efficiency" when the industry it was supposed to regulate had so much to do with the worst economic crisis since the Great Depression.

Go figure.

About Those Derivatives

Some people think gambling is illegal outside of Las Vegas, Atlantic City, and Native-American reservations, but that's not quite the way it is. The stock market itself is a form of gambling. We call it investing, but seriously, who are we kidding? When we do business on any of the one-hundred-plus "exchanges" around the world, such as the old New York Stock Exchange or the Chicago Board Options Exchange, we are placing bets on an uncertain outcome. Much like a casino, where we can choose among slot machines, blackjack tables, or the craps dice tables, these exchanges offer a variety of bets, and one of the biggest is a product known as derivatives (pronounced "duh-riv-uh-tivs").

Derivatives are contracts where the value of the deal is *derived* from something else. The something else could be just about anything, including interest rates, energy prices, currency exchange rates, hell, even the weather!

For example, for a fee, you can get the right to buy some amount of bacon at a set date in the future based on today's price (it's called pork-belly options). If pork prices are higher in the future than what you agreed to pay when you made the deal, you make a profit; if prices are lower, you lose money.

Options like this, called *commodities futures,* are a type of derivative you might find on one of the large exchanges. Not all derivatives are sold on exchanges though—some specialized products are sold directly from one investment bank to another. The transaction is called over-the-counter (OTC) trading. It's these OTC products that generate a lot of worry because they are frequently misunderstood, and they had been largely unregulated. They caused huge problems at companies like Enron, Fannie Mae, and Freddie Mac.

Here is an example of a very popular OTC derivative to protect against changes in interest rates, called an *interest rate swap.* Assume that your bank paid a customer 3 percent for a big deposit account and used the money to make an adjustable-rate loan at 6 percent to one of their big business customers. Your bank may be happy with the three-point spread (6 percent loan - 3 percent deposit), but if the rate on that business loan changes from 6 percent to 5 percent next year, your bank might not be as happy with only a two-point spread (5 percent loan - 3 percent deposit).

Fortunately, there are gamblers who are willing to bet that the rate on the loan will not go down at all next year, or if it does, by only a little. One of them might be willing to offer the bank a deal: for a fee, the gambler will pay the bank any difference between the 6 percent rate they earn today and any rate lower than that next year.

The gambler is willing to do so because the odds are good. If rates go up or stay the same, he does nothing and gets paid by the bank. Gosh, even if rates go down less than the fee he charged the bank, he is still happy. Only if rates go down more than his fee would it be a bad deal for him. He figures on winning three out of four times. If rates go up, stay the same, or go down only a little, he wins.

The bank also likes the deal because it's similar to buying an insurance policy where it pays for protection from falling interest rates. The banker has eliminated the risk that interest rates could go down and make the loan less profitable. It's as though they have managed to *swap* (get it?) their floating-rate loan for a fixed rate. It's an interest rate swap.

In this example, the gambler is a risk taker and likes the odds. The bank is risk averse and more than happy to buy this "insurance" in case interest rates fall. In fact, the risk-averse banker may even want to protect thousands of individual loans at his bank, so he buys interest rate swaps against a bunch of loans he has "pooled" together. Now the bank has hedged its bet, or as they say in the business, they are *hedging the risk.* This is exactly what companies like Fannie Mae, Freddie Mac, Bear Stearns, Lehman Brothers, commercial banks, thrifts, and others would do—use derivatives like these interest rate swaps to reduce risk.

But suppose the bank or the gambler wants to get out of the contract. Maybe the contract cost too much. Maybe he can get more money by selling it to somebody else, or maybe he just wants the cash. It hardly matters because there are others out there who might want to buy this derivative. Either party can call their broker to get in or out of the game. The brokers will usually sell derivatives to other dealers directly in an OTC transaction. It happens a lot more often than you think. In 2008, the Bank for International Settlements valued the transactions at over six hundred trillion dollars!

Derivatives can be used to protect against other risks too, such as credit risks. Suppose your bank has a bunch of home loans they want to package and sell as a mortgage-backed security. If enough borrowers don't pay on their loans, the bank has a serious *credit default*, and the security would lose a lot of its value. In fact, who would want to buy the security if there was even a small chance of a credit default? Fortunately, you could buy a *credit default swap* for protection, and the other party to the transaction would pay you if there was a problem with the loans.

You would have swapped the risk of default with somebody else. Of course, the buyer would want some assurance that the loans were not too risky. That's why sellers would have the securities reviewed by a credit rating agency. With a high rating from these agencies, buyers had some confidence they weren't getting ripped off. They would assume the loans had normal risk, not excessive risk.

Buying derivatives, in fact, is a lot like gambling, and that's perfectly fine as long as everybody understands the risks. There are operational risks, such as computer software glitches or human errors; legal risks, such as a poorly written contract that can't be enforced; credit risks, such as when one party to the contract can't pay the other guy; market risks, such as when the value of the deal falls significantly and you can't sell it at a good price; and liquidity risks, such as when it becomes difficult to sell the contract because nobody wants to buy the darn thing. None of these risks are unusual—investors face them with almost all products. But they are substantial just the same.

So what protects investors? Detailed disclosures are helpful, and the Financial Accounting Standards Board (FASB) has specific rules for disclosing these investments. But problems at Enron, Fannie Mae, Freddie Mac, and many others shown us that these disclosure requirements are at best, well, let's just say *insufficient*.

Disclosure requirements about having enough liquidity are important because they ensure that if anybody has to pay, they can. In addition, capital disclosure requirements are important to ensure that everybody in the game has enough shareholder money to back the deal if necessary. But failures at Bear Stearns and AIG are two prime examples where these standards proved to be, well let's just say *insufficient*.

Nobody deserves praise for managing

the risks with these products. Never mind the huge losses at Enron, Bear Stearns, AIG, Fannie Mae, and Freddie Mac that were tied to derivatives. The losses are huge, but that news isn't new.

Procter & Gamble lost $102 million in 1994. Orange County, California, lost $1.6 billion in 1994 and went bankrupt.

The 233-year-old British bank, Barings, lost $60 billion and failed in 1995. Long-Term Capital Management, a Connecticut hedge fund, lost $4.5 billion and was bailed out by fourteen investment banks at the Federal Reserve's "request" in 1998.

Now don't get the wrong idea. These products really benefit the companies who use them carefully. But the fact remains that the risks from derivatives to the US and world economies are very real and worrisome. A few smart people have tried to enact more robust regulation, but those efforts were defeated.

In fact, when Brooksley Born was appointed chair of the Commodity Futures Trading Commission in 1996, she specifically and heroically proposed developing regulations to limit their potential damage. Her efforts were aggressively opposed by Federal Reserve Chair Alan Greenspan, Treasury Secretaries Robert Rubin and Lawrence Summers, and others. She was even called before Congress and given a verbal beating from Senator Phil Gramm for even suggesting it.

But Brooksley Born was right to propose more oversight! Alan Greenspan, Robert Rubin, Larry Summers, and Phil Gramm were wrong. Very, very wrong.

In 2009, Treasury Secretary Timothy Geithner changed course and proposed the SEC and Commodities Future Trading Commission share the burden of regulating derivatives. Their authority and success is far from certain.

Credit Rating Agencies

Seriously Overrated

When lenders or others want to know if you are creditworthy, they may ask for a report from one of three large credit *reporting* agencies (Equifax, Experian, or Trans Union) and these reports will sometimes include a credit score to make the lending decision less subjective. Get a high score, and you can get a good interest rate on your loan. A low score, and you may be denied the loan or have to pay a higher interest rate. Well, the same thing holds true for big companies. Financial institutions, securities firms, and insurance companies are also "scored" by one or more private companies, credit *rating* agencies. Get a good rating, and get a good deal; a bad rating will cost you.

The credit rating agencies also score specific products you might sell, such as mortgage-backed securities. Credit ratings distinguish between acceptable risks, called "investment grade," and those with high risks, or "noninvestment grade." Each company has its own specific system, but as an example, an investment-grade rating might range from the highest score of "AAA" to the lowest of "Baa." Below that might also be called junk bonds. A "noninvestment" grade will often mean that regulated companies, such as banks or thrifts, couldn't buy the products.

In 1975, the SEC began to make explicit references to credit ratings in its various rules and regulations. Instead of developing a system where the government assigns a credit rating, they outsourced the work to the private sector. At the time, there were three well-known private companies that provided credit ratings, and the SEC decided that the ratings from these "Nationally Recognized Statistical Ratings Organizations (NRSROs)" could be used to meet SEC regulatory requirements. Other state and federal government agencies decided to follow along and use the NRSROs' ratings for their purposes too.

The private companies were **Moody's Investors Service Inc., Standard & Poor's Ratings Services, and Fitch Inc.**, and although the list of NRSROs has recently increased to ten companies in all, from 1990 to 2005, the SEC would only recognize these three companies as official NRSROs. Even now the companies maintain their dominance. The three had over 90 percent of the market share in 2011.

The three companies became highly profitable because anybody who wanted to sell securities wound up at their doorstep seeking a favorable "grade." In the past, Moody's, S&P, and Fitch were on the outside, working hard to sell their opinions about investment companies and their products. Now, these same investment companies would have to pay Moody's, S&P, and Fitch for those opinions! They were in bed with the investment companies like never before.

Thanks to the SEC, profits for these three companies rose like crazy! Revenues doubled from $3 billion in 2002 to $6 billion in 2007. It was driven by a ton of "private label" mortgage- backed securities that entered the market, especially during the housing boom in 2006. The private label securities were those being peddled by companies like Countrywide, Washington Mutual, GMAC, Bear Stearns, and Lehman Brothers.

But the three credit rating agencies blew it during the housing boom from 2005 to 2007 by overrating virtually all of these securities backed with subprime and Alt-A loans. They made a lot of money, paid their executives handsomely, and helped destroy the economy.

Without a doubt, the credit rating agencies contributed to the economic collapse in 2008. There are many reasons for their failures.

- Only three companies were recognized by the SEC with their NRSRO status, and these three didn't have to worry much about their reputation because people had to do business with them anyway.
- The three of them were under considerable pressure from their top ten customers, who dominated the private label securities business. These ten companies wanted the NRSROs to *quickly* rate their products, or they would take their business to one of the other two companies. That meant there was not enough time for due diligence. It was either fast money or due diligence. They chose fast money.
- Agencies had an incentive to be less stringent in evaluations in order to keep or gain market share.
- Issuers were allowed to preview their ratings first—without paying significant fees. That allowed them to go with the agency that offered the highest rating, and that rating agency would then get the big fee income when the security was issued.
- The agencies were double-dipping by receiving one fee to provide consulting services on how to structure the deal and then receiving another fee to rate the same deal highly.
- The computer models used by the agencies were rotten because they were based on historical performance and didn't recognize that current underwriting standards had changed substantially. They were using these poorly tested models on a very large scale.
- The agencies never confirmed loan underwriting standards on mortgage-backed securities or ever looked at loan files. They used mathematical models without checking whether the data was accurate (for example, that a proper appraisal had been done).
- The agencies claim that many consumers committed fraud by lying on their mortgage-loan application—and there is certainly some truth to that——but they never bothered to verify the data before they gave the high ratings.
- The agencies were overly optimistic that the housing market would remain strong.
- The products were becoming increasingly complex. Mortgage-backed securities were being merged into "collateralized debt obligations" and then again into even more complex products

called "collateralized debt obligations squared." The agencies were in over their heads.

- The agencies were never paid money to downgrade a rating, so they rarely did.

There is no question that the credit rating agencies had seriously overrated the US private label mortgage-backed securities. When the securities began to default big time, the credit rating agencies had to begin downgrading their scores. *Fortune* magazine reported that rating agencies had downgraded ratings on nearly $1.9 trillion from mid-2007 to mid-2008.[117] Another report from Fitch announced that they had downgraded 11,418 US residential mortgage-backed securities in 2008—an astonishing downgrade rate of 55 percent—that was caused mostly by the subprime and Alt-A loans originating between 2005 and 2007.[118] S&P downgraded more than two-thirds of their ratings, and Moody's had to downgrade over five thousand similar securities![119]

These large-scale and sudden downgrades meant that the financial institutions that owned the security must now hold more capital against them.

In response to the pitiful performance by these government-promoted credit rating agencies, Congress passed the Credit Rating Agency Reform Act in 2006 to force the SEC to step up its oversight responsibilities.

In 2008, Representative Jackie Speier (D-CA) called the credit agencies' conduct a "bone-chilling definition of corruption." That same year Senator Christopher Shays (R-CT) said, "The ratings agencies are useless now."[120] In 2009, the companies faced numerous lawsuits, and the SEC announced they were hiring a new group of examiners to oversee these agencies.

Better late than never.

Bear Stearns Companies Inc.
1923–2008

In 2006, Bear Stearns was celebrating its twentieth year as a public company, and its fifth consecutive year of record profits. According to CEO James E. "Jimmy" Cayne, the progress had "been built on a firm foundation." He proudly touted the company's "dedication to risk evaluation and management" that gave them the ability to "expand carefully and conservatively." Bear Stearns's stock had climbed as high as $172 a share in 2007, and his company had reached the prestigious title of fifth-largest investment firm in the country.

Less than a year after its 2006 annual report was published, the company was in such dire straits that it was forced to sell itself to JPMorgan Chase, which initially offered only $2 a share. JPMorgan Chase raised the offer to $10 a share after employees, who owned about one-third of the company, and shareholders screamed bloody murder.

Even then, JPMorgan Chase would only do the deal if the Federal Reserve agreed to loan them $29 billion at the Fed's dirt cheap discount rate, which at the time was 2.25 percent.

Bear Stearns was one of the early promoters of mortgage-backed securities (MBS) back in the 1980s, and before they went under they were ranked #1 in MBS originations, and #1 in adjustable-rate mortgage originations.

They built a tremendous mortgage franchise with their fingers in every aspect of the real estate lending pie: originating loans, servicing loans, packaging them into securities, and then selling the securities. They went at it with gusto, growing one of their subsidiary's loan originations to more than $5 billion in less than two years.

When combined with their newly acquired subprime mortgage company (Encore Credit), they were projecting an absolutely astounding $1 billion of loan originations in the United States for *each month* of 2007! Not satisfied, they were seeking substantial mortgage origination growth in Europe too, focusing on Great Britain through their Rooftop Mortgage Company, and France through their Bearimmo Mortgage Company.

Bear Stearns was on a roll, and with the combination of subprime mortgages to package with its conventional mortgages, they were able to offer institutional investors, such as hedge funds and pension funds, great returns on these highly rated products. They used complex financial instruments, such as interest rate swaps and credit default derivatives to enhance the product's value. Bear Stearns was so convinced these investments were safe and highly profitable that they even borrowed money to buy these securities for themselves. They had a lot of eggs in this one basket, and it led to disaster.

Bear Stearns faced big problems when so many adjustable-rate and subprime borrowers began to default on their loans. Institutional investors who saw the problem with these loans wanted out of the investments.

In particular, two of its own hedge funds that had invested large sums in subprime mortgages were in trouble, and Bear Stearns tried to keep them afloat by dumping an additional $1.6 billion into them. Ultimately, these two funds failed and were allowed to "unwind," which is a nice way to say liquidate at a loss, or better yet, crash and burn.

As a result, the faith their investors had in Bear Stearns began to unravel. The company tried to regroup, and they did convince China's government-controlled company, Citic Securities, to invest $1 billion in them, but even that proved too little too late. More and more investors began withdrawing their money from the company, and Bear Stearns' position became more and more precarious.

Finally, with Bear Stearns on the verge of bankruptcy and unable to raise money or arrange for its own quick sale, the SEC, and Bear Stearns's senior management called the Federal Reserve to request an emergency loan. The Federal Reserve System has the power to make emergency loans to nonbanks like Bear Stearns, but it required special approval and had to be an extreme situation.

In fact, the Fed had never done it before, but after consulting with the Treasury, the SEC, and its own board, the Fed decided that the risk of a total market meltdown was too high, so they made a twenty-eight-day loan on March 14, 2008. Two days later, the Fed helped arrange the sale of Bear Stearns to JPMorgan Chase.

The fire sale of Bear Stearns was mainly the result of their having purchased an excessive amount of mortgage-backed securities. While this presented its own risk, when they borrowed so much money to buy a large volume of these high-risk subprime mortgages for themselves, hedge funds, and other institutional investors, it created a recipe for disaster.

He who has the gold, rules. Bear Stearns had the gold, they made the rules, and they did nobody any favors booking, packaging, and selling shoddy loans that could not be repaid. It cost them the company.

Regardless, CEO Jimmy Cayne was still paid over $33.8 million in 2007.[121]

Lehman Brothers
1850–2008

In 2007, Lehman Brothers was the fourth-largest investment bank in the United States. They had come a long way from their humble beginnings in 1850 when the three Lehman brothers, Henry, Emanuel, and Mayer, founded a cotton brokerage firm in Montgomery, Alabama. They became a public company in 1994 and moved into a lush new headquarters in midtown Manhattan in 2002. In January 2007, Lehman Brothers' stock climbed as high as $82 a share.

Lehman was on a roll after going public, acquiring investment companies and real estate, and arranging high-profile mergers and acquisitions. For example, with their help Cingular Wireless acquired AT&T Wireless, and Sprint acquired Nextel Communications.

Lehman was making record earnings and saw its S&P debt rating climb to A+. They garnered awards around the world, including "Best Investment Bank" by *Euromoney* in 2005 and "Most Admired Securities Firm" by *Fortune* in 2007. In the ten years ending in 2007, the company had grown from almost $154 billion to over $691 billion! *Bigger is not always better.*

But their "Factbook 2007" annual report claiming to have "effectively managed" risk, balance sheet, and expenses while carefully managing "liquidity, capital commitments, and balance sheet positions" proved to be … well, let's just say it was not all "factual."

Lehman Brothers suffered a miserable, painful collapse over the next nine months before it filed the largest bankruptcy in our nation's history on September 14, 2008.

Lehman was a major player in the market for subprime mortgages and, much like Bear Sterns, was a significant player in the hedge funds market. Among other problems, a series of portfolio write-downs, i.e., losses on their own mortgage-backed securities, hurt their reputation. The "mark-to-market" accounting rule required them to mark down their portfolio to the market value (what they could get if they sold the securities that day), and contributed to "short sellers" aggressively trading their stock, which drove their stock price even lower.

They announced a $2.8 billion loss in June 2008, and panicked shareholders began to sell their shares as quickly as they could. Lehman tried raising capital but couldn't. They announced plans to sell assets to raise cash, but they couldn't do it fast enough. When they announced a third-quarter loss of $3 billion, it was clear the end was near.

They asked for a bailout from the federal government, but were denied.

In his testimony to Congress on October 6, 2008, Lehman CEO Richard Fuld took "full responsibility for his decisions" and then began to play the blame game.

The Federal Reserve had failed to be more responsive to their company.

The media had inappropriately reported rumors and negotiations.

The uncontrolled amount of short selling had inappropriately driven their stock value down.

The SEC's accounting rules were also to blame.

Everybody was at fault, except apparently, Lehman executives.

In his testimony, Fuld acknowledged seeking $20 million in bonuses for three of his executives just four days before filing for bankruptcy. However, he denied receiving compensation of $484 million over seven years as the company was engaging in higher and higher risks.

He said it was closer to $350 million. He made no apologies for greed.

Chapter 6

Federal Bank Regulators

One of the greatest political battles of all time was between Thomas Jefferson and Alexander Hamilton, and what happened has a lot to do with our banking system today. In one corner, we have Thomas Jefferson, shown on the left and on the front of our nickel coins and two-dollar bills, author of the Declaration of Independence, the third president of the United States, and founder of the University of Virginia. In the other corner, we have Alexander Hamilton.

A lawyer.

From New York.

Hamilton is like the great comedian Rodney Dangerfield, a guy who used to complain he "don't get no respect." Have you been to the Hamilton Memorial in Washington DC? There isn't one. But Hamilton, right photo and on the front of the ten-dollar bill, was also one of our founding fathers, primary author of the *Federalist Papers* supporting and interpreting the US Constitution, and our nation's first secretary of the Treasury. His work gave us the foundation for the economic and financial system we have today.

He was never a president, could be a jerk (he cheated on his wife), didn't care much for the middle class, and died young (49), so it makes sense that Jefferson gets a bigger statue. But these two guys fought long and hard over the direction of the country, and a big part of this battle was whether we would have a strong centralized economy and government or a decentralized association of agricultural states. Hamilton's views won out.

When President George Washington appointed him the first ever secretary of the Treasury, Hamilton led the successful efforts in 1791 to establish the

"First Bank of the United States." It was to be a type of central bank similar to what the British had with their "Bank of England," only ours was chartered for just twenty years.

The country was in deep debt, about $50 million or so, and the First Bank of the United States was founded to help manage the nation's finances by, among other things, refinancing the debt, issuing currency, serving as the federal government's fiscal agent (meaning they would handle most financial affairs, such as paying interest to those holding government bonds), and helping banks exchange their currencies with each other.

Hamilton managed a lot of complex financial matters, such as selling stock in the bank; assuming, refinancing, and repaying the debt incurred by *both* the federal government and the colonial states during the Revolutionary War; and stabilizing our currency. By just about all accounts, he was a great administrator and did a remarkable job as secretary of the Treasury. Here's a great summary about Hamilton from a 2004 *Wall Street Journal* article.

> Even Hamilton's detractors, including members of the Aaron Burr Association, concede that he was a brilliant administrator, who understood financial systems better than anyone else in the country. He laid the groundwork for the nation's banks, commerce and manufacturing, and was rewarded by being pictured on the $10 bill. "We can pay off his debts in 15 years," Thomas Jefferson lamented, "but we can never get rid of his financial system."[122]

The debt Jefferson was talking about was our national debt. Remember that, unfortunately, and not unlike a lot of third world countries today, as a nation of states we were at the point of saying, "to hell with it! Let's just default on our debts to other countries even if those countries helped us get independence. We simply owe too much." But Hamilton stressed that because the war was a national war, all states should share the burden of repaying the debt instead of leaving it with each state to manage. So he pushed to have the federal government assume all of the state debts, which was great if you had a lot of debt (like Massachusetts). But states that didn't have a lot of debt (like Virginia) were angry. Even so, Hamilton pressed ahead, and Congress agreed. He then refinanced all debts, and the United States established a lot of financial credibility that remains with us today. The good ol' USA has a pretty decent "credit score" in spite of its excessive debts.

To stabilize the currency, Hamilton required all state banks to back their individual currencies with gold or silver. This really made some state bankers and rural communities mad. They were trying to expand rapidly, and they backed their currency with all of the bank's assets, including the loans they made to others, rather than just by gold and silver. At the "central bank," Hamilton enforced these tougher currency standards by refusing to accept any other currencies as deposits to buy government securities, to pay on loans, or to exchange with other banks. Rural communities were not happy that these policies slowed their growth, even if it did strengthen their currencies.

The First Bank of the United States was the only "national" bank in the country, and, although technically a private bank, it was the only one to receive federal government deposits. This too angered many of the state bankers.

A lot of people hated Hamilton's policies, especially Thomas Jefferson, who argued that the First Bank of the United States was itself an illegal institution. Jefferson was serving as George Washington's secretary of state at the time and was a strong advocate for less federal government, but he lost the battle to charter the national bank. In fact, when it came to financial matters, George Washington relied heavily on Hamilton and implemented a tremendous number of his programs.

Much has been written about the political battles between Jefferson and Hamilton, and it's clear that Hamilton was an outspoken, highly regarded and influential leader of the Federalist, his political party. Jefferson could claim the same in the Democratic-Republicans, the opposition party. Hamilton's political opponents hounded him everywhere, but he never hesitated to retaliate, sometimes viciously and without merit. Yes, our nation's first secretary of the Treasury had plenty of enemies. They tried to impeach him, they tried to discredit him, and eventually the vice president killed him.

Yes, our nation's first secretary of the Treasury had plenty of enemies. They tried to impeach him, they tried to discredit him, and eventually the vice president killed him.

His death occurred not long after his son was shot dead, and even his son's death stemmed from politics. It seems that nineteen-year-old Philip Hamilton got caught up in a public argument with a twenty-seven-year-old lawyer named George Eacker over his father's views on President Jefferson. Defending his father's honor resulted in some nasty words, a duel in Weehawken, New Jersey, and young Phillip's death. The devastating loss of his son, along with many other factors, led to more erratic behavior and to Hamilton's own death when he was shot in 1804 by (Jefferson's) Vice President

Aaron Burr. Would you believe that it happened in Weehawken, where young Hamilton had been shot? It was probably the most famous political shooting in US history, although (George W. Bush's) Vice President Dick Cheney shooting his lawyer in the face was a close second. What is it with our vice presidents and their guns?

By the way, in a strange twist of fate, the *same guns* were used in both duels that killed father and son. Chase Manhattan Bank (now called JPMorgan Chase Bank) purchased them in 1930 and still owns them. It's appropriate for the bank to own them: Burr was a founder of the Bank of the Manhattan Company in 1799 and at the time competed with a bank Hamilton had founded, the Bank of New York (now called Bank of New York Mellon). I bet if you open a large enough checking account at JPMorgan Chase Bank, they would let you touch them. You should ask.

The point here is that while Hamilton may not have been the most popular guy in town, he was financially astute and succeeded in establishing a financial framework for the new US government economy. His job as secretary of the Treasury was officially created by an Act of Congress on September 2, 1789, when the US Treasury Department was created. The programs he helped implement and the success he had when using the charter of the First Bank of the United States are still with us.

Famous Secretaries

There have been seventy-five different Treasury secretaries through 2010. If you enjoy history and want more trivia, you might get a kick out of their individual backgrounds. In such a high-profile, important cabinet position, you would expect prominent citizens, and you would be right. After all, the Treasury secretary is fifth in line to replace the president upon his or her incapacity, death, resignation, or removal from office.

Hamilton himself was also a founder of the Bank of New York in Lower Manhattan, five years before he became the Treasury secretary. The Bank of New York merged in 2007 with Mellon Financial Corporation, parent company of Mellon Bank, NA, to form the Bank of New York Mellon (total consolidated assets of $238 billion at year-end 2008).

The old Mellon Bank, NA, could trace its history back to 1869 when Thomas Mellon and his two sons founded it as T. Mellon & Sons Bank. One of the sons, Andrew Mellon, went on to become the forty-ninth Treasury secretary from 1921 to 1932. Andrew Mellon faced an impeachment trial in

1932 over conflicts of interest he had as Treasury secretary with businesses he and his family controlled. After the trial, but before the vote to impeach was taken, he resigned as Treasury secretary and accepted an appointment by President Hoover as US ambassador to the United Kingdom (known as ambassador to the Court of St. James's at the time). It sure doesn't appear his trial had gone well![123]

The fourth Treasury secretary was Albert Gallatin, founder of New York University. He was the longest serving US Treasury secretary in history, serving almost thirteen years under Presidents Jefferson and Madison. It was under his watch that we financed the Louisiana Purchase. He was probably a great guy but was somewhat creepy-looking too. It's no wonder people fear the government.

The twenty-fifth was Salmon P. Chase, who was honored four years after his death when Chase National Bank named its institution after him even though he had no financial interest in the company. Chase National acquired the Bank of Manhattan (started by Vice President Aaron Burr) and was itself acquired in 1996 by Chemical Bank of New York. A few mergers later, it became JPMorgan Chase & Co, a $2 trillion institution.

The thirty-first Treasury secretary was John Sherman, who was also the Ohio senator who wrote the Sherman Antitrust Act to prevent business monopolies. His brother was General William Tecumseh Sherman, famous from the Civil War's Atlanta Campaign and the March to the Sea (Savannah), and who is still not especially popular in the Deep South.

The forty-seventh was Carter Glass, who served in the House of Representatives, where he sponsored (with Sen. Robert Latham Owen) the bill establishing the Federal Reserve System. After leaving the Treasury, he became a US senator and introduced the bill (along with Rep. Henry B. Steagall) establishing the Federal Deposit Insurance Corporation (FDIC).

The sixty-first was John Connally, who was also a passenger in the car with President John F. Kennedy when Kennedy was assassinated in 1963. People forget, but Connally was the Texas governor at the time and was also shot and seriously wounded on that sad day. Connally believed the assassin was trying to kill both him and the president, not just the president.

Timothy Geithner is the seventy-fifth. He was previously the president of the Federal Reserve Bank of New York. According to President Obama, "There has never been a secretary of the Treasury, except maybe Alexander Hamilton, right after the Revolutionary War, who's had to deal with the multiplicity of issues that Secretary Geithner is having to deal with—all at the same time. And he is doing so with intelligence and diligence. Nobody is working harder than this guy. He is making all the right moves in terms of playing a bad hand."[124] Time will tell if the president is correct. Let's hope so.

The United States Department of the Treasury

The Treasury Department is a very large federal agency responsible for managing the government's finances and promoting economic growth and stability. It is organized into two areas: departments, where policy is set, and bureaus, where policy is implemented. There are nine separate departments, including Domestic Finance, which covers banking and finance.

It is here, in the Office of Domestic Finance, where some very serious work goes on related to our nation's banking system, securities firms, insurance companies, government-sponsored enterprises, and others. It is also where the *final* decisions on currency designs are made, so if you think the rarely seen two-dollar bill is ugly, these are the folks to call.

In March 2008, the previous Treasury secretary, Henry Paulson, released a "Blueprint for a Modernized Financial Regulatory Structure," which was written by two top officials from the Office of Domestic Finance, Robert Steel and David Nason. The blueprint accurately showed a screwy system of regulating financial institutions. This system has evolved over a seventy-five-plus-year period, which is to say that it's not a system that had some great master plan. At the time of the blueprint, it was a system with five federal depository institution regulators in addition to regulators in every state.

The federal regulators included the Office of the Comptroller of the Currency (OCC) for national banks, the Office of Thrift Supervision (OTS) for federal thrifts, the Federal Reserve System for all companies that own the banks (holding companies) and for some state banks, the FDIC for state-chartered banks, and the National Credit Union Administration (NCUA) for credit unions.

This system really needs an overhaul, and the blueprint was a serious effort to do just that. But serious efforts have been on the table before, and like others, this one had limited traction and went nowhere.

Policy matters aside, the rubber meets the road in the Treasury bureaus because although policy is set in the departments, 98 percent of the workforce is in the bureaus. There are twelve bureaus in the Treasury Department, including for example:

- **Bureau of Engraving and Printing**, which makes military ID cards, immigration and naturalization certificates, the Federal Reserve paper currency you carry in your wallets, and other important documents. (If you want to purchase sheets of really cool uncut currency, you can get them from this bureau.)
- **US Mint,** which designs and manufactures coins. It stores all government gold and silver at its vaults in Denver, Colorado; West Point, New York; and Fort Knox, Kentucky.
- **Bureau of Public Debt**, which borrows money to finance the national debt.
- **Community Development Financial Institution Fund**, which provides incentives such as the $16 billion New Markets Tax Credits to revitalize distressed communities.
- **Internal Revenue Service (IRS)**, which is the largest bureau of them all and collects federal taxes.
- **Office of the Comptroller of the Currency (OCC)**, which charters, regulates, and supervises national banks.

Besides the state bank and thrift regulators, at one time we had four different federal bank and thrift regulators: the OCC, OTS, Federal Reserve, and FDIC. Let's take a look at these agencies and what they regulated ... sometimes well and sometimes badly.

For the record, in 2009 the OCC comptroller, FDIC chair, and OTS director were all on a government pay scale (listed at Executive Level III), with a starting annual salary of $158,500. The Treasury secretary is a Level I position that pays $191,300 and serves at the discretion of the president; the Federal Reserve Board chairman is a Level II position that pays $172,200.[125]

Now compare those salaries with what the executives of the companies that they regulated receive. For just one example, the president and CEO of Wells Fargo and Company, John G. Stumpf, was paid almost $14 million in 2008 while the secretary of the Treasury was paid less than $200,000.[126] "Absurd" is defined as "ridiculously incongruous or unreasonable," and that surely applies here.[127]

In 2006, *BusinessWeek* magazine listed the OCC as #48 on its list of "Best Places to Launch a Career." The OCC, whose employees are represented by the National Treasury Employees Union, pays an average annual base salary for entry level hires of $40,000 to $45,000. Unlike the Peace Corps, IRS, or CIA, which have all made the top fifty list more than once during the first three years it was published, the FDIC, Federal Reserve, and OTS, had not made the list by 2011.[128]

US Secret Service

Among its many responsibilities, the US Secret Service has two roles: (1) prevent counterfeiting and (2) protect national leaders. Fortunately, outside of occasionally allowing uninvited guests into White House dinners, major scandals rarely happen, and the agency quietly does what appears to be a fine job of protecting our people and our money.

But today's integrity and prestige is quite a contrast to their shady beginnings. According to their official (2010) website, the Secret Service Division of the US Treasury was officially "created to suppress counterfeit currency" when Chief William P. Wood was sworn in by Treasury Secretary Hugh McCulloch. What the website didn't say was that their founder, William Patrick Wood, was an unscrupulous schemer who frequently operated outside the law to get what he wanted.

In the 1850s, Wood managed to get himself appointed Superintendent of the Old Capital Prison, which at various times housed runaway slaves, spies, prisoners of the Civil War, hostages, deserters, and others. Here, he began calling himself "Colonel Wood," even though he was a former corporal.

Wood ran his own show and ruled over a regular "Guantanamo Bay-style" prison (Gitmo). He often denied his prisoners their right to lawyers or bail and used harsh interrogation techniques and fake confessions to get information.

As you may recall, Gitmo was where "enemy combatants" were also denied their rights (from 2001 to 2006) in violation of international law (the Geneva Conventions) until the Supreme Court intervened.

Coincidentally, the lawless Old Capital Prison was located on the exact same site where the lawful Supreme Court Building is today. Talk about irony!

In 1864, Wood teamed up with a detective named Lafayette Baker, a man who was providing a *secret service* for the secretary of war by investigating fraud against the government and tracking down counterfeiters. Funded by the sale of cotton that was captured during the Civil War rather than by the more accountable government appropriations, this secret service housed its prisoners in Wood's Old Capital Prison.

Eventually Treasury Secretary Hugh McCulloch "officially requested" President Lincoln to authorize a more legitimate structure. McCulloch asked Lincoln to hire Wood as "chief of the detective force" in the Treasury Department to combat counterfeiting, but there is no official record that Lincoln ever approved it.

Allegedly, Lincoln got the paperwork the day before he was shot and approved the deal but just didn't have a chance to sign the paperwork. That's hard to believe.

Regardless, Wood was sworn in July 5, 1865, and thus began the Secret Service's role to "safeguard the nation's financial infrastructure and payment systems."

Oddly, the Secret Service was also involved in foiling a plot to steal Abraham Lincoln's body. In 1876, the Secret Service arrested master counterfeit engraver Ben Boyd. To secure his release, a counterfeiter named "Big Jim" Kinealy teamed with Lewis G. Swegles and two hired grave robbers to steal Lincoln's body from Oak Ridge Cemetery in Springfield, Illinois.

The plan was to steal the body on November 7, an election day, and then hide the body in the sand dunes of northern Indiana until Boyd was released and the criminals received $200,000 in gold (the equivalent of about $4 million today).

As it turned out, Big Jim chose his friends poorly: Lewis Swegles was a Secret Service agent. Although the thieves managed to break into Lincoln's tomb and pry open the marble lid holding the casket, they were chased away and arrested in Chicago ten days later. They received the maximum sentence: one year in Joliet State Prison. Lincoln's body is still in Oak Ridge Cemetery.

It wasn't until the assassination of President William McKinley in 1901 that Congress directed the Secret Service to protect the president full time. That role has now been expanded to include the vice president, the president-elect, the vice president elect, their immediate families, former presidents and their spouses for ten years after leaving office, their children until they reach age sixteen, visiting heads of state, and others.

In 2003, the Secret Service became a part of the US Department of Homeland Security and is no longer a part of the US Treasury Department. They continue to do an exceptional job, for which we should all be grateful.

Office of the Comptroller of the Currency (OCC)

National Bank Regulator

When the National Bank Act was passed in 1863 to finance the Civil War and establish a national currency, a national bank charter was also created that would be regulated by the Office of the Comptroller of the Currency (OCC), part of the Treasury Department. The OCC is headed by a comptroller, who is appointed by the president for a five-year term.

Working at a bank regulatory agency draws a variety of quality people. Some are starting their careers in banking, and others are winding theirs down. Many are "lifers" who spend their entire careers involved not so much in the daily aspects of a bank but more in the macro role of monitoring banks and the industry. The pay is not as good as in some of the private sector, but all agencies work hard to maintain competitive pay at staff levels, even if executive pay is impossible to match. You may hear harsh comments about regulators and bank examiners, but they perform a public service and a noble profession working as detectives, consultants, cops, and umpires to protect the soundness of our financial system, and, more importantly, your deposit accounts.

The OCC is a major player. They regulated 1,678 national banks in 2008, about 20 percent of all banks, but these banks were quite large with total assets of $8.3 trillion! That represents 62 percent of all banking assets. You can tell if the bank is regulated by the OCC because it will have the word "National" or the letters "NA" for national association in its title. The OCC is able to regulate all these banks without our tax dollars because they charge fees for their examinations. These fees provide 96 percent of their revenues.

They manage their expenses very well, but charging examination fees does seem awkward. "Hello, I'm your government regulator. I've just spent a few months examining your bank. Here is a report of everything you are doing wrong. Fix them."

"Oh, one more thing. Here's my bill."

One problem all regulators have to deal with is the turnover of good examiners. If examiners are especially good, commercial banks often recruit them to work for higher pay than a regulatory agency can offer. That's why having a self-funded agency that doesn't depend on government appropriations for money is important. A self-funded agency can pay more competitive salaries and recruit higher-skilled staff. State regulators have to deal with this issue all the time. Many state regulators have limited budgets and can't attract and keep highly skilled examiners, and yes, more than a handful of bankers complain about the quality of some state regulatory agencies.

Just as in any large company, some of the examiners are flat-out exceptional and some of them are … not. But overall, the OCC has generated some very good results and has earned the respect of their colleagues. When you attend conferences and joint agency meetings with OCC folks, you see that they are often a cut above the average. (Hey, almost as good as you, right?)

Even so, the recent bailout has also shown that the large banks regulated by the OCC have all needed varying levels of government assistance to keep them from failing (they were deemed "too big to fail"). The OCC, along with the other regulators and politicians, will surely be criticized and investigated by the inspector general and others for allowing financial institutions to become so large that they were and still are a risk to the entire economy when recessions occur.

Regulator Watchdogs

The Inspector General (IG) is a watchdog that independently audits and investigates agencies to "prevent and detect fraud and abuse" and to recommend policies that promote "economy, efficiency, and effectiveness." In other words, the Inspector General gets to criticize government agencies for screwing up!

The Inspector General Act of 1978 and its amendments created nearly sixty Offices of Inspector General at a multitude of government agencies: the CIA, HUD, Farm Credit Administration, Treasury, Federal Reserve, FDIC, National Credit Union Administration, the SEC, and SBA to name just a few.

The Federal Deposit Insurance Corporation Improvement Act of 1991 also requires the IG to conduct a review on all bank or thrift failures when the cost to the FDIC insurance fund exceeds $25 million. Beginning in 2010, that threshold was raised to $200 million.

It's a healthy process to have an independent third-party review when things go bad. The IG recommendations may not always be right (Are anybody's?), but the common themes they identify must be addressed, and the IG seems to do a very good job.

Everybody takes these reports seriously, of course, and always tries to correct the issues. You can review the "Material Loss Reviews" by going to the IG web page for each of the agencies, which can be found at:

http://www.ignet.gov/igs/homepage1.html (accessed on March 18, 2011).

The recent banking crisis has put all regulators under a spotlight, and that's appropriate. In their own 2008 annual report, Comptroller John C. Dugan even raised some of the OCC's own deficiencies and errors, and that's commendable. Interestingly, he recognized that the recent bank failures were not necessarily a result of low capital levels (although that is an issue and a common problem with failed banks) but of weak liquidity positions.

He didn't name names, and they weren't OCC-regulated banks, but if you look at failures of institutions like IndyMac, which lost $1.3 billion in deposits in eleven days, and WaMu, which lost $16.7 billion in ten days, what finally killed them was their inability to quickly convert investments to cash without big losses. Regulators were not thorough enough when they were reviewing liquidity positions at a lot of institutions. Of course, they would not have needed the liquidity if they had not made or bought so many bad loans in the first place. Bad loans caused a panic, and a liquidity problem followed. *It's almost always bad loans.*

Besides the banks and thrifts not having enough liquidity, another mistake examiners made was relying too heavily on credit agencies that overrated investment securities the bankers were buying. Examiners assumed that if the agencies rated investment securities as good, they must be good, and examiners could move on to the next item on their checklist. The credit reporting agencies blew it, and the regulators and bankers were foolish enough to buy into it.

And finally, Dugan noted two obvious items: rapid growth and loan (or investment) concentrations. When a bank grows so rapidly, it misses the "blocking and tackling" basics, to use a sports analogy, which leads to higher risk. Combine that with a high concentration of bad real estate loans, and you got T-R-O-U-B-L-E. In the case of Countrywide, which the OCC regulated until it suddenly converted to a thrift institution seven months before crashing, the bank's growth rates ranged from 513 percent in 2002 to 111 percent in 2004. That's crazy! And when the hyper-rapid growth is driven mostly by subprime and Option ARM real estate loans, it shouldn't take a rocket scientist to recognize the excessive risk.

The OCC did not do a good job regulating Countrywide. Hindsight is twenty-twenty, and it's easy to criticize after the fact. But it's important to look over the "game tape" and see what went wrong. Comptroller Dugan wasn't the first OCC leader to do that. Looking back at their "Annual Report" in 1881, Comptroller John Jay Knox did the same thing by not only listing the bank failures by name, but by going into a great amount of detail on the role of a bank examiner following the failure of the Mechanics' National Bank of Newark, N.J. People were particularly sensitive about failures back then because depositors got screwed out of a big chunk of their money. Their losses frequently ranged from 10 percent to 35 percent of their deposits in national banks.

Knox's description of the role of the OCC examiner was interesting, and his contention that the board of directors has primary responsibility for the bank's actions, not the examiner, holds every bit as true today. According to Comptroller John Jay Knox in 1881:[129]

> The duties of the board of directors are plainly defined, and however innocent they may be of any intention of wrong, they are responsible for the safety of funds committed to their care.
>
> [Regulator's] restrictions are intended to protect these institutions, by imposing on them general rules, which experience has shown may be properly done by the government *without its thereby becoming the guardian of the bank, or the moneys of its depositors or stockholders, or being in any way responsible for the management of its funds.*
>
> It is a supervision and labor not seen or known of the general public, whose attention is only arrested when some sudden or unexpected failure occurs; and this simply illustrates the fact that, with the best endeavors, and the most careful supervision by this Office, such disasters may happen ... if directors neglect to exercise that continuous vigilance for which they were elected, and which they have sworn to perform.

It bears repeating: Board members, not government agencies, are primarily responsible for their institutions. That's the way it was in 1881. That's the way it is supposed to be today.

Office of Thrift Supervision (OTS)

Thrift Regulator

The OTS is also housed in the Treasury Department, but it wasn't always that way. Originally, the Federal Home Loan Bank Board was the regulator for all national thrifts, but after a series of widespread failures in the 1980s resulting in a $159 billion government bailout, they were stripped of those responsibilities, and the OTS was formed in 1989 to assume the role.

During the Panic of 2008, the agency was under considerable pressure for a series of self-inflicted blunders that caused tremendous and unfair reputational damage to the good people that work at the OTS and in the thrift industry. Taxpayers had a right to be mad. The OTS's crime was failing to rein in the excessive high-risk lending and investment programs and then presenting false information about some thrifts' financial condition during the recent crisis. In short, the leadership is guilty of failing to regulate and in some cases lying.

There is always the risk that regulators will get too close to the industry they oversee, an issue called "regulatory capture." Put yourself in the regulator's shoes. You work with people in this business every day, and you come to know them well. You have a similar skill set. You took the same classes in college or at industry training programs as they did. Sometimes you have even worked on the other side of that fence before you became a regulator. You appreciate the issues they confront and the problems they have to overcome. Almost all are honest, hardworking men and women who live very similar lifestyles as you. It's rarely an adversarial relationship between banker and regulator unless the institution is in trouble, the head honcho is antagonistic, or the regulator has come down unnecessarily hard on the institution. In fact, regulators have to be careful not to become an industry advocate. They have to avoid regulatory capture.

By law, the bank and its regulator are married to each other—for better, for worse, for richer, for poorer, in sickness and in health, until failure do them part.

By law, the bank and its regulator are married to each other—for better, for worse, for richer, for poorer, in sickness and in health, until failure do them part. Like most good marriages, the relationship has many aspects: friendship, respect, open communication, and honesty. The big difference is that the regulators are not allowed to "get cozy" with the banks. As awkward as it may seem, they absolutely must be a bit less of an advocate for their spouse and, instead, more of a critic. It's one of those lessons never learned: *Don't sleep with each other.*

Unfortunately, the OTS leadership failed to avoid regulatory capture. The warning signs of this excessively cozy relationship have been there for years. *We should have seen it coming.*

It's a simple example, and yes, it is trivial, but wasn't the language odd at the "About the OTS" page on the regulators' website (www.OTS.gov) in April 2009? In red print they listed three reasons to get a charter from the OTS: (1) nationwide branching *without restriction or condition*, (2) *only one* federal regulator, and (3) no *subjecting* institutions to state and local laws. The italics were added by this author to draw your attention to their message. It's as if this regulator was advertising leniency. It says a lot "About the OTS."

The first page of their 2007 annual report touts "preemption" whereby OTS regulations will *trump state and local laws*, and reduce *regulatory burden.* They flaunted their relationships with Lehman Brothers, AIG, Washington Mutual, World Savings Bank, and Countrywide. Today those same companies are for all practical purposes gone, gone, gone, gone, and gone. It is as if the agency was calling out, "Marry me. I'm easy." And I need the money.

Perhaps that was true. The OTS was funded by fees from the institutions they regulated, just like the OCC. But the OTS was a small agency with 1,069 examiners, and its staff regulated only 818 thrift institutions with assets of $1.8 trillion. (They also regulated 469 thrift holding companies with assets of $8.1 trillion in 2008). In contrast, just one OCC-regulated bank, Bank of America, had assets totaling $1.4 trillion—nearly the same as all 818 thrifts combined. And because OTS fees were based on asset size, the larger the institution they regulate, the higher the fee income they generate. Without a sufficient base of institutions to regulate, your relevance as a regulator decreases.

In a scathing article about the OTS in the *New York Times*, journalist Robert Cyran stated what many people had been thinking. "This [fee] structure," he wrote, "gives O.T.S. a potential incentive to first try to lure financial institutions into becoming savings and loan associations and then look the other way if they enlarge their asset bases through questionable lending."[130]

He wasn't alone. The *Washington Post* had also run an article by Binyamin Appelbaum and Ellen Nakashima which said, "When Countrywide Financial felt pressured by federal agencies charged with overseeing it, executives at the giant mortgage lender simply switched regulators in the spring of 2007. The benefits were clear: Countrywide's new regulator, the Office of Thrift Supervision, promised more flexible oversight of issues related to the bank's mortgage lending. For OTS, which depends on fees paid by banks it regulates and competes with other regulators to land the largest financial firms, Countrywide was a lucrative catch."[131]

They went on to say that the OTS "stands out" for missing signals or making bad decisions and that the agency adopted an "aggressively deregulatory stance" toward the institutions they regulated.

Leadership matters, and leadership at the OTS had a recent history of poor judgment. Just look at some of these actions.

- In 2004, OTS Director James Gilleran stated, "Our goal is to allow thrifts to operate with a wide breadth of freedom from regulatory intrusion." He reduced full-time supervision staff from 821 in 2003 to only 797 for each of the next two years. He did this in spite of the fact that the number of thrifts under his watch was increasing in number (from 726 to 747), in size (total assets of $573 billion in 2003 to $841 billion in 2005), and in complexity.[132]

- In February 2005, Gilleran unilaterally changed the thrifts' examination process for the Community Reinvestment Act (CRA), (a law promoting lending and investments in low- and moderate-income areas), beyond that of any other federal regulator. These changes were in spite of the fact that over 95 percent of the four thousand letters received from the public opposed the move. That's a lot of opposition letters! They included twenty-eight from members of Congress and forty-five from US mayors. Gilleran became so unpopular with community-based organizations that they began calling on President George W. Bush to request his resignation, which occurred on April 29. [133]
- In 2006, OTS Director John Reich opposed OCC efforts to crack down on high-risk Option ARM products, saying, "[Thrifts] have demonstrated that they have the know-how to manage these products through all kinds of economic cycles."[134] In 2008, IndyMac and Washington Mutual, two of the nation's largest thrifts, failed because of these same loans.
- In 2008, West Division Director Darrel Dochow (who supervised Washington Mutual, Countrywide, and IndyMac) was removed from his position when the IG discovered that he had allowed IndyMac to publicly lie about its capital levels in its quarterly report (a public document). By letting the thrift "backdate" (lie about) when it raised capital, they allowed the thrift to avoid harsh public scrutiny and additional mandatory regulatory oversight.
- In January 2009, OTS Director John Reich acknowledged four cases in which the OTS allowed thrifts to backdate their capital. In other words, to meet the required capital standards, the thrifts could claim they raised money earlier than they had actually done so. It made the thrifts look like they were in better financial condition than they were. He resigned one month later.
- In 2009, Acting Director Scott Polakoff was removed from office while being investigated for allowing BankUnited of Coral Gables, Florida, to backdate its additional capital.

By being such a friend of the institutions they regulated, it was no wonder that a major industry trade association, the Independent Community Bankers

Association (ICBA), gave such lavish praise on their regulator's leadership. Why wouldn't they?

ICBA President and CEO Camden Fine said Director Gilleran was "a man of action, not just words," and that "he stood out as a gutsy public official who did not abandon his convictions or buckle from the pressure of others with different views."[135] They also honored Director Reich with the ICBA Main Street Hero Award for his leadership in supporting the community banking industry. If you are a thrift looking for less government regulation, then the praise from your (thrift) trade association was well deserved for both men. But sleeping with each other is never a good idea.

The ICBA is actually a very good organization serving its members well. And, of course, nobody likes government regulations. By definition, they are intrusive and costly and a general hassle. But weak regulations, or, more specifically, a weak regulator, is likely to fail in its mission "to supervise savings associations and their holding companies in order to maintain their safety and soundness."[136] And the OTS had the worst track record of all regulators.

Using the quick and dirty method of "who died under your watch," the OTS regulated institution failures totaled $359 billion, an astonishing 23 percent of total assets under their domain.[137] Defenders of the OTS might argue that if you exclude the two largest institutions, IndyMac and Washington Mutual, the dollar amount of failed assets would be only $21 billion, not $359 billion. But that is exactly the point! Even without their two largest failures, the percentage of failed assets (1.75 percent) is still unreasonably high. Those kinds of losses can cripple an insurance fund. Add that having two of its largest institutions fail is probably the most damning evidence that the OTS's deregulated approach was, at best, a *terrible* approach!

It's a risk to reference numbers like this because it can be misleading. The other agencies had many significant failures as well. It's true that other large commercial banks, such as Citigroup, received significant government assistance to make sure they stayed afloat. They were considered "too big to fail." But the OCC had been a strong regulator, including being vocal about its concerns with high-risk products, such as Option ARMs and subprime loans, while the OTS had soft-pedaled on the same issues.

No, there is no getting around it. The OTS had done a disservice to the industry they tried so hard to protect when they failed to step in sooner and more forcefully to reduce the growth of high-risk loans funded by high cost and volatile deposits.

It would be nice to stop here and leave all the blame on the leadership. But the examiners themselves were not entirely innocent. I am somewhat reluctant to point out their mistakes because so many of them have worked tirelessly to clean up this mess. They will receive little praise and lots of grief from the industry and the public, and it wasn't usually their fault. But in some cases they did fall down on the job.

In its February 2009 report on the failure of IndyMac, the IG was quite direct about mistakes that the examiners made.

- IndyMac's high-risk business strategy warranted more careful and much earlier examiner attention. (*We should have seen it coming.*)
- Examiners incorrectly viewed growth and profitability as evidence of capable management. (*Bigger is not always better.*)
- Examiners were painfully slow to react and didn't even downgrade the thrift's 2 rating (on a 5-point scale, 1 is the highest) until just a few months before the thrift failed.
- Examiners identified poor lending practices but were not aggressive enough to stop them. (*It's almost always bad loans.*)
- As many as forty bank examiners were involved in the thrift's supervision, but the examination results failed to reflect IndyMac's risky business model and practices. *(We should have seen it coming.)*
- Examiners uncovered significant problems that never made it into the examination report. *(Don't sleep with each other.)*.

In fairness, the OTS is not at fault for the hard times all thrift institutions had during the recent housing crisis. All thrifts suffered losses, and many failed because their charter required that they maintain 60 percent of assets in home mortgages and other types of consumer loans. The tax breaks they received in return for generating so many housing loans did not compensate for the severe losses they suffered when housing markets collapse. That is one reason why it was not unreasonable to suggest the thrift charter should change or be eliminated.

Given the widespread OTS deficiencies and thrift failures, change at the agency was required. On July 21, 2010, the Dodd-Frank Wall Street Reform and Consumer Protection Act was signed into law. It abolished the OTS as an independent agency and transferred nearly all of its responsibilities and its staff into the OCC. Only the supervision and regulation of state savings associations went to the FDIC and the savings and loan holding companies went to the Federal Reserve. The thrift charter has been abolished.

The lessons are harsh but important. *It's almost always bad loans. Bigger is not always better. Don't sleep with each other. Good government is necessary.*

Federal Reserve System

The Nation's Central Bank

Wouldn't it have been fun to live in the early 1920s when it seemed like everybody was listening to great music, wearing different clothes, and going to clubs to dance and drink? It just seems that era was similar to a Bonnaroo-style Music and Arts Festival, only it lasted longer than four days. [138]

In the '20s, there were thousands of "speakeasies," and as long as you knew the password, you were welcome to sit at their bar, toss back a few, and perhaps hear some amazing jazz from folks like Bessie Smith, Duke Ellington, and Louis Armstrong , or even dance the foxtrot, waltz, tango, Charleston, or lindy hop. Baseball's Babe Ruth was smacking home runs, boxing's Jack Dempsey was smacking heads, football's Knute Rockne was smacking football teams around, and golf's legendary Bobby Jones was smacking a little ball a long, long way.

Panic of 1907

The contrast to the period leading up to the Roaring '20s couldn't have been more dramatic. For one, World War I began in 1914, and the United States entered the war three years later. But even before then, times were tough, in large part because of the earthquake that hit San Francisco in 1906. It could be felt from southern Oregon to south of Los Angeles and inland as far as central Nevada. It measured 8.3 on the Richter scale, killed an estimated three thousand people, left 225,000 homeless (out of a population of four hundred thousand), and caused widespread fires for three days.[139] Damn! Can you imagine that? It lasted right at one minute, which is just short of forever if you were there.

The financial shock was also devastating. Besides the immediate property damage, estimated at $400 million (that's about $9.5 billion today), the disaster out West drew gold out of the world's major money centers, creating a liquidity crunch and leading to a major recession starting in June of 1907. [140]

You see, confidence in the banking industry was not especially high at the time. About a year before the earthquake, on April 24, 1905, the Comptroller of the Currency was notified that Frank Bigelow, the president of First National

Bank of Milwaukee, had stolen $1.4 million (that's over $33 million today) from his bank. He had then lost it by investing in stocks and by trying to corner the wheat market. Bigelow had been president of the prestigious American Bankers Association and was widely known and respected. He got caught when an employee sensed that something was wrong with the bank's books and notified a director.

Note that it wasn't a bank examiner who caught the obvious fraud. The bank examiner in charge here had been submitting clean reports to the Comptroller because he trusted the president of the bank, and he failed to verify anything on the bank's books. At the time, examiners were paid a fee for each examination they completed, and he was apparently more concerned with generating fee income than he was in properly examining the bank's books.[141] Fortunately, bank examiners are no longer paid that way—they earn salaries instead. The bank examiner here was fired: he should have been jailed.

Bigelow had no attorney representing him at his trial. His old friend, Judge Joseph Quarles, showed no mercy and sentenced him to ten years of hard labor at the federal penitentiary in Fort Leavenworth, Kansas. Bigelow expressed no remorse and offered no apology or explanation for his greed.[142] What an ass.

Much to their credit, the directors of the bank all pitched in and quickly purchased enough additional stock to cover what the president had stolen! They also secured a line of credit from some Chicago banks, from which $2 million in currency was quickly transported to the bank. When word got out about the fraud, the combination of these efforts kept the run on the bank from becoming a disaster. They saved the bank, and their depositors did not lose any money.

The bank survived the crisis, but other banks began to look more closely at their books, and several found problems, although none as big as this. Negative publicity inevitably hurt bankers' reputations, and consumer confidence fell.

It wasn't long after this bank fraud (and its damage to consumer confidence) and the San Francisco earthquake (and the liquidity crisis that led to a recession) that a huge banking crisis, the Panic of 1907, occurred. As with other panics, it happened quickly, over a six-week period beginning in November, when the New York Stock Exchange fell dramatically, two brokerage firms failed, and the resulting shock sent depositors rushing to their banks to retrieve their money. In response, the bankers called on individuals to pay off loans they had used to finance stock market purchases. Thousands of companies failed.

John Pierpont Morgan

President Theodore Roosevelt's Treasury secretary (George Cortelyou) acted quickly, and gave seventy-year-old J. P. Morgan $25 million in government deposits (at no interest) to control the panic. Morgan was able to lend this money to the institutions he thought were important to save. You might be saying: "What the hell? Why would the Treasury turn to this one guy outside of the government, J. P. Morgan, to stop the panic?"

Well, Morgan was very well respected in financial circles and had experience in developing rescue packages when financial panics occurred. He even managed to bail out the federal government itself in 1895 when he organized a group of bankers to lend the US Treasury 3.5 million ounces of gold (worth over $3 billion in early 2009). A panic had occurred; people converted their dollars to gold and moved the gold back to their European banks. Pictured here is Morgan, who looks eerily similar to the mascot from the well-known Monopoly board game.

In his exceptional book about the Federal Reserve System (and more), *Secrets of the Temple*, William Greider said this about Morgan:

> The Morgan Banks could execute dazzling and ruthless manipulations in the stock market—cornering, crushing, swallowing their corporate prey. At the same time, Morgan was the ultimate guarantor of stability and order in the banking system, the man whom other bankers turned to in distress. With a few confident strokes, it was said J. P. Morgan could stop bank panics. Some critics were convinced that he also started them.[143]

When Morgan and his men organized loan syndicates to rescue select banks when panics occurred, the rescued paid a lot of money to survive, and Morgan prospered at their expense. "Naturally," according to Greider, "he was hated. He was also indispensable."

Morgan and his banking associates worked hard to resolve the Panic in 1907, and it took several weeks to calm the markets enough to stop widespread bank runs and failures. Some made it. Others, which Morgan and his associates didn't try to save, failed. But this panic simply drove home the point that the country's banking system had serious problems.

Banking System Problems

On a very practical matter, one of the problems with the banking system was that the amount of currency in circulation did not increase when people needed it most. For example, communities needed more currency during boom times, when businesses were trying to grow fast enough to meet the demand. Imagine you are a good business owner with great credit and were not able to get an affordable bank loan because they didn't have enough currency to lend. (It is not hard to imagine, because it happened again to a lot of businesses and homebuyers in 2008.) The same holds true with seasonal borrowing needs. Imagine you are a qualified farmer who couldn't get an affordable crop loan because the bank was low on currency.

In the early 1900s, bankers could lend you gold or silver, but they were obviously limited by the amount that had been produced. They could lend you gold or silver certificates (currency backed by gold or silver), but they were also limited by the amount that had been produced. They could lend you greenbacks (from the Civil War era), or they could lend you their national bank notes, but they too were in limited supply. So when the economy was humming along and more currency was needed, the banking system had nothing in place to support it. Simply put, there was not enough money to go around in support of the good times.

Another problem causing the currency shortage was the reserve requirements. Banks were required to keep some cash reserves in their vaults for business transactions. Fair enough. But to ensure a sound system nationwide, the country banks had to also keep some reserves at larger banks, called "reserve city" banks, and these banks then had to keep some money at one of three "central reserve city" banks in New York, Chicago, or St. Louis. The idea was to spread the money around so that when areas needed money to meet surges in loan demand, they would have ready access through this distribution system. The larger bank could lend it to smaller banks, and they could then relend it to their customers. Good idea.

But in a growing economy with seasonal borrowing needs, the system did not always work. For example, when country banks needed currency, especially during the crop-planting season, they would draw down their reserves at the larger banks. These banks would then draw down their reserves at the largest banks in New York, Chicago, and St. Louis. These very large banks, such as the one owned by J. Pierpont Morgan, had tons of currency in their vaults and, if not, could get more if given enough time to do so. They could organize syndicates of lenders who wanted to lend their money. They could borrow gold from European banks that they could then use to acquire more US currency. Or they could raise the interest rates on their own borrowers and reduce the local demand for loans, thus increasing the currency available for areas where loan demand was hottest.

Unfortunately, on more than one occasion with a rapidly growing economy there wasn't enough cash or time to get more currency, and a panic would occur. Significant financial panics of 1873, 1884, 1893, and especially 1907 occurred in part because of this "pyramid" scheme.[144] The banking system was just not able to meet the demand.

It gets better. Imagine you are a banker with a sudden shortage of cash. You do the obvious and call your stockbroker with instructions to sell some of the stocks he has bought with your extra deposits. If a lot of bankers do this, the stock prices fall rapidly. People notice. They panic and run to the bank for their cash. Bankers need more cash and order the sale of more stock, and, well, the whole process repeats, and the economy, as they say, "goes right down the toilet." The banking system was not designed to handle this problem. In fact, it could cause it.

On a practical matter, it was also becoming more costly and time consuming to clear customers' checks. There were other problems too, such as very rigid reserve requirements that did not allow banks any flexibility to fund more loans during good times.

The banking system was just not able to address all these problems, and after the Panic of 1907 the wheels were set in motion to form the Federal Reserve System (the Fed).

Love him or hate him, the truth remains that J. Pierpont Morgan was very good at addressing panics such as the one in 1907. But Morgan and his peers were all getting older (he was seventy), and, at the same time, the number of banks was quickly increasing, and the population was growing farther and farther away from New York, the nation's financial capital. Given the size and complexity of the banking system and its currency problems, it was no longer possible to use the private sector alone to solve liquidity needs or to prevent panics. A new system was needed: one that would no longer be dominated by Morgan and his peers but instead would operate more formally. A new Federal Reserve System would come into being. *We got this way for a reason.*

The Fed's Origin

Research will show that the people who develop policies, programs, and organizations to address shortcomings in the US economy have almost all been educated in the school of hard knocks. The folks who developed our national banking system and the Fed are graduates of this prestigious school. After all, it was in large part the failings of the state banks and the need to more effectively finance the Civil War that led to the development of a national banking system. And it was the national banking system's failings that led to the creation of the Federal Reserve System.

Some people contend that the Federal Reserve System was devised by a handful of rich white guys at a secret meeting held behind closed doors at an exclusive country club on Jekyll Island, Georgia.

They would be right.

But it isn't as sinister as it sounds. After the Panic of 1907, Congress reacted by forming an eighteen-member commission (nine from the Senate and nine from the House), chaired by Senator Nelson Aldrich (R-RI) to review the problems of the US banking industry. After travelling around Europe looking for "best practices," Aldrich hosted a conference of select people at the Jekyll Island Club. The club was an exclusive hunting preserve catering to millionaires, including J. P. Morgan, who was a member and arranged for the group to use it.

By then, Morgan was seventy-three years old (he died two years later) and did not attend. But his business partner Henry Davidson did, along with Arthur Shelton (Aldrich's secretary); Dr. A. Piatt Andrew, former Harvard University professor of economics; Frank A. Vanderlip, former assistant secretary of the Treasury and at the time president of National City Bank (now called CitiBank); and Paul M. Warburg, partner at the investment firm of Kuhn, Loeb, and Co., a strong competitor of the J. P. Morgan Company. (Kuhn, Loeb, and Co. eventually ended up as part of Lehman Brothers.)

They met in secret in 1910 for a practical reason: if the proposal was seen as one developed by "Wall Street," it would never pass the House of Representatives, which was controlled by the Democrats. The plan they devised became, in fact, the prototype for legislation that was eventually introduced by Congressman Carter Glass (D-VA) and Senator Robert Latham Owen (D-OK).[145] The Carter-Owen Bill was signed into law as the Federal Reserve Act by President Woodrow Wilson on December 23, 1913. But there were some differences.

The Jekyll Island meeting proposed a "National Reserve System," while Glass proposed the "Federal Reserve System." In both names, the word *reserve* was used to emphasize the need to keep currency reserves available to pay depositors. But while the Glass proposal would have had fifteen regions, the final law authorized eight to twelve. Glass proposed that the board of directors be controlled by commercial bankers; the final law required a combination of bankers *and nonbankers*. Most importantly, the law mandated there would be a Federal Reserve Board in Washington, whose directors would be appointed by the president and approved by the Senate. This board would oversee the independent Reserve Banks.

The Federal Reserve System was originally meant to be an association of independent and autonomous Reserve Banks. What cities these *Federal Reserve District* banks would be in was left to a committee comprised of the secretary of the Treasury, William McAdoo; the secretary of Agriculture, David Houston; and the comptroller of the currency, John Skelton Williams. The committee decided that the maximum number of locations would be twelve, and thirty-seven cities requested they be chosen as one of the sites.

The twelve cities that were selected were Boston, New York, Philadelphia, Cleveland, Richmond, Atlanta, Chicago, St. Louis, Minneapolis, Kansas City, Dallas, and San Francisco. Over time, each Reserve Bank built a few branch locations too, but most have now closed, and the size of the ones that still exist is getting smaller. The branches were heavily involved in processing checks, and checks are now being replaced by debit cards, electronic check clearing, and other innovations.

Naturally, anytime there are winners and losers in a selection process, allegations of political favoritism arise, and choosing these twelve locations was no exception. In Greider's book, he states that while the selections seemed a "reasonable delineation of the nation's economic regions" the choices were "not entirely free of politics" because Cleveland, home of Secretary of War Newton Baker, beat out Cincinnati and Pittsburgh; Richmond, home state of Congressman Carter Glass, beat out Baltimore; and Missouri, home of House Speaker Champ Clark, was awarded two cities (St. Louis and Kansas City).[146] Others have questioned why Atlanta and Dallas were selected over New Orleans and why Kansas City was selected over Denver or Omaha. All complaints aside, and there were sure plenty of them at the time, the evidence of political partisanship is purely anecdotal.

Citing studies that say the Reserve Bank cities were chosen in an honest and fair manner sounds like baloney. But, to be fair, several studies have shown just that.

If you need more proof, check out an interesting essay by Dr. Michael McAvoy of the Division of Economics and Business at the SUNY College at Oneonta. Oneonta used probability choice models for the thirty-seven cities considered and concluded that politics didn't play a meaningful role in the selection of the District Federal Reserve Bank locations. Columbia University Professor David Weiman and Scripps College Professor Kerry Odell concluded the same thing in their study: the committee "did not behave in a partisan manner." Even more to the point, according to McAvoy, "the selection committee is shown to have behaved impartially and not arbitrarily."[147]

In any event, the committee's decision was to locate the District Reserve Banks in those cities, and if a Reserve Bank moved to a new headquarters building, it had to be in the city. So the Atlanta Federal Reserve Bank, for example, could not have built their new headquarters in 2001 in nearby Cobb, Gwinnet, or Clayton Counties outside of the city limits. Besides, what better location for the Atlanta Fed than right next door to the historic home and museum of Margaret Mitchell, author of *Gone with the Wind*?

Fed Structure

The Federal Reserve System was established to address several shortcomings in the banking system such as the lack of currency to support growth (known as an *inelastic* currency because it cannot expand or contract to meet public demand). Then there were the problems with check-clearing operations and with preventing bank runs and panics by having enough liquidity for the banks.

The Federal Reserve's charter was granted by the US Congress. The Fed is an *independent* company with a public purpose. Its congressional charter *required* all national banks (and *invited* state banks) to purchase stock in their District Federal Reserve Bank, thereby becoming "member banks." The District Reserve Banks were structured as any private company would be. The shareholders receive dividends (the law requires a 6 percent return on shareholders' stock), and the Fed earns its own income to cover expenses. Unlike the private sector, however, the Fed's stock can't be sold or traded with others.

The Federal Reserve System isn't supported by taxpayers. In fact, the Fed earns its own sizable income, primarily from the interest on US government securities it owns, but also from the interest on loans to banks (and in rare events, to others) and on fees to banks for its services.

Because the law requires banks to keep some cash on reserve at the Federal Reserve Banks, the Fed uses these cash reserves to buy government securities and make loans. In a sense, it's very similar to any other bank that opens a checking account for its customers and then uses the money they deposit to make loans and buy government securities. The difference here is that the national banks have no choice and are required to open an account with the Federal Reserve Banks. Up until October 2008, the banks' deposits at the Fed earned no interest, which really bothered the bankers. After years of their moaning and groaning about it, Congress passed the Financial Services Regulatory Relief Act of 2006, which forced the Federal Reserve to pay them interest on their deposits.[148]

Although the Federal Reserve System is exempt from federal, state, and local taxes, in an odd twist, because it is technically owned by private companies (commercial banks), it is still subject to state and local *property* taxes, which amounted to $38 million in 2008. For the record, at year-end 2008, the consolidated assets of all Federal Reserve Banks totaled $2.2 trillion. You can find the Feds' annual financial statements at www.federalreserve.gov.

In effect, the banking industry owns a company that returns tremendous amounts of its profits back to the taxpayers each year. In 2008, for example, the Federal Reserve System paid to the Treasury $31.7 billion (which the Treasury can use to either buy gold or pay down the national debt). The amount paid to the Treasury is considered "interest" expense on the Federal Reserve Notes (and coins) that the Treasury loans to the Fed and that we all use as currency. Remember, the Federal Reserve borrows the currency from the Treasury after putting up suitable collateral. The collateral is primarily government securities.

Over the years, folks would propose that the Federal Reserve System use some of its profits to fund a specific program, such as affordable housing or small-business lending. These proposals never went far. Having the Federal Reserve System pay bank industry money directly to the government to pay down the national debt (or buy gold) was considered a much better thing for taxpayers. For almost one hundred years, having an *independent* Fed was considered much too important than to favor any particular housing or business interest. Until now!

Following the recent financial crisis, Congress established a Bureau of Consumer Financial Protection, to be housed within the Federal Reserve

Board.[149] In a solid slap at the Federal Reserve System for being too cozy with the banking industry and callous to consumers, Congress required the Federal Reserve Board to house and pay all costs of this new independent consumer protection agency. The agency is not subject to the Fed's oversight; they just send the Fed their bills!

Board Composition

As with all private companies, the composition of the board of directors is critically important. The Federal Reserve Act required that the District Reserve Bank boards include nonbankers, much to the dismay of the banking industry when the law was passed in 1913. To them, this was a private bankers' bank, funded by the banks to provide services to the banks. The banks were the shareholders, and they thought they should be able to elect their own boards without outside interference. But to get approval from Congress and the president, who worried that "Wall Street" would be too powerful and dominant, a compromise was necessary, and the boards of the District Reserve Banks have nine directors, split among three classes.

Three Class A directors are commercial bankers. Three Class B directors represent commercial, agricultural, industrial, labor, consumer, and public interests. The stockholders (bankers) elect these six directors. The Board of Governors in Washington DC, chooses the other three Class C directors to balance the composition of the board. They also represent commercial, agricultural, industrial, labor, consumer, and public interests. The job of the District Reserve Bank boards is to not only provide guidance and direction on typical business concerns, such as personnel matters (hiring new officers, for example), but to have a say in economic policy matters too.

The directors' views on the economy are very important. It may vary some among the District Reserve Banks, but the basic structure is to have the board members specifically solicit input from their constituents about the economy. The information is used in combination with other government reports, economic analysis, and other forecasts to help guide economic policy decisions. The anecdotal information is compiled into what was once a beige colored book and is published eight times a year. Called the Beige Book, for obvious reasons, it is widely noted and quoted by the media.[150]

Originally, the District Reserve Bank presidents were called governors, and they considered themselves equals (or more) with the Board of Governors in Washington DC. The inherent conflict between District Reserve Banks and board were in part caused by the unusual corporate structure from its charter and the need for the District Reserve Banks to operate independently of each other to serve local credit needs. The board had "oversight responsibilities," but the Reserve Banks would battle with the board when necessary to maintain their independence.

The appointment of Federal Reserve Board Chairman Marriner S. Eccles changed these dynamics considerably. Based on his proposal to President Franklin D. Roosevelt, the Banking Act of 1935 was passed. The Board of Governors won out in a big way with major influence over District Reserve Banks, including the power to oversee and overrule everything from budgets to new buildings to staff salaries. As if to drive home the point, the title of the District Reserve Bank *governors* was changed to *presidents*. Members of the board in Washington, however, are still called governors. With Chairman Eccles, the power had clearly shifted from the District Reserve Banks to the board. Eccles served as board chairman from 1934 to 1948, and the building that houses the main offices of the Federal Reserve Board was named in his honor by an act of Congress in 1982. The District Reserve Banks, on the other hand, haven't named any buildings for him.[151]

The Banking Act of 1935 also changed who sat on the Board of Governors in Washington DC. Before 1935, the Federal Reserve Board consisted of the secretary of the Treasury and the national bank regulator, the comptroller of the currency, along with five other people appointed by the president and confirmed by the Senate. These people served for ten years (it's now fourteen years). This structure meant that the board was balanced politically because the Treasury secretary and the comptroller worked for the president and could be replaced when a new president was elected. The other five "governors" had longer terms and would be less influenced by presidential politics. The Federal Reserve System got even more removed from politics when the new law in 1935 removed the Treasury secretary and the national bank regulator from their board.

The Fed got even more removed from politics when the new law in 1935 removed the Treasury secretary and the national bank regulator from their board.

Today, although the Federal Reserve System is still subject to congressional oversight (there are required reports and testimony), it operates very independently because the members of the board are appointed for fourteen-year terms and can outlast a president. More importantly, the Board of Governors isn't tied to congressional "purse strings" to cover its expenses. Instead, the board will assesses each Reserve Bank a fee based on that Reserve Bank's size (more specifically, its total capital and surplus). In 2008, these assessments by the board totaled $853 million.

The president appoints seven Federal Reserve Board members and the Senate confirms them to serve fourteen-year terms. The chairman and vice chairman are also appointed and confirmed, for four years. On February 1, 2006, Ben S. Bernanke was sworn in as a full board member for fourteen years and as chairman of the board for four years. He was reappointed for a second term as chairman in 2010.

Bernanke, who was born in Augusta, Georgia, and raised in Dillon, South Carolina, is sorta smart. That is, if you consider a Harvard University summa cum laude graduate who has taught at Princeton, MIT, Stanford, and New York University smart. In contrast, legendary singer James Brown was also from Augusta, Georgia, and although he never attended Harvard or taught at Stanford, he did become the Godfather of Soul and, of course, was much cooler.

Bernanke photo (left) courtesy of Federal Reserve Board. Brown photo (right) courtesy of WENN.

To his credit however, Bernanke, like James Brown, does have his own nickname. He was delivering a speech on *deflation* to the National Economists Club, where he indicated a willingness, if absolutely necessary, to combine monetary policy with congressional tax cuts to boast spending and fight deflation.[152] A bit boring perhaps, but he went on to call it the "equivalent to Milton Friedman's famous 'helicopter drop' of money" idea, where the Fed dumps a bunch of money into the economy as quickly as possible. His willingness to drop money from a helicopter, metaphorically speaking, earned him the nickname "Helicopter Ben." It's not as hip as being the Godfather of Soul, but for a central banker from Augusta, Georgia, it's as good as it gets.

Discount Window

Originally, the primary function of the District Reserve Banks was to allow their stockholders (called member banks) to borrow money when they needed it. These banks would use the short-term business loans (commercial loans) they had made as collateral. They could exchange the commercial loans for more currency and thus remove one of the problems of having a limited amount of currency in circulation. The money supply could now expand when times were good and bankers were making more business loans. The supply could contract when the loans were repaid.

The loans that were serving as collateral would be *discounted* from their face value and the borrowing would be from the District Reserve Bank's "Discount Window" at an interest rate called the discount rate. This discount rate was originally higher than what commercial banks would offer each other. This made the Federal Reserve the *lender of last resort* because banks wouldn't typically borrow here if they could get it cheaper somewhere else. Banks were sometimes reluctant to borrow except for seasonal needs because they were afraid that people, including their regulators, would think they were in trouble, but that's not really the case anymore. For the record, there is no literal window. Today it's simply a computer monitor.

Up until 1935, each District Reserve Bank could set its own interest rate, although the board had the right to review the rates. The rates were often different in each District Reserve Bank. That sounds odd now, but at the time agricultural regions were different from manufacturing regions, and the discount rates reflected those differences. Then, as now, the law requires that rates be set by the District Reserve Banks every fourteen days (typically one time at a board meeting, the other by conference call). The board gained so much power in 1935 that it can override these rate decisions, so now all Reserve Banks offer the same rate. The District Reserve Banks recommend the rate, but the Board of Governors makes the final decision.

When people talk about the discount rate, they mean the traditional "primary credit" rate because beginning in 2003 the Discount Window offers several interest rates depending on the type of loan. Banks in good shape can get a primary credit loan, typically overnight and usually to meet their reserve requirements. Banks that are not in such good shape and that have higher risk can get a "secondary credit" loan, which is also a short-term (typically overnight) loan, but they have to pay a higher interest rate. A seasonal credit is a longer-term loan to banks that need money just part of the year to meet seasonal needs, often because they are located in agricultural or tourist areas.

There is a fourth loan available at the Discount Window—emergency credit—and it's very rarely used. The other three loans are for depository institutions, but this one makes loans to *nondepository* institutions, even the ones that are not directly regulated by the Federal Reserve. It's only for emergencies, or more specifically "unusual and exigent circumstances," and it hadn't been used since the 1930s. But then came the Panic of 2008, and with that came Bear Stearns, the nation's third-largest brokerage firm. Bear Stearns got a $12.9 billion loan on March 14, 2008, and then one of the largest insurance companies in the world, AIG got an $85 billion loan commitment.[153] The loans have been repaid now, but yes, they were a really big deal and are discussed more fully in chapter 9.

Open Market Operations

Banks borrow extensively from the Federal Reserve Banks today, but that's something new. In the beginning, demand wasn't particularly strong. That made it tough because then and still today, the District Reserve Banks must earn enough income to cover their expenses. Although this has not been a problem for quite some time, it certainly was a struggle in the beginning because many of the District Reserve Banks weren't making enough loans. Some Reserve Banks, such as Atlanta, didn't have many national banks in their districts. After all, although the South had lost the Civil War almost fifty years before the Fed was born, the thought of joining a national bank system instead of staying with a state banking system was still a tough sell in some parts of the country. That meant fewer banks were requesting Discount Window loans, and that made it hard for the District Reserve Banks to generate enough income to cover overhead expenses. Not surprisingly, the District Reserve Banks would buy US Treasury securities to earn interest and cover their expenses. They even formed a committee to make these trades.[154]

It's against the law for the Federal Reserve Board or District Reserve Banks to purchase securities directly from the US Treasury. Just like the rest of us, if they want to buy or sell securities, they call a broker and conduct business on the open market. Like any good company, they have a screening process to choose their brokers, and as of April 2009, the Fed was using sixteen different securities dealers. The dealers have to meet size, reputation, expertise, and other criteria. If you want more details and to see a current list, you can find it all at the New York Federal Reserve Bank's website.[155]

It's rather interesting to know that the District Reserve Banks used currency held in their vaults to buy securities. When they bought securities, the currency left their vaults and rather quickly ended up on deposit at commercial banks as their brokers used the money to buy securities. With all that new cash going into the commercial banks, those banks had more money to lend, and interest rates would decline. When the District Reserve Banks sold securities, the currency they received came out of the commercial banks, and interest rates would increase because the bankers had less cash available to lend.

Early on, the District Reserve Banks decided to coordinate buying and selling securities both to save on costs and, more importantly, to reduce the disruptions to market interest rates. The District Reserve Banks decided to form an Open Market Investment Committee (OMIC) to coordinate purchases and sales and to ensure sensitivity to the influence it has on market interest rates. They didn't want to cause interest rates in any particular district to disrupt those economies. At their request, the Board of Governors passed a resolution supporting the OMIC and officially appointing the five committee members. The members were from the New York (Governor Strong, the chairman), Boston, Chicago, Cleveland, and Philadelphia Federal Reserve Banks.

So now, the Federal Reserve System found itself with a surprising amount of influence. By changing the amount of reserves a bank was required to keep with them (roughly 10 percent of transaction accounts today), or by offering loans through the Discount Window at higher or lower interest rates, or when buying and selling government securities, the Reserve Banks could have a very powerful influence on short-term interest rates, and thus the economy. These three tools—reserve requirements, discount rates, and open market operations—are still the main tools the Fed uses to manage the money supply.

As you may know, when the Federal Reserve System influences the economy with these tools, it's called *monetary policy*. When our elected officials influence the economy with government spending, saving, or investment programs, it's called *fiscal policy*.

Federal Open Market Committee (FOMC)

The District Reserve Banks hadn't really meant to have such a huge influence over the nation's economy when buying and selling securities to cover their expenses; it was more incidental. But some District Reserve Bank governors figured out pretty fast that the Fed could have a lot of influence on the economy (especially controlling inflation and fighting deflation) and no one was more powerful than the New York Federal Reserve Bank governor, Benjamin Strong (from 1914 until his death in 1928).

It is true that many Fed governors and officials didn't agree with Governor

Strong. They didn't think that the Federal Reserve should have such a powerful role in fighting inflation and deflation. Philadelphia Federal Reserve Bank Governor George W. Norris, for instance, was outspoken in his opinion that the role of the Fed should be strictly limited to providing credit to banks and letting other agencies (Commerce Department or Labor Department) deal with price stability. Federal Reserve Board Governor Adolph Miller argued that any such role should be handled by the board, not the District Reserve Banks. And the board's head of research, Director Emanuel Goldenweiser, argued that when the Fed bought and sold securities, it didn't have any real effect anyway.[156]

These varying views aren't surprising. This was all unchartered territory, and because the District Reserve Banks were independent and autonomous (the charter specifically avoided the words "central bank" to ensure that Congress passed it), the role of the OMIC was very interesting. Supplying enough currency was one thing, but making monetary policy was something else completely. The District Reserve Banks were frequently challenged from within and from outside the Fed about their role in managing the economy. In a May 1922 response to a request for clarification from Treasury Secretary Mellon, the OMIC governors even declared that their policy was "to invest in Government securities only to the extent that it may be necessary from time to time to maintain earnings in amounts sufficient to meet expenses, including dividends and necessary reserves."[157] That wasn't an especially wise declaration.

The problem with the OMIC governors misunderstanding the effect their securities decisions and other activities have on the economy is that it could lead to disastrous results. For example, most people would agree that the harsh and prolonged Great Depression was caused in large part by the Fed's failure to increase the money supply (by lowering the discount rates and buying government securities, for example) following the stock market crash in 1929.

There are a lot of opinions and thousands of articles and books on the topic of the Fed's role during the Great Depression. It is a topic we won't delve into in this book. But there is no doubt that the Federal Reserve System was under a great deal of scrutiny, and rightfully so, after the stock market crashed in 1929. Not long afterward, with a new President (Roosevelt) and new Fed chairman (Eccles), a whole new era for the Fed began. When the Banking Act of 1935 was passed, the OMIC was replaced with the Federal Open Market Committee (FOMC), a new group made up of the Federal Reserve Bank presidents and the Federal Reserve Board governors.

Learning from the errors made during the Great Depression, the FOMC is today more inclined to act in a "countercyclical" way. That is, it implements policies that slow the economy down when business is booming (to fight inflation) and that pump up the economy during downturns (to prevent recession). As William McChensney Martin, the longest serving Board of Governors chairman in history, described it in the 1950s, the Fed's role was that of "leaning against the wind" to prevent extremes during the good or the bad times. The Fed was "the people who take away the punch bowl just when the party is getting good."[158]

That's somewhat ironic coming from a guy who didn't drink.

It's an unusual structure; now all the Federal Reserve Bank presidents attend and participate in the FOMC meetings, but only the seven Board governors, the New York Federal Reserve Bank president, and four District Reserve Bank presidents can vote. The four District Reserve Bank presidents serve a one-year term, and they rotate among four groups: (1) Boston, Philadelphia, and Richmond; (2) Cleveland and Chicago; (3) Atlanta, St. Louis, and Dallas; and (4) Minneapolis, Kansas City, and San Francisco.

Today's Fed has clearly established monetary policy as a primary responsibility, and it uses a variety of tools to influence short-term rates. Reserve requirements, the discount rate, and open market operations (securities purchases and sales) remain its main tools, but it has an arsenal of weapons at its disposal if necessary. Although the Fed has other very important functions, since 1935, and regardless of what they may tell other employees who work outside of their research departments, the Fed's most important responsibility is still forming monetary policy in "pursuit of maximum employment, stable prices, and moderate long-term interest rates."[159]

Supervision and Regulation

The research department is critical to the Federal Reserve System, but that's not to say that the other departments aren't important. Supervising and regulating banking institutions, and providing financial services to depository institutions, the US government, and foreign institutions are also very important. In fact, supervising and regulating banks is particularly important because Federal Reserve officials have long claimed that they can't implement good monetary policy without direct insight into how banks operate. The Federal Reserve has been quite outspoken that regulation and monetary policy have to go together to have a safe and sound financial system.

Congress has agreed that good monetary policy depends on knowing firsthand what is going on in the banks, and it has passed laws that give the Fed responsibility for overseeing other financial entities besides bank holding companies.[160] Now the Federal Reserve Board is the federal supervisor of three kinds of financial companies: (1) all US bank and thrift holding companies (that own banks or thrifts), (2) financial holding companies (that own banks, insurance, and/or investment firms), and (3) state-chartered commercial banks that are members of the Federal Reserve System. This third group is a mouthful, but it just means state banks that choose the Fed *and* the state to be their regulators. For many of them, the choice was easy because the Fed already regulated their holding company or financial services company.

As a practical matter, the Federal Reserve Board has "delegated" responsibility of examining banks and inspecting bank holding companies to the District Reserve Banks. Bank examiners usually come from the District Reserve Banks, and are paid by those Reserve Banks. But the work they perform and the reports they write are done so for the Board of Governors. Decisions to implement enforcement actions or to close a bank are done in consultation with the Reserve Banks but are the board's call.

According to the Board of Governors' 2007 annual report, the Fed regulated 878 state-chartered banks, which was about 12 percent of all FDIC-insured commercial banks in the United States. The Fed also regulated over five thousand bank holding companies, and these companies held about 96 percent of all insured commercial bank assets in the United States. Among the holding companies that the Fed regulated, 597 were financial holding companies, meaning they owned insurance and/or investment companies too. All of this makes the Fed a very important regulator to keep banks and other institutions healthy and to protect consumers.

Is it necessary for the Fed to be a bank regulator? The Fed thinks so and argues that having hands-on experience in regulating banks is very important. They have always fought back challenges to their authority to do so. In his 1998 speech at Widener University in Chester, Pennsylvania, former Federal Reserve Board Governor Laurence H. Meyer offered this rationale:

> The central bank, in my experience, needs direct, hands-on involvement in the supervision and regulation of a broad cross-section of banks in order to carry out the Fed's core responsibilities of conducting monetary policy, ensuring the stability of the financial system, acting as the lender of last resort, protecting the payments system, and managing a financial crisis. Meeting all of these responsibilities is not

> just an academic exercise; it requires practical knowledge of financial institutions and markets, knowledge that comes with being deeply involved in supervising individual banking organizations. Without such involvement, the Federal Reserve would be much less able to maintain both its practical knowledge of banking and other financial markets, and the influence and authority necessary for macroeconomic policy and crisis management. [161]

The best line in his speech was this: "Ivory towers are great for universities, but they are not desirable for central banks."

It almost seems crazy to say that the Fed shouldn't have its role of supervision and regulation. Would we want the Federal Aviation Administration to ensure the safety of the airline industry if they weren't also allowed to see firsthand how planes are made?

On the other hand, some folks see this argument as a lame excuse to protect one's turf. After all, countries like Australia, Canada, France, Germany, Greece, Japan, Mexico, Spain, Sweden, and the United Kingdom have all separated their regulatory function from monetary policy, and it has worked out okay.

Panic of 2008

The recent economic crisis has rightfully called into question several assumptions about the Federal Reserve System and other regulators. What are the appropriate roles for so many regulators? Why wasn't there one centralized authority to understand and lessen the "systemic risk" of so many large institutions, whether they are mortgage, insurance, investment, or financial companies? Systemic risk is when something causes losses to our entire financial system, not just one part of it. For example, if the largest bank in the country fails, it could take down other companies too. The losses become contagious. Systemic risk is a very real and serious threat.

The most recent near total collapse of our economy is a clear example of a systemic risk that was not well managed. Nobody, including the Fed, had the tools or the authority to control the systemic risk. It doesn't matter. The Fed was blamed anyway for not using its existing authority to prevent the 2007–2009 financial crises. Right or wrong, the Fed was criticized for helping to cause it too.

The Federal Reserve System was blamed for keeping interest rates too low for too long, which caused an unnecessary housing boom that would eventually explode. People have criticized its "ad hoc response" to the Panic of 2008, saying that the Fed seriously underestimated problems with subprime lending. People complain the Fed rarely supported important consumer protection laws, favoring banks over consumer rights. Critics claim that the Fed let the banking industry regulate itself and that doing so was dangerous and costly.

Critics also claimed the Fed provided a bailout to the elite only. They allege that if you were a subprime borrower with a liquidity need, you got nothing. But if you were running a troubled hedge fund, or you were a rich guy running a megacompany, you could pledge any crap you owned and get money from the Fed. They criticized the Fed for corporate welfare when it loaned money to General Electric Co., Caterpillar Inc. and Harley-Davidson Inc. They complain the Fed did nothing to directly support small businesses and working-class families. They deride the Fed as being a banker's bank, instead of a people's bank. They wanted the Fed's independence revoked.

In one of his most famous songs, musician Greg Allman would sing with a great deal of anguish, "sometimes I feel like I've been tied to the whipping post."[162] If you worked at the Fed during this time, you could certainly relate to the lyrics. There were so many accusations, so many complaints, and so many folks grabbing hold of that vicious whip to pummel the Fed for its perceived failures.

Undoubtedly, far too many of the allegations against the Fed were simply politically motivated, self-serving, and without merit. But there is certainly at least some truth to many of them as well. Analysts will study these topics extensively for years. Their studies will come too late to prevent the reputational damage to the Fed. Right or wrong, perceptions matter, and it appears the Fed failed to recognize some important lessons from the past. *Good government is necessary. People matter. It's easy to misplace blame.*

Whether the criticisms about the Fed prove true or not doesn't really matter. Once you find yourself tied to the whipping post, you are in for a whuppin'. In this case, the Fed found itself working overtime to protect its role as an independent central bank. They had to fight back congressional proposals to strip it of its authority to regulate smaller community banks. They had to defeat efforts to change the New York Federal Reserve Bank president from a position appointed by its board of directors (with the approval of the Board of Governors) to one that was appointed by the US president. They fought back attempts to have each District Reserve Banks' board chairperson also appointed by the White House.

When the dust settled, Congress had passed a new comprehensive law named for its sponsors, Senator Christopher Dodd (D-CT) and Congressman Barney Frank (D-MA). The Dodd-Frank Wall Street Reform and Consumer Protection Act (Dodd-Frank Act) had several measures directed specifically at the Fed.

For example, the Fed was required to reveal details of their various emergency lending programs undertaken during the financial crisis. They had to name names. They had to reveal the amount and type of assistance provided, the terms for repayment, and the collateral used. The Fed fought this proposal because they believed if the companies that borrowed were revealed, the public's reaction to those companies might make matters worse. They were right to be concerned. The same issue had also occurred with the Reconstruction Finance Corporation (RFC), which was established by President Hoover during the Great Depression to make similar emergency business loans. When some of the companies that borrowed from the RFC were made public, folks rushed to sell their stock or quickly withdraw their deposits. Of course this only made matters worse for those companies, and it scared away some who needed the money but couldn't afford the reputational risk. The Fed didn't want to create the same problem with their emergency loan program.

The Dodd-Frank Act directed the Comptroller General (Congress's watchdog) to conduct a one-time audit of all actions taken by the Federal Reserve System during the economic crisis.

The Fed was subject to a wide range of audits before, but never one that covered monetary-policy actions or decisions. It was never subject to audits that would reveal discount-window lending or actions by the Federal Open Market Committee (the group that influences short-term interest rates). Before this bill, its transactions with foreign governments or foreign central banks were not audited. The Fed opposed these audits because they worried the government audits could lead members of Congress to second-guess Fed decisions about interest rates. They worried that the Fed would be politicized, with Congress calling on Fed governors and bank presidents to explain or change their specific interest- rate decisions. It could create political pressure for the Fed to stimulate economic growth in the short run (perhaps when politicians are running for reelection), which might lead to inflation in the long run. The independence of the Fed to conduct monetary policy (including interest-rate decisions) would no longer be separated from Congress's job to conduct fiscal policy (government spending programs). The Fed considers this separation of duties very important.

In the end, a compromise was struck, and the Fed was subject to a one-time audit of all actions they took during the economic crisis. Of course, it leaves open the door to future congressional actions and audits. You may be familiar with the old proverb: once a camel gets his nose under a tent, his body will soon follow. Well, Federal Reserve officials certainly know this proverb and will have to remain diligent to protect their tent from anything more than a camel's nose.

The Dodd-Frank Act had many more important provisions, such as establishing the Financial Stability Oversight Council to prevent systemic risk. At one time you might have thought a council like this would be run by the Federal Reserve, but with its reputation tarnished, Congress decided instead to have the council comprised of ten different agencies (including the Fed).[163] It will be chaired by the Treasury Department.

In another interesting provision, the act established a Bureau of Consumer Financial Protection, to be housed within the Federal Reserve Board. This consumer protection agency is fully independent, but the Fed must still pay the agency's salaries and overhead expenses. In the end, this may prove to be a small price to pay for public anger. Repairing its reputation is far more expensive. *People matter.*

Federal Deposit Insurance Corporation (FDIC)

It's grim to think about bank failures before we had deposit insurance. Imagine that you have a checking account at a bank that is in financial trouble. Unless you're sure that your deposit is safe, you would be crazy to leave any big deposits at that bank. Just the thought of the bank getting into trouble is enough to make you race to the bank to pull out your money.

Banking is all about confidence. We want to be sure that the people running the joint are competent. We want to be sure that they will return our deposits immediately when we ask for them. We want to be sure that they have enough shareholder money to cover any of their losses so we can still do business with them. Any loss of confidence can cause a bank to fail.

When confidence is shaken, a crisis can occur, and that was a huge part of the problem in the 1920s and '30s. Simply put, banks did not have enough money to protect against bad loans *and* the loss of consumer confidence. When problems became evident, banks failed big time. In fact, over 12,500 banks and thrifts failed in the ten years ending in 1933. In contrast, we had just fewer than 350 failures in the ten years ending in 2010.[164]

In the banking crisis of the 1920s and '30s, politicians responded like you might expect: they called for special committees and silly laws. For example, in his annual address to Congress in 1929, Republican President Herbert Hoover declared "it might be advantageous to create a joint commission" to report back on the problem and offer solutions. You think!? Meanwhile, Charles Brand (D-GA) proposed a law prohibiting the circulation of false rumors about banks, and Edgar Howard (D-NE) wanted to make it illegal for bankers to circulate false reports about people.[165] Nice work, guys. Glad you brought your "A-game" to the table.

Banks were scaling back their lending programs, and efforts by the Federal Reserve System to improve liquidity and get credit flowing again were sporadic and unsuccessful. At one point, Secretary of the Treasury Ogden Mills complained about "the psychology of fear which has affected bankers quite as much as their depositors" and kept them from booking loans.[166] Some might observe that this same psychology gripped the bankers again in the more recent crisis in 2007–09.

Rather than form a joint commission as President Hoover suggested, both the Senate and the House formed their own committees, one chaired by Senator Carter Glass (D-VA) and the one in the House chaired by Louis McFadden (R-PA). In 1932, Senator Glass teamed up with Representative Henry Steagall (R-AL) to pass the first of two bills named after them. The Glass-Steagall Act of 1932 allowed the Federal Reserve Banks to make loans to banks secured by assets other than commercial loans and US Treasury securities. It had limited effect, but it did pave the way for the Federal Reserve Banks to accept mortgage loans during later crises, such as the Panic of 2007.

Despite President Hoover's modest attempts to revive the economy, his and Congress's programs didn't work, and he was soundly defeated in his reelection bid. The Republican Party also took a beating, and the Democrats gained control of 72 percent of the House seats in1932. The country was clearly in no mood for halfhearted measures, and with this kind of popular support, President Roosevelt and Congress were able to be more aggressive in establishing new government programs.

That's when a second Glass-Steagall Act was passed in 1933, only this one was much more comprehensive. Not only did it separate banking, insurance, and investment companies from common ownership, it created the Federal Deposit Insurance Corporation (FDIC).

In 1934, the FDIC was to be a temporary agency that would provide insurance on deposit accounts up to $2,500 (about $41,000 in 2009 dollars). Not all bankers opposed the measure, but a lot of them did. For example, in Senate hearings on the proposal, Percy H. Johnson of the Chemical Bank and

Trust Company of New York said that insurance wasn't needed "unless we are going to guarantee all elements of society against misfortunes and evils of all kinds. Of course, if we are going to have socialistic government, then we ought to guarantee everybody against all manner of things." Ronald Ransom, president of the Georgia Bankers Association, said that banks in Georgia were 100 percent against it. A.L.M. Wiggins, president of the South Carolina Bankers Association, said that it would lead to panic and more failures.[167] And Morton Bodfish, head of the United States Savings and Loan League (the thrift's trade association) called it an "unwise and unsound program."[168] Even so, the public pressure for some form of deposit insurance prevailed, and the FDIC was born to protect commercial bank deposits. Savings and loans were excluded from coverage.

The program worked. The year after the FDIC insurance went into effect, only nine banks failed. Given that over twelve thousand had failed in the ten years before Glass-Steagall was passed, this was a remarkable turnaround. It wasn't surprising, then, that the FDIC insurance program became permanent in 1934, and the coverage limit was increased to $5,000.

Federal Savings and Loan Insurance Corporation (FSLIC)

The FDIC insurance program for commercial banks was so successful that it began to draw deposits away from thrifts and put thrifts at a competitive disadvantage. As a result, the thrift trade association did a complete turnaround and began pushing for a deposit insurance program for thrift institutions. They eventually got it in the National Housing Act of 1934. Thus was born the Federal Savings and Loan Insurance Corporation (FSLIC, which was commonly pronounced "fizz-lick").

All federal thrift charters had to have FSLIC deposit insurance, but it was optional for state charters. A lot of states had their own deposit insurance programs, and the bankers thought these state programs provided enough protection. Unlike the FDIC, which was a separate independent agency, FSLIC was housed in the FHLB board and was run by FHLB members. And unlike the FDIC, where depositors could get all of their money back within a few days because banks offered checking accounts (demand deposit accounts), it could take as long as three years for somebody to get back a savings account insured by the FSLIC.

Not all state savings and loan associations joined the FSLIC program, and that led to some pretty painful results. State insurance funds failed in

Ohio in March 1985 and in Maryland in May 1985. In the Ohio debacle, the governor declared a bank "holiday" and closed the savings and loans until they could reopen with federal deposit insurance. Depositors typically had to wait several weeks to get all of their money. In Maryland, taxpayers had to foot a $185 million bailout. These two screw ups made huge headlines and quickly ended state deposit insurance funds nationwide.

FSLIC itself couldn't survive the savings and loan crisis of the 1980s and had to be bailed out with federal taxpayers' money. First, it became insolvent (more debts than assets) in 1986, and then Congress created the Financing Corporation. To raise enough money to bail out FSLIC, the Financing Corporation sold thirty-year bonds totaling $8.1 billion to the thrift industry. These bonds don't completely mature until 2017. That's a lot of debt for a long time! Initially, it was just the thrifts that had to pay the money back, but eventually the program was expanded to include all financial institutions that have FDIC deposit insurance.[169]

Most of us think of the savings and loan crisis from the 1980s as a thing of the past. But bankers still pay these debts when they send the FDIC their quarterly insurance premiums. Generally speaking, the quarterly fee the banks pay the FDIC to cover these bonds was about 0.011 percent of their assessed deposits. So, for example, if you ran a small $50 million bank with a dozen full-time employees, and you had $35 million in deposits, you would have paid about $3,850 each quarter ($15,400 a year) to bail out the thrift industry back in 1987. That's a bitter pill to swallow when you think of how your small bank could spend fifteen grand a year instead of paying for a problem somebody else caused.

That would have been bad enough if only it had been enough. But, sadly, even an extra $8 billion wasn't anywhere close to being enough to save FSLIC, so it was merged into the FDIC in 1989. The S&L crisis eventually cost taxpayers about $153 billion.

FDIC Structure and Results

The FDIC still provides deposit insurance, much in the way that the insurance was originally intended. They have a $100 billion line of credit from the Treasury Department if they need it, and the deposit insurance coverage has been increased to $250,000. Like other insurance policies, there is some fine print, but the FDIC makes it easy. They developed a website called EDIE (Electronic Deposit Insurance Estimator) to help you ensure that you are insured. It's at www.fdic.gov/edie.

The FDIC's mission is straightforward: insure deposits, examine and supervise state chartered banks that have insurance with the FDIC, and manage the assets of failed banks. As of September 2008, the FDIC insured $4.5 trillion in deposits for 8,384 banks and savings banks, of which they directly supervised 5,134. That's more than half of all the banks in the country, mostly community banks.

The FDIC announced a new premium structure effective April 1, 2009, to replenish the insurance fund. The premiums will range from 7 cents per $100 of deposits for the strongest banks to as much as 77.5 cents per $100 of deposits for the weakest, higher-risk banks. FDIC insurance is a lot like health insurance. Folks with good health who exercise and have good diets pay lower premiums than say, chain-smoking, beer-drinking slobs. High-risk banks are the equivalent of those chain-smoking, beer-drinking slobs who pay more for insurance.

Unfortunately, it's not just the slobs who pay. In the new assessment program, large, healthy banks will have to pay more than smaller, equally healthy banks because the formula for deciding the premium is based partly on asset size. Although megathrift IndyMac caused a tremendous and high-profile loss to the insurance fund, this formula was controversial because *most* of the bank failures that used up the insurance fund were actually the smaller banks. FDIC Chairman Sheila Bair defended the premiums. "A lot of large banks haven't failed because of massive government assistance," Bair said. "If it weren't for those, some big banks would have failed and there would have been costs."[170] She was right.

The FDIC headquarters is in Washington DC, with offices in Atlanta, Boston, Chicago, Dallas, Kansas City, Memphis, New York, and San Francisco. Taxpayers don't fund the FDIC; the banks and thrift institutions fund it with their premiums. The FDIC also earns money from its investments in US Treasury securities. It has a five-person board of directors, all of whom are appointed by the president and confirmed by the Senate. The head of the OCC also serves on the FDIC board.

To their credit, they got a glowing report from the Inspector General in 2008. The IG reported that "the FDIC has brought stability to the banking system" and that "amidst the current turmoil in the nation's economy and the resulting liquidity crisis, the FDIC has persevered in its mission, risen to meet new challenges, and helped maintain the public's confidence during these extraordinary times."[171] That's quite a glowing report!

In their own 2007 annual report, the FDIC touted their "long and continuing tradition of excellence in public service" and their success in "effectively and efficiently carrying out its insurance, supervisory, and receivership management responsibilities." While this type of bragging is self-serving, in fairness they do seem to manage their affairs well, and they deserve praise for how well they handle their bank supervision and receivership responsibilities. Their bank examiners do a very fine job with a high level of integrity. Their receivership responsibilities are done professionally and with dignity, and that job, by the way, is not without some risk to the men and women who do the work.

Closing a Bank

Think about it. A bank officially fails when its regulator determines (in consultation with the FDIC) that it is unable to meet its obligations to depositors. Not every banker will agree with that decision, especially when they have worked so long and hard to keep the bank afloat and when they have their life's work and wealth tied to that bank. As you can imagine, it's a rotten experience for the bankers and owners. In a bank closure, the FDIC must serve as the "receiver" of the failed bank. That means they literally take over running the bank until they can sell everything to another institution or sell it off in pieces. They try to sell it outright using a bidding process among interested buyers.

The FDIC keeps a database of banks that are eligible to bid on a failed institution and that have expressed an interest in buying based on the institution's size, type, geography, etc. When the time comes, the FDIC reviews the safety and soundness of the potential bidders to be sure they can manage the purchase if they are the winning bidder. If it all looks good, they trim down the list to a manageable number and then invite them to review the failed bank's assets and place a bid. The highest bid doesn't guarantee a winner because the FDIC has to decide if the bid is good enough or if they can get a better deal some other way.

The senior people working at the bank to be closed know they may be shut down, but are almost always unaware of when it will be closed. It is all done secretly for a lot of reasons. For one, if the bank is aware it is about to be shut down and reveals it to the customers, the customers might panic and come running in for their deposits. They already have deposit insurance for up to $250,000, but their panic can make a bad problem worse. Also, some bankers may have done something illegal and might be arrested when the bank is shut down. You never want to tip them off in advance so they can destroy evidence. In some cases, a banker might approve and fund (bad) loans or otherwise impair the bank's assets before closing. But most importantly, and not to sound alarmist, it might be dangerous for the FDIC staff that physically comes into the bank if an unstable bank officer, owner, or employee has decided to become confrontational. With time to plan, sick and twisted folks might bring weapons into the bank or otherwise prepare for a battle, and that's a risk you don't need to take.

When the FDIC shuts down a bank, they will typically determine the winning bidder by midweek and have the details worked out with the buying bank by that Friday. They then quietly travel to the area, and their staff will wait until the senior team goes into the bank in the late afternoon to announce the closure. Closures are not *totally* unexpected because everybody knows the bank had problems, but it is still a surprise to the folks working there. The FDIC will have security with them, and the bank's senior staffs are usually escorted out of the building. The FDIC staff then enters the bank to begin working long hours—counting cash, securing assets, and separating items that the winning bidder will keep with their purchase from those that the FDIC will keep. A note is posted on the door that it has been taken over by the FDIC and that the bank will reopen on the next business day.

When it reopens, it is under new ownership. In a good scenario, the entire operation, including all loans, deposits, and investments, is sold, and there is no exposure to the FDIC insurance fund. In other scenarios, the bank is sold piecemeal, with a bank buying only the deposits, for example, or buying the loans under a loss sharing agreement (where the FDIC assumes losses up to some dollar amount). Sometimes the FDIC can't find a buyer and will simply hire another bank to manage the deposits for a set amount of time (such as six months) as they go about trying to collect outstanding loans and sell off assets. They have been known to be quite unrelenting and occasionally uncaring when collecting loans, even good loans, they obtained from failed institutions. Clearly, they exist to protect depositors. They make fewer friends with borrowers.

In the recent financial crisis, some have suggested that the FDIC consider running the failed bank itself until markets stabilize, and it can get a better sale price. The problem now is that many potential buyers will wait for the bank to fail outright and then bid on the remaining good assets and loans at very low prices—leaving the FDIC with tremendous losses. If the FDIC could manage the bank until markets stabilized and they could get a better price, losses to the insurance fund and expenses for taxpayers might be a lot less. This proposal has a lot of merit. But there is no guarantee that the FDIC officials could run the bank any better than the bankers themselves did, and there is no guarantee that the market price would improve. The taxpayers or the insurance fund might also be worse off.

The challenge may have less to do with the proposal's financial merits than with the public's perceptions. If the FDIC took over a failed bank until the bank could be sold at a profit, that would mean that we have "nationalized" it, and for many people that is something only a communist or socialist country would do, not a capitalist country. To them, it doesn't matter how much it is now costing the industry or the taxpayers. Just the thought of our government running a bank is unacceptable to them.

The FDIC often sells the bank assets (furniture, computers, and repossessed vehicles) through auctions. You can get a list of all assets for sale at www.fdic.gov.

The FDIC sells a fair amount of real estate too, through hired brokers and auctions, and directly. Their website does a nice job of posting all eligible properties, with contact information and photographs. In fact, the website is full of really good (and free) information covering everything from a list of all failed institutions to consumer protection rights. The free online subscription service also does a good job alerting the public of everything from fraudulent bank checks to recent bank failures.

Summary

Running a regulatory agency is not easy. There are plenty of critics, and it is difficult to please everybody. The successes are expected, typically go unnoticed, and are not often rewarded. The failures are very different: unexpected, high profile, and unacceptable. Sometimes it's hard for government regulators to attract and retain the most skilled staff because the private sector can offer better compensation packages to steal away the best people. Somehow regulatory agencies manage to hold their own anyway. They earn their respect.

I suppose it's the same with any government agency. Not everybody wants to do the job or deal with the criticism that comes with it. It's unfortunate that some people find the work distasteful. They shouldn't. It can become a very rewarding and satisfying career.

He wasn't always that way, but my father became one of those people who came to dislike public service. As a younger man, he was one of many World War II military heroes. My father, Robert F. Dufries, was awarded the Bronze Star, the US Armed Forces' fourth-highest award for bravery, and four other medals. He was a good man, a family man. He loved our country and our government.

He died of natural causes in 2009, but like so many super seniors in their early nineties, he also experienced mild dementia. Nighttime is especially hard for many elderly people because they are sometimes confused, a condition known as "sundowners syndrome."

I remember him calling me early one night. Dad believed he had been kidnapped and was being held hostage downtown. He was furious at his captors, who had forced him into the worst possible labor, and he wanted to be rescued immediately. He couldn't bear the work one minute longer. He wanted out. Now! He was angry and agitated. And who could blame him?

His captors had made him the mayor of Atlanta.

Federal Financial Institutions Examination Council (FFIEC)

The current regulatory structure is confusing, and, until recently, nobody was interested in doing away with banks having a choice between a state and a federal charter. The result is that we have a system with many regulators. They sometimes have different laws, rules, and regulations, and this creates problems, especially for larger bank holding companies that may own several different types of banks and could be subject to conflicting regulations and reporting requirements. To make matters worse, banks can and do "shop around" and switch their charters depending on the regulator they think will be the most lenient.

Politicians have never had the appetite or the ability to truly eliminate the redundancy, but they did manage on March 10, 1979, to establish the Federal Financial Institutions Examination Council (FFIEC), which is charged with making the examinations of banks, thrifts, and credit unions consistent.

The five original members of the FFIEC—the Federal Deposit Insurance Corporation (FDIC), the Federal Reserve System, the National Credit Union Administration (NCUA), the Office of the Comptroller of the Currency (OCC), and the Office of Thrift Supervision (OTS)—helped develop uniform principles, standards, and reporting along with uniform examination procedures. In 2006, the State Liaison Committee (SLC) was added to the council to be sure the states also had a voice. This group included state bank supervisors, state savings supervisors, and state credit union supervisors. In 2009, the new regulator for Fannie Mae, Freddie Mac, and the Federal Home Loan Banks—the Federal Housing Finance Agency (FHFA)—was also added to the council.

Although there will always be cultural and philosophical differences among the agencies, the FFIEC has done a very good job at promoting consistency and providing examiner training programs. The extensive programs are impressive, and since 1979 the Council has provided training for over eighty-eight thousand participants, including state regulators, which is a healthy way to ensure consistency and professionalism in the regulatory system.

By law, the FFIEC receives no tax dollars and instead is funded by assessments charged to the Federal Reserve, OCC, OTS, FDIC, and NCUA. The FFIEC is headquartered in Arlington, Virginia.

Chapter 7
Government-Sponsored Enterprises

Sometimes things just don't turn out the way you figured.

Consider the Barbie bandits: nineteen-year-old Ashley Nicole Miller and twenty-year-old Heather Lyn Johnston. These women teamed with twenty-three-year-old Benny Allen III and twenty-seven-year-old Michael Darrell Chastang, to rob a Bank of America grocery store branch in Acworth, Georgia. The two pretty strippers (exotic dancers, if you prefer) wore designer sunglasses and tight jeans and were laughing as they robbed the bank of $11,000 in February 2007 from bank teller and cohort Benny Allen.

Pictured clockwise are Miller, Johnston, Chastang, and Allen. Miller and Johnston photo courtesy of Cobb County Police Department. Chastang and Allen photo courtesy of Cobb County Sheriff's Office.

Following the robbery, the women went on a local spending spree at some nearby upscale malls and then got their hair done at a fancy salon. When the Cobb County Police Department released the bank's surveillance camera photo, local media quickly capitalized on the story. Given their good looks, the media began calling the women Barbie bandits (after the famous Barbie doll). Of course, hundreds of tips came in (mostly from men, I presume) identifying the two popular strippers, and they quickly became an international media sensation and a big hit on the Internet.

They were arrested two days after the heist. Johnston, who was more honest and forthcoming to the police than the others, received ten years on probation, had to repay the bank, perform community service, and pay a

$2,000 fine. Miller received a two-year prison sentence followed by eight years of probation.

Allen advised the women what to write on the robbery note they handed him. (All loose bills. No strapped cash. Remember I will not hesitate to kill you. Keep hands where I can see them. Do not pull switch.) He also had to give the women directions to his bank when they called his cell phone. They had gone to the wrong branch earlier that day. Because he was already on five years' probation for a previous drug offense, he received a five-year prison sentence. Miller's boyfriend at the time, Chastang, was the guy who devised the plan. He had a previous felony record for theft, drugs, and weapons, and was given a twenty-five-year prison sentence: ten years for the robbery on top of fifteen years for prior felony conviction.

So the women got probation or a two-year jail term. The men got five years and twenty-five years in jail.[172] I think it's safe to say things didn't turn out as they planned.

These stories are unrelated, of course, but like so many of the government programs we have today, things rarely turn out exactly as you might think. At least with government programs, many of which were done in response to hard or even desperate times, it's actually worked out pretty well for us, and that is covered in this chapter. The two very notable exceptions (Fannie Mae and Freddie Mac) are covered in the next chapter.

We got this way for a reason.

Consider the process of getting a loan. Most of us go directly to a lender at a bank, thrift, or credit union, or we may find a money broker, such as a mortgage lender, who will shop around for us. These financial institutions all have built-in limitations—our deposits. If they can't get other sources of money besides our deposits, especially long-term sources, they will run short of cash and be reluctant to lend for anything other than for a short time, around ten years max. That's just one of the reasons our government developed some housing and business lending programs. It was to ensure everybody who was creditworthy would have access to the money needed to prosper and to achieve what has been called the American dream: home ownership or owning a business, or both.

The first of these government programs was designed to help farmers get credit in parts of the country where there were few if any banks. What banks they had didn't have enough deposits to meet the loan demand. Later, government programs were established to provide longer terms and less expensive housing loans. These longer-term loans helped the (nonprofit) thrift industry provide affordable loans for middle-income families to buy a house. Other programs also emerged to encourage lenders to give loans to business owners who have *slightly* higher risk profiles. These government incentives include guarantees to the lenders that they'll get their money back in case the borrower defaults on the loan.

In some cases, the government administers these programs through government agencies, such as the Small Business Administration (SBA) and the Federal Housing Administration (FHA). But we also have many hybrid organizations, those *private* companies that were chartered, supported, and broadly regulated by the government. These hybrid organizations, known as government-sponsored enterprises (GSEs), include institutions as diverse as the Tennessee Valley Authority and the US Postal Service.

Because they are so large and contain substantial risk, two of them—the Farm Credit System and the Federal Home Loan Bank System—are featured in this chapter.

Farm Credit System: *Our First GSE*

A lot of people have no idea that around a third of all farmers, ranchers, and agricultural cooperative loans come from a government program called the Farm Credit System, our nation's first and oldest government-sponsored enterprise (GSE). The GSE was chartered in 1916 with twelve Federal Land Banks across the country, much like the Federal Home Loan Bank System and Federal Reserve System. It allowed lenders to make longer-term loans for farmers and ranchers to buy land. Several years later, in 1923, the Agricultural Credits Act was passed to give farmers access to shorter-term loans to buy crops and machinery.

None of these programs were able to withstand the Great Depression, when falling prices kept farmers from repaying their loans, so the federal government stepped in with a couple of huge bailout plans. One law provided $200 million in emergency loans (about $516 million today) specifically to farmers to refinance some of their existing loans for longer terms and lower monthly payments.[173] Another law restricted the ability of banks to foreclose on their family farms.[174] A third law, the Farm Credit Act of 1933, established the system that resembles what we have today.

That last law, the Farm Credit Act, nationalized lending programs for farmers. In a bit of a screwy manner, its twelve Federal Land Banks gave long-term land loans, and its twelve Federal Intermediate Credit Banks gave loans for crops, machinery, and other short- or *intermediate*-term loans to new local Production Credit Associations, which would then lend it to farmers and ranchers, and to rural residents for housing. The act also established twelve banks for cooperatives, to provide loans to farmers' cooperatives, and a central bank for cooperatives, to handle the loan requests that were too large for the smaller co-ops. All these organizations were to be supervised by the Farm Credit Administration.

It would appear that whoever came up with the Farm Credit System structure must have been drunk.

So we had federal land banks, federal intermediate credit banks, production credit associations, banks for cooperatives, and a central bank for co-ops. It would appear that whoever came up with the Farm Credit System structure must have been drunk. Like the regulatory structure for banks and thrifts, the current Farm Credit System has evolved over time. But its origin was necessary because banks and thrifts were not able to meet the credit needs of people living in rural areas. At the time, commercial banks were not even permitted to make real estate loans. They also had restrictions on opening branch offices that limited them from better meeting rural credit needs. So these government programs reflected the political reality of the times when farmers' and ranchers' interests were a major concern to their elected congressmen.

A government-sponsored credit system like this for farmers and ranchers shouldn't be too surprising. Farmers in particular have always been a special interest group that receives favorable legislation from the federal government. For example, crop subsidies alone totaled an astounding $177 billion from 1995 to 2006, including $13.4 billion in 2006 alone (to 1.4 million recipients).[175] Apparently, Americans don't object to family farm subsidies. A University of Maryland study in 2009 found that 77 percent supported giving small farmers (under five hundred acres) subsidies, although 61 percent opposed giving subsidies to large farming businesses.[176]

We have a long history of giving cash subsidies and passing other laws in support of family farms. In 1933, one law allowed the federal courts to just reduce a farmer's bank loan to the value of the land. If the farmer could then afford the reduced loan amount (over six years at 1 percent interest), he wouldn't have to pay anything more. If he couldn't afford the new loan, he could still farm his land and be a paying tenant.[177] Bankers cried foul, and the Supreme Court did rule the law was unconstitutional because it allowed the farmer to take land from the mortgage holder without due process. So Congress passed another law in 1935 that allowed bankrupt farmers to stay on their land for three years if they paid a fair rent. This one passed legal muster and was renewed several times before it expired in 1947.[178]

A major way of supporting farmers has always been the Farm Credit System, especially with the changes during the 1930s and '50s. But the biggest changes occurred with the bailout of the system after a farm crisis occurred in the late 1980s.

1980s' Farm Crisis

Looking back, it is easy to see how the farm crisis happened. In the 1960s and '70s, technology was improving. New machinery, pesticides, and irrigation products were making greater levels of production possible. Interest rates were relatively low. The prime rate was under 6 percent for most of the 1960s, and farmers could borrow from the Farm Credit System at lower rates than commercial banks were offering. Farmers were expanding operations rapidly, and they were incurring big debts to buy new equipment, land, seeds, fertilizers, and pesticides. Lenders were more than happy to provide the credit because land values were increasing, and using land as collateral gave more than enough protection to support the loans. More importantly though, foreign markets, particularly the Soviet Union, which had suffered a severe drought, were willing to pay higher food prices that supported the farmers' increased debt levels. *Bigger is not always better.*

It all began to change in the late 1970s and early '80s when inflation became such a problem that the Federal Reserve began raising short-term interest rates to slow the economy. The Fed had reduced the money supply, which meant that the dollar got stronger and other countries had to pay more for US crops. Foreign demand for crops also declined a lot because third-world countries were having problems repaying their debts. Then too, the United States suspended food shipments to the Soviet Union after it invaded Afghanistan in 1980. Because of higher interest rates, overproduction, and less demand for grain, we had a serious debt crisis. Farmers simply couldn't repay their loans. The bubble had burst, and land prices that had been climbing rapidly during the 1960s and '70s came crashing down.

From 1980 to '86, farm real estate value dropped so much ($293 billion) that it became very difficult to use the land as collateral to refinance debts or get new loans. Even worse, it became impossible for many farmers to sell their land and pay off their debts.[179]

By 1985, the Farm Credit System was in a serious bind. By one estimate, two hundred thousand to three hundred thousand farmers were facing financial ruin. The Farm Credit System of lenders that provided these loans reported net losses of $2.7 billion in 1985 and another $1.9 billion in 1986. According to the system's regulator, the Farm Credit Administration (FCA), these losses were the largest in history for any US financial institution![180] *It's almost always bad loans.*

It was under this cloud and the near complete collapse of the Farm Credit System that Congress *again* stepped in with two bailout bills. The Farm Credit Act Amendments of 1985 beefed up the FCA's enforcement powers and required that their direct-lending institutions be examined annually, similar to commercial banks and thrifts. The Agricultural Credit Act of 1987 went even further when it reorganized the Farm Credit System, created an insurance fund for the lenders, and pumped in $4 billion to the troubled lenders (equivalent to about $7.5 billion in 2009). The bill also created a new government-sponsored enterprise, the Federal Agricultural Mortgage Corporation (Farmer Mac).

Farmer Mac was chartered to create a secondary market for the agricultural real estate and home mortgage loans. This secondary market would raise money cheaply by selling bonds on Wall Street and would use the proceeds to buy the farm and ranch loans. This would free up money to lend again and reduce interest rates for farmers.

The Farm Credit System today is a $215 billion-plus network. Take a deep breath because you won't believe how many institutions are in this network. It's got a regulator (Farm Credit Administration), a trade association (Farm Credit Council), a funding company to raise money (Federal Farm Credit Banks Funding Corporation), a leasing company to support low-cost and tax-advantaged leases for vehicles and equipment (Farm Credit Leasing), a secondary market to buy and package loans for resale (Farmer Mac), and five wholesale cooperative banks that provide loans to over ninety smaller cooperatives and lending companies.

A bit much, isn't it? These massive programs have evolved over time in no small part because our elected representatives believe a privileged and protected food supply is in our national interest. Is there a better way? Perhaps. But one thing is certain: *we got this way for a reason.*

The Farm Credit System is a GSE owned by their members, not by the government. All the profits besides what they keep to support future growth or to protect against potential losses are for their members, not the government. Farmers and others who borrow from the Farm Credit lenders have to purchase stock (usually between $1,000 and $5,000) in their association as a condition for getting a loan. No problem. The money to buy that stock is usually included in the loan amount, so the borrower doesn't have to pay anything out-of-pocket to join the association. The borrower gets his or her money back when the loan is repaid.

Because history has shown taxpayers will bail out the farm lending system when needed, a strong regulator is necessary to keep us from having to do so. That's why this system is regulated by an independent federal agency, the Farm Credit Administration (FCA) in McLean, Virginia. They examine all banks, associations, and related entities in the system, including Farmer Mac. This regulator receives no tax dollars and is funded from assessments that the institutions it regulates must pay. *Good government is necessary.*

Farm Credit Funding

The Farm Credit System has an interesting loan distribution system. There are five huge wholesale lenders set up to fund and support about ninety smaller local lending associations. These lending associations have several hundred branches around the country operating as agricultural credit associations, production credit associations, or the nonprofit federal land credit associations. Their differences are mainly in what kinds of loans and terms they offer. These associations lend directly to farmers, ranchers, and others.

No member of the Farm Credit System, including the five wholesale lenders, the ninety or so associations they support, or any of their local branches in rural America are *depository institutions.* None of them offer FDIC-insured checking or savings accounts. Instead, they get money to lend from a company called the Federal Farm Credit Banks Funding Corporation (Funding Corporation) that sells debt securities to Wall Street investors.

The buyers of these securities include mutual funds, commercial banks, savings banks, international banks, pension funds, hedge funds, insurance companies, foundations, and state and local governments. These are not officially "government-guaranteed securities," but of course investors believe the government will bail them out in a crisis—which is always the case—so credit agencies rate these securities very highly. With a high rating and an implied government backing, the interest rate that investors will accept is pretty low. This means that the Farm Credit System lenders can get their money cheaper, and their borrowers can frequently get their loans cheaper than they could at a commercial bank or thrift.

Although our government is not officially on the hook to bail out the Farm Credit System or any other GSE, we have a history of doing exactly that, not only with Farm Credit System but more recently with Fannie Mae and Freddie Mac (covered in the next chapter). For example, Farmer Mac already has substantial government backing, including a $1.5 billion line of credit with the US Treasury in 2009. Congress has tried to create a program to prevent any future taxpayer farm lending bailouts, or at least reduce the cost if one was necessary. The last big bailout of the Farm Credit System, in 1987, required that, going forward, the associations must contribute to a separate insurance fund just in case things got bad again. It's called the Farm Credit System Insurance Corporation.

This insurance fund is a good idea. It is supposed to ensure payment on these Funding Corporation securities so the investors don't lose money or the government doesn't get stuck with the bill. Generally speaking, the fund has to equal at least 2 percent of the associations' borrowings. This $3.3 billion Farm Credit insurance fund (at year-end 2009) might seem big, but we've seen that it really isn't when there's a deep or prolonged economic downturn. What's even more alarming than the modest fund size is that it is *legally prevented* from exceeding 2 percent. Anything more than that must be refunded to the associations. That's not to mention that the fund was *below* the 2 percent obligation for five years in a row (beginning in 2003)! Look, insurance funds are great, but they can get depleted fast in a crisis. Underfunded insurance funds get depleted even faster! It appears their new premium structure setup in 2009 will help keep the fund from falling short again. Here's hoping. The fund isn't all that big to start with. *Accounting is not a game.*

Wholesale Lenders

As mentioned, there are five huge wholesale lenders set up to fund and support about ninety smaller local lending associations. They have some overlapping jurisdictions and include four farm credit banks and one nationwide agricultural credit bank.

- AgriBank, FCB (for Farm Credit Bank) is a $70 billion company in St. Paul, Minnesota, that lends money to agricultural credit associations. For comparison, if they were a commercial bank instead of a farm credit bank, they would be the twentieth largest bank in the country! That's bigger than Morgan Stanly Bank (New

York), Compass Bank (Alabama), Northern Trust Co. (Illinois), and Bank of the West (California) *Bigger is not always better.*

- CoBank, ACB (for Agricultural Credit Bank) is a $61 billion company in Denver, Colorado, that lends money to cooperatives engaged in agribusinesses, agriculture, rural energy, rural communications, and rural water companies. They also fund five larger agricultural credit associations (ACAs), which in turn lend the money to farmers, ranchers, aquatic producers, rural home owners, and rural businesses. In December 2010, they announced a proposal to merge with US AgBank, which, if approved by shareholders and their regulator, would make them the largest wholesale lender in the system. If they were a commercial bank, they would be the seventeenth-largest bank in the country, bigger than Union Bank (California) and KeyBank (Ohio).
- US AgBank, FCB is a $30 billion company in Wichita, Kansas.
- AgFirst Farm Credit Bank is a $32 billion company in Columbia, South Carolina.
- Farm Credit Bank of Texas is a $20 billion company in Austin, Texas.

Male Dominance

The five wholesale lending companies are governed by their own boards of directors, elected by their membership. Although their regulator suggests diversity among their board (including gender), they are all male-dominated institutions. Over 93 percent of the boards and 92 percent of their executive teams are men. Consider these numbers from 2009:

- Fourteen of sixteen board members (87.5 percent) and seven of eight senior officers (87.5 percent) at CoBank were men.
- Seventeen of eighteen board members (94.4 percent) and ten of eleven executive officers (90.9 percent) at AgriBank were men.
- Nineteen of twenty board members (95 percent) and the seven executive officers (100 percent) at AgFirst were men.
- Sixteen board members (100 percent) and six executive officers (100 percent) at US AgBank were men.
- Six of seven board members (85.7 percent) and five of six executive officers (83.3 percent) at Farm Credit Bank of Texas were men.

Choosing good board members and executive officers is difficult. But the low percentage of women in leadership roles at these multibillion-dollar companies is ridiculous. At a minimum, it's a missed opportunity to get a healthy diversity of views, another opportunity for business networking, and, of course, an improved reputation. In short, lack of diversity weakens the company. After all, the 2007 Census of Agriculture reported that women operated over 306,000 farms, with 64.3 million acres, and represented 27.2 percent of all farmers. Too bad these boards don't better reflect that constituency. *People matter.*

To their credit, it appears the FCA regulators are well aware of the issues confronting the wholesale lenders. That's good news for everybody. There are still some red flags worthy of mention though.

One of the red flags that is hard to ignore and yet hard to prevent is an institution's rapid growth. Regulators know that rapid growth often leads to problems with internal controls, asset quality, and capital. And although growing from $100 million to $200 million might be manageable, it is a whole different ball game for multibillion-dollar institutions. That's why we all hope that the FCA regulators are closely watching institutions like AgriBank and CoBank. AgriBank grew from $42 billion to $70 billion over five years, and CoBank's size nearly doubled, from $31 billion in 2004 to $61billion in 2008, over the same time period.[181]

CoBank would increase in size another 49 percent assuming it merges with US AgBank, in 2011, making it a $91 billion lending institution. It is worrisome to see this kind of rapid growth. If the deal goes through as expected, CoBank would have grown 194 percent over seven years! That's getting big fast! *Bigger is not always better.*

Sure, it is nice to have a wider variety of loans spread over a larger geographic area. But you have to be concerned about how hard it is for these institutions to have enough capital to keep up with the growth. The amount of capital at CoBank, for example, has struggled to keep pace. The ratio of total capital to assets has gone steadily down from 8.58 percent in 2005 to only 5.88 percent in 2008.

They haven't gotten in deep trouble with their regulator because the Farm Credit Administration allows a "permanent capital ratio" of 7 percent. This ratio includes preferred stock and term stock with maturity over five years. CoBank has relied on these expensive capital sources to fund growth. For example, they borrowed $500 million priced at over 7 percent, and they had $200 million of preferred stock that pays a guaranteed 11 percent dividend. Both were issued in 2008, both count as capital, and both are alarming.[182]

The debts are not guaranteed by the insurance fund or the US government, but this is really expensive debt that CoBank can count as capital, and it's not very comforting that the company is using it to support its rapid growth. After all, the more expensive your debt, the more you have to earn to cover the cost. For some lenders, that requires taking higher risks to get higher interest and fees. Let's hope that the lender and their regulator really understand these risks and that the FCA doesn't get caught up in "regulatory capture" like other regulators have. It could be one of our lessons never learned: ***we should have seen it coming.***

Competitor Complaints

Although they still hold a much larger market share, commercial and thrift bankers who compete for the larger, highest quality loans have said it is hard to beat a Farm Credit System lender for those customers' business. The Farm Credit lender obtains their loan money from the sale of low-cost securities that have an implied government guarantee. That means they can offer lower interest rates to their customers. Sometimes commercial and thrift lenders can offer other advantages to their customers: superior customer service, less stringent underwriting standards, or faster response times, for example. But given the Farm Credit System's built-in, government- subsidized lower cost of funds, it has a decided advantage in competing for the best quality loans.

Banks and thrifts are sometimes frustrated that some Farm Credit lenders look like they are "cherry-picking" loans. They seem to be funding strong, large, and high-quality borrowers while ignoring the smaller, higher-risk borrowers. The concern isn't new, and after hearing enough people complain about it, Congress responded. Amendments to the Farm Credit Act in 1980 began requiring that each Farm Credit System institution develop a program to furnish "sound and constructive credit" for young (under thirty-five years old), beginning, and small farmers and ranchers. They have to develop a "YBS" Report each year on their success in lending to these borrowers.[183] ***People matter.***

Banks and thrifts are also concerned that Farm Credit lenders can finance "off-farm" loans as long as they are in the interests of farmers and ranchers. That means that Farm Credit lenders can loan money for restaurants, condominiums, veterinary clinics, rural estates, weekend getaways, and hunting preserves, etc. Sure, Farm Credit lenders may want to book the off-farm loans to reduce their concentration of agricultural loans. After all, Farm Credit lenders will feel the full brunt of a bad ag economy, and they like the product diversity. But these loans are not entirely consistent with their charter, especially the nonprofit charters.[184] Not all Farm Credit lenders have expertise in these types of loans either.

Overall, the Farm Credit System is doing what it was designed to do: It gives a lot of low-cost loans to US farmers and ranchers. The challenges the Farm Credit System face are just that: challenges. To their credit, they are successfully managing those challenges. They have avoided disasters, and that says a lot about the Farm Credit System as the Panic of 2008 and the recession that went with it took down two other GSEs, Fannie Mae and Freddie Mac.

But it is not unreasonable to ask whether we really need a Farm Credit System as a GSE. The system was originally established because access to credit in rural areas was scarce, especially before and during the Great Depression. That's not true anymore. Having the Farm Credit System or something like it around to ensure access to credit in all rural areas, and in particular during economic downturns, is a good idea. But as we learned from the experience with Fannie Mae and Freddie Mac, having a government guarantee, assumed or actual, can result in a very expensive taxpayer burden if problems arise with this special interest group again. We may clamor for less government or a smaller government, but with billions of taxpayer dollars at risk, we must have strong controls too. It is very hard to have it both ways: less government *and* strong oversight. Either we do it right and manage our risks fully and directly, or we privatize the system completely and reduce the risk to taxpayers in the process. *Good government is necessary.*

Federal Agricultural Mortgage Corporation (Farmer Mac)

Farmer Mac is a government-sponsored enterprise that buys agricultural or rural housing mortgage loans, packages them into securities, and sells them to investors. Farmer Mac also buys some securities for their own investment portfolio. In fact, Farmer Mac does about the same thing as Fannie Mae or Freddie Mac did, except that Farmer Mac focuses on agricultural loans, rural mortgage loans, and rural utilities loans

Having a secondary market for these loans is a great way to increase the availability of credit. In the past, lenders from banks, thrifts, and the Farm Credit System could lend until they ran out of cash. Having secondary market programs like Farmer Mac enables lenders to sell the loans at a small profit. They can often keep the rights to collect loan payments (servicing rights) that generate fee income and keep the customer relationship intact. The secondary market will free up cash for more loans and solve a big liquidity problem where banks simply run out of money to lend.

The downside with programs like this is that once a loan is sold to the secondary market, any losses on the loan go along with it unless there is some specific recourse in the deal (like a government guarantee). So if Farmer Mac buys the loans, they make the profits or suffer the losses on the loans too. When they package the loans into securities they sell, they still have some risk.

How well has Farmer Mac managed the risk? Well, 2008 was the worst year in their twenty-one-year history. They lost $154.1 million.

Part of the loss ($18 million) was caused by loaning too much to the ethanol industry, which was doing poorly. But it was owning Fannie Mae preferred stock and Lehman Brothers bonds that cost them $106 million! They also had to write down $85 million on financial derivatives they purchased to manage interest rate risk.

The interest-rate risk derivatives were like an insurance policy against changes in interest rates. If rates go one way, they get paid; if rates go the other way, they pay the other guy. The value of the derivatives products they owned plummeted, and, as a result, Farmer Mac had to write down their values substantially.

In 2008, Farmer Mac was a $10 billion stockholder-owned company regulated by the Farm Credit Administration. They had a $1.5 billion line of credit with the US Treasury to ensure payments on the securities, and, let's face it, they have more than an implied government guarantee. History has shown us: it's quite real.

Federal Home Loan Bank System: *Our Largest GSE*

Let's go back to the Great Depression, which led to dramatic changes in how thrift institutions are chartered and regulated. At the time, local building and loan associations and mutual savings banks had a reputation of being safe havens for money, but changes were necessary because even they were not exempt from the horrendous economy. In spite of their good reputation, they too had failures just like their commercial bank counterparts. And remember, because there was no insurance on the deposits, customers lost money at the failed thrift institutions.

When the stock market crashed in 1929, Herbert Hoover was only eight months into his presidency, and, unfortunately for everybody, his term expired before the crisis ended. It's hard to find kind words for President Hoover. He never visited breadlines or Hoovervilles, the poorest sections of towns, which were derisively named in his "honor." Crudely built shacks and tents housed homeless men, women, and children, and food was in short supply. He once declared, "No one is actually starving," and claimed to know of "one hobo in New York who got ten meals in one day." Nice.

When campaigning for reelection, President Hoover proclaimed, "Let no man tell you it could not be worse. It could be so much worse that these days now, distressing as they are, would look like veritable prosperity." Comforting. He initially opposed federal aid to reduce the suffering and advocated instead for volunteerism and self-initiative. Lame. At the same time, he was promoting a balanced budget and less government. In fact, he was given the nickname "President Reject" for opposing so many programs. Rejecting government help met his ideological views, but it did nothing to reduce hunger, homelessness, unemployment, bankruptcy, depression, and suicide, all of which were increasing during the Great Depression.

The suffering was horrendous, and his words and actions were out of touch and callous. Looking back, some of the opposition to his administration was somewhat funny, such as the time he was booed with chants of "We want beer" at a baseball game because he opposed repealing the prohibition of alcohol. Other times, the anger was far more dangerous. During his campaign for reelection, his train was pelted with eggs and tomatoes on several occasions. In Detroit, the crowds chanted "Hang Hoover! Hang Hoover! Hang Hoover!" *People matter.*

But before anybody at Stanford University, home of the Hoover Tower building and the Hoover Institution Research Center founded by the former president, starts burning this book, let's give him credit. He was one of only two presidents to ever refuse his salary (John F. Kennedy was the other), and he generously gave his time and money to charity, particularly to the Boys Club of America, and especially after his presidential term ended. He was also an advocate of public-private partnerships, where limited government funds could be combined with private funding to accomplish social and economic goals. Public-private partnerships take work to implement, but they are a good idea. And late in his term he did change course by implementing two significant financial programs. *Good government is necessary.*

The first program he supported would charter the Reconstruction Finance Corporation, an agency that gave direct loans to troubled banks, railroads, savings and loans, and life insurance companies. At first, its impact was limited, but it eventually served its purpose well.

The second significant legislation during Hoover's term was the Federal Home Loan Bank Act of 1932 (FHLB Act). The FHLB Act created a new GSE that provided cash (liquidity) to thrifts and other mortgage lenders so they could refinance mortgage loans and originate new ones.

FHLB Structure

Writing the FHLB Act wasn't particularly hard because a similar proposal—the Federal Building Loan Bank Act—had been prepared in 1919, but after a series of House and Senate hearings, it went nowhere. This new bill created something that mirrored the Federal Reserve System, which was written into law nineteen years earlier. The Federal Home Loan Bank System had twelve regional Federal Home Loan Bank (FHLB) offices. Each one had its own employees, board of directors, and management, and each operated independently of the others.

Together, they received $122 million from the government to get started (which has since been repaid) and were purposely headquartered in cities where the Federal Reserve Banks were *not* located.[185] They now have their offices in Atlanta, Boston, Chicago, Cincinnati, Dallas, Des Moines, Indianapolis, New York, Pittsburgh, San Francisco, Seattle, and Topeka.

Membership in an FHLB is voluntary. The FHLB members (stockholders) were originally just thrifts but now include banks and others. Members join because they can get low-cost loans (called advances) from their regional FHLB, which they use to fund loans to their banking customers. The banking customer loans serve as collateral for even more advances from the regional FHLB, and the process repeats itself. The interest rates members pay for the advances varies among the regional FHLBs depending on the product type and term. At one time, the rates were publicly available and published on the regional FHLB's websites, but only a few do so now.

Collectively, the twelve FHLBs form the nation's largest government-sponsored enterprise.[186] Their combined total assets were $1.4 trillion at the end of 2009! That's far less than the $2.5 trillion Federal Reserve System, but for perspective, if they were a commercial bank, they would be the fifth-largest bank in the United States. However, they aren't the Federal Reserve, and they aren't a bank. The regional FHLBs may have been chartered by the government and backed by the government, but they are still separate legal entities formed as cooperatives. Their stockholders (membership) in 2009 included 1,167 thrifts, 5,849 commercial banks, 952 credit unions, and even 184 insurance companies.[187] Generally speaking, these members must be a "community financial institution" or have over 10 percent of their assets in products having to do with mortgages.

The regional FHLBs' stock is not publicly traded or quoted. The FHLB of San Francisco is the largest in the group, with total assets of $244.9 billion, followed by Atlanta with assets of $140.8 billion. The smallest is Des Moines, with assets of $42 billion, but Des Moines has the most members too (1,247 institutions), followed by Atlanta (1,210 institutions).[188] Unlike the District Federal Reserve Banks, whose independence from the Board of Governors was constrained following the Great Depression, the regional FHLBs have still maintained a lot of their independence.

Federal S&L Charters

I would probably have to temper my favorable opinion of the FHLBs if I had known them when they first began in 1932. They were supposed to refinance large numbers of distressed mortgage loans, but they only approved three loans *out of 41,000 applications* in their first two years! They had the authority, and they had the mandate, and they failed on both counts.[189] I'm not sure who got those three loans, but it sure smells rotten, doesn't it?

It was no laughing matter at the time either. Their regulator at the time, the Federal Home Loan Bank Board, Washington DC (FHLB Board), reported that in 1933, about one thousand home loans were foreclosed *every day*! A Department of Commerce study in 1934 found that 44 percent of all urban home owners with mortgages were in default and had been past due on payments for an average of fifteen months![190] That's just incredible! In comparison, the Mortgage Bankers Association reports that the combined past due and foreclosure rate at year-end 2008 was 11.93 percent, the highest level since they began tracking the data back in 1972, but, fortunately, nowhere close to the worst of the Great Depression. Of course, claiming that things were not as bad as they had been in the Great Depression provides no comfort.

Although the FHLB charter allowed them to lend directly to home owners, it wasn't practical. The regional FHLBs had such limited resources that instead of lending directly to homeowners, they spent most of their first two years getting organized and lending to their building and loan association members. They made no real progress in stemming the tide of foreclosures or delinquencies either.

To try to get gun-shy lenders back into the game and at the same time be sure that rural areas were not overlooked, the Home Owners' Loan Act of 1934 authorized a new agency to buy bad loans from banks (see the HOLC sidebar). The HOLC was supervised by the FHLB Board. But the big deal here was that HOLC also authorized the FHLB Board to charter new federal savings and loan associations. If state chartered thrifts weren't going to make loans, perhaps a federally chartered thrift would get the job done! *We got this way for a reason.*

Not everybody liked the idea of a new federal charter. Some states rights advocates and state regulators did not like the idea of the federal government invading their turf, and some local thrifts didn't like the idea of more competition. But in spite of their opposition, the legislation was in place, and thus began the federal charter for savings and loan associations. It was a dual banking system, allowing the associations to choose between a state charter and a federal charter, just like we have now with commercial banks.

Roosevelt wasn't done yet. His administration also recognized that it needed to assure thrift lenders that the new loans they booked could be done safely. That assurance came in the form of a government insurance program, administered through an agency called the Federal Housing Administration (FHA). FHA was established specifically to provide insurance on mortgage loans so lenders would start booking them again. *We got this way for a reason.*

Reconstruction Finance Corporation (RFC)

Reviewing details of government programs is often boring unless the law authorizing the programs was named after one of your relatives. However, the RFC is interesting because the issues we faced at the start of the Great Depression are the same ones we faced seventy-five years later.

The RFC Act created a government agency to lend money to troubled banks, railroads, savings and loans, and life insurance companies. The idea was to keep these large private companies afloat because if they failed, the negative impact on the economy would be tremendous. If these large private companies failed, people not even on their payrolls would lose their jobs too. Their failure presented a "systemic risk" that would lead to other failures, such as their suppliers and vendors. In a sense, the loans were for companies considered too big to fail. Sound familiar? The $700 billion bailout authorized under the Emergency Economic Stabilization Act in 2008 was not the first time our government has stepped in to lend directly to private companies. The RFC did it before, lending $6.5 billion in its first five years alone (about $102 billion in 2009 dollars)!

The RFC was widely criticized in the beginning. There were insider transactions, unfulfilled commitments to state and local governments, and a focus on big businesses at the expense of small businesses and banks. Against the wishes of President Hoover, the public demanded to know where their money was being spent, so the names of the companies that borrowed were made public, and when that happened, folks rushed to sell their stock or withdraw their money from those companies. The same issue would arise again with similar emergency loans made by the Federal Reserve Bank to private businesses in 2008. Of course this only made things worse for those companies during the Great Depression, and it scared away a lot of companies that needed the money but couldn't afford to risk their reputations. They simply sat on the sidelines, reduced expenses as much as possible, and waited for a better day to come. Nobody won.

The Reconstruction Finance Corporation evolved significantly from its birth in 1932, assuming many different roles to support everything from agricultural programs to wars. It was formally dissolved in 1954.

Home Owners' Loan Corporation (HOLC)

Within the first one hundred days of his administration, Franklin Delano Roosevelt developed his "New Deal," which created some forty-two different agencies to address the depressed economy. Because of the criticism the FHLB System was getting for its lack of progress in refinancing troubled mortgage loans, President Roosevelt replaced all FHLB board members with his own team, and then he set out to get rid of the refinancing obstacles on these home loans. One of his solutions was a new law that established the Home Owners' Loan Corporation (HOLC), an agency within the Federal Home Loan Bank Board. The HOLC was authorized to refinance bad mortgage loans, thus removing the loans from the lenders' books and allowing families to stay in their homes as owners. The HOLC was a bank for bad assets, or, as we might call them today, toxic assets.

The HOLC was a hot topic again in 2008 when the country faced a similar dilemma of high delinquencies and foreclosure rates, and folks began pushing for a "Bad Assets Bank" modeled after the HOLC. But we should be careful when we compare the two crises because the Great Depression's real estate woes were caused by a very bad economy that led to job losses and *then* to housing problems. The 2008 crisis, on the other hand, was caused by excessive risk in housing loans that then led to a bad economy and job losses.

Even so, it wasn't unreasonable to suggest an HOLC strategy again because, although the HOLC may not have been 100 percent successful, it did generate a $14 million profit that was returned to the government when its mission ended.

The HOLC success is overstated a bit because in reality nearly half of the applications they received were either rejected or withdrawn. According to Morton Bodfish, one of the board members that the president replaced (and the head of the thrifts' trade association), the HOLC was intended to take care of the "exceptional borrower," whose loan problems were due to "his honest inability to discharge his obligation." It wasn't designed for folks who couldn't afford the loan in the first place. Even so, about 20 percent of the HOLC loans still ended up in foreclosure.

But, hey, these were weak loans to start with, and the number of foreclosures would have been a hell of a lot higher if the government hadn't done anything. Considering what might have happened, the number of HOLC foreclosures at that time doesn't seem so bad.

Federal Housing Administration (FHA)

Your Door to FHA HOMEOWNERSHIP

Solving the real estate problems during the Great Depression would clearly have taken more than a new federal thrift charter and federal deposit insurance program to protect customers. The problem then, as it was again in 2008–09, was persuading lenders that it was safe enough to begin lending again. One way to do that was to offer government insurance. That's exactly what FDR tried to do with the National Housing Act that created the Federal Housing Administration. The FHA is **not a government-sponsored enterprise**; it is a wholly owned agency of the government set up to provide mortgage insurance on loans originated by private lenders to buy, repair, or construct a home. The program is still working well today.

Although FHA mortgage insurance is costly, it allows people to get loans they might not otherwise get. The FHA is not the only mortgage insurance available—there are private mortgage companies too—but the FHA is the only government-sponsored mortgage insurance program. And it isn't especially cheap. Before 2008, its typical upfront fee was 1.5 percent of the loan amount (usually financed with the loan) plus an annual fee of 0.5 percent of the outstanding loan balance.

For example, on a $220,000 loan, the insurance premium is $3,300 upfront plus $91.67 a month for the first year. Generally, the monthly insurance premium continues until the loan is repaid or the loan-to-value ratio is 78 percent and the borrower has paid the premium for at least five years. Some borrowers today are required by their lenders to buy a similar insurance product with their mortgage, called PMI. But that's ***private mortgage insurance***, not the one from the FHA.

Before and during the Great Depression, most lenders would offer only loans up to 60 percent of the home's appraised value, and with a repayment schedule that required a full repayment within at least eleven years. The down payment was pretty hefty, and middle-class Americans had a hard time qualifying. Lenders were afraid to go with lower down payments because if they had to foreclose on the home, the home might not have enough value to cover the loan.

With mortgage insurance, any shortfall would be covered by the insurance policy. So lenders got protection and had more incentive to lend. With insurance backing the loan, lenders were more likely to allow smaller down payments and higher loan-to-value ratios of up to 80 percent in 1934, which was increased to 90 percent in 1938, and is now at an astonishing 96.5 percent.[191]

In 2009, borrowers could actually buy a house under the FHA insurance program with only a 3.5 percent down payment if they meet all the other underwriting standards. But that's what the government program is designed to do: encourage lenders to take more risks. Are there too many risks?

The delinquency rate for **all types of loans** outstanding in September 2008 was really high. It reached 5.06 percent for conventional, or "prime," loans; 13.73 percent for FHA loans; and 21.88 percent for high-risk, or "subprime," loans. These high past-due rates are worrisome, but while loans insured by the FHA perform far worse than conventional loans, they are not nearly as bad as subprime loans. But they are bad just the same.

More importantly, the government insurance fund has been able to handle the risk so far even though the fund dropped from 6.4 percent of loans outstanding in 2007 to only 0.50 percent in 2009. This drop in funds meant that the program was close to needing more money because federal law requires the insurance fund to have a reserve equal to at least 2 percent of its total insured loans.

It appears FHA has weathered the storm. In 2011, the premium structure changed, with a slight reduction in the upfront premium but a larger increase in the monthly premium. These changes were designed to replenish the fund without any taxpayer bailout.

But before we speak poorly of FHA, consider this: the FHA insurance pool (technically called the Mutual Mortgage Insurance Fund) was overfunded for many years, and it actually returned more than $13.5 billion in profits from 2001 to 2007 to the Treasury![192]

This raises a reasonable policy debate. Why should the Mutual Mortgage Insurance Fund give its profits back to the Treasury? Should it have reduced insurance premiums instead? Should it have plowed more into the insurance pool, which might have caused grumbling that the pool was "excessive"? That "excessive" pool would sure look better today! Should it have developed new programs with the money? Should it have rewarded its employees with higher salaries? Or should it have just given the money back to the government and let our elected officials figure out how to use it? All of the arguments have their pros and cons. But it seems a shame to tax the middle-class borrowers who use the program with higher premiums when they had already paid so much extra into this system.

The FHA became a part of the US Department of Housing and Urban Development (HUD) in 1965. FHA is self-funded. It earns its own income and doesn't require any tax dollars. It is the largest insurer of mortgages in the world. It does not lend money, and it does not plan or develop housing. In spite of complaints about its insurance premiums or potential taxpayer bailout risks, it has generally performed pretty darn well over the years.

FHLB Regulator

The FHLB Board was originally supposed to oversee the FHLBs, charter federal thrifts, and serve as a thrift regulator. They did a reasonably good job until the 1980s, when the S&L crisis hit. When it became evident that the FHLB Board was doing a terrible job regulating thrifts leading up to the savings and loan crisis in the mid-1980s, the federal government passed the Financial Institutions Reform, Recovery, and Enforcement Act of 1989 (FIRREA), a one-thousand-page law that covered a lot of ground.

FIERRA abolished the FHLB Board and transferred oversight of the regional FHLBs to a government agency called the Federal Housing Finance Board. It was funded by fees assessed to the FHLBs, not by taxpayers. The federal savings and loans themselves would now be chartered and regulated by a new agency too, the Office of Thrift Supervision. The FHLB Board had received the death sentence. Not the people, just the institution, of course.

In 1992, the Federal Housing Enterprises Financial Safety and Soundness Act created a new regulator for Fannie Mae and Freddie Mac called the Office of Federal Housing Enterprise Oversight (OFHEO). More recently, because Congress started worrying about weak oversight of GSEs in general, and Fannie Mae and Freddie Mac in particular, they passed the Housing and Economic Recovery Act of 2008. That act created a new regulator for Fannie, Freddie, and the FHLB: the Federal Housing Finance Agency (FHFA). The FHFA regulates all three GSEs. *Good government is necessary.*

When congress developed an S&L bailout plan in 1989, people were

With the 2008 collapse of Fannie Mae and Freddie Mac, Congress passed the Housing and Economic Recovery Act, which replaced their old regulator, the Office of Federal Housing Enterprise Oversight, with the Federal Housing Finance Agency (FHFA). This new agency was created to address the problems of the past and, in particular, to strengthen the regulator's budget, staffing, independence, and, most importantly, authority.

At the same time and even though they had fewer high-profile issues, Congress also eliminated the Federal Housing Finance Board, which was responsible for regulating the Federal Home Loan Banks, and placed them under the authority of the FHFA.

The FHFA is an independent agency headed by a director who is appointed by the president and confirmed by the Senate for a five-year term. It receives no federal tax dollars and instead pays its own expenses by charging fees to the institutions it regulates.

Sadly, it may very well have the lamest logo of any independent government agency, domestic or foreign.

mad. Then, as now, nobody likes to bail out an industry loaded with greed and excess. The name of the law itself—Reform, Recovery, and Enforcement—reflected public outrage that the FHLBs and thrifts had participated in unsafe banking practices that almost destroyed the industry. And why wouldn't the public be outraged? There is a long list of reasons, but to get a sense of some of the abuses, look at some of these high-profile thrift bankers from Texas.

- Stanley Adams, CEO of Lamar Savings and Loan Association in Austin, actually applied to open an S&L branch on the moon in 1985, had plans to build a sixty-two-story skyscraper in China, and (along with other thrift officers) was charged with looting more than $121 million through sham real estate transactions. The thrift failed in 1988.
- Don Dixon, CEO of Vernon Savings and Loan Association in Dallas, used bank money to buy a Colorado ski chalet for $1.9 million, a 112-foot yacht for $2.6 million, a Texas hunting lodge for $2.4 million, luxury cars for $1.8 million, a beach house for $2 million, and six jets for God knows how much. The thrift failed in 1987.

- Edwin T. McBirney, CEO of Sunbelt Savings Association of Texas, in Dallas, used bank money to throw lavish parties at his home, pay for his chauffeured limousine, and purchase **seven** planes, which he used for his frequent trips to Las Vegas. That thrift failed in 1988.

Part of the blame lay with the federal regulator, the FHLB Board, which succumbed to regulatory capture, exercised weak oversight, and made bad decisions. *Don't sleep with each other.* People were mad that so many thrifts were run by self-serving owners. These thrift managers had forgotten or never cared about their roots, in particular that of providing low-income people access to affordable loans. *Greed has a price.*

FHLBs don't receive any federal tax dollars to cover overhead expenses. They earn enough income themselves to pay their own way. Like the Federal Reserve Banks, the FHLBs are also exempt from all federal, state, and local taxes. However, the FHLBs aren't entirely free of taxes. They still pay taxes on real property, such as land and buildings. Also, as part of the industry's penalty for greed and excess, FIRREA requires the individual FHLBs to pay a 20 percent income tax to repay the $30 billion in government bonds that were issued to help fund the industry bailout.[193]

AHP and CIP

There was another penalty for the greed and excess that became evident during the S&L crisis. This one was designed to make sure that thrifts do more to serve low- and middle-income communities. After all, they had been given special tax breaks to provide affordable mortgage loans, and they had drifted pretty damn far from their origin as a savings bank for the working poor. That's why FIRREA requires each FHLB to contribute 10 percent of their profits to an Affordable Housing Program (AHP). *Greed has a price.*

The AHP is a huge program that provides grants (not loans) to support local housing programs. The grants are used by nonprofits, government agencies, and others that are working closely with FHLB members to provide affordable housing and to help revitalize distressed communities. The FHLBs also have a Community Investment Program (CIP) that offers below-market-rate loans (not grants) to their members for similar housing and economic development projects. It's remarkable that the FHLBs had lent $56 billion through the Community Investment Programs and had distributed about

$3.7 billion through their Affordable Housing Programs from 1990 to 2009. That's a whole lot of money!

Many folks may question the merit of the law and its taxes, but few would argue that the AHP money hasn't made a difference. In Atlanta, for example, the FHLB reported committing over $363 million since 1990 to help construct or repair more than sixty-five thousand homes. In San Francisco, it was $551 million over the same period. These are truly impressive programs for which the folks who put them together at each FHLB have every right to be proud. The AHP is just one of several programs for low- and moderate-income families and communities. Other programs also serve community and economic development projects and rural development projects. If you visit the FHLB websites, you can get a summary of the programs as well as information about how to apply for some of the money. It may not always be the case, but these programs have been run by some really good people committed to doing the right thing.

Financials

There is substantial risk to having a $1.4 trillion financial system like the FHLB System so heavily involved in mortgage-lending activities. Their primary source of funds is raised by selling bonds, primarily to investors on Wall Street. These debt instruments are "consolidated obligations" because all FHLBs are on the hook to pay the debt even if the proceeds only went to one FHLB. The debt instruments are given the highest possible ratings by the credit rating agencies in no small part because they have an implied government guarantee on their debts, much like Fannie Mae, Freddie Mac, and Farmer Mac.

The "implied" guarantee isn't just smoke and mirrors. The FHLBs could borrow over $100 billion from the US Treasury through year-end 2009; they are still authorized to sell $4 billion in debts to the Treasury if necessary; they don't use commercial banks but instead have a special account at the US Treasury to process their debt payments; they receive special consideration under national bankruptcy laws; and they have a superior lien (the FHLB gets first dibs) on a member bank's assets if their loans to the banks go bad. That superior lien is even higher than the FDIC would have![194] So we should all be concerned. It hasn't always been easy for them, especially following the financial Panic of 2008, as the table below shows:[195]

FHLB 2008 Financial Summary	Assets (in billions)	Total Capital Ratio (4% required minimum)	Net Income (in millions)	Return on Average Assets	President/CEO Compensation
Atlanta	$209	4.3%	$253	0.13%	$1.84 Million
Boston	$80	4.6%	($116)	(0.14%)	$2.18 Million
Chicago[196]	$92	4.7%	($119)	(0.13%)	$2.21 Million
Cincinnati	$98	4.5%	$236	0.25%	$2.28 Million
Dallas	$79	4.5%	$79	0.11%	$1.64 Million
Des Moines	$68	4.7%	$127	0.18%	$1.22 Million
Indianapolis	$57	4.8%	$184	0.32%	$1.63 Million
New York	$138	4.4%	$259	0.22%	$2.15 Million
Pittsburgh	$91	4.6%	$19	0.02%	$852 Thousand
San Francisco	$321	4.2%	$461	0.14%	$1.31 Million
Seattle[197]	$58	4.6%	($199)	(0.29%)	$1.06 Million
Topeka	$59	4.2%	$28	0.05%	$1.70 Million

The FHLBs' profits in 2008 were terrible. At year-end 2008, the Federal Home Loan Banks reported a combined profit of $1.2 billion, which may seem impressive at first but is actually 57 percent less than the year before and reflects the same problem noted at the individual FHLBs: losses in securities and derivatives. The road to full recovery is rocky because so many members (thrifts and banks) have themselves experienced significant financial trouble, and many have failed.

Not all FHLBs are created equal, and three of them lost a lot of money in 2008: Boston, Chicago, and Seattle. The FHLB of Boston lost $116 million, and the FHLB of Seattle lost $199 million in 2008, mostly because they both purchased private label mortgage-backed securities that had higher risk subprime and Alt-A loans (loans with limited documentation). Unfortunately, Boston and Seattle, like all the other FHLBs, didn't fully analyze the credit risk when they purchased these securities. It's hard to blame them. The national rating agencies, including Moody's, Standard & Poor's, and Fitch, had all rated the securities very highly before the bottom fell out. It was divisions of companies like Credit Suisse Group AG, Deutsche Bank AG, JPMorgan

Chase, Morgan Stanley, and Goldman Sachs that were peddling these crappy securities. The FHLBs paid billions of dollars for their recommendations and these securities. They are still paying a high price for buying them. Several FHLBs have filed lawsuits against these dealers claiming the dealers were less than honest about the risks. Good luck with that, right?

It's amazing the FHLBs have survived as well as they have following the 2008 financial panic. Fortunately, they had more capital than the roughly 2.5 percent ratio required at Fannie Mae and Freddie Mac. When Congress deregulated the banking industry (the Gramm-Leach-Bliley Act of 1999), it required each FHLB to adopt a new capital plan. By 2009, all of them have done so except Chicago (theirs was pending). The capital levels have all improved substantially since 2008 but are still tight. (The one exception is the FHLB of Seattle, which was "undercapitalized," and they had to sign a consent order, in October 2010, with their regulator requiring the FHLB develop a plan to fix it.) That's why they all agreed that when the S&L bailout bonds are repaid (in January 2012), they will continue to set aside the 20 percent of profits they would have been paying on these bonds to a special capital reserve. It's a very good idea.

The strength of the FHLB System is still considered strong, and it maintains an AAA/A-1+ rating because of the implied government guarantee. Because the FHLB System has "consolidated obligations," that is, its debts are shared among all FHLBs, it also prepares consolidated financial statements so investors can evaluate their condition as a whole. The FHLB's Office of Finance prepares these statements and publishes them on their website. The individual FHLBs also file financial statements with the SEC.

The Chicago Story

It's one thing to be ripped off by a securities dealer who sold you some bad investments, but self-inflicted wounds hurt even more. The FHLB of Chicago stands out because they led the charge into their own unsuccessful product, which not only resulted in losses to the company, but also led to a cease and desist order with their regulator. A cease-and-desist order is not to be taken lightly: it is a very loud statement that there's been a major screw up.

In this case, the FHLB of Chicago had developed a Mortgage Partnership Finance program (MPF) with noble intentions. The FHLB would purchase from one of their members a mortgage loan and then keep it in their own investment portfolio. The member bank or thrift that sold them the loan would collect and then send the monthly payments to the FHLB. The thrift would also buy back the loan if it went bad. The advantage here would be that the FHLB would worry about funding the loan for a long time at a fixed interest rate, and the thrift would worry about collecting the loan payments and keeping the customer relationship going. It was such a good idea that several other FHLBs began offering something similar, but none were as gung-ho about it as Chicago.

At one point these loans were about 60 percent of the Chicago FHLB's assets, and even after their regulator demanded that the bank change the program, these unique mortgages in Chicago's portfolio were still almost 35 percent of total assets at year-end 2008! For comparison, all FHLBs combined held less than 6.5 percent of their assets in loans like this. Wow—that's 35 percent versus 6.5 percent! Talk about too much of a good thing.

The bigger problem was that it was too much of a *bad* thing. Over time, the program evolved, and the Chicago FHLB was taking more and more risk while allowing the thrift to take less and less risk. One product even allowed the thrifts to sell the FHLB loans *without* recourse (the thrift didn't have to buy back the loans that went bad) and with credit scores as low as 580. Oh sure, the FHLB sincerely thought they could manage it, and they began using more complex methods to measure and mitigate risk, but, let's face it, a bad loan is a bad loan. *It's almost always bad loans.*

So the loans began to sour, and their regulator not only demanded changes to the program but also required a new capital plan to protect against potential losses. The regulator also prevented the Chicago FHLB from paying any dividends without prior approval. Ouch. In cases like these, you would expect the top executives to lose their job, and it happened here. In April 2008, the president and CEO, J. Mikesell Thomas, was "separated" from the bank. But don't feel too bad for him. His compensation for the year was still $1.48 million.

Accounting

The FHLBs have done well to avoid failing like Fannie Mae and Freddie Mac, but they too invested in a large number of higher-risk, mortgage-backed securities. At the end of March 2009, the FHLB System was looking at $6.6 billion in losses on these securities at eight of the twelve FHLBs. Of that amount, only $618 million had been recognized on their income statement, and the remaining $6 billion was recorded on the balance sheet as "Accumulated

Other Comprehensive Income," which is a fancy new accounting trick that allows them to put off recognizing these losses.

On the one hand, it means that the FHLBs don't have to write off losses on these securities, which were difficult to value anyway until the markets were more stable. If the FHLBs had written off these losses early in 2009, it would have wiped out their capital and (unnecessarily) caused some of them to fail. Besides, investors can easily see for themselves the condition of these FHLBs because the amount is clearly disclosed on the balance sheets. But on the other hand, although the accounting standard is necessary, reasonable, and fair, it still just doesn't feel right. It's like getting a mulligan in golf. Sure, it improves the scorecard, but it's not entirely forthright either. *Accounting is not a game.*

It wouldn't be surprising and might even be healthy to have some of these FHLBs merge. The combined strength and the cost savings could make it worthwhile. The FHLBs recognize this, and some have even seriously considered it. If you look closely at the 2009 compensation packages of some of the CEOs, especially the ones in Pittsburgh and Seattle, they even have provisions to pay the CEO if a merger results in his being left without a job. And in 2008, the FHLBs of Dallas and Chicago specifically discussed a potential merger. Good for them.

The Federal Home Loan Bank System was created during the Great Depression. They have been through plenty of trials and tribulations. Sure, they've made mistakes. We all have. But they continue to provide a great service to the country. Even so, there is no question that their mammoth size is a problem. Their lobbyists might argue otherwise, but they are clearly backed by our government, and this backing has allowed them to grow too large. Their outstanding debt levels are second only to the US government. At year-end 2008, they had $1.25 trillion in debts outstanding![198] That's not good. Should they ever require a bailout, and history has shown that nobody is exempt from failing, the costs would be ridiculous. It isn't clear that the country could afford to do that either. Can you imagine! Politically and financially, it would be overwhelming! *Bigger is not always better.*

Chapter 8

Government-Owned Enterprises

Sometimes things happen so fast, you just act. You don't have time to think about it or analyze the situation. You just act.

It happened to me one evening at dinner with the president of a well-run Midwestern bank and his two senior officers. Things were going great until the president began to choke on his food, so I performed the Heimlich maneuver. Anybody who knew how would have done the same thing, but the president was still very gracious about it. The next morning, as a large number of the bank's leadership team had gathered for my consulting session, the president went out of his way to thank me. He explained to the group that I had helped him avoid disaster the night before.

The room was dead quiet for a moment or two before somebody in the back blurted out, "*Why!?*"

It's a true story that reminds me how much I enjoy working with bankers. It also reminds me that we all instinctively do what's necessary. Sometimes we are just compelled to act. Whether it's a simple gesture like opening a door for a stranger whose hands are full or something more important, such as opposing discrimination or homelessness, we typically rise to the occasion. We may not agree on specifics, but we know we should at least do something to make things better.

Such was the case during the Great Depression. People wanted something done to eliminate homelessness, hunger, and unemployment, and our elected officials recognized that one of the obstacles was getting the lenders back in the game. Without being able to get credit, especially not being able to get loans for affordable housing, the economy would never get back on track. That's when the idea of developing national mortgage associations became reality. These private associations could be used to promote a public benefit. It was a great idea, so we just did it.

As we have discovered, if properly managed, these national mortgage associations can in fact help solve many public policy issues and concerns.

The trick, though, is to ensure that these associations are properly managed. Unfortunately, if poorly managed, the reverse is also true, and they aren't a great idea at all.

The story of Fannie Mae and Freddie Mac presents the best and worst of these programs, and, in spite of the downside, it's hard to imagine not having something like them. They are incredibly beneficial to our economy and to our country.

Federal National Mortgage Association (Fannie Mae)

To battle the Great Depression, the National Housing Act that President Roosevelt signed in 1934 would provide a federal charter for folks to form "national mortgage associations," private companies that would raise money to originate home loans (mortgages). The original idea was to allow these national mortgage associations to go head-to-head with savings and loan associations and lend money directly to homebuyers. Not surprisingly, the thrift industry was against the idea, and in the final bill the national mortgage associations weren't tax exempt like the savings and loans, and their direct lending authority was eliminated.

Instead, for only $5 million and a minimum of five people, you could get a charter to become a national mortgage association, and your private company could then sell some bonds at a low interest rate, buy some mortgage loans that paid a higher interest rate, and make money off the difference.

Unfortunately, you would also have to put up with federal government regulations and examinations, and, frankly, there were a lot of strings attached. The federal government set limits on how much you could borrow from banks, and the feds also dictated where you could keep the cash. Not all ideas are great, and this one totally flopped. After three years, only one association was formed, so the federal government ditched the program in 1938 and instead created their very own National Mortgage Association.

This was a "federal" National Mortgage Association, known as—you guessed it—the Federal National Mortgage Association (FNMA). Politicians are not especially good at naming things, and "Federal National" is clearly lame. Also, the letters FNMA made a weak acronym, but if you get a running start after a few drinks, pronouncing FNMA can sound like "Fannie Mae," and thus the nickname was created. So there you have it. Fannie Mae was derived from Jack Daniels. For the record, on January 6, 1997, Fannie Mae's stock started being listed under the name "*Fannie Mae*" rather than "*Federal National Mortgage Association.*"

Fannie Mae was originally housed in the Reconstruction Finance Corporation (RFC), a government agency that put up $10 million to buy all of the stock in the new company. Over time, its home and government oversight responsibilities were bounced around a bit before it all landed in the Department of Housing and Urban Development (HUD) in 1965.

Initially, Fannie Mae was supposed to offer their own IOUs to investors (debt securities) and use the money they raised to buy mortgage loans that were insured by the Federal Housing Administration (FHA). Fannie could either keep the loans in their own portfolio or sell them to other private investors. This new market (buying loans that were originated by others) was called a "secondary market" and gave lenders the confidence to originate FHA-insured mortgages. The investors could turn the loans into cash and originate even more mortgage loans. The program got bigger in 1949 and included purchasing loans that were guaranteed by the Veterans Administration to veterans.

A nice benefit of the Fannie Mae program was that areas of the country that had cash to invest, like the Northeast, could now safely invest in communities outside their region. In particular, the South and the West had fewer deposits to support growth, but they could now get more loans.

Following World War II, the housing industry began to boom. Returning home, men and women found loans with low down payments, such as those insured by the government under the VA Home Loan Guaranty Program of 1944. Naturally, they bought homes, and the home ownership rate grew from 44 percent in 1940 to 55 percent in 1950. Fannie Mae grew right along with the boom.

Fannie Mae grew so rapidly that people began to worry that they were getting too big, and, in response, Congress passed the Federal National Mortgage Association Charter Act in 1954. The act required mortgage lenders to buy nonvoting stock in Fannie Mae if they wanted to sell mortgages to them. When the mortgage lenders bought the nonvoting stock, it added capital to Fannie Mae that supported its growth, and with a few dips here and there, Fannie Mae continued to chug along as a strong and profitable government agency.

It all started out so well.

Vietnam War

We sometimes forget that wars are incredibly expensive, and the costs have serious repercussions. A March 2009 report by the nonpartisan Congressional Research Service estimates that we spent $648 billion waging the Iraq War, which by the time it is over will surely surpass the previous record holder for the most expensive war in US history: the $686 billion Vietnam War.[199]

Now an expensive war, whether in Vietnam or Afghanistan, takes its toll on the economy and leads to tough choices. We try to save money wherever we can, and during the Vietnam War we tried to save a few bucks by privatizing Fannie Mae. It was a bad move. The high cost of the war and the resulting 1968 budget deficit became a major problem for President Lyndon Johnson and Congress.

Nobody could blame the president for hoping his legacy would be more than having waged an expensive war in Vietnam. He also spent a lot of money on his "Great Society" set of domestic programs aimed primarily at poverty and racial injustice.[200] But rather than cut more from the war budget or from these social programs, the Johnson administration chose to sell assets, in this case the profitable Fannie Mae government agency for $160 million (about $932 million in 2009 dollars). Bad move!

More specifically, on September 1, 1968, Fannie Mae was allowed to sell subordinated capital debentures, a type of IOU whose interest is paid before common stock dividends but after other debts. Fannie Mae could then use that new money to repay $160 million in preferred stock that was owned by the US Treasury Department. Fannie Mae became a government-sponsored enterprise, a private company with a public purpose of supporting affordable mortgage lending. It received no tax dollars to fund operations, and it became responsible for managing its own affairs.

Some people might argue that selling Fannie Mae was not done *just* to raise money, but that it was time to return Fannie Mae to the private sector. It had served a public purpose and now had reached the point that it could prosper on its own. Folks may argue that selling Fannie Mae was done because the experiment had worked, and it was not only unnecessary but also undesirable to have a government agency rather than the private sector run a profitable business. Some politicians were undoubtedly inclined to support privatizing Fannie Mae for these reasons, but there is also no doubt that at the time the sale was precipitated first and foremost by the need to raise money and remove the debt from the government's balance sheet.

> *... the financial cost of the Vietnam War led to the sale of Fannie Mae for what now appears to be a paltry amount.*

Unfortunately, the sale has not panned out very well, and the government had to bail out Fannie Mae in 2008, along with their competitor Freddie Mac. These bailouts are estimated to have cost taxpayers a whopping $300 billion![201] Simply put, the financial cost of the Vietnam War led to the sale of Fannie Mae for what now appears to be a paltry amount. Had we kept it as a government agency, we would have been much better off.

Fannie Mae's Generous Benefits Package

When we originally removed Fannie Mae from the government's balance sheets, we divided it into two companies. Fannie Mae would become much more independent as a privately owned company, but it would still serve a public interest. It would also be allowed to purchase conventional loans, those with no government guarantee but whose appraised value of the property was 80 percent or less of the loan amount. The other company was a new government-owned national mortgage association called the Government National Mortgage Association (GNMA), or "Ginnie Mae" (thanks again, Jack Daniels!). Ginnie Mae had a similar public interest mission as Fannie Mae.

The spin-off of Fannie Mae from a government agency to a private company came with many very generous benefits that your typical private company does not get. For one, there are not many companies that had a $2.25 billion line of credit with the US Treasury, but both Fannie Mae and Freddie Mac had one!

Fannie Mae was exempt from state and local income taxes. Bankers could use Fannie Mae's IOUs (debt securities) as collateral when they borrowed from the Federal Reserve, which made selling these debt securities to thousands of banks and thrifts much easier. Fannie was also exempt from SEC registration fees and was not required to file reports with the SEC like other private companies. It could operate with less capital than other government-sponsored enterprises, thrifts, and banks. And, most importantly, Fannie Mae had the "implied" guarantee of the US government, which meant it could borrow money at very low interest rates because the risk of those debts not getting repaid was very low. Furthermore, a 1984 federal law required that securities that Fannie Mae (or Freddie Mac) issued or guaranteed must be treated as obligations of the US government for purposes of state investment laws.[202]

Although Fannie Mae had been explicitly clear in selling securities and filing financial statements that "the U.S. government does not guarantee, directly or indirectly, Fannie Mae's debt securities or other obligations," everybody knew that was hogwash.

Given the size of Fannie Mae and Freddie Mac, their government charter, government benefits, and their economic importance, investors around the world knew damn well that the US government would bail them out in a crisis. Fannie played it up quietly as well, even arguing in a letter to the OCC that its securities were safer than other AAA-rated debt because of the "implied government backing."[203]

In a fascinating and widely read report from the Congressional Budget Office, the government benefits provided to both Fannie Mae and Freddie Mac were an astounding $6.5 billion in 1995.[204] That didn't include the combined $362 million annual benefit they got from their exemptions from taxes and registration fees. Fannie Mae obnoxiously called the report "the work of economic pencil brains who wouldn't recognize something that works for homeowners if it hit them in the erasers."[205] But that study actually paled in

Freddie Mac

Federal National Mortgage Association

When Fannie Mae converted from a government agency to a government-sponsored enterprise in 1968, Ginnie Mae became their only significant competitor. But Ginnie had certain restrictions limiting their scope. For example, unlike Fannie, they could not buy loans directly. Ginnie could only offer guarantees that certain mortgage-backed securities would be paid as agreed. Two years later, recognizing that the exclusive legal advantages provided to Fannie Mae were not good public policy, and in an effort to address a shortage of affordable housing, Congress passed the Emergency Home Finance Act. This law established an organization to compete directly with Fannie Mae. Regulated by the Federal Home Loan Bank Board, it was called the Federal Home Loan Mortgage Corporation, or as we call it today, Freddie Mac.

comparison to the one by Federal Reserve Economist Wayne Passmore in 2003 that put the value of the government's implied guarantee to Fannie and Freddie at between $119 billion and $164 billion![206] With these incredible benefits, there should be strings attached—a lot of strings!

Risky Rapid Growth

Fannie Mae's charter has been amended by the government many times, but its purpose has always been clearly defined: to support housing by providing a secondary market for mortgage loans. Beginning in 1972, Fannie Mae started buying its first "conventional" loans, those not insured by the FHA or guaranteed by the VA. Two years later, it began buying multifamily loans. All loans were at fixed interest rates, which created problems when interest rates were rising, and they did rise a lot in the early 1980s. Fannie Mae found itself in the same boat as most thrift institutions: they had a lot of loans that earned low interest rates and a lot of debts where they had to pay higher interest rates.

To its credit, Fannie weathered the storm and began buying adjustable-rate mortgages (ARMs) and selling mortgage-backed securities (MBSs). Ginnie Mae had been the first company to do this back in 1970. Fannie Mae guaranteed that it would pay interest and principal on the securities, which generated fee income for them. By 1990, Fannie had issued more than $140 billion in mortgage-backed securities, had over $133 billion in assets, and generated a $1.2 billion profit. Not bad.

But, as always, there was good news and bad news. Fannie Mae had a nice profit, but it was getting dangerously large and doing so very quickly. From 1990 to 2000 it had grown an astounding 407 percent, reaching $675 billion in assets. It had become the twenty-sixth-largest company in the United States according to *Fortune* magazine's annual list, and the 824th-largest company *in the world*, according to *Forbes* magazine's annual list. By the time Fannie Mae collapsed in 2008, it owned or guaranteed over $3 trillion of mortgage assets in the country—approximately 26 percent of total US mortgage debt! It had become even bigger than the Federal Reserve System. *Bigger is not always better.*

To grow this large, Fannie Mae had begun selling debt securities (IOUs) that were then used to buy loans and mortgage-backed securities. There was no limit on this activity, and Fannie Mae created incredible profits. It was really quite simple. Step one: issue IOUs (debt securities) at really low interest rates because you have an implied government guarantee backing them. Step two:

use the proceeds to buy loans from banks, thrifts, and others and package them into mortgage-backed securities (charging fees along the way, of course). Step three: buy a variety of mortgage-backed securities for your own portfolio because the difference in what you pay for your money and earn on these securities is great! Step four: repeat the process.

Along with Freddie Mac, Fannie Mae quickly became the largest mortgage holder in the country. As such, it faced considerable credit risk and interest-rate risk. Credit risk was what would happen if borrowers began defaulting on their loans. Fannie could run out of capital very quickly and would require a government bailout. Interest-rate risk was what would happen if interest rates changed significantly and enough borrowers *prepaid* their loans. Fannie Mae would then be stuck with paying off their expensive IOUs compared to earning low interest on their new loans. Losing that much interest on loans could be serious.

In both cases, Fannie Mae rightfully argued that it could reduce these risks by buying mortgage insurance and derivatives. The mortgage insurance would cover the credit risk. And Fannie could cover the interest rate risks (or "hedge" the risk, as they say) by buying derivatives, a product similar to an insurance contract where somebody else pays you if interest rates turn against you. It works well as long as the other guy honors the contract. It can be a pretty good hedge against interest rate changes.

***ARMs** are **a**djustable-**r**ate **m**ortgage loans whose interest rate is tied to some index that will adjust periodically. For example, the interest rate on an ARM loan tied to a US Treasury bill interest rate index will typically change every time that index changes. Some ARMs contain very low initial interest rates, called "teaser rates," followed by much higher interest rates later.*

MBS is a mortgage-backed security, a type of IOU that is secured by home mortgage loans.

Government National Mortgage Association *(Ginnie Mae)*

The National Housing Act in 1968 that spun off Fannie Mae into the private sector created this new National Mortgage Association to support mortgage loans with government insurance or government guarantees. The new *Government* National Mortgage Association, nicknamed Ginnie Mae, doesn't actually buy or sell loans or even issue mortgage-backed securities. Instead, it offers federal government "guarantees" that timely principal and interest payments will be made on certain mortgage-backed securities.

While Fannie Mae was spun off to provide a secondary market that included conventional loans, Ginnie Mae was established to support a secondary market for government guaranteed loans. Ginnie Mae is a **government-owned enterprise** that competes with Fannie Mae, Freddie Mac, and other companies that issue their own private-label securities.

The difference here is that Ginnie is fully owned by the US government and there has never been any "implicit" guarantee. It's a clearly defined taxpayer guarantee. We own the agency.

The amount of loans they can guarantee is set by Congress. The US Department of Housing and Urban Development, HUD, reports that since 1970, Ginnie Mae guarantees totaled over $2.8 trillion, which supported loans for well over thirty-two million US families. They had *outstanding* guarantees of $576 billion as of September 30, 2008, and over 95 percent of them were either FHA or VA loans. By far, their largest concentration of single-family loans was in Texas (14 percent), followed by Florida (5.6 percent) and Georgia (5.5 percent).

It works like this: Banks, thrifts, and other lenders make home purchase-loans to you and me. Those lenders then sell to private companies any of those loans that are either insured or guaranteed by federal government agencies. Those agencies include the Federal Housing Administration, the Veterans Administration, the Department of Agriculture's Rural Housing Services, and HUD's Office of Public and Indian Housing. The private companies buying the loans will then package them into a mortgage-backed security that Ginnie Mae guarantees will be repaid. This makes those securities very valuable and very easy for these private companies to sell to investors around the world.

At one time, Ginnie Mae was a dominant player in large part because it sold the first ever mortgage-backed security product in 1970. Naturally, it didn't take long for Fannie Mae and Freddie Mac to catch on and do the same thing, but even as late as 1985, Ginnie Mae still held a dominant 42 percent of the market share. The competition from Fannie Mae and Freddie Mac ate away at their dominance, and with the proliferation of private-label securities, their market share has fallen consistently and was only 4 percent in both 2005 and 2006.

The collapse of their competitors who all engaged in higher-risk subprime and Alt-A loans—products Ginnie could not legally guarantee—caused a spike in market share to 19 percent in 2008! As a result, Ginnie Mae estimated they would need authority to guarantee $500 billion in new securities in 2010.

Ginnie Mae outsources a significant amount of it operations (over 80 percent in 2004) and operates with a small staff (less than 78 people in 2009). Outsourcing can save money, but it is also risky and can lead to substantial problems, such as those experienced in the mid-1980s when lax supervision of its mortgage originators and loan underwriting standards led to substantial losses.

Today, Ginnie Mae operates without taxpayer funds to cover overhead expenses. It generates significant fee income (mostly from its guarantees) and although its capital measures only 2.38 percent of its $14.9 billion in assets, it has been very profitable. In 2008 it generated a $906 million profit (an exceptional 6.3 percent return on average assets) for the taxpayers. Federal law requires they use their profits to buy US Treasury securities to help finance the country's national debt.

That was a big "if" at Fannie Mae though. The problem was that Fannie was choosing to self-insure more and more of the higher and higher credit risk, and it was buying more complex derivatives with unknown parties. There was no transparency, so Fannie's shareholders and other analysts didn't know much about these transactions. After all, Fannie didn't have to file annual reports with the SEC. As we found out later, Fannie's accounting of these transactions was, at best, dubious.

An editorial in the *Wall Street Journal* on February 20, 2002, sounded warnings when it said:

> As for interest-rate risk, Fan and Fred hedge with a giant and complex program using all manner of derivatives. At the end of 2000, their combined derivative position was valued at $780 billion. Even scarier, these hedges are only as good as the counterparties' ability to pay up. But Fan and Fred don't disclose the identity of their parties, so investors have no idea how much risk comes from possible counterparty failure. (By the way, last year Fan's derivative strategy went, um, somewhat amiss and she had to write down shareholder equity by $7.4 billion.)
>
> We aren't trying to scare readers here, and perhaps all of these concerns will come to nothing. So far during this recession, the housing market has held up well, knock on wood. Then again, unlike Enron, where only shareholders got taken to the cleaners, in the case of Fannie and Freddie taxpayers will take any bath.

If only we had listened. *We should have seen it coming.*

Back in 1992, Congress got worried about Fannie and Freddie's growing risk and worried that they were getting too far removed from their charters. Their charters said that they were supposed to promote financing of affordable housing for low-, moderate-, and middle-income Americans, but their activities had obviously grown beyond their original purpose. So Congress created the Office of Federal Housing Enterprise Oversight (OFHEO) as a new regulator for both Fannie and Freddie.

Housed within HUD and funded by assessments on Fannie Mae and Freddie Mac, OFHEO could act on a range of issues including minimum capital standards for Fannie and Freddie and on the maximum sizes of loans Freddie and Fannie could buy. HUD also required Fannie and Freddie to establish annual goals for mortgages they purchased or guaranteed in support of low- and moderate-income housing and underserved areas.

It was not unreasonable to require them to serve a public purpose in return for the tremendous number of government benefits they had obtained (i.e., tax exemptions, multibillion-dollar lines of credit with the Treasury, SEC filing exemptions, implicit government guarantees, etc.). Besides, these companies were experiencing tremendous growth, paying very high salaries, and generating strong profits. They should have been held accountable to their charter. Between 2001 and 2008, the housing goal ranged from 50 percent to 56 percent of loans.

Surprisingly, the OFHEO still had to get congressional approval for its budget every year, which meant the companies it regulated, Fannie and Freddie, could pressure politicians to cut OFHEO's budget if they didn't like the way the regulators were running the show. In 1993, the sparks began to fly when OFHEO Director Aida Alvarez suggested that Freddie Mac actively opposed her efforts to expand staff so they could monitor both Fannie and Freddie. "I did say [to the CEOs of both companies] I was hearing reports of lobbying activities on the Hill ... and I thought that that would be detrimental," she told the *American Banker* newspaper.[207]

Two weeks before, an *American Banker* article was more direct, saying, "For their part, the two companies stoutly deny any role in the D'Amato-Bond amendment. But Hill sources said repeatedly that they believed Freddie Mac was behind the move to cap Ms. Alvarez's staff."[208]

Needless to say, the OFHEO and Fannie Mae weren't exactly buddies, and OFHEO's effectiveness was limited. Then again, the regulator wasn't exactly getting anybody's respect. An editorial in the *Wall Street Journal* once described the OFHEO as a "hapless regulator."[209]

An article in *Fortune* said, "OFHEO is not like most regulatory agencies; it is much weaker."[210] Rep. Richard H. Baker (R-LA), who served on the House Banking Committee, admitted that Fannie and Freddie were "extremely complex, enormously sophisticated companies, and frankly are at a mismatch with OFHEO's resources."[211] Left largely unchecked, Fannie Mae continued to grow, assume greater risks, and become more arrogant.

Arrogance and Accounting

My friend Rob once reminded me, "The trouble with trouble is that it always starts out as fun." And it's true. It's fun to watch baseball players who use steroids smack some really long home runs—until their bodies break down. We love the music from artists who use drugs—until they end up in rehab or drop dead from an overdose. It's fun to work with or own stock or bonds in a high-flying, award-winning company—until it crashes and burns.

It's not like we don't know better. Don't we all occasionally see things happening that we just know will lead to bad endings? At one time or another, haven't we all seen red flags? If there are only one or two red flags, we can dismiss the danger signs. But if we see a lot of them, they scream out at us. The collapse of Fannie Mae and Freddie Mac was one of those train wrecks we knew was coming, but like deer in the headlights, we just couldn't crank up the ol' Chevy and get the hell off the tracks.

It is a compelling story, and it's a great topic for the many books that will undoubtedly be published. Because Fannie and Freddie play such an important role in our economy, and because their failure put the taxpayers at such tremendous risk and cost taxpayers a fortune, we can spend some extra ink here. The stories behind failures at Bear Stearns, Lehman Brothers, Countrywide, Wachovia, and others are disturbing because they revealed so much greed and excess, but this isn't our nation's first rodeo and while disappointed and perhaps even angry, we aren't really shocked that privately owned companies—even those subject to government oversight—are so greedy. We may not be shocked, but we certainly have the right to expect better from our government and, by extension, our government-sponsored enterprises.

Fannie and Freddie should have been different. These GSEs (government-sponsored enterprises) were established to promote a specific national objective—affordable housing—and got tremendous government support to do it. We gave them a $2.25 billion line of credit from the US Treasury, for goodness sake! We exempted them from a ton of taxes. Unlike other companies of their size, we excused them from onerous regulatory filing requirements with the SEC. We even let them operate with a razor-thin amount of capital, a benefit we would never allow our nation's banks and thrifts.

They let us down. We should be pissed off. But the sad truth is, they failed because we allowed it to happen. For way too long, we liked the idea that a program we developed to ensure affordable home loans for everybody could continue to work with government support but without government intervention. We merely grumbled about the high salaries but didn't complain too loudly because credit was readily available, and the money, it flowed like wine. We bought into the simplistic slogan of less government is always better without giving enough thought to the repercussions. We bought into the hype.

Hey, it's easy to get caught up in the euphoria of a booming housing market and the comments from its charismatic cheerleaders like those at Fannie Mae. And what's not to like about a great American success story with Fannie Mae's former Chairman and CEO Franklin Delano Raines?

Born in 1949 to a father who worked in the Seattle Parks Department and whose mother was a maintenance worker at the Boeing aviation company, it was yet another great story of a kid with modest beginnings who went on to achieve remarkable success.[212] He served as a senior officer and board member of Fannie Mae beginning in 1998, and was their chairman of the board and chief executive officer from January 1999 until his official resignation on December 21, 2004. He had everything going for him, but he blew it.

It was Raines's arrogance and failed leadership that not only caused irreparable damage to Fannie Mae's reputation but to his own reputation as well. He resigned from the board and settled with the government for $24.7 million in exchange for not having to face charges for fraud.

As noted before, Fannie and Freddie were growing by leaps and bounds, and they were becoming so dominant that competitors began to complain openly that their being sponsored by the government was unfair, unnecessary, and risky. In June 1999, an advocacy group was formed to confront the unbridled expansion of both Fannie and Freddie. They cited Fannie Mae's expansion into private mortgage insurance, home equity lines of credit, and home improvement loans (purchased from Home Depot stores) as examples of activities that exceeded Fannie's charter. As if Fannie's expansion wasn't enough, such rapid growth also presented risks to taxpayers. After all, why should the taxpayers subsidize people buying hot tubs and chandeliers from Home Depot?

This advocacy group was called FM Watch, and its board included some very powerful CEOs.[213] Raines fired back at FM Watch in his May 12, 2000, interview with *National Journal* magazine, declaring, "We have a very well-organized group of financial companies who have banded together with the express purpose of doing harm to Fannie Mae. If you spend enough money in Washington on lobbyists and PR people, you will have an impact."[214] He should know. Fannie Mae spent $7 million lobbying that year alone and over $45 million during his tenure at Fannie Mae from 1999 to 2004![215] Did you catch that? They spent $45 million to lobby the politicians for favorable treatment!

At the same time, Fannie helped form the Homeownership Alliance. Its members also included some heavy hitters: Freddie Mac, the National Association of Homebuilders, the National Urban League, the National Association of Real Estate Brokers, and others. The Homeownership Alliance wanted to counter opposition from FM Watch and others who opposed Fannie and Freddie's unbridled growth. In an obvious overreaction to FM Watch, the new Alliance president, Rick Davis (former presidential campaign manager for Arizona Republican Senator John McCain) declared, "Some critics of the system are implicitly calling for policy makers to reconstruct the system so it can be more like that of other industrialized countries. Forty-percent down payments, like they have in Germany, and huge prepayment penalties that are the norm for refinancing in some European countries are things we did away with decades ago, and we certainly don't want to turn the clock back."[216] Wow, the only word missing in his diatribe was Nazi. Davis was paid over $30,000 *a month* for five years—until the group disbanded in 2005.[217]

In another volley against FM Watch by the two GSEs, Gerald L. Friedman, chairman of the FM Watch board, issued a press release stating, "Each member of our board of directors has been systematically approached and threatened by these government-sponsored enterprises. In each instance the message was the same: Stop supporting the activities of FM Watch or be prepared to see your business opportunities and products suffer."[218]

Meanwhile, Fannie Mae continued to grow and report enormous profits. By the end of 2001, they owned or guaranteed about 43 percent of the country's residential mortgage loans and were funding 60 percent of all multifamily loans. "We knew Fannie and Freddie were very aggressive and very hungry," says Jay Brinkmann, the Mortgage Bankers Associations senior director of research and economics, "but no one expected [them] to grow [multifamily loans] that much in such a short time. That's a little sobering,"[219]

But heaven forbid you should complain about Fannie. In response to a critical article printed in the *Washington Business Journal* (April 2001), Arne Christenson, Fannie Mae's senior vice president for regulatory policy (and chief of staff to former House Speaker Newt Gingrich, R-GA) wrote a blistering, over-the-top 1,296-word letter to the *Washington Business Journal* complaining about the paper's bias and the "disservice to its readers" in accepting the "arguments of [their] competitors."[220] She went on to describe Fannie as having a "safety and soundness regime that is second to none" and complained that in many cases Fannie's critics' "anti-consumer goals are obvious." The letter proved to be utterly absurd, with comments such as the one praising OFHEO as providing "cutting-edge regulatory supervision" and her claim that their "capital standards, liquidity, transparency and market discipline, are considered unsurpassed by any financial institution in America," and finally—wait for it—"Fannie Mae is one of the safest, strongest financial institutions in the world." *Riiiight.*

In February 2002, even the *Wall Street Journal* (WSJ) couldn't bear to witness the madness of it all and, to their credit, ran an editorial titled "Fannie Mae Enron?" that criticized Fannie's regulator, decried its low capital levels, and raised concerns about its growth, risks, and lack of transparency.[221] They were right on target.

Accounting Integrity

Fannie Mae's response to the WSJ editorial was predictable. Among many other things, Frank Raines wrote a letter to the WSJ denouncing the editors as "glib, disingenuous, contorted, and even irresponsible."[222] But his timing was bad because Enron's accounting scandal had been revealed just five months earlier, and it not only caused that company's bankruptcy (the largest in US history at the time) but also bought down its accounting firm, Arthur Andersen. Given that Arthur Andersen was also Freddie Mac's accounting firm, regulators, politicians, financial analysts, and the public were in no mood for any more shenanigans, and the writing was on the wall.

In April, Fannie Mae's regulator announced it would begin a joint review of Fannie's and Freddie's financial disclosures, and in July, Senator Christopher Shays (R-CT) and Senator Edward J. Markey (D-MA) sponsored a bill that would strip Fannie's exemption from filing reports with the SEC. In May, the Bush administration weighed in with a serious demand for greater accounting transparency. By July, Fannie and Freddie caved and signed a "voluntary" agreement to begin filing their company's financial statements (but not their debt securities offerings) with the SEC.

It didn't take long to understand why they didn't want greater transparency.

After Enron, Freddie Mac had no choice but to fire Arthur Andersen, and their new accountants, PricewaterhouseCoopers, began an extensive review of the books. In June 2003, Freddie Mac disclosed that it had misstated earnings by some $4.4 billion for the past four years. That's right—$4.4 billion. Uh oh! The company's chairman and chief executive were fired. It was shocking, but, in hindsight, Fannie Mae's response was not shocking. Here's the report from *Fortune* magazine:

> Fannie responded to Freddie's problems with astonishing self-righteousness. Raines held a press conference in which he accused Freddie of causing "collateral damage." The Frequently Asked Questions section of Fannie's website included the following statement: "Fannie Mae's reported financial results follow Generally Accepted Accounting Principles to the letter … There should be no question about our accounting."[223]

A somewhat self-righteous Raines went even further to distance Fannie Mae's reputation from that of Freddie Mac, telling the *American Banker* newspaper, "It would not take 500 people for us to go back [and make corrections] even if we made the same mistakes."[224] Three months later (in October 2003), he wrote what appears to be a disrespectful letter to Treasury Secretary John Snow complaining about the way Treasury was treating his company. As that same *Fortune Magazine* article put it, "In political terms the letter was astonishment—what other CEO would dare dress down the Treasury Secretary, much less address him as 'Dear John'?"[225]

One of the biggest setbacks to Fannie Mae's bravado was the December 2003 report by Federal Reserve Board Economist Wayne Passmore. His analysis showed that Fannie and Freddie together received an incredible $143 billion in direct and indirect subsidies from the government. What made it worse, if that's possible, was that more than half of that government subsidy was paid to shareholders, officers, employees, and other insiders. Furthermore, the study showed that the subsidies provided by the government resulted in savings to borrowers of just 0.07 percent interest on their loans, and it's a far cry from the quarter to half a percent the companies had claimed! This study followed a critical speech in March by William Poole, president of the Federal Reserve Bank of St. Louis, that openly challenged the financial stability of Fannie and Freddie and warned of significant problems if they faltered.

Fannie Mae's board of directors consisted of eighteen people: thirteen elected by shareholders and five appointed by the US president. The terms of the five presidential appointees expired on May 25, 2004, and President Bush didn't reappoint or replace them—a highly unusual move that sent a clear vote of no confidence from the White House.

In September 2004, it was curtains for Fannie Mae's senior executives and board chairman. Fannie's regulator released a major investigative report that questioned Fannie Mae's financial results over the past six years. The OFHEO report completed a yearlong investigation that, with the help of the accounting firm of Deloitte & Touche, reviewed over twenty thousand documents and e-mails and conducted hundreds of interviews and depositions. The OFHEO report concluded that Fannie was routinely cooking the books to report unrealistic earnings. OFHEO claimed that there was improper accounting to portray Fannie Mae as having consistent earnings and (even worse!) to ensure executives' bonuses. OFHEO trashed Fannie Mae's internal controls, especially the lack of controls to prevent these accounting breakdowns. Clearly, Fannie Mae was playing tricks with their accounting.

The 211-page OFEHO report covered a lot of ground and basically accused Fannie Mae's management of fraudulently manipulating earnings in violation of generally accepted accounting procedures (GAAP). Fannie's actions included these blunders:

- Deferred $200 million in expenses in order to pay the maximum executive bonuses (outgoing CEO James Johnson was paid $1.19 million; incoming CEO Frank Raines was paid $779,625)
- Created a "cookie jar" of cash reserves that executives could add to in good years, (presumably when bonus goals had been met and the extra earnings weren't needed) and draw from in bad years (presumably to cover up weak performance and meet bonus goals)
- Installed software to produce reports on the most desirable financial statements based on different scenarios and assumptions—in effect, running reports to create the most favorable financial statements regardless of whether they were accurate or not

- Classified a huge number of derivatives improperly to avoid showing losses on its income statement (over $12.2 billion in losses were deferred this way)

You can easily guess the reaction from Fannie and its allies, including a number of nonprofit organizations that were receiving grants from Fannie Mae. The talking points ran the gamut from the "regulator was wrong and its actions were politically motivated" to "these were complex accounting matters and any inadvertent errors simply reflected differences of opinion and interpretations."

But people who may have viewed the OFHEO as hapless, weak, and overmatched would find that their report was very clear about generally accepted accounting principles (GAAP), and they were not backing down. The report stated that "the misapplications of GAAP are not limited occurrences, but appear to be pervasive."[226] OFHEO directly questioned Fannie Mae's capital adequacy, reported earnings, management ability, and safety and soundness. Almost immediately, Fannie Mae was required to develop a plan for increasing capital by $9.4 billion. *Accounting is not a game.*

Fannie Mae fought back by not only openly criticizing its regulator but by hiring a prestigious law firm to conduct its own independent review.[227] And Frank Raines went a step further, insisting that the SEC itself review and validate their regulator's accounting allegations. The heat was on, and even before these two reviews were completed, Congress held hearings, the SEC launched an inquiry, and the Justice Department began a criminal investigation.

In the October 2004 congressional hearings, Fannie Mae had many defenders. Representative Maxine Waters (D-CA) claimed "we do not have a crisis at Freddie Mac and in particular at Fannie Mae under the outstanding leadership of Mr. Frank Raines."[228] Representative Lacy Clay (D-MO) called it a "rush to judgment" and implied race was a factor when he called the congressional hearings a "political lynching" of Mr. Raines, who is African American.[229] In fairness, there was no credible evidence that the attacks on Raines were racially motivated, and, in fact, the investigation was driven in large part by the evidence provided by "whistleblower" Roger L. Barnes, a Fannie Mae accountant who is also African American. Barnes had been forced out of the company after his repeated attempts to get the board and the auditors to address financial irregularities were ignored.

There is, however, plenty of evidence that the hearings were politically motivated. The White House, Senate, and House of Representatives were all controlled by Republicans, and the 2004 election was less than a month away. The hearings were held in the Capital Markets, Insurance, and GSE Subcommittee, chaired by Richard Baker (R-LA). At this point, the SEC had not released its findings, and clearly there wasn't going to be any meaningful legislation before its report was released, and certainly not before the election. As Equity Research Analyst Henry Blodget so clearly explained, "the Fannie investigation represents a Republican payback for Enron and Halliburton. Conservatives are delighting in the gutting of Raines and Fannie Mae—a Democratic boss of a Democratic-leaning company."[230] Unfortunately, while the public pressure and congressional hearings were probably biased and definitely motivated by politics, they were also warranted.

In December, the SEC completed its review of OFHEO's accounting accusations and completely backed the regulator, dealing a fatal blow to the senior officers of the company. Raines retired from the company on December 21, 2004, saying "I previously stated that I would hold myself accountable if the [Securities and Exchange Commission] determined that significant mistakes were made in the company's accounting. By my early retirement, I have held myself accountable."[231]

Four years later, following Raines's appearance before a House Congressional Committee, where he restated this same "accountable" quote, Senator Christopher Shays reacted harshly, saying, "Frank [Raines] left when it was disclosed that their books didn't meet any of the (federal) standards and that they had overstated—by billions—their profits, that's why he left."[232]

Former Senator Warren Rudman (R-NH) chaired Fannie Mae's internal investigation, which was reported to have cost a whopping $80 million. The findings from that internal investigation were eventually published on February 23, 2006, and confirmed that management's accounting practices "in virtually all areas that [they] reviewed were not consistent with GAAP" and that management knew that to be the case.[233] The Rudman Report agreed that management had cooked the books to show stable earnings over time; however, except for 1998, the Rudman Report didn't find any evidence that management did so to meet performance bonus plans. The report said that senior management had placed unqualified people in their accounting, reporting, and auditing functions and that these people gave incomplete or misleading information to the board of directors. The report described the company's accounting systems as "grossly inadequate."

And here is how the company hired by the Fannie Mae board of directors described Fannie's former chairman and CEO Franklin Raines:

> We did find, however, that Raines contributed to a culture that improperly stressed stable earnings growth and that, as the Chairman and CEO of the Company from 1999 through 2004, he was ultimately responsible for the failures that occurred on his watch.[234]

Because part of the compensation package was tied to the inflated earnings, in December 2006, the OFHEO filed 101 charges against Raines, former Chief Financial Officer J. Timothy Howard, and former Controller Leanne Spencer in large part to recover some of the money. That's right—101 charges. Executive compensation had always been a sensitive subject at Fannie Mae, and the company aggressively fought efforts to disclose their compensation. For example, in the October congressional hearings, Chairman Baker revealed that when he sought records on the compensation paid to Fannie Mae's top twenty executives in 2003, Fannie had hired Ken Starr (the lawyer who investigated President Bill Clinton and his affair with Monica Lewinsky) to oppose the request. Starr threatened civil legal actions against Chairman Baker himself if the information was released. Baker backed down.

Raines received compensation of more than $90 million from 1999 to 2004, of which $52 million was from bonuses tied to earnings.

It took three years, but Fannie Mae did resubmit its earnings reports from 2002, 2003, and 2004, reporting $6.3 billion in losses that it had failed to recognize before. They paid a $400 million fine, with $50 million going to the government and the other $350 million to a special fund for harmed shareholders. Fannie also agreed to limit the number of mortgages in their portfolio to year-end 2005 levels.

Sixteen months later Raines agreed to a $24.7 million settlement with the government that included his donating $1.8 million to a charity approved by the OFHEO that assisted home owners threatened with foreclosure. He also had to pay a $2 million fine to the Treasury (which was covered by Fannie Mae's officer liability insurance policy) and to surrender $15.6 million in stock options (that were worthless when the settlement was reached anyway). Raines, Howard, and Spencer were also prohibited from working with Fannie Mae ever again. *Greed has a price.*

"This settlement is not an acknowledgment of wrongdoing on my part, because I did not break any laws or rules while leading Fannie Mae," Raines proclaimed defiantly. "At most, this is an agreement to disagree."[235]

OFHEO Director James Lockhart called it "a satisfactory conclusion" to their enforcement actions against the three executives.[236] A *Wall Street Journal* editorial disagreed, calling it a "paltry settlement," and even that critique may have been charitable.[237] The settlement seems to indicate that the regulators either had a weak case or weak knees.

The story with Frank Raines and Fannie Mae is compelling and sad. To their credit, journalists around the country did a fine job reporting the story, and they presented reasonable views from both conservatives and liberals. Certainly one of the better jobs of reporting came from Bethany Mclean, who said this in her January 2005 *Fortune Magazine* article on "The Fall of Fannie Mae":

> The Fannie story is not like other accounting scandals, though. Yes, the company broke the rules to produce a smooth stream of earnings, just as Enron, Tyco, WorldCom, and all the others did. But that's only one of a half-dozen different story lines. The Fannie Mae saga is also about a company that lost sight of its original mission. It's about power politics run amok, and the combustible blend of politics and business. It's about a company whose huge debt terrified top government officials, and whose very existence drew ideological opposition. It's about an orchestrated, behind-the-scenes campaign to rein in a financial powerhouse. It's about a regulator who learned to fight back against a much more formidable foe.
>
> It's about all these things and one more. Fannie Mae thought itself so different, so special, and so powerful that it should never have to answer to anybody. And in this, it turned out to be very wrong.

Government Takeover

It would be easy to blame the failure of Fannie Mae on Frank Raines, but it would also be wrong. Yes, he deserves blame for their excessive growth, insanely weak capital position, and terribly damaged reputation, all of which contributed to Fannie's failure, and it all occurred under his watch. But the government takeover of both Fannie Mae and Freddie Mac occurred four years after he left. More directly to blame were the massive losses from Fannie's foray into the Alt-A lending business and, to a lesser extent, subprime lending. The allure of Alt-A loans, also called "low-doc" loans or, better yet, NINJA loans (No Income—No Jobs) helped take down many companies, including Wachovia Bank and Countrywide Mortgage. Fannie Mae's massive size limited the government's alternatives in addressing the large portfolio of bad loans that accumulated under the leadership of the guy who replaced Raines: Daniel H. Mudd.

Daniel Mudd was the son of the famous award-winning TV journalist Roger Mudd. The son was a very talented and respected figure in his own right. When he assumed Fannie's leadership role after Raines resigned, he had been on the board of directors of both the company and the Fannie Mae Foundation since early 2000. A decorated US Marine Corps officer from his combat service in Beirut, he had worked at the World Bank and at Xerox Corporation before moving on to serve as CEO of GE Capital, Japan, and as president of GE Capital, Asia Pacific. He certainly had the credentials.

Mudd has been credited with doing a very good job of improving relationships with Fannie Mae's shareholders, employees, regulators, politicians, and the public. But his decisions to lead the company into high-risk loans and securities caused Fannie Mae to fail.

Like most companies, competition can be fierce, and Fannie Mae was feeling the pressure. Previously, Fannie's and Freddie's market share was so dominant that they controlled the national underwriting criteria used to originate home purchase loans. But given the opportunity to make some fast bucks, investment firms began to invade Fannie's and Freddie's turf by offering their own private-label securities. The products they were peddling included jumbo mortgages, which are those large-dollar loans in high-cost areas like much of California or in larger high-cost cities like Miami and New York that Fannie and Freddie could not legally buy. Even more dangerous were the subprime and Alt-A loans that had yet to stand the test of time.

In 2003, Fannie Mae dominated the market. It issued almost $1.2 trillion in mortgage- and asset-backed securities, about 44 percent of the market. But for several reasons—the debacle of Frank Raines and the Fannie Mae accounting issues, intense scrutiny by the regulators, and significant competition—their securities production fell to $527 billion the next year, and their market share fell to only 28 percent. The private-label companies, however, did not falter and increased production by 47 percent (to $864 billion) as their market share climbed from 22 percent in 2003 to 46 percent in 2004. The private-label business was eating Fannie Mae's and Freddie Mac's lunch! As it turned out, it was some really bad food.

In an early encounter, cocky Countrywide Financial Chairman and CEO Angelo Mozilo told Daniel Mudd, "You're becoming irrelevant." As Fannie Mae's largest customer, he went on to tell Mudd, "You need us more than we need you and if you don't take these loans, you'll find you can lose much more."[238] The loans he referred to were the subprime and Alt-A loans that ended up wreaking havoc on the country.

These were terrible products that Countrywide was booking and packaging into private-label securities, and Mozilo wanted Fannie Mae to buy both the loans and the securities. By mid-2006, Countrywide had become the largest issuer of Alt-A securities in the country.[239] By February 2007, its stock price had reached $45 a share, but then the bottom fell out. Countrywide's high concentration of Alt-A and subprime loans were not performing, and investors began dumping the stock because they were afraid the company might fail. Countrywide's corporate debt reached junk bond status in May, and the stock price crashed to $6.71 before Bank of America bought the distressed company at a fire sale price.

Incidentally, the second-largest issuer of Alt-A mortgage-backed securities was Bear Stearns, which saw its own stock price collapse from $172 a share in 2007 to $10 a share when it was sold under duress to JPMorgan Chase in March 2008. The third largest was IndyMac, which failed in July 2008. The list goes on, but you get the picture. By mid-2006, the combined subprime and Alt-A mortgages were an astonishing 76 percent of all private-label securitizations. Everybody who peddled these risky loans eventually got burned.

Fannie Mae did not have the same level of exposure to subprime and Alt-A loans as these companies, but it was not immune to the problems because it too began to buy these "toxic" securities. By year-end 2007, Fannie Mae's investments in Alt-A and subprime securities totaled $73.9 billion. They could buy these because at the time, 99 percent of those securities received the highest possible credit rating from at least one of the three SEC nationally recognized credit rating agencies.

But we soon found out that the credit rating agencies were *horrible* at rating these securities, and they could not have been more wrong. In congressional hearings, Chairman Henry Waxman (D-CA) accurately described the credit rating agencies when he stated, "the story of the credit rating agencies is a story of a colossal failure. The credit rating agencies occupy a special place in our financial markets. Millions of investors rely on them for independent objective assessments. The rating agencies broke this bond of trust, and Federal regulators [at the SEC] ignored the warning signs and did nothing to protect the public."[240] He was right.

The rating agencies completely sucked at their job, and even that's being too kind.

But Fannie Mae owned the securities anyway, and, regardless of the rating, they too should have known better. It was their job to know better! Now they had to deal with the consequences. By June 30, 2008, the sixty-day-or-more past-due rates on the loans underlying the securities they owned were shocking, ranging from a very high 3.36 percent for the best quality Alt-A loans to over 36 percent for the weakest subprime loans! Alt-A loans were especially troubling, and by year-end, although they were only 10 percent of the Fannie Mae loans (in their mortgage portfolio or in securities), they represented 31 percent of the properties in foreclosure.[241] Fannie was reporting a $5.1 billion loss for the six months, and the trend was looking very, very bad. In fact, by the end of 2008, Fannie had suffered an astounding $59.7 billion loss for the year!

Banking is all about confidence, and after years of public disclosures and accounting irregularities at both Fannie and Freddie, the mess at both companies made it hard for investors to believe that either one was strong enough to survive. To boost investor confidence, in July 2008, the Federal Reserve Board offered both companies access to the Fed's Discount Window, and Treasury Secretary Henry Paulson proposed a larger line of credit at the US Treasury. He even indicated a willingness to use tax dollars to buy stock in the companies.

But it was all too late. The credit agencies, which previously couldn't rate a mortgage-backed security worth a damn, now began systematically lowering their ratings on all but the most senior debt at both Fannie and Freddie. These securities were becoming less marketable, and an estimated $89 billion in debt in the second half of 2008 was coming due and needed to be refinanced. There was no chance this debt could have been refinanced without government help.

Both companies' capital positions had fallen to dangerously low levels, and there was no chance of raising the additional capital in 2008. The alternative was to sell assets, but dumping securities and other assets into the market would have only lowered their values even more and resulted in more losses to the companies.

Allowing the two companies to fail outright would have devastated the economy. The private-label securities market was almost completely gone at this point, and there was nobody with an ounce of brains willing to step into this role.[242] As Federal Reserve Chairman Ben Bernanke explained later, "Developing an effective securitization model is not easy—according to one economic historian, mortgage securitization schemes were tried and abandoned at least six times between 1870 and 1940."[243] As bad as they had become, Fannie

Mae and Freddie Mac (and Ginnie Mae too) were still the best thing going. In fact, they were the only thing going.

Without Fannie, Freddie, and Ginnie, mortgage rates at the time would climb significantly and mortgage lending would decline substantially, completely killing any chance of a housing-market recovery for many, many years and throwing the country into an even deeper recession—deeper and longer than the eighteen-month recession the country was already in (from December 2007). That recession resulted in a very high unemployment rate of 10.6 percent (January 2011)! The housing industry dominated the US economy (in 2005 it was an amazing 17 percent of the country's GDP), and its further collapse would have been devastating.[244] This was nothing to be flippant about.

In addition, we can't forget that the Fannie Mae and Freddie Mac securities and preferred stocks were (and are) held by central banks, commercial banks, pension funds, and other institutions around the world. Fannie's and Freddie's collapse could have caused an even bigger international financial panic, unlike anything we had ever seen. Foreign investors (who held about $1.3 trillion of these securities) would have little choice but to begin dumping the investments, driving down their value and leading to tremendous losses, which would have carried over to other securities and investments as well. After all, if the securities people thought were backed by the US government were no good, then every other investment they owned would be suspect and less valuable too.

The credit score of the US government itself would have suffered, and the low interest rates we now pay on our government debt would have gone a lot higher. People would have no longer trusted that the United States would honor all of its debts.

At the time, and even now, a lot of the popular sentiment was, "Well, let's just let Fannie and the private banks fail. After all, they brought it on themselves. They made their bed. Now let them lie in it." But we couldn't just walk away and let these institutions fail. The systemic risk where Fannie's and Freddie's failures would have led to wide-scale company failures across the nation was very real, and much too high. A government takeover was the only option.

Fannie Mae's New Owner: Taxpayers

On September 6, 2008, James Lockhart, director of the Federal Housing Finance Agency (the new regulator for Fannie and Freddie) became conservator of both companies.[245] The Federal Reserve and US Treasury announced their full support. A conservator acts like a bankruptcy judge and gives the companies an opportunity to work things out in a structured way. But unlike a bankruptcy judge, who may approve a plan put in place by the company executives working with debtors and an appointed court representative, when the US Treasury takes over, they really take over. As Fannie Mae's annual report described it, Treasury would now have seniority over "*all rights, titles, powers and privileges of the company, and of any shareholder, officer or director of the company with respect to the company and its assets.*"[246]

Now that's a takeover! When it happened, Treasury Secretary Paulson stated that the government's three objectives were to (1) stabilize the financial markets, (2) support the availability of mortgage finance, and (3) protect the taxpayers.

The markets did in fact stabilize after the takeover because it was clear that the guarantees from Fannie Mae would be honored by the government, and mortgage financing would continue to be available. In fact, Fannie was authorized to increase its portfolio up to $850 billion (over fifteen months) to try to help stabilize mortgage lending nationwide, which at this point had dwindled to a trickle. However, because Fannie and Freddie were considered too big to start with, they were also required to begin reducing their size by 10 percent a year beginning in 2010 until they got down to a slim $250 billion.

It remains to be seen how well the third objective—protecting the taxpayers—will pan out. It doesn't look good. One thing is certain: this wasn't a sweetheart deal for the shareholders. With the government's action, common stock shareholders saw their investments virtually wiped out (a share was valued at about 50 cents in July 2009), and both the common and preferred stock dividends were eliminated. As part of the takeover, at any time until September 2028, the Treasury could buy up to 79.9 percent of the company's common stock for only $0.00001 per share.

The US Treasury agreed to lend Fannie Mae up to $200 billion (it is now an unlimited amount) when it needed capital, but the terms are not exactly generous. Whenever Fannie's capital becomes a negative figure, they must sell the US Treasury senior preferred stock that pays10 percent interest. If Fannie doesn't pay the interest, the rate goes up to 12 percent. Fannie Mae will also pay Treasury a quarterly fee for the Treasury's commitment to make these investments (beginning March 2010). The money isn't cheap, or as my friend Alicia put it, "The Treasury prices its loans like a 'payday' lender!"

Former President and Chief Executive Officer Daniel Mudd was paid a $952,000 salary the year the company failed, but there were no severance payments or golden parachute when he was fired. Even so, his compensation package for salaries and benefits (not counting stock awards, options, and pension plans) from 2003 to 2008 was more than $15.7 million. Although it was far less than his predecessor Raines had received, it wasn't a bad paycheck for a company that had failed under his watch.

Federal Home Loan Mortgage Corporation (Freddie Mac)

Several factors made homes unaffordable in the late 1960s: inflation, higher interest rates, and a shortage of loan money The situation was made worse by the large number of baby boomers (born between 1946 and 1964) who were now beginning to enter the housing market. The problem with baby boomers seeking loans was simple: as a group, they didn't deposit enough money in the banks to pay for the loans they wanted.

Congress considered several solutions. Some people advocated giving direct government subsidies to borrowers to reduce interest rates to less than 7 percent. Some people advocated eliminating "discount points" when pricing loans. A discount point is equal to 1 percent of the loan amount, and in their view, the points were simply another unnecessary and expensive fee being charged to borrowers.[247]

Another solution people suggested was requiring the Federal Reserve System to lend the regional FHLBs up to $3 billion a year to use for housing loans. That way, interest rates on loans would be lower because there would be an increased supply of low-cost money being used for mortgage loans. But interest-rate subsidies were too expensive, and eliminating discount points was too controversial, and involving the Federal Reserve was in President Nixon's view, "an intolerable invasion in the Federal Reserve." He didn't think the Fed should favor one industry over the others, like housing loans over small-business loans.[248]

The bill that President Nixon signed to help support home ownership created a new government-sponsored enterprise whose rights and responsibilities were pretty much identical to those of Fannie Mae. The new GSE's shareholders were decidedly different, however, as their name implies. This was a national mortgage association owned by the Federal Home Loan Banks. It was called the Federal Home Loan Mortgage Corporation, dubbed Freddie Mac.

Freddie Mac's shareholders comprised the twelve FHLBs that purchased a combined $100 million in common stock. The investment was very good too, and by 1985, it was valued at almost $2 billion. Under the original charter,

Freddie could buy loans only from FHLB members or from commercial banks and mutual savings banks. But in 1978, Freddie's charter was amended to allow it to buy loans from any HUD-approved mortgage lender. In 1981, Freddie began paying dividends, and the next year it got congressional approval to issue preferred stock, which it did to the tune of $150 million.[249]

Unfortunately, the savings and loan crisis in the mid-1980s culminated in restructuring the FHLB System, and Freddie Mac was separated from the FHLB in 1989.[250] Freddie's preferred stock was converted into common shares, and its board of directors was structured like Fannie Mae's thirteen shareholder-elected directors and another five appointed by the president.

Leland Brendsel was elected chairman of the board when Freddie Mac became publicly owned. He moved up the corporate ladder quickly at Freddie Mac and became the CEO in 1985 and chairman of the board in 1989. He held those positions until he was reportedly "forced to retire" in 2003 following a huge accounting scandal.

The theme for Freddie Mac's 1999 annual report was "Our Future Looks Very Bright," and at the time, it did. Celebrating its tenth year as a public company, it managed to increase net income 31 percent from the year before to an astonishing $2.2 billion profit and a 26 percent return on equity. The company had reached $386 billion in assets, a far cry from the $35 billion in assets ten years earlier. Although overhead expenses increased some while Freddie prepared for "Y2K," the date change that had all major companies updating their computer software, net income was still climbing because borrowing costs were falling. Credit quality was rock solid too, with a very low ninety-day-past-due rate of less than 0.39 percent on both single-family and multi-family loans. Freddie was doing a nice job of managing risk, primarily by buying private mortgage insurance on loans with less than a 20 percent down payment (or, more specifically, a loan-to-value ratio exceeding 80 percent). Yeah, those were the days!

But Freddie was also growing its portfolio of "non-Freddie Mac securities," which included low-risk, government guaranteed Ginnie Mae securities. The problem was that Freddie's portfolio also included higher-risk securities, such as home equity loans, commercial real estate, and prefabricated housing. At the time, the securities were performing well and although all of them had "A" ratings or better, they signaled an appetite for taking more risk at the company. Freddie was also using derivative financial instruments to mitigate these risks, particularly the interest-rate risk.

Accounting Problems

Bankers have undoubtedly attended scores of seminars and training programs on how to use derivatives, and we can all agree that it's really tricky to understand the products. The presenters in these seminars and training programs are often economists who begin with some lighthearted comment ("As you can see from my bio, I have accurately forecasted nine of the last five recessions.") before speaking glowingly of these "bilateral contracts that have been systematically introduced, modified, and expanded over many years and whose more popular and widely understood albeit occasionally speculative products, such as futures and forward contracts, are being supplemented with a multitude of hedging instruments to mitigate financial risks such as options and swaps, especially interest rate and credit default swaps."

It gets boring after that.

And that is exactly the problem. These are complex products that are often misunderstood, and yet they have become a standard feature on large corporate balance sheets. Enron had a very profitable derivatives business, but they used a variety of accounting tricks with their derivative products to hide some very unprofitable, offshore businesses. Both Freddie Mac and Fannie Mae knowingly used improper accounting methods to hide their profits. The irregular accounting helped them smooth out their earnings and impress investors with their steady, consistently rising profits.

The senior management at companies like Fannie Mae claimed that the complexities of the products and accounting standards led to differences of opinions about financial reporting, but nobody should buy into that nonsense. Seriously, if you are paid multimillion-dollar salaries and benefits, it's your job to get it right! There is certainly a little room for subjective interpretations, but significant multibillion-dollar errors are inexcusable. Costly "mistakes" like these demonstrate either management's incompetence or faulty ethics. Or both.

Freddie Mac was engaging in derivatives, especially interest-rate swaps, in part because it had introduced several new products under Brendsel's leadership, including the adjustable-rate mortgage securities. These ARM loans were important because long-term fixed interest rates were very high (over 10 percent) from the late 1970s through the 1980s. At the time, most properly underwritten ARMs were good products. They generally allowed homebuyers to lock in lower interest rates for a set time period, such as five years. The interest rates would then change every year to the same rate as a one-year

Treasury bill rate plus a modest 2½ to 3 percent over that. These ARMs were nothing like the subprime and Alt-A ARM loans that were introduced years later, where the initial interest rates were high, the lock-in periods short, and the rate adjustments significantly higher. But in the beginning, Freddie would buy these good ARM loans, package them with others into a mortgage-backed security, and wisely use interest-rate swaps to lessen the interest-rate risks. The problem wasn't with the product. It was with the accounting.

The issues with accounting for derivatives at Freddie Mac didn't come to light for many years. Like their larger competitor Fannie Mae, Freddie was not subject to SEC-regulated reporting standards and requirements. Instead, Fannie and Freddie published their own "Information Statements." It all looked perfectly fine. But the derivative products were becoming more complex, and the accounting for them was becoming less honest.

Freddie's 2000 annual report, "Again and Again: Freddie Mac Delivers," reported a 15 percent increase in net income in 1999 and a $2.6 billion profit. Freddie bragged about an unbroken thirty-year record of profits and a return on equity of over 20 percent for the past nineteen years. The numbers were impressive, and credit quality was sound. Chairman and CEO Brendsel was generously rewarded. His compensation totaled $7.9 million in 2000, including $4.8 million in stock awards.

In 2001, Freddie's annual report, "Bringing America Home," reported a huge 66 percent increase in net income and a $4.2 billion profit. It was selling 35 percent of its debt overseas because with profits like this and an implied government guarantee, who wouldn't want in on the deal!? The company's return on equity had averaged 22 percent the previous four years but had now climbed to 29 percent in 2001. *Business Ethics Magazine* rated them tenth on its list of 100 Best Corporate Citizens that year.

Freddie's stock price had reached a high of almost $71 a share that year, up from a low of $38 the year before. The numbers were impressive, and credit quality was sound. Leland Brendsel was held in high regard by his stockholders and was reelected to the board of directors that year with over 98 percent of the votes. He was richly rewarded with compensation totaling $8.2 million, including $4.7 million in stock awards. Brendsel was apparently on a roll, earning even more than Frank Raines, his counterpart at Fannie Mae.

There was limited public outcry at the time over the salaries at Fannie and Freddie. Because nonprofits and community activists were receiving big grants, they were not going to make a fuss. Politicians were also receiving big donations from the companies, and few wanted to go up against their lobby machines. Few business organizations would ever want to draw attention to executive salaries. Some organizations, such as FM Watch and the Federal Reserve System, did speak out against the unsafe growth of these two GSEs, but the focus in 2001 and 2002 was not on compensation. It was on excessive growth and risk. Complained former Federal Reserve Board Chairman Paul Volcker, Fannie and Freddie's mandate "was solely to develop a secondary market, and they've gone way beyond that."[251]

There was reason to worry because, like Raines at Fannie Mae, Leland Brendsel and his management staff were leading Freddie Mac at a dangerously rapid growth rate that eventually exceeded their management abilities. After all, Freddie had grown from a $100 *million* company at birth in 1970 to $386 *billion* thirty years later, making it the sixty-fourth largest company in the United States according to *Fortune* magazine. Just two years later Freddie had $617 billion in assets, and was ranked #41. Growth like that is dangerous. *Bigger is not always better.*

But earnings at the time were stable, consistently rising, and impressive. Analysts and reporters nicknamed the company "Steady Freddie." Things were going so well, it almost seemed too good to be true. In fact, it was. Freddie was misrepresenting its earnings to meet analysts' projections of its performance and to maintain its Steady Freddie reputation. In fact, its 2000 reported profit was *understated* by a *billion* dollars, and the 2001 profit was *overstated* by a *billion* dollars![252] Freddie Mac later disclosed that it had misstated earnings by some $4.4 billion over three years. *Accounting is not a game.*

The earnings "mistakes" were the result of using the derivatives transactions to hide earnings. In one example of accounting misconduct, in 2001, Freddie made a series of interest-rate swaps. They would pay an investment firm a fee of over $400 million up front, when they had plenty of profits to meet earnings expectations and could afford to do so. They would then have it paid back to them in later years when they may need the income to meet earnings expectations. These particular swaps were not made to lower interest-rate risk but to reduce earnings in 2001 (after earnings goals and bonus plans had been met) and to be sure of future earnings (which would help meet future earnings goals and bonus plans).

Freddie had also been putting more money than necessary into the loan loss reserve from 1998 to 2002 in an effort to reduce reported earnings (a type of "cookie jar" accounting later found at Fannie Mae too). There were many other issues, such as refusing to disclose accounting errors of up to $285 million because these "errors" were considered "immaterial," and hiring two top-level executives in 2001, the chief financial officer and the controller, who were responsible for ensuring proper accounting and reporting but who lacked accounting expertise (they were not even certified public accountants).[253]

To be clear, the problem with understating earnings in one year is that the earnings that aren't reported can then be used to overstate earnings later. This maneuver helps ensure that there will be enough money to pay executive bonuses later on, even if it was undeserved that year. But more importantly, understating earnings can hide very important issues that shareholders should probably know about. By the time those issues surface, it could be too late for the investors to get out of harm's way. It is immoral, improper, and if done knowingly, illegal.

Accounting irregularities with derivatives were found shortly after serious accounting issues at Enron Corporation came to light. Enron declared bankruptcy in December 2001. Shockingly, senior officials at their accounting firm, Arthur Andersen, had engaged in a massive document shredding program immediately following revelations of wrongdoing at Enron. In June 2002, a jury convicted the senior officials of obstruction of justice (the convictions were overturned by the Supreme Court in 2005).

When Arthur Andersen's integrity was shattered it went out of business, and Freddie Mac hired PricewaterhouseCoopers, LLP (PWC), as its new accountants beginning with year-end 2002 statements. Unfortunately, PWC told Freddie's board that Freddie needed to refile its financial statements for 2000 and 2001, and delay filing for 2002 until PWC could complete a more in-depth review of accounting problems. With news like that, it was no wonder the board hired the law firm of Baker Botts LLP to conduct an extensive review of its accounting problems. Former SEC General Counsel James Doty led the review. Their findings were contained in the Botts Report.

Unfortunately, Armando Falcon Jr., director of the OFHEO (Freddie's regulator) didn't see the disaster that was coming. In January, he issued a press release stating that Freddie Mac had "sound internal controls and prudent risk management." He went even further by offering a glowing appraisal of Freddie Mac in his June 2003 annual report to Congress, declaring among other things that "the policies, procedures, internal controls and management reporting relating to interest rate risk are effective," that the "Board is appropriately informed of the condition, activities, and operations," and that "management effectively conveys an appropriate message of integrity and ethical values." Boy, was he wrong.

Within days of this report to Congress, Freddie's board received a copy of the Botts Report and quickly forced Chairman/CEO Leland Brendsel to retire and Chief Financial Officer Vaughn Clarke to resign. Freddie's board outright fired its President and Chief Operating Officer David Glenn. The 107-page Botts Report listed a lot of issues, including allegations that Chairman Brendsel and President Glenn directly participated in accounting and investment decisions to manipulate how Freddie reported profits and that the three men kept the board and shareholders in the dark about the controversial practices. The outside auditors at PWC had expressed a "lack of confidence" in Glenn to the board a month earlier, and he was fired outright because he got caught intentionally altering and removing pages from his extensive journals that the Botts's team had requested.[254]

The firing and forced resignations left egg on the face of the OFHEO's Armando Falcon, who was blindsided by the news. OFHEO had even been in meetings with the accountants, the audit committee, and the board throughout the process. Those meetings had left Falcon with enough confidence to publish the glowing report to Congress about Freddie. One can only imagine how angry the folks at OFHEO must have been after hearing that the top three executives were being forced out for misconduct. At best, Freddie Mac officials violated their regulator's trust by failing to keep them in the loop; at worst, they intentionally withheld information. Either way, the gloves were off at the OFHEO.

Political Obstacles

It wouldn't be easy for the regulator to get tough. Both Fannie and Freddie had powerful allies in Congress. Both companies contributed heavily to the campaigns of Democrats and Republicans, and they weren't afraid to call on them for support. "The lobbying ability of Fannie and Freddie is second to none in Washington," said Congressman Richard H. Baker (R-LA). "They have not only unlimited financial resources but good personnel who maintain good relations with many members of Congress. When their interests are threatened, the response is almost army-like. They're tactical, and they're everywhere."[255]

Consider this exchange between *Congressman Gregory Meeks (D-NY) and Director Falcon at a House Financial Services Committee* hearing, Sept. 25, 2003:[256]

> *Rep. Gregory Meeks* … I am just pissed off at OFHEO because if it wasn't for you I don't think that we would be here in the first place. And

> Freddie Mac, who on its own, you know, came out front and indicated it is wrong, and now the problem that we have and that we are faced with is maybe some individuals who wanted to do away with GSEs in the first place, you have given them an excuse to try to have this forum so that we can talk about it and maybe change the direction and the mission of what the GSEs had, which they have done a tremendous job …
>
> *OFHEO Director Armando Falcon Jr.:* Congressman, OFHEO did not improperly apply accounting rules; Freddie Mac did. OFHEO did not try to manage earnings improperly; Freddie Mac did. So this isn't about the agency's engagement in improper conduct, it is about Freddie Mac.

Freddie had abundant resources and was not afraid to use them. In the 2000 election cycle, it directly contributed $2.5 million to federal candidates and political parties (57 percent to Republicans). In 2002, it increased its donations to $4.2 million (again, 57 percent to Republicans). In fact, Freddie Mac has given so much money to federal candidates, parties, and political action committees that the nonpartisan Center for Responsive Politics ranks them seventy-fifth on its list of top one hundred donors of all time (from 1989 to 2009), with 56 percent of the donations going to Republicans. In fact, many of the overly aggressive contributions from 2000 to 2003 were illegal, and while "admitting no wrongdoing," Freddie paid a record $3.8 million fine to the Federal Election Commission (FEC) for eighty-five illegally reported or funded events that raised $1.7 million.[257]

The largest FEC fine in history started with a complaint filed by Public Citizen, a consumer advocacy group founded by Ralph Nader in 1971, alleging that Freddie Mac and its chief lobbyist, Mike Delk (senior vice president for government relations) hosted at least forty-five illegal fund-raising events. The consumer group was especially concerned about the twenty-four events that Freddie sponsored that would feature as its advertised "special guest" Congressman Michael Oxley (R-OH) who was the chairman of the House Financial Services Committee. His committee had oversight of Freddie Mac, Fannie Mae, and their regulator, the OFHEO. It just so happened that nineteen of the twenty-four times Oxley spoke, the fund-raiser benefitted one or more of his Republican *committee* members. Public Citizen included in its official complaint the Associated Press story:

"Freddie Mac lobbyist staged 50 GOP fundraisers as Congress let legislation die."[258] In that article, author Pete Yost noted that eighteen fund-raisers were for *subcommittee* members who helped fight several attempts by Capital Markets Subcommittee Chairman Richard Baker (R-LA) to strengthen OFHEO regulation of the two GSEs.

Freddie Mac contributions favored Republicans, but Fannie Mae, which was not nearly as big a campaign donor and didn't make the Center for Responsive Politics' top one hundred list of contributors, favored Democrats. Fannie's contributions were more indirect and were done through the Fannie Mae Foundation, which in 2006 was still the largest foundation in the United States devoted to affordable housing and community revitalization. But the foundation, which was chaired by Franklin Raines and significantly influenced by the Fannie Mae Company, was often accused of using donations to buy influence or punish critics. "It is clearly used as hush money to buy silence" of groups that might otherwise be critical of Fannie Mae, said well-known housing community activist Bruce Marks. According to Peter Wallison of the American Enterprise Institute, the Fannie Mae Foundation makes "contributions to community groups in the states and districts of members of Congress who can be helpful, especially to community groups that are favorites of the congressmen or senators."[259]

The *St. Petersburg Times* reported in 2000 that Fannie showed bias toward Democrats, especially black and Hispanic Democrats who represented poor communities. *The Times* cited many examples, including a study that showed of the twenty congressional House districts that received $9.6 million of foundation money in 1998, all but one was represented by a Democrat, and 97 percent of the money went to their districts. The foundation argued that giving so much money to the Democrats was coincidental; it was simply a case where the poor communities tend to be represented by Democrats.[260] That explanation seems pretty lame —a lot of the evidence shows a clear bias toward Democrats.

It wasn't just political and charitable donations that the agencies used to ensure favorable political treatment. They lobbied like hell too! Freddie reported spending $9.8 million in lobbying expenses in 2002 (fourteenth biggest spender in the country), up from $7.2 million the year before. In 2003, Freddie spent over $15 million, and it spent that much again in 2004! Its sister, Fannie Mae, spent $7.6 million in 2002, up from $6.1 million the previous year.[261] Because of these donations to lobbyists and politicians, accusations of trying to "buy influence" were rampant. And legitimate.

Freddie Mac always fought against congressional proposals to restrict its extensive lobbying. Years later and just before its failure in 2008, then Chairman and CEO Dick Syron argued, "We have well organized and well funded critics. We have every right to protect shareholder interests and advocate our positions ..." Proving that the pen is mightier than the sword, the journalist running the quote in *U.S. Banker* magazine, Joseph Rosta, ended his article with this observation, "What rights do taxpayers have, sir?"[262]

Fannie and Freddie were two peas in a pod in spending so much to influence politicians of both parties. In April 2004, about six months after the OFHEO began investigating Fannie Mae's accounting irregularities, Senator Christopher "Kit" Bond (R-MO) ordered the HUD Inspector General to investigate OFHEO on how they were investigating Fannie Mae. The Inspector General report revealed dissension among the agency's staff about how the OFHEO was getting Fannie Mae's cooperation but found no cause for formal action. But it is simply amazing that a politician would order an investigation of the regulator's investigation while it is under way!

Here's what the *Washington Post* said about Senator Christopher S. Bond in 2004:

> Bond has had a long-running conflict with OFHEO. The senator has requested repeated investigations of the agency, has sought to limit its role and staffing over the years, and is trying to withhold $10 million of the agency's proposed $59 million budget until its director, Falcon, is replaced ...
>
> The Missouri senator, who chairs the subcommittee that oversees OFHEO's budget, has received thousands of dollars of political contributions from Fannie Mae employees, including chief executive Franklin D. Raines, a veteran of the Clinton administration.[263]

Between 2001 and 2006, Senator Bond received $23,700 in campaign contributions from Fannie Mae's political action committee and employees. Fannie was ranked twentieth on the list of top donors to Bond's campaigns.[264]

Bond should be ashamed. But attacking the regulator on behalf of Fannie Mae was really a bipartisan affair. Following the IG investigation, Congressman Barney Frank (D-MA) claimed, "The senior management of OFHEO appears to have run roughshod over the judgment of professional staff and seriously compromised OFHEO's credibility as a financial regulator. ... It is clear that a leadership change at OFHEO is overdue."

Regulatory Backbone

Falcon was not deterred by the pressure when the accounting issues came to light, and he was not holding back. Almost immediately after the June 2003 Botts Report caused Freddie's board to change its executive management, Falcon announced that OFHEO was deploying its own special investigative team to review accounting issues, internal controls, and employee misconduct. He hired a heavy hitter named Stephen A. Blumenthal, former counsel to the House Commerce Committee and a former director of regulatory relations at the Securities Industry Association, to head the special examination. Here's what Blumenthal said about the IG investigation that Senator Bond instigated. "We are beginning to wonder if, a la the Keating Five in the past, there is some sort of an attempt … to somehow chill or otherwise interfere with the investigation of Fannie Mae."[265] Blumenthal went on to state, "We will not be deterred in any way."[266]

They were not alone. The SEC and the US Attorney's Office also announced investigations, and a total of nineteen different class-action lawsuits would eventually be filed. A month later and before the OFHEO investigation was completed, Director Falcon issued a startling press release:

> In the course of the special examination, OFHEO has reviewed the conduct of certain senior executives. Based on that review, I have concluded that [Leland Brendsel's replacement] CEO & President Greg Parseghian and General Counsel Maud Mater should be replaced. I have informed Freddie Mac's Board of Directors of my decision and they have agreed to comply.

There was nothing subtle about that statement. The regulator had just fired Freddie Mac's top dog and top lawyer. Parseghian appeared to have approved and participated in some of the accounting decisions at the root of the scandal, and OFHEO would not allow him to stay. Freddie's general counsel was believed to have withheld information from the regulator, and he too had to go.

Two weeks later (September 4), OFHEO initiated action to recover Brendsel and Clarke's generous compensation. Instead of allowing the two officers to resign, Falcon wanted them "terminated with cause" so that the OFHEO could go after their $37 million severance payments ($33 million of it to Brendsel).

Freddie's former president, David Glenn, agreed to cooperate fully with the OFHEO's investigation, pay a $125,000 fine, and never work with Fannie and Freddie again. CFO Vaughn Clark held out before agreeing to the same terms in September 2007. He also agreed to forgo any bonuses that he might have received. Finally, Chairman/CEO Leland Brendsel agreed in November 2007 to pay $2.5 million in fines to the government, return $10.5 million in previously paid salary and bonuses, and forgo any bonuses that he might have been due (valued at about $3.4 million). *Greed has a price.*

When the OFHEO released its nearly two-hundred-page examination report in December 2003, it was even more damning of the company executives *and board members* than the Botts Report, especially for their lack of accounting competence. OFHEO ended up fining Freddie Mac $125 million, required Freddie to make the chairman and CEO positions separate, and forced Freddie to sign a consent order addressing the deficiencies. The SEC also fined the company $50 million.

These were very difficult times for the OFHEO and Armando Falcon. Bruising battles with both Fannie Mae and Freddie Mac and their extensive political and financial resources had created a hostile environment. OFHEO was caught between conservative and liberal politicians who had very different views on the role of GSEs. OFHEO made mistakes and had to defend themselves against all types of unfounded accusations. They suffered through years of disrespect, numerous battles with Congress, insufficient funding, and extensive media coverage. In the end, the agency stood up for itself and fought back. Hell yeah!

Grudgingly perhaps, they earned respect. Senate Banking Committee Chairman Richard Shelby (R-AL) said that Director Falcon has "shown a lot of courage."[267] He later said, "After all is said and done, you have to give him an A+ for pointing out a lot of problems in the GSEs, particularly Fannie and Freddie, when a lot of people were not listening. He stuck by his guns. He's distinguished himself."[268] The *New York Times* ran one of the few favorable articles written about the agency: "Man Who Toppled Chief of Fannie Mae Is Seen as a David Who Beat Goliath." In that article, banking expert and consultant Bert Ely noted that in the beginning Falcon "was not particularly convincing or inspiring. He just came across as someone who was not up to the job." But in the end, Ely said, "he has been powerfully vindicated."[269]

In his 2004 annual report to Congress as his five-year term was coming to an end (he ended up staying for six), Director Falcon dedicated the report "to the employees of OFHEO," whose "expertise and tireless dedication" made the company successful. He noted that challenges with Fannie and Freddie had "tested the mettle of each employee, yet they rose to the challenge and got the job done."

Freddie Retools and Fails

Meanwhile, Freddie had no choice but to rebuild its brand, and choosing Richard F. Syron as its new chief executive officer and chairman of the board seemed like a good way to begin. So in December 2003, Richard (Dick) Syron started his tenure with Freddie. Syron had been the CEO and chairman of Thermo Electron, a large company ($21 billion in assets) but he was more widely known for having been chairman and CEO of the American Stock Exchange, president of the Federal Reserve Bank of Boston, and president of the Federal Home Loan Bank of Boston.

Dick Syron had an impressive resume, and few people would question his integrity. However, many rightfully questioned his business decisions and his paycheck while he was at the helm of Freddie Mac.

The Freddie Mac debacle looks a lot like the Fannie Mae failure. Both were very large government-sponsored enterprises that purchased or guaranteed way too many bad loans and mortgage-backed investments. *It's almost always bad loans.* Like Fannie, Freddie didn't have enough capital and liquidity to survive the repercussions. Its top executives got high salaries and bonuses in spite of the failures.

When Syron took the helm at the end of 2003, Freddie was still struggling to get its books in order and meet GAAP requirements. But by the end of 2004, although the company had shrunk in size by about 1 percent from the year before, Syron was boasting of a $2.9 *billion* profit, and a 17 percent increase in common stock dividends. The company had grown to almost $795 *billion* in assets and was fast approaching the size of the Federal Reserve System ($811 billion).[270]

In hindsight, the 2004 annual report revealed some issues that would haunt the company just three years later. In Syron's letter to shareholders, he said that Freddie had lost customers in 2003 but was able to turn the situation around because it offered better service, more competitive pricing, and the "introduction of more new products last year than in the previous four years combined."[271] As a result, he reported that Freddie's market share had climbed six percentage points. Freddie Mac was clearly seeking continued growth and increased market share with its new products. To do so, it chose to take on higher risks.

Surprisingly, Freddie's balance sheet showed modest growth, only about 1.25 percent over the next two years, but Freddie was falling into the same trap as Fannie Mae. It was purchasing or guaranteeing subprime and Alt-A loans and securities. At first, things didn't seem so bad. But that began to change in 2005 when Freddie revealed that it had bought a lot more interest-only and Option ARM loans (they made up 11 percent of the portfolio vs. 2 percent the year before). Freddie indicated that in spite of the higher risk, it would be buying even more. In another bad move, Freddie was offering guarantees on subprime loans that others had packaged into mortgage-backed securities. Freddie guaranteed $4.5 billion of these loans in 2004 and another $2.3 billion in 2005.

Management's decision to purchase and guarantee crappy loans, such as the Alt-A and subprime mortgages, bit Freddie in the ass and led to its failure.

On the plus side, Freddie also had a large, multifamily loan portfolio that was performing very well. Its market share was climbing steadily, from 37 percent in 2003 to 45 percent in 2005! There was a negative side though. Management's decision to purchase and guarantee crappy loans, such as the Alt-A and subprime mortgages, bit Freddie in the ass and led to its failure.

Freddie reported a $2.1 *billion* profit in 2005, which was very good considering it had to pay off fines and lawyers from the previous accounting scandals, work through losses from Hurricane Katrina, and work with narrowing net interest margins. It increased dividends twice during the year and rewarded its executives generously. In 2005, Chairman and CEO Syron received compensation totaling $8.4 million

But as we all learned later, the profits were misleading because management was engaging in high-risk subprime, Alt-A, and Option ARM lending that would soon bankrupt the company. In particular, the number of subprime and Alt-A loans led to increasing loan defaults, and by the end of 2008, many single-family loans that were originated only a year or two earlier were already in default! As these defaults came to light, investor confidence eroded, liquidity dried up, and the government had to step in.

FHFA as Conservator

Simply put, Freddie reported a $3 billion loss in 2007 and a stunning $50.8 billion loss the next year. The jig was up. Freddie was nationalized on September 6, 2008. Freddie was no longer a government-sponsored enterprise. It was now owned by Uncle Sam.

Its regulator had changed from the OFHEO to the Federal Housing Finance Agency (FHFA) in early 2008, and now the FHFA had became both Freddie's and Fannie Mae's *conservator*. We use that word because it implies a "timeout" for the company. It's a chance to regroup before getting back into the game. It may offend people to say that the company had been *nationalized* because that's the kind of thing a small-country dictator would do to a profitable American company. But let's be honest. We may not be small, and we certainly are not dictators or communists, but we definitely took over this company to protect our national interests.

We had no choice. As noted before, without Fannie and Freddie, mortgage rates would climb significantly and mortgage lending would decline substantially, completely killing any chance of a housing-market recovery for many years. The economy would have suffered a very steep and prolonged recession, or worse. Fannie's and Freddie's collapse could have caused an even bigger international financial panic, unlike anything we had ever seen. We had no choice.

In his testimony before the House Committee on Oversight and Government Reform on December 9, 2008, Mr. Syron presented his views on the collapse of the US economy and the failure of Freddie Mac. In his prepared testimony, he blamed others for the economic problems and Freddie's failure. These "others" included investors who had too much money to invest ("the prolonged glut of credit"), homebuyers who accepted the loans Freddie was buying ("ultimately, not without cost if the choices made by individual home owners are unaffordable"), Congress ("the pressures on Freddie Mac and Fannie Mae were enormous"), Freddie's charter ("the lack of diversification was extremely challenging"), and the poor ("if you are going to take the mission of promoting low-income lending seriously, then you are, by definition, going to take on a somewhat greater level of risk").[272]

He denied responsibility for subprime and Alt-A loans (they were "developed largely by private label participants"), claiming that Freddie provided a market for these loans only because it was required of them ("to carry out its public mission" and to remain "relevant").[273]

Congressman Christopher Shays (R-CT) represented a lot of people in a very nonpartisan way when he later responded, "That's just bullshit. The bottom line to this was they were entering into a market they didn't have to."[274]

Committee Chair Henry Waxman (D-CA) said that internal documents showed that the companies made "irresponsible investments that are now costing federal taxpayers billions." He went on to say, """Their own risk managers raised warning after warning about the dangers of investing heavily in the subprime and alternative mortgage market. But these warnings were ignored."[275]

Syron's remarks didn't say anything about meeting Freddie's internal growth objectives and taking the GSE to a dangerously large size ("too big to fail") by peddling government-supported securities to foreign powers, most notably China. He didn't say a word about Freddie's foray into the unaffordable subprime, Alt-A, and Option ARM loans when analysts in his own company warned him specifically against it. He didn't explain why he never separated the position of chairman and chief executive officer, as required by Freddie's regulator five years earlier. He never said anything about how the huge sums his company spent lobbying Congress and the millions they spent on political donations "failed" to allow them to diversify and perhaps reduce the 90 percent market share for the mortgage-backed securities they shared with Fannie Mae. And he never explained how the low-income family who borrowed their gold at absurd interest rates was able to destroy the economy and the company.

Damn those little people.

Mr. Syron's compensation as the head of a government-sponsored enterprise totaled over $54 million from when he was hired in 2004 until the company's bankruptcy in 2008.

The executives and board of directors of both Fannie and Freddie were replaced with an entirely new slate of officers when the FHFA took over. David Moffett, former CFO and vice chairman of US Bancorp, agreed to be the new CEO, and John Koskinen, former president and CEO of Palmieri Company, agreed to be chairman of the board. David B. Kellermann, former senior vice president and controller (since March 2008), was named acting chief financial officer.

The pressure on these men to manage a trillion-dollar-plus company would be intense. Freddie was losing money every day and under intense public scrutiny. This new management didn't cause the problems at Freddie, and fixing them wasn't going to be easy because, as a practical matter, they weren't authorized to engage in any meaningful programs or activities without the specific approval of their regulator and, in effect, the US Treasury. Every move they made was subject to considerable armchair quarterbacking.

It's not especially hard to run a company into the ground, but it can be very hard to help that company recover when the stakes are so high. When David Moffett resigned after only six months, it was musical chairs for the rest of the management staff. John Koskinen assumed the role of interim chief executive officer, and Robert F. Glauber, former chairman and CEO of the National Association of Securities Dealers, became interim chairman.

Moffett's resignation left a big hole in the company, and finding a replacement was about to get a lot harder. Shortly after he resigned, the news broke that American International Group Inc. (AIG), the insurance company that had received $170 billion in a federal government bailout, was planning to pay $165 million in retention bonuses.

The public outcry was swift and loud. President Obama was slow to react, but when he recognized the widespread public outrage, he instructed Treasury Secretary Geithner to "pursue every single legal avenue to block the bonuses and make the American taxpayers whole." Reflecting the public's very real anger, he asked "How do they justify this outrage to the taxpayers who are keeping the company afloat?"[276]

AIG caught a lot of flak when its plan to pay exorbitant bonuses was announced, and you can imagine the outrage when the public learned a few days later that failed Fannie Mae had planned to pay bonuses of $71.9 million, and failed Freddie Mac had planned to pay bonuses of $74.5 million. The bonuses were part of an employee retention plan established by their regulator (the FHFA), in consultation with the US Treasury and HayGroup, an international compensation consulting firm. An average of $32,000 went to thirty-five hundred employees at Fannie Mae, and four thousand employees at Freddie Mac received an average of $24,000. FHFA Director James Lockhart was forced to respond to the public and political outrage and in particular to both House and Senate oversight committees.

Congressman Barney Frank (D-MA) wrote a classic understatement to Lockhart: "I remain very skeptical that retaining and rewarding people who made the mistakes that contributed to the unsatisfactory performance is a good idea."[277] He called on the FHFA to eliminate the bonuses at both agencies and asked that employees repay their bonuses when the two companies were placed under government control.

Senator Charles Grassley (R-IA) was even more blunt, saying, "It's an insult that the bonuses were made with an infusion of cash from taxpayers. The elite in Washington and New York need to realize that bonuses for poor performance and at taxpayer expense do a lot of damage to public confidence."[278]

In a very poor choice of words, Senator Grassley went even further when he told an Iowa radio station (WMT) on March 16, 2009, that AIG executives should "follow the Japanese example and come before the American people and take that deep bow and say, 'I'm sorry,' and then either do one of two things: resign or go commit suicide."[279] Realizing that such a statement was reckless, he softened the statement the next day when he said, "What I'm expressing here obviously is not that I want people to commit suicide. That's not my notion. But I do feel very strongly that we have not had statements of apology, statements of remorse, statements of contrition on the part of CEOs of manufacturing companies or banks or financial services or insurance companies that are asking for bailouts."[280]

Employees of Fannie Mae and Freddie Mac now found themselves in a very hostile environment. Their leadership had led them down a very bad path and was now gone. Their companies had failed, but they still believed in their mission and were committed to carrying it out. Yes, they had been well paid in the past, but their salaries certainly hadn't been in the same class as the top executives' compensation. They were on the front line—and still are—but the company stock they had socked away in their retirement plans was now worthless.

It was particularly harsh for newly appointed CFO David Kellermann. He had begun working for Freddie Mac when he was twenty-five years old and had methodically climbed the corporate ladder for over sixteen years until he was suddenly thrust into the role of CFO. He also lost a ton of money. The half million dollars in stock options he owned were now worthless, and so was the $461,000 in restricted stock awards.

An article in the *New York Times* described his work environment as a "poisonous political atmosphere." He had pressure coming from the SEC to accurately certify their financial statements, from company executives who wanted him to emphasize in his disclosures that the company was being run "for the benefit of the government rather than the shareholders," and from the media's mob mentality as they were seeking him out because of the recently announced retention bonuses.[281]

FHFA Director Lockhart would not release details on who was getting large retention bonuses out of concern for their safety, but the media still knew Kellermann was set to receive $850,000 over sixteen months. The media went nuts about Kellermann's compensation. Reporters and camera crews began to park outside his home, disrupting the family life he had with his wife and their five-year-old daughter and creating a dangerous atmosphere at his home.

The long hours of work, political pressures, company legal issues, corporate infighting, media coverage, regulatory pressures, and loss of net worth would surely take its toll on any of us. Sadly, on April 22, 2009, David Kellermann hanged himself in the basement of his home.

He was forty-one. He was a good man. He didn't deserve this.

Part III

In the End

Chapter 9
The Panic of 2008

I once owned a used 1970 Volkswagen bus. I miss it.

Back in the early 1980s, I loaned it to one of my brothers when he and a few pals went on a fishing trip. They drove awhile before eventually heading down a long and winding, washed-out, red dirt road. The day after setting up camp at the river bank, one of his buddies was tying a fishing line to his hook by gripping it between his teeth so he could pull the knot real tight. Too tight. He yanked that ol' hook right into his lip. I wasn't there, but I'm pretty sure Budweiser was.

Photo courtesy of Rich Taylor.

In any event, even though the talented fishermen managed to get the hook out of the poor guy's mouth, they decided to hurry back to the van and get further treatment back home. They didn't panic.

Some of you might recall that these old VWs had the engines in the back. A thin cable ran from the gas pedal, along the bottom of the van, and up to the rear engine compartment. Unfortunately, as my brother drove back to town, a rock kicked up from the dirt road and broke the gas pedal cable. The clutch pedal on the four-speed manual transmission still worked, but pressing the gas pedal to go would do no good. They didn't panic.

Working as a team, they tied their shoestrings together and attached it to the throttle in the back of the bus. The string wasn't very long, but could still make it through the rear window to the backseat. It was there that one of the more talented crewmates controlled the VW's speed as my brother drove.

You can imagine the scene as my brother would holler over the loud noise to the middle-row passengers: "Slowing down!" "Stopping!" "Changing gears!" They would relay the messages to the backseat driver who controlled the speed and their destiny.

You just can't make these things up.

It was a small crisis, but the story ended happily because they didn't panic. It's not always that way. Over the years, we have seen a wide variety of financial disasters where people panicked. Unfortunately, they rarely end well.

There is no way to properly cover the 2008 financial crisis in one book, let alone one chapter. But because there are so many lessons never learned that resulted in this crisis, this chapter will at least summarize the financial meltdown that has led to so much public anger, banker frustration, and political attention. This chapter will review the **Panic of 2008**.

Our country has a history of financial disasters, and you can find plenty of material about panics, for instance, the panics of 1819, 1837, 1857, 1873, 1884, 1893, 1907, 1920, 1921, 1929, 1937, 1974, and 1987. As you can see, panics are not entirely uncommon, and although we have gotten better at preventing them since World War II, obviously, some, like the Panic of 2008, are far worse than others. For the record, a financial panic occurs if people believe that one or more financial institutions will be unable to pay its obligations and they try to withdraw large amounts of their money. When enough people are afraid that the banks will lose their money and rush to withdraw it, the situation can quickly become a self-fulfilling prophecy, and their panic can *cause* the banks to fail.

The Panic of 2008 was exactly that. People rightfully feared they couldn't get their money out of some investment banks; they panicked; suddenly there wasn't enough cash available for everyone, and a crisis ensued. That's the story. You can put your pencils down now.

But the larger questions remain. What caused people to panic? How did we respond? What have we learned??

It really is fascinating and at the same time frustrating to read the wide range of opinions and analyses as to what caused the financial meltdown that began in 2007 and hit a very dangerous level in September 2008. Some explanations have merit, some are absurd, some are weak excuses, and others are simply ideological positions restated. In no particular order, here are just a few of the common and frequently competing explanations of why the meltdown occurred:

- The Federal Reserve kept interest rates too low and caused a housing bubble that collapsed.
- Fannie and Freddie were allowed to get too large and engage in risky lending activities.
- There was a glut of money to invest, particularly from China.

- Politicians demanded more affordable housing loans from lenders, and they forced lenders to take excessive risk.
- The credit reporting agencies were asleep at the wheel.
- There was too much regulation, and the Federal Reserve and Treasury blew it by bailing out Bear Stearns.
- There was not enough regulation, and the Federal Reserve and Treasury blew it by not bailing out Lehman Brothers.
- Borrowers lied.
- Lenders lied.
- Congress dropped the ball.
- Investment banks had too little capital and borrowed too much.
- Commercial banks had too much capital and loaned too much.
- Unregulated hedge funds were allowed to get too big.
- Credit default swaps and other derivatives were poorly designed and regulated.
- The Community Reinvestment Act of 1978 forced banks to make bad loans.

In the end, none of these "causes" of the financial meltdown matter, and it really doesn't matter what academics, bankers, politicians, radio jocks, television personalities, or any other talking heads might claim either. The only thing that matters is the public perception. And the public was less concerned about the third-party responsibilities with credit default swaps or the intricate details of a twenty-five-year-old community reinvestment law.

They were concerned that a boatload of mortgage loans were going bad, and they wanted out before it got worse. They panicked when it became clear that they *might not* get their money back.

Panics

One of the more interesting economists around is former St. Louis Federal Reserve President William Poole. He is an outspoken guy, widely quoted and noted earlier in this book for his public attacks on the structure of Fannie Mae and Freddie Mac. Without trying to label him too narrowly, he is more of a libertarian (or, if you prefer, a "market-liberal") than most.[282] Years ago in a speech, he talked about financial panics in an interesting and accurate way. According to Poole:

> ... periods of great market instability arise when three conditions are met. First, something happens that has widespread significance—is

large enough to matter to lots of people. Second, the triggering event is a surprise. Ordinarily, events long anticipated are not troublesome because corrective action occurs before problems arise. Third, substantial uncertainty clouds resolution of the problem. It is especially difficult for investors to know what to do when the government's response to an unfolding situation is highly uncertain.[283]

The Panic of 2008 met all three conditions. *First, something happens that has widespread significance.* In this case, a ton of higher-risk yet highly rated mortgage-backed securities began to flood the markets.

Second, the triggering event is a surprise. In this case, Bear Stearns's struggle to come up with the cash to pay off investors in two large, nonperforming hedge funds (totaling $1.6 billion) was shocking and triggered a crisis. Further, when nobody stepped up to bail out Lehman Brothers, and they were forced to file for bankruptcy (on September 14, 2008, six months to the day after Bear Stearns received their emergency financing from the Federal Reserve) it was *surprising* and marked what many are calling the unofficial starting date of the financial meltdown.

Third, substantial uncertainty clouds resolution. In this case, our government stepped up and forced the sale of Bear Stearns, this huge bankrupt company. Following that, we did some apparently inconsistent things, like bailing out AIG but letting Lehman Brothers fail. Events were just happening much too quickly for politicians and Treasury and Federal Reserve officials to develop and communicate a comprehensive plan. It was difficult if not impossible for investors to know with confidence what to do with all the uncertainty.

So there you have it. The market was flooded with risky mortgage-backed securities, Bear Stearns couldn't handle it, and Wall Street investors freaked out. The government's response was erratic and inconsistent. The result was panic.

A lot of factors contributed to the crisis, but we'll emphasize some more than others simply because they have (or should have) grabbed more of the headlines and public outcry. There is a reason so many people have been outraged and outspoken and so much media coverage has been focused on the crisis. Some of the noise was warranted, and some was people justifying bad behavior or an ideological perspective. All kinds of regulatory and market-driven changes are taking place, and the situation will undoubtedly make this chapter old news before it is even published. These changes will surely be earnestly debated.

What is not acceptable is a debate without context or a debate that allows broad accusations to go unchallenged.

Tempting as it might be, this chapter tries not to be too harsh on any one particular institution for the Panic of 2008 because in fairness, many people, policies, and institutions should share the blame even though *some clearly deserve more blame* than others. We won't try to measure how much fault one factor had over another, and we won't offer suggestions on how to fix things. It is clear that some of the issues in the Panic of 2008 could have been prevented or the impact mitigated if we had not forgotten the lessons from past panics. Sadly, after reading this chapter one thing will become painfully obvious: *We should have seen it coming.*

Housing Is a Right and a Priority

Housing has always been a national priority. We have extensive tax breaks for home builders, home buyers, and investors. Builders, for example, can often get tax credits or tax abatements to build in designated areas; home buyers can use interest and property tax deductions on federal tax returns; and investors can purchase low- income tax credits to fund more affordable housing. Faith-based organizations, housing advocates, and political leaders frequently declare that safe, decent, affordable housing is a *right* in this country, and we take it seriously. In fact, when Congress passed the National Housing Act in 1949, President Harry S. Truman set the stage for the many government-sponsored housing programs that we have today when he declared:

> *"... a decent home and a suitable living environment for every American family."*

> The Housing Act of 1949 also establishes as a national objective the achievement as soon as feasible of *a decent home and a suitable living environment for every American family*, and sets forth the policies to be followed in advancing toward that goal. These policies are thoroughly consistent with American ideals and traditions. They recognize and preserve local responsibility, and the primary role of private enterprise, in meeting the Nation's housing needs. But they also recognize clearly the necessity for appropriate Federal aid to supplement the resources of communities and private enterprise.[284]

In the past, a great deal of our national focus was on eliminating blight, improving tenement housing, and addressing substandard or dangerous rental housing. Over time that focus has shifted to home ownership because with rising levels of home ownership comes an investment that we believe helps create financial security, promotes a sense of individual pride and responsibility, helps stabilize neighborhoods and reduce crime, and creates job opportunities and economic growth.

Some argue that the wide range of tax breaks and incentives to promote housing of any kind is misdirected and should be eliminated, if for no other reason than to remove the focus on housing loan programs that contributed to this panic. At a minimum, they say, these incentives should be reduced substantially if not entirely phased out.

But as my friend Hugh once observed, "If you are going to have government involved in anything, it should be in the necessities of life: food and housing."

Historically, most Americans agreed, and that's why we have so much government emphasis on agricultural and housing programs. We wanted these programs! *We got this way for a reason.* Besides, the government programs that support home ownership were put in place because they provide tremendous individual and collective benefits. Although these government programs have side effects, the positive impact of the housing industry exceeded the downside, and home ownership has generally created more wealth for everybody. And it

***Mortgages** are the written agreements to borrow money to buy property that specifically says the lender may take possession of the property if the loan is not repaid.*

The Oxford English Dictionary *claims the word was used as far back as 1267and comes from the old French word **mort,** meaning dead, and **gage,** meaning pledge. Roughly translated it means pay me and the land you pledged will be dead to the lender (they have no rights to it). It does not mean" pay me, or I'll kill you." But wouldn't that make a more interesting legal agreement?*

***ARMs** are **a**djustable-**r**ate **m**ortgage loans whose interest rate is tied to some index that will adjust periodically. For example, the interest rate on an ARM loan tied to a US Treasury bill interest-rate index will typically change every time that index changes. Some ARMs contain very low initial interest rates, called "teaser rates," followed by much higher interest rates later.*

***Option ARMs** are also adjustable-rate mortgage loans with interest rates that adjust periodically. However, these loans have another feature: an option on the amount of money borrowers will pay each month. Most give the borrower the option to make small monthly payments initially, followed by much higher payments later* does so without penalty: the increasing net worth of one family rarely happens at the expense of another.

But none of this is without risk, and, time and again, excessive investing in real estate leads to the inevitable boom-and-bust cycle. This one was a real doozy.

Loans, Loans, Loans

You could trace the beginning of the Panic of 2008 as far back as you wish. Perhaps it all started with the Industrial Revolution that led to the need for housing in the cities that led to lending innovations and new institutions, such as building and loan associations. Perhaps it was the National Housing Act of 1934 that created FHA insurance and loosened loan underwriting standards. Maybe it was those pot-smoking hippies from the 1960s. You can start wherever you want and probably justify it somehow. But at least in this case, although we can argue about the exact beginning of the panic, no one can say that it wasn't tied to making bad loans. In this case, it was public concern over the high concentration of subprime and Alt-A loans that led to the crisis, especially when those loans were priced as adjustable-rate mortgage loans (ARMs or Option ARMs), packaged, and then sold as private-label mortgage-backed securities.

Some reports have said that the subprime mortgage crisis was not caused by the more popular explanations, such as lending to borrowers with bad credit, by using weak underwriting standards, or by declining home values. For example, Senior Research Economist Yuliya Demyanyk at the Federal Reserve Bank of Cleveland summarily dismisses many of the most popular explanations about the subprime crisis.

Instead, she says that causes were more complex than that and had been building for many years before the financial meltdown.[285] In a study she wrote with Otto van Hemert, assistant professor of finance at New York University, they claim it was a classic lending "boom-bust scenario with rapid market growth, loosening underwriting standards, deteriorating loan performance, and decreasing risk premiums" that led to the collapse of the market. In their view, we could have seen it coming in 2005. "Loan quality had been worsening for five years in a row at that point." Their viewpoint is consistent with one of our Lessons Never Learned: *We should have seen it coming.*

But others dispute her findings and place greater significance on unscrupulous borrowers, unsound underwriting criteria, or unreasonable loan pricing as the root cause of the crisis. It hardly matters because in the end the Panic of 2008 was a crisis of confidence. The root causes are still very important, but it doesn't matter so much whether the facts prove or disprove the *reasons* subprime and Alt-A loans went bad and caused a crisis. What matters more are the public *perceptions* of what caused it. Loans undeniably went bad. Investors undeniably wanted their money back. Bank runs undeniably occurred. It was a nasty reminder that panics still happen.

At the center of it all were the borrowers, the lenders, and the buyers. In the next three sections, we review each party at the dance.

The Borrowers

To prevent panics, you have to get rid of or reduce the causes, and in this case, the perception that high-risk loans were going bad was certainly a problem. But eliminating all bad loans is impossible, and, frankly, undesirable. I know that sounds odd, but lenders learn early on that those who have never made a bad loan are not good lenders. They are too risk averse. They haven't learned where the line in the sand should be drawn, and as a result, they let good, profitable customers go to the competition. When they adopt too conservative an approach, they don't serve good customers' needs or their own institution's needs.

Naturally, there is a process with safeguards to limit making bad loans and to protect against losses when loans do go bad (with collateral and personal guarantees, for example). There is no reason to be dumb about it. All institutions place dollar limits on individual lenders, so that each one has only so much authority to book a loan without more review. Good bankers have good credit review systems in place. Of course it would be absurd to roll the dice on large loans if those loans didn't have enough protection, or on a large number of loans whose underwriting criteria were untested.

And yet, we did just that with subprime and Alt-A loans.

Alt-A Defined

As background, not everybody uses the same definitions of what an Alt-A or subprime loan is, but the two loans share some of the same characteristics. Alt-A loans have been called "low-doc" loans because they didn't require income or employment verification and relied instead on credit scores. Originally, they were good products for self-employed individuals whose income fluctuated from year-to-year but who consistently paid their bills on time, and these loans were priced a little higher to account for the increased risk.

They were also called "near prime" loans because although not perfect in documentation, they were for borrowers with very good credit histories, and less documentation was the only thing that separated them from a conventional, or prime, loan.

Others called them more derisively NINJA loans, claiming, "No Income, No Job," no problem. Or even "liar loans" because people could simply lie about their income since nobody was checking for accuracy. There are some claims that lenders would even tell the Alt-A borrower what income he or she needed to qualify for the loan and encourage the borrower to list that income on his or her loan application, regardless of whether it was true or not.

Did these mostly white and middle- or upper-income borrowers (as discussed below) cause the meltdown by fraudulently reporting their income in order to get loans, especially loans for the speculative homes where they never intended to live? There is some anecdotal evidence to support this claim, and there is no doubt that it was a contributing factor. It's called fraud, it's illegal, and anybody who intentionally lies on a loan application is a crook. But nobody really knows the extent of the liar problem, and it is hard to believe that there were so many liars that it caused a complete financial meltdown. NINJA loans, or liar loans, were a problem, but they were only a part of the problem.

Besides, blaming people who are encouraged or allowed to lie on a loan application diverts attention from the lesson we never learn: *We should have seen it coming*. We all know that some people will lie or do crazy things for money. Have you watched any television reality shows? Didn't anybody consider that even high credit-scoring borrowers might actually lie? Sure, the borrowers probably thought about their honesty every time they signed a loan document. But what about the lenders—you know, the ones with the gold? Did it ever dawn on the lenders that liar loans could come back to haunt us? Hindsight is 20/20, but, seriously, we should have seen it coming and prevented the problems with fraud.

Subprime Defined

Subprime loans, on the other hand, were different and were a step below the quality of an Alt-A loan. The commercial bank and thrift regulators issued a statement that offered the following characteristics of a subprime loan:

> Subprime borrowers typically have weakened credit histories that include payment delinquencies and possibly more severe problems, such as charge-offs, judgments, and bankruptcies. They may also

> display reduced repayment capacity as measured by credit scores, debt-to-income ratios, or other criteria that may encompass borrowers with incomplete credit histories. Subprime loans are loans to borrowers displaying one or more of these characteristics at the time of origination or purchase. Such loans have a higher risk of default than loans to prime borrowers. Generally, subprime borrowers will display a range of credit risk characteristics that may include one or more of the following: two or more thirty-day delinquencies in the last twelve months, or one or more sixty-day delinquency in the last twenty-four months; judgment, foreclosure, repossession, or charge-off in the prior twenty-four months; bankruptcy in the last five years; relatively high default probability as evidenced by, for example, a credit bureau risk score (FICO) of 660 or below (depending on the product/collateral), or other bureau or proprietary scores with an equivalent default probability likelihood; and/or debt service-to-income ratio of 50 percent or greater, or otherwise limited ability to cover family living expenses after deducting total monthly debt-service requirements from monthly income.[286]

What is most interesting about the regulators' view of subprime lending is that they never said, "Don't do it." Instead, they said, "Be careful." More specifically, they said, "the Agencies continue to believe that responsible subprime lending can expand credit access for consumers and offer attractive returns. However, we expect institutions to recognize that the elevated levels of credit and other risks arising from these activities require more intensive risk management and, often, additional capital."[287] You know, be careful.

The regulators went on to provide some specific guidance for any institution choosing to make subprime loans. If an institution chose to make subprime loans, it needed additional capital and loan loss reserves. It also needed strong risk-management controls, and it needed to stress test the loan portfolios (for example, determining the impact of increased loan defaults in case there was a downturn in the economy). So subprime lending became an accepted product, but with strings attached. If you were a regulated depository financial institution, you could do it, but be prepared if things go bad.

Subprime lending was going strong anyway, but the regulators' blessing surely didn't slow down the rapid growth rates. In fact, the subprime market was booming and had grown from $210 billion in 2001 to $625 billion in 2005, about 20 percent of all originations that year.[288]

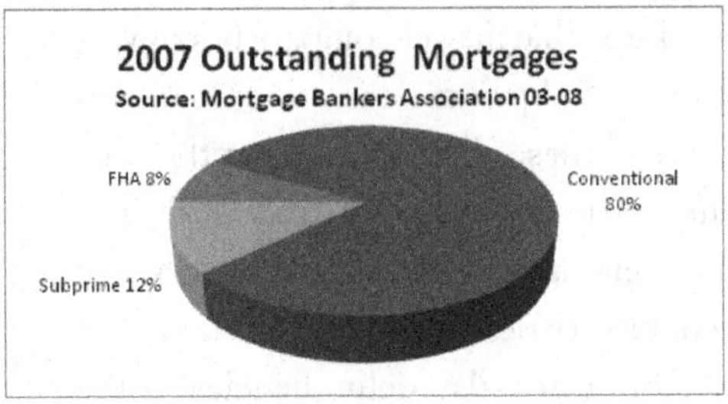

Although 80 percent of the outstanding mortgages in 2007 were still conventional loans, subprime loans were growing fast, and they comprised 12 percent of all outstanding mortgages that year. In fact, according to a report from the Federal Reserve Bank of Dallas, subprime and near-prime loans shot up from 9 percent of newly originated securitized mortgages in 2001 to 40 percent in 2006.[289] That's a lot of growth for higher risk products! *Bigger is not always better.*

Low-Income and Minority Subprime Concentrations

A lot of people thought that subprime lending was loan programs for poor people or for minorities, and when these borrowers couldn't repay their loans, that caused the financial meltdown. Neil Cavuto, FOX News Channel anchor and managing editor of *Business News*, foolishly declared, "Loaning to minorities and risky folks is a disaster."[290] And Orson Scott Card, Southern Virginia University professor, claims, "This housing crisis didn't come out of nowhere. It was not a vague emanation of the evil Bush administration. It was a direct result of the political decision, back in the late 1990s, to loosen the rules of lending so that home loans would be more accessible to poor people."[291] But these allegations are simply political and ideological views. *It's easy to misplace blame.* Don't believe the hype.

Most subprime loans were made to whites and wealthier households, not to minorities and the poor. The problems that began in 2004 that did lead to a financial meltdown three years later were due to the large-scale higher-risk subprime and Alt-A loans, but of the 5.2 million subprime loans between 2004 and 2006, over 57 percent (2.9 million) were made to white borrowers. At this point, there is no evidence that the other 43 percent of (minority) borrowers defaulted on such a large scale, that they alone caused the financial panic.

Whites had more subprime loans than *all minorities combined.* Similarly, of the 7.1 million higher cost loans (especially ARM loans) booked in just the year 2006, over 70 percent (five million) went to white borrowers. Furthermore, middle- and upper-income borrowers accounted for 75 percent of these loans.[292]

In fact, neither minority nor low-income mortgage borrowers have ever caused a financial meltdown in this country, in part, because there just haven't been enough of them to do so. For example, in 1940 the homeownership rate among black households was approximately 20 percent. The rate of ownership for black households had more than doubled to 48 percent by 2003 because of generally safe, sound, and profitable lending programs and a reduction in credit barriers (things were very different for minorities in the 1940s, '50s, and '60s!). The lending programs that led to this increase in black ownership had no systemic risk and didn't result in a financial disaster.

Blaming minorities and the poor for the Panic of 2008 is factually wrong. The data just doesn't support it. That's not to say that focusing on housing in lower-income and minority populations is unwarranted. In fact, a lot of lenders focused on these two demographics for a very good reason: *There was money to make there!* These markets are the main opportunities for home builders and mortgage lenders to grow their businesses.

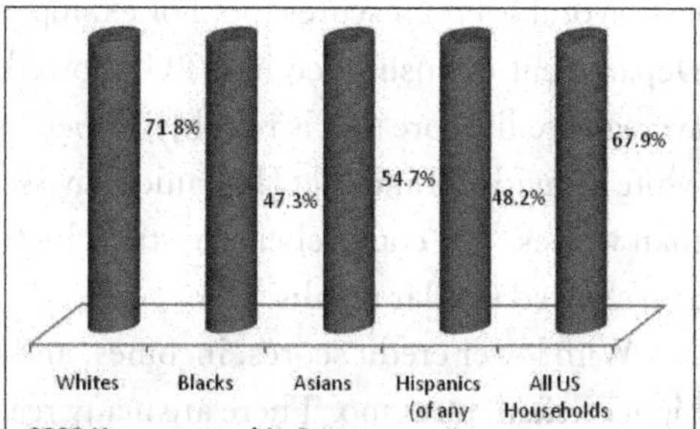

2002 Homeownership Rates

As it turns out, most white families and middle- and upper-income families already own their homes. In 2002, the Census Bureau reported that an incredible 72 percent of white families owned their homes, while less than half of black and Hispanic households could say the same.[293]

In addition, an astounding 83 percent of all households with incomes higher than the national average ($54,400) owned their home, while only 52 percent below that income owned theirs.[294]

In other words, builders, lenders, government agencies, and others all target low- and moderate-income households and minority households because that is where the growth opportunities are!

It's easy to blame politicians for advocating lending to minorities, and that's not to say that they were too aggressive, as some would contend. It's just that placing blame here misses the simple fact of the matter: the market was going in that direction in a very big way, regardless of the politicians.

It isn't surprising to see more *subprime lending* in some minority communities. Subprime lending thrives in communities that have lower incomes, lower net worth, and lower credit scores.

As for incomes, the US Census Bureau reports that nationwide, the median (average) household income in 2009 was $51,425. But Hispanic households (of any race) had 20 percent less income ($40,946); African American households had 33 percent less ($34,445).[295]

Hispanics and African American households had a lower average net worth too. In 2008, the Census Bureau reported the nationwide median net worth (the difference between everything a household owned minus what they owed) was $58,905. But Hispanic households (of any race) had an 87 percent lower average net worth ($7,950); African American households had 91 percent lower ($5,446). They used 2002 data in their study, but the results are still astonishing![296]

Several studies have shown that Hispanics and African Americans have less favorable credit scores too. For example, a widely read study by the Texas Department of Insurance in 2004 showed that African Americans have an average credit score that is roughly 10 percent to 35 percent worse than that of white individuals and that Hispanics have scores 5 percent to 25 percent worse than whites.[297] A comprehensive study by the Federal Reserve Board in 2007 also showed similar results.[298]

With lower credit scores, incomes, and net worth, we would expect to see higher default rates too. There are many reasons for these problems, including the lingering effects of historical, discriminatory education, employment, and housing opportunities. But regardless of the cause or the solution, the raw fact remains that all things are still not equal. We have come a long way but have a long way to go.

So it isn't surprising to see *subprime lending* in minority communities. But even with these statistics, it is still surprising to see the *high concentration* of subprime lending in minority communities that may not go along with the differences in credit scores, net worth, and income.

We know a lot of minority borrowers have problems qualifying for loans. Heck, a lot of minorities won't even apply for a loan because they don't want to be denied. But between 2004 and 2006, for the folks who did get approved for mortgage loans, an astounding 53 percent of mortgages to African American borrowers and 41 percent of mortgages to Hispanic borrowers were subprime loans.[299]

It begs the question: did all those minorities have issues that forced them into subprime loans? In particular, are fewer than half of all black borrowers worthy of a loan that *wasn't* subprime? This includes government-sponsored loans, such as loans to veterans. Something is amiss.

In 2006 alone, subprime lending comprised 39 percent of all mortgages to minorities (compared to 18 percent for white borrowers). Some states reported very high levels of subprime lending to minorities, for example Michigan (60 percent of all mortgages), Rhode Island (49 percent), and Missouri (48 percent). In fact, over 60 percent of mortgage loans to African Americans in Michigan and Wisconsin were subprime loans![300]

The nonprofit Center for Responsible Lending reported that "for most types of subprime home loans, African-American and Latino borrowers are at a greater risk of receiving higher-rate loans than white borrowers, even after controlling for legitimate risk factors."[301] If true, this would constitute predatory and illegal lending activities. Don't be surprised to see significant controversy on this subject over the next several years.

Nobody brings the issue of subprime and Alt-A loans to light better than the very funny Larry Wilmore, senior black correspondent for *The Daily Show* in his interview with comedian and host Jon Stewart:[302]

> **Jon Stewart:** How actually does someone with no money and a poor credit history even qualify for these loans in the first place?
> **Larry Wilmore:** To get one of these loans, you only need to fill out something called a "stated income form." Now, you put down whatever salary you want without getting it checked.
> **Stewart:** I'm sorry. Can I just go back to that very quickly? What was that under cosigner?
> **Wilmore:** Oh, yeah. That's Oprah, Jon. They don't check that out.
> **Stewart:** They don't check out that Oprah's cosigning these loans?
> **Wilmore:** Nope. Absolutely real. We are allowed to use her as collateral.
> **Stewart:** If poor people in the black community, if they know that these loans are spurious, they're not good loans, why take them out, why let themselves be duped by unfair lending practices?
> **Wilmore:** Duped? Believe me: we know these loans are unfair. That's why we stopped paying them back.
> **Stewart:** I didn't realize that.
> **Wilmore:** I mean who's duping who, Jon?
> **Stewart:** But if you don't pay back, you lose your house.
> **Wilmore:** Yeah, but *they* lose a trillion dollars.

"They" refers to the investment bankers (and hedge funds), commercial bankers, and thrift bankers who provided the money for these loans, and this would be even funnier if it weren't so close to the truth. And the impact on minority and poor neighborhoods is very harsh too. Although beyond the scope of this book, it's worth mentioning that there are many issues with high concentrations of subprime lending in minority and low-income communities, not the least of which is the high rate of foreclosures, which will devastate the net worth of families living nearby because their housing prices are going down. That's because for most US families, our wealth is concentrated in our homes, and this is especially true for minorities and low-income households. The US Census Bureau reports that in 2002, 42 percent of our household's net worth (about $73,700) was in our home, versus only 11 percent (about $10,000) in stocks and mutual funds. Among minorities, the concentration of net worth in homes was a whole lot higher, 61 percent of black households' net worth and 59 percent of Hispanic households' net worth.[303] Imagine the impact on your family as your net worth crumbles every time a foreclosure sign appears in your neighborhood. Regardless of your race or "class," this problem affects everybody.

"Generally, subprime lending and the foreclosure crisis is presented as if it is only an issue for minority and low-income borrowers," said Maurice Jourdain-Earl, managing director of Compliance Technologies, a firm known for significant home-mortgage analysis. "However, the data shows that the problem is much broader than just with minorities and low-income households. My beliefs are, if we widen our lenses to see that this problem affects all segments of society, we will change the tone and context of our approach to solutions."[304] Well said.

Adjustable Rate Loans and Prepayment Penalties

To make matters even worse, most subprime loans had higher default risk because they were priced aggressively with adjustable-rate loan features and with stiff prepayment penalties. Looking back, you can see a disconcerting picture: subprime *adjustable-rate loans* climbed from less than 60 percent of originations in September 2003 to over 76 percent in June 2005![305] In contrast, the Federal Reserve reported in March 2007 that while adjustable-rate mortgages (ARMs)

> *... a dumb mistake in assuming that property values would continue to rise and refinancing would always be available.*

were only about one of every eight high-quality loans, they were between half and two-thirds of all subprime mortgages![306]

Because these loans were often provided at low initial interest rates (called "teaser rates") to help marginal borrowers meet their loan payments, they were at risk of defaulting when the homebuyers' mortgage interest rates adjusted upward, which they almost always do unless market rates fall significantly.

Lenders would frequently reassure borrowers who were concerned about higher interest rates that they could refinance the loan if rates got too high, and because property values were continuing to rise, most borrowers and their lenders assumed that was true. There is plenty of anecdotal evidence that a lot of lenders unethically or illegally coerced borrowers into these risky loans. But there appeared to be less of an evil intent to defraud the borrowers with ARMs than a dumb mistake in assuming that property values would continue to rise and refinancing would always be available.

> *... prepayment penalties on such a high concentration of subprime loans may not have been illegal, but for most subprime borrowers, it sure as hell was a rip-off.*

Many bankers will argue otherwise, but an evil intent does seem evident with prepayment penalties attached to high-cost subprime mortgages, especially those that were priced with adjustable interest rates.

Advocates of prepayment penalties will contend that they serve a useful role. They ensure that lenders will generate enough income to cover expenses and provide a fair return on investment. They protect against interest-rate risk that can occur when lenders borrow longer-term money to fund a loan and then get stuck with the high cost of borrowed funds when loans are repaid. Prepayment penalties also help assure lenders they will generate a steady income stream over a few years.

Most importantly, prepayment penalties are necessary when lenders offer teaser rates on ARMs because borrowers could refinance as soon as the teaser rate was repriced, thus preventing lenders from obtaining a fair return on their loan. After all, the teaser was offered with an expectation that the lost income in the first year would be recovered in later years.

But while prepayment penalties were seldom included on conventional loans (about 2 percent of the time), they were included on almost 80 percent of all subprime loans![307] And while there may be some merit in charging prepayment penalties to lessen interest-rate risk for the small percentage of lenders who keep the loan in their own portfolio, it rings hollow for the overwhelming majority of subprime lenders. They sell their loans to be packaged into mortgage-backed securities, where there are other low-cost and equally effective ways to mitigate the interest-rate risks. For example, interest-rate swaps are well-established, low-risk derivative products that can serve this purpose.

No, prepayment penalties on high-priced subprime loans were done for one reason and one reason only: to make a killing.

Let's face it: subprime loans rarely offered *teaser* rates that were even close to conventional market interest rates. They were higher. A whole lot higher!

Remember, a well-structured ARM would start at a somewhat low rate and then adjust upward. But while a high-quality ARM loan at the time might start at a comfortable 2.5 percent interest rate, these subprime disasters were starting at around 8.5 percent and then adjusting up from there!

More specifically, according to a study by Senior Research Economist Yuliya Demyanyk (Federal Reserve Bank of Cleveland) the average subprime ARM rates at origination "were in the 7.3 to 9.7 percent range for the years 2001–2007, compared to average prime hybrid mortgage rates at origination of around 2–3 percent." As she said, "the subprime figures are hardly 'teaser rates'."[308] And you couldn't get out of the deal without paying a penalty either! You know, prepayment penalties on such a high concentration of subprime loans may not have been illegal, but for most subprime borrowers, it sure as hell was a rip-off.[309]

The pricing on prepayment penalties varies, but, generally speaking, lenders received about a 1 percent premium on the amount of the loan they sell if it has a prepayment penalty. The borrower's penalty is usually calculated as a percentage of the outstanding loan balance at the time of prepayment (such as 2 percent of the loan amount), or as the interest that would be paid over a period of time (such as six months interest). The prepayment penalties usually decline or disappear completely after five years. Sometimes lenders will offer prime borrowers a lower interest rate in return for accepting a prepayment penalty. But subprime borrowers were not likely to get a lower rate in exchange for the prepayment penalty because, frankly, they were in no position to negotiate loan terms.

The regulators considered mortgage loans to be *predatory* if the repayment was based on the assets of the borrower instead of the borrower's ability to repay (typically) with employment income or with liquid assets, such as cash savings, stocks, and bonds. Predatory loans also included convincing a borrower to refinance a loan repeatedly so the lender could charge high points and fees each time. Enforcing stiff prepayment penalties was certainly one way to obtain higher fees! Some states, such as Texas and Vermont, prohibit state-chartered banks from originating prepayment penalties with high-cost home loans. But federal enforcement of laws and regulations to prevent predatory prepayment penalties like these rarely if ever occurred. That's one reason why Congress now requires the Federal Reserve System to pay the bills for a new, *independent* agency, the Bureau of Consumer Protection, which will assume responsibility for enforcing federal consumer protection laws (covered in the next chapter). *People matter.*

The final numbers aren't in yet, but credit losses on mortgage loans are going to be huge. As of year-end 2008, the Mortgage Bankers Association reported that 28.3 percent of subprime loans were at least sixty days past due, and nearly 40 percent of subprime ARMs were past due. For any readers who are not familiar with past-due rates, these levels of nonperforming loans fall into a category known in finance as, "Are you friggin' kidding me!" Estimates vary widely, but Lehman Brothers analysts estimated in December 2007 that credit losses on the outstanding stock of all mortgages would range between $250 billion and $320 billion. In November 2007, Goldman Sachs was estimating between $243 billion and $495 billion.[310]

The Lenders

You can't point to any one lending company for causing the Panic of 2008, but you can still direct your attention to California and its high concentration of mortgages originated by large subprime and Alt-A lenders. In fact, according to the National Mortgage News rankings, seven of the top ten subprime mortgage lenders were headquartered in California, and although they financed houses nationwide, the high concentration of defaults in California made up a lot of their problem loan portfolios.[311]

High concentrations of subprime lending and then foreclosures have spread nationwide, and some communities have been hit harder than others. A study by the Center for Responsible Lending reports that subprime loan foreclosures will result in home values declining nationwide by over $202 billion.[312] Losses this high can crush state and local governments that rely on property taxes for funding.

The top five states projected to suffer the biggest loss in home values were California, New York, Florida, Illinois, and New Jersey, but you almost have to list every state in the country because the impact of foreclosures and the resulting loss of property values hurt everybody. Individual communities such as Miami, Phoenix, and Minneapolis also had serious and very real problems. The table on the next page lists the top fifteen communities hit hardest by foreclosures.

There are many ways to measure the largest US subprime loan companies. You can compare asset size, loan originations by number or by dollar amount, total capital, etc. You can also look at any period of time you wish, such as a five-year period showing various levels and trends or a one-quarter period representing a snapshot of the industry. In any case, although the rankings are very interesting, the underlying problems were the same, and most of the big players have been shut down by now. By the end of 2006, at least twenty-two of the thirty largest subprime lenders in the United States had gone bankrupt or were otherwise out of business.[313]

Some folks might think it unfair to say that the largest subprime lenders in the country paid a *well-deserved* very high price when they tossed sound underwriting standards out the window and promoted aggressively priced loans with strong prepayment penalties. And you might think that using these short-term profits to line the pockets of their executives, staff, and shareholders was okay too.

But I would disagree.

First, there should be a high price for unethical behavior, and many lenders did in fact behave unethically and take advantage of uneducated or unknowing borrowers. And, yes, it is absolutely true that a lot of borrowers were treated illegally. That's why the attorneys general in so many states are pursuing lawsuits and settlements for the illegal predatory practices of these lenders. The lawbreakers should be punished to the absolute full extent of the law, and it is in everybody's best interest to be sure that the punishments are strong enough to deter these illegal activities in the future. A high price for predatory or discriminatory lending protects good lenders from damaged reputations when criminals get involved. Prosecution is well deserved. *Greed has a price.* Let's hope it is high.

As an example of the problem, in an interview with host Steve Inskeep on National Public Radio, some former employees of Ameriquest Mortgage (one of the largest subprime lenders in the country) admitted to unethical behavior and said they were encouraged to "conceal rate terms" and make "fake fixed-loan documents that pushed customers into loans they couldn't afford."[314] Richard Bitner, former subprime lender and author of *Confessions of a Subprime Lender:*

An Insider's Tale of Greed, Fraud, and Ignorance, says that "three out of four subprime mortgages originated by brokers were misleading or fraudulent." He notes that "now that the entire thing has crashed, every subprime lender is viewed as a scumsucker."[315] No surprise there.

Top 15 Metropolitan Statistical Areas Projected Foreclosure Rates for Subprime Loans Originated in 2006

RANK	MSA	%
1	**Merced, CA**	25.0
2	**Bakersfield, CA**	24.2
3	**Vallejo-Fairfield, CA**	23.8
4	**Las Vegas-Paradise, NV**	23.7
5 (tied)	**Fresno, CA**	23.5
5 (tied	**Ocean City, NJ**	23.5
7	**Stockton, CA**	23.4
8	**Reno-Sparks, NV**	23.2
9 (tied)	**Santa Ana-Anaheim-Irvine, CA**	22.8
9 (tied)	**Washington-Arlington-Alexandria, DC-VA-MD-WV**	22.8
11	**Riverside-San Bernardino-Ontario, CA**	22.6
12	**Carson City, NV**	22.5
13 (tied)	**Atlantic City, NJ**	22.2
13 (tied)	**Visalia-Porterville, CA**	22.2
15 (tied)	**Los Angeles-Long Beach-Glendale, CA**	22.0
15 (tied)	**Nassau-Suffolk, NY**	22.0
15 (tied)	**Saginaw-Saginaw Township North, MI**	22.0

Source: Center for Responsible Lending[316]

But it's not fair to cast such a wide and nasty net over all subprime lenders. Even if Bitner was right, that still means *at least some* subprime lenders were honest, ethical, and honorable. In fact, people who support subprime lending see it as an effective capitalist approach to serving borrowers' needs, especially, *but not exclusively*, low- and moderate-income borrowers. While we may not agree with the loan pricing, most people believe the government does not have enough reasons to outlaw subprime lending if certain conditions are met, such as complying with states usury interest-rate laws. As long as the lenders are honest—the underwriting standards are not abusive (for example, if they do not saddle borrowers with excessive debt payments relative to their income), there is no fraud, the borrower understands the agreement because the lender has disclosed all of the terms, and borrowers are aware of alternatives—most people are okay with it. The federal regulators certainly have been.

Oh, there are better loan programs for sure (FHA loans, for example), and state usury interest rate ceilings are sometimes ridiculous. For example, the maximum interest rate allowed in Georgia was set at 60 percent on loans over $3,000.[317] That's right. 60 percent! Even so, informed people should have freedom of choice in this country. As long as we have financial literacy (And that's a problem. We often *don't* have financial literacy.) and better enforcement of lending laws, subprime advocates and others think we should have a fair amount of latitude and allow subprime lending to continue. I'd like to think we can do better than to allow this to continue, but that's just me.

That doesn't mean that there isn't a price for the lenders though. Aside from the costs of illegal or predatory lending, in a capitalist economy there is often a high price to pay for bad business decisions when so many loans default. The men and women running subprime lending companies are not and should not be exempt. Not only have their professional reputations been severely damaged, but their companies' profits and equity have been decimated. *Greed has a price.*

The list of failed subprime lenders is extensive because subprime lending became so profitable in the short run that everybody tried to get in on the game. But it's important to get a sampling of the types of companies engaged in subprime lending because they were major contributors to the 2008 financial meltdown. The following is a snapshot of the largest subprime lenders in the fourth quarter of 2006.

HSBC Finance

Based on originations, **HSBC Finance,** a finance company in Prospect Heights, Illinois, was at the top (we'll call it **No. 1**). In the fourth quarter of 2006, it was the largest subprime loan originator in the United States. You might know them as Household Finance, a company whose history dated back to 1878. It was owned by HSBC North America, a holding company owned by HSBC Holdings in London.

HSBC Finance originated about $12.3 billion of subprime loans in 2006, primarily through its US consumer lending business (1,382 branches, 13,300 employees, and forty-six states). It also bought pools of loans from over 220 unaffiliated, third-party lenders, primarily through its subsidiary, Decision One Mortgage Company.[318] Most of its business was in California and Florida.

It doesn't look like management fully grasped the scope of the pending financial disaster lurking around the corner. Profits were falling in their consumer lending business from a 1.77 percent return on average assets in 2004 to only .71 percent two years later, and in spite of the decline in profits and the hefty increase in nonperforming loans, the company kept on expanding its loan portfolio by 13 percent in 2006. They also purchased two mortgage companies—Solstice Capital Group Inc. for $49 million and Champion Mortgage for $2.5 billion—to try to keep the loan portfolio growing. *We should have seen it coming.*

By the end of 2007, HSBC Finance was reporting a $4.9 billion (yes, *billion*!) loss. They closed branches, stopped originating subprime loans, and shut down both Decision One Mortgage Company and Solstice Capital Group.

Siddharth (Bobby) Mehta was appointed chairman and chief executive officer of HSBC Finance Corporation in May 2005 and became chief executive officer of the parent company, HSBC North America Holdings Inc., in March 2005. Working at the company paid very well, and from 2003 to 2005, his compensation totaled $37.1 million.[319] He was highly paid for his wisdom, and in January 2006, the *Times* newspaper in London quoted him as saying, "We don't believe that there is any credit cataclysm coming." That same year he was paid $6.88 million.

Thirteen months later, Mehta "resigned" (on February 15, 2007) and was paid $6.15 million for his work that year. That's right, folks. Mr. Mehta worked forty-six days in 2007 but was paid over $6 million in compensation while the company went on to lose *$4.9 billion* in that same year (yes, *billion*!).

Once again, management's response to the horrendous results in 2007 was puzzling. Wisely, they began calling customers to modify ARM loans in anticipation of their first rate adjustments because they knew their borrowers would have trouble paying these loans. If the borrowers couldn't pay the loans, it would send HSBC's past-due, nonaccrual, and foreclosure rates through the roof. But the proposed repricing was good for only a year, and it certainly doesn't look like their plan was designed to provide much relief for borrowers. Renegotiating the loans was not a community service. It was purely self-serving.

And it was too late. By the end of 2008, HSBC had closed over five hundred branches, borrowed $520 million from the Federal Reserve, and contributed $3.5 billion in additional capital to keep going.[320] They also reported a $2.8 billion (yes, *billion*!) loss for the year. In February 2009, they decided to stop lending. By June 2009, the subprime finance company was reporting a $5.1 billion (yes, *billion*!) loss *for the first six months* of the year and was closing *all* consumer lending branch offices. They announced that approximately fifty-four hundred employees would lose their jobs as a result.

Let's be very clear: they reported losses of about $12.8 *billion* in two and a half years! That's a lot of money down the drain. From July 2007 to December 2008, the subprime lender and its subsidiaries faced five separate class-action lawsuits alleging discriminatory lending. In addition, the City of Cleveland, Ohio, filed two lawsuits (one state, one federal) naming the subprime lender and others as defendants. The financial and reputational damage here is very real. *Bigger is not always better. Greed has a price.*

The very large, $2.4 trillion, bank holding company that owns HSBC Finance will continue to operate out of London. But the US-based subprime lender, HSBC Finance, has now disbanded almost all of its consumer lending business (where most of the subprime loans were made or purchased) and is a shell of its former self, with only a very narrow focus on collecting the remaining outstanding loans.[321] In any event, the financial losses caused by their awful loan underwriting standards and overly aggressive loan pricing were well deserved. *It's almost always bad loans.*

Other subprime lenders

No. 2 on the list of largest subprime loan originators in 2006 was **New Century Financial, Irvine, California**, a real-estate investment trust that operated a wholesale lending division in eighteen states and thirty-five regional offices (purchasing forty-seven thousand mortgages). They also owned a retail division, Home123, (with 222 sales offices), a 1-800-HOME123 phone application, and a HOME123.com website. They originated $12.2 billion in mortgages in 2006. They filed for bankruptcy on April 6, 2007.

No. 3, Countrywide Financial, Calabasas, California, was sold in a fire sale for a mere $6.71 a share (down from $45 six months earlier) to Bank of America shortly after Countrywide's corporate debts were rated as junk bonds. A few months later, Bank of America said it would spend up to $8.7 billion to settle predatory lending charges filed by eleven state attorneys general against Countrywide.

The next five largest subprime lenders were all California-based companies and included the following:

No. 4, WMC Mortgage, Burbank, California, was owned by GE Money, a subsidiary of the General Electric Company. GE bought the company, formerly known as Weyerhaeuser Mortgage Company, from Apollo Management LP in 2004. After incurring an operating loss of $900 million in 2007, GE sold the subprime lender in December 2007.[322]

No. 5, First Franklin Financial, San Jose, California, was purchased by Merrill Lynch from National City Corporation in December 2006 for $1.3 billion. By the end of the next year, Merrill Lynch was reporting $3.1 billion in losses in subprime lending (and $542 million in losses with Alt-A loans) and had shut down all subprime loan originations.[323] (Do we need to say "yes, *billion*" anymore? Hopefully everybody gets it. This is a ton of losses!)

No. 6, Wells Fargo Home Mortgage, San Francisco, California, is a subsidiary of Wells Fargo & Company and produces conventional and subprime loans. By the end of 2007, the parent company was no longer buying subprime loans, had placed $11.9 billion of these loans into liquidation, and had added $1.4 billion to its loan loss reserves for these loan products.[324]

No. 7, Option One Mortgage Corporation, Irvine, California, was a subsidiary of H&R Block, and its operations were discontinued in November 2006. The subsidiary had lost approximately $808 million in 2007 and another $1.2 billion in 2008. What remained of it was sold to American Home Mortgage Servicing Inc. (an affiliate of WL Ross & Company), in April 2008.[325]

No. 8, Fremont Investment and Loan, Santa Monica, California, was one of fourteen California industrial banks, which means it couldn't accept demand deposits—checking accounts—but was still subject to the same basic laws as commercial banks. Freemont's subprime lending led to losses of $143 million in 2006, $879 million in 2007, and $206 million in the first six months of 2008.[326] The FDIC issued a cease-and-desist order in 2007; the bank's parent company declared bankruptcy on July 17, 2008, and a few days later, sold what remained of its bank's branches and deposits to CapitalSource Bank, a new industrial bank in Chevy Chase, Maryland.

The Buyers

We are all familiar with the Golden Rule. No, not that one. The other one: *He who has the gold, rules.* It's important because without the gold rulers, there would have been no Panic of 2008. Although many say that the panic was because homebuyers defaulted on their loans or because unscrupulous lenders made the loans in the first place—and both certainly were at fault—the Panic of 2008 could not have occurred without large-scale financing. The financiers must be held accountable because they had the gold, and they set the rules. There are plenty of guilty parties, but it was the commercial banks, thrifts, and investment banks with most of the gold. They used this money to purchase subprime and Alt-A loans, package them into securities, and sell them to others (or even back to themselves). And they made money all along the way.

To understand how this contributed to the panic, we need to understand how a mortgage-backed security (MBS) works because it was the higher-risk securities (and their offspring) that were in the center of the storm.

> ***MBS** is a mortgage-backed security, a type of IOU that is secured by home-mortgage loans.*

Let's assume you want to buy a house so you get a typical (conventional) thirty-year, fixed-rate loan from your local bank or other mortgage lender. You agree to make monthly principal and interest payments on that loan to the company that provided the money, usually a bank, thrift, credit union, or large mortgage company.

From a lender's perspective, keeping a long-term fixed-rate loan on a bank's books is risky because over time what the bank pays on deposits could actually cost more than what they earn on the loan. That's why banks frequently choose to sell the loan instead of keeping it. Besides, if they sell the loan they can earn a decent fee (typically around $1,200 on an average loan in 2008) and get their cash back to make even more loans.

The loan purchaser could be just about anybody, but it is usually a company that has expertise in grouping your mortgage loan with other similar mortgages (known as *pooling* the mortgages). Those companies have MBS underwriters who then sell an IOU backed by this pool of loans, including yours, to investors.

Technically, the investors are only buying the cash flow from the principal and interest payments on the mortgage loans in the MBS. They don't want the hassle of actually calling people to collect late payments, after all. So we have mortgage "servicing companies" who specialize in collecting the loan payments. They collect all loans, take a fee, and pass on the rest to the MBS underwriters. The MBS underwriters take a fee and pass on the rest to the MBS investors. So far, the only one actually paying money every month instead of earning money every month is the home buyer! But they get the home of their dreams, or something like that, so it's all good.

In fact, it's a nifty little system developed right here in the USA where everybody gets something out of the deal. Home buyers get their home, lenders make money and get their cash back quickly, the MBS underwriters sell securities for a profit, and MBS servicers also turn a profit. Other than outright fraud or theft, the only breakdown that could occur is if a large number of the underlying loans went bad.

In the beginning everybody understood that, which is why the underwriters had very strict standards of what loans they would purchase from lenders. That's in large part because to sell these securities to investors, the MBS underwriters paid Fannie Mae, Freddie Mac, or Ginnie Mae a fee in return for a *guarantee* that if necessary, these agencies would ensure the prompt payment of principal and interest on the MBS. If you were an MBS underwriter, once you had this guarantee, you knew it would be no problem getting a very good credit rating from one of the big three nationally recognized credit rating agencies—Moody's, Fitch, and Standard & Poor's. A guarantee and a great credit rating would further assure investors around the world that this was a good deal.

Their guarantee was so important that Fannie Mae and Freddie Mac and, to a much lesser extent, Ginnie Mae were able to set the loan underwriting standards for just about everybody.[327] If you wanted their guarantee or if you might want it later, you had to *standardize* the transactions to their satisfaction, from debt-to-income ratios, down-payment requirements, and credit scores, right down to the actual loan documents used at the loan closing.

To see just how dominant these companies were, if you borrowed money to buy a home in the past fifteen years or so, take a look at the loan closing documents. There is a very good chance they have the Fannie Mae or Freddie Mac names in the footers. It makes sense too; if you are going to buy and sell mortgage loans on a large scale, you must document them consistently. And if the products are standardized, it makes it possible to package the loans into mortgage-backed securities. For the most part, this was a safe and profitable product that helped millions of people own their own homes.

Fannie Mae dominated with about 44 percent of the market in 2003. But because of the accounting debacle with Frank Raines, intense scrutiny by the regulators, and significant competition from private-label issuers, Fannie's market share fell to only 28 percent the next year. Similarly, Freddie Mac was also embroiled in an accounting scandal, and their market share had gone down as well. It's easy to blame these two GSEs for buying the subprime and Alt-A loans that caused the panic, but it's incorrect. They were so embroiled in their own accounting controversies that they were late to the game, and they were still first and foremost providing the secondary market for conventional loans. *It's easy to misplace blame:* Fannie Mae and Freddie Mac.

The investment banks' private-label companies, however, did not falter like Fannie and Freddie, and these companies increased production considerably as their market share more than doubled, from 22 percent in 2003 to 46 percent in 2004. They were becoming significant competitors in the secondary market and were taking more risk to do so. They were the leaders in packaging subprime and Alt-A mortgages. As they grew, the risks grew with them.

At its peak in 2006, companies like Bear Stearns and Lehman Brothers were heavily invested in these products and had considerable exposure. Both Bear Stearns's and Lehman Brothers's 2006 annual reports clearly state they were leaders in mortgage-backed securitization. Bear had packaged $99.3 billion of primarily private-label securities that year alone.[328] What happened next was a disaster and was a sober reminder of all ten lessons never learned. Within eighteen months, the economy faced a complete and total meltdown.

As noted before, panics occur when three conditions are met. *First, something happens that has widespread significance*, which in this case was the increase of higher-risk, yet highly rated, mortgage-backed securities flooding the markets. We have just reviewed the borrowers, the lenders, and the buyers who made that possible. Now let's look at the second and third conditions: *the triggering event is a surprise,* and *substantial uncertainty clouds resolution.* The chronology that follows presents the surprising series of events leading to the Panic of 2008. Each one was noteworthy and a bit surprising, and the failures of Bear Stearns, Lehman, AIG, and others were downright shocking. In hindsight, *we should have seen it coming.*

Triggering Events

April 2007

The first red flag and one of the first big companies to fail was the second-largest subprime lender in the country. **New Century Financial** declared bankruptcy mainly because they had to buy back large numbers of bad loans they had previously sold "with recourse." Bad loans, insufficient liquidity, and legal woes took them down. Unfortunately, they were just one of many failures. *It's almost always bad loans.*

May 2007

A large hedge fund operation, **Dillon Read Capital Management**, a subsidiary of Swiss investment bank UBS, closed after huge losses in US subprime, mortgage-backed securities. It resulted in a $375 million (US dollars) loss to the company.[329] The losses included $200 million in severance packages for company executives at the failed hedge fund operation.[330] This was a very generous payoff for a failed venture, and the public began to notice excessive compensation. *Greed has a price.*

June 2007

As the number of past-due rates and defaults began to skyrocket, the value of the mortgage-backed securities continued to fall. Two large hedge funds (about $2 billion in total equity) managed by Bear Stearns were heavily invested in subprime, mortgage-backed securities, and because the fund managers borrowed heavily (about $10 billion in loans) to purchase the securities, as their value fell, the hedge fund was required to put up more cash as collateral for these loans. Both funds lost nearly all of their value.[331] Bear Stearns put in another $1.6 billion to meet the liquidity needs in June. Perhaps sensing blood in the water, other competing hedge funds and investors began betting that the value of mortgage-backed securities would continue to fall. That would force Bear to either put up more cash or sell more securities (at a loss), and the value of their stock would drop. The bets paid off. Bear was forced to sell more securities, driving their value lower, which then required Bear to sell even more securities, and the process would repeat. Bear was facing financial ruin.

This was not the first time a very large US hedge fund had faced financial ruin. **Long-Term Capital Management (LTCM)** in Greenwich, Connecticut, was founded by two Nobel Prize winning economists, Myron Scholes and Robert Merton, in 1993, but faced near bankruptcy in 1998 (when Russia defaulted on its debts). The Federal Reserve Bank of New York held a meeting of investment bankers who stood to lose a lot of money if the hedge fund declared bankruptcy. The Reserve Bank helped broker an industry bailout that helped protect the lenders and avert a financial crisis. No government money was used for the bailout, and it worked. The debts were all repaid, a crisis was averted, and the hedge fund was liquidated in 2000. To their credit, fourteen of the fifteen investment banks who were asked to step up and provide the necessary loans did just that, thus saving themselves from losses and preventing an economic crisis.

Only one investment banker refused to participate in the bailout. Bear Stearns CEO Jimmy Cayne was reported to have bluntly said, "Let them fail."[332] He walked. Needless to say the other investment bankers and Federal Reserve officials were not pleased with his tone or his refusal to participate in a matter that they believed posed tremendous risk to the economy. It shouldn't be surprising then that when Bear Stearns faced its own liquidity crisis nine months later, nobody showed up to help them out, leading to the company's collapse in March 2008. Some people speculate that this was payback for Cayne's attitude with the LTCM bailout. *Greed has a price. People matter.*

July 2007

Bear notified its hedge fund investors that one fund had lost more than 90 percent of its value, and the other had lost virtually all of its investor capital. The two funds filed for bankruptcy. As the investment fund manager, Bear Stearns also took a hit and reported approximately $200 million of losses associated with the failure. It marked the beginning of the end for Bear Stearns. *It's almost always bad loans.*

August 2007

President George W. Bush stated in his presidential news conference on August 9 that "the fundamentals of our economy are strong" and that it appeared we would not have a "precipitous decline in housing" but instead we were likely "headed for a soft landing."[333]

That same day, BNP Paribas, France's largest bank, announced that they would not honor withdrawal requests from three large investment funds totaling $2.2 billion because they couldn't raise enough cash to meet those requests. The funds were heavily invested in US mortgage-backed securities, and, at this point, there was really no market for their sale. BNP Paribas issued a statement saying, "The complete evaporation of liquidity in certain market segments of the US securitization market has made it impossible to value certain assets fairly regardless of their quality or credit rating."[334]

The following week, the Federal Reserve lowered the discount rate (the rate they charge banks for overnight or short-term loans) by half a percent, from 6.25 percent to 5.75 percent, announcing that "financial markets have deteriorated" and expressing concern that "tighter credit conditions and increased uncertainty" could hurt the economy. The Fed acknowledged that the economy was in trouble, and the "downside risks to growth have increased appreciably."[335]

In an effort to stay alive, Countrywide Financial sold $2 billion of preferred stock to Bank of America. It wouldn't be enough to save them.

American Home Mortgage, the tenth-largest mortgage lender in the country, filed for bankruptcy.

September 2007

The Federal Reserve lowered the discount rate another half percent, to 5.25 percent, to try to increase liquidity and spur the economy because tightening of credit conditions was making housing problems worse.

The international ramifications of subprime lending become painfully evident when Britain's eighth-largest bank, Northern Rock, was faced with a run on the bank by worried depositors who feared the bank would fail. The British eventually nationalized the bank, and depositors were spared losses. However, shareholders lost their entire investments. *People matter.* Of course, some people will matter more than others, and, in this case, depositors mattered more than shareholders.

October 2007

Merrill Lynch CEO E. Stanley O'Neal was forced to retire October 31 after Merrill Lynch reported a $2.2 *billion* quarterly loss, the largest in its ninety-three-year history. The loss occurred because this third-largest investment company in the country had invested heavily in subprime, mortgage-backed securities, and their value had sunk by about $8.4 billion. O'Neal was also criticized and lost the confidence of the board when he held "undisclosed" meetings with Wachovia Bank without telling the board. He was trying to arrange a merger of the two companies before announcing these huge losses, but going behind the board's back is never a good move. Unbelievably, his compensation package when he was fired was valued by Merrill Lynch as of October 29, 2007, at $161.5 million![336] He is one of the reasons lawmakers began efforts to restrict executive pay. *Greed has a price.*

Meanwhile, profits at the largest US banking company, Citigroup, fell 60 percent for the third quarter because of subprime loan concentrations. Citigroup announced they had approximately $55 billion in direct exposure to subprime lending. Of that amount, $43 billion was in securities backed by subprime loans, and $12 billion was in direct subprime loans. Their stock price plummeted 25 percent, from $55.70 per share in January to under $42 in October. *It's almost always bad loans.*

November 2007

After the company wrote down $5.9 *billion* in subprime-related losses, Citigroup's chairman and chief executive officer, Charles O. Prince III, resigned. By the end of the month, Citigroup's shares had deteriorated to about $30 a share, and analysts began questioning whether the company was too big to manage, and whether it had enough capital to withstand its subprime loan problems. At the end of the month, Citigroup announced it had sold 4.9 percent of the company for $7.5 billion to the Abu Dhabi Investment Authority, an investment fund benefitting the Emirate of Abu Dhabi, one of seven emirates (states) of the United Arab Emirates. When the Abu Dhabi sale was combined with the stock owned by Prince Walid bin Talal of Saudi Arabia, Middle Eastern investors would own about 10 percent of the company. (Although they owned a large amount of stock, the Federal Reserve still places restrictions on all foreign investors' ability to manage, govern, or serve on their board.) The sale to these foreign investors was expensive—in the form of preferred stock paying an 11 percent yield, and that has to be converted into common stock from March 2010 to September 2011.[337] All other shareholders had their dividends cut 41 percent. Prince's separation agreement exceeded $51 million.[338]

Let's be very clear. In 2007 Citigroup had to write down $19.6 billion of subprime loans. Their profits fall 83 percent. Their return on equity dropped like a rock, from 18.6 percent in 2006 to only 3 percent. Their shares, which had been selling for over $55 a share the year before, were selling for $30 when Prince quit. (They were worth less than $5 in early 2011.) They were forced to raise $30 billion of additional capital and paid a very high price to do so. They cut shareholder dividend payments 41 percent (it was down to a penny a share in 2009). And somehow, their board still found it proper to reward their CEO Prince royally. (Within three years of the Prince resignation, two-thirds of the board had been replaced.)

Hedge Funds

Got a million dollars? Then feel free to invest in a hedge fund.

Hedge funds are privately organized investment funds run by highly paid professional managers for the benefit of wealthy investors.

By limiting the fund to a small number of investors and requiring large minimum investments (typically $1 million or more), the hedge funds can avoid important government regulations, such as those imposed on a typical mutual fund.

While a typical mutual fund might invest almost exclusively in stocks or bonds, a hedge fund has no such constraints. Each fund has its own unique investment strategy, and their managers use a variety of investment methods.

Hedge funds raise massive capital, borrow a lot more, and invest heavily to get very high returns for their wealthy clients. Investments can include anything from short selling (betting a company stock price will go down) to derivatives to quants (short for quantitative investing—using mathematical formulas to determine investment strategies). These investment professionals originally used a wide range of hedging techniques to mitigate risks, but that isn't necessarily the case anymore.

Hedge fund managers and staff are well paid, often receiving a management fee of 2 percent of the fund's net asset value each year and a performance fee of 20 percent (up to 45 percent in some cases) of the fund's profits. Compensation based on performance often leads to taking higher risks and, in particular, to borrowing large amounts of money to generate big returns.

According to the Federal Reserve, by the end of 2006, there were more than nine thousand hedge funds managing about $1.4 trillion in assets.

Although we have experienced significant systemic risk when these hedge funds failed, politicians and regulators have been reluctant to regulate an industry made up of rich people who are investing freely. Instead, we all relied on their voluntarily complying with "guidelines and principals" developed by the industry, regulators, and politicians in 2007. Changes are coming, and that's a good thing. Let's hope it's enough. *Good government is necessary.*

December 2007

The Federal Reserve lowered the discount rate to 4.75 percent, because economic growth was slowing, the housing industry was falling apart, and people were sensing a recession (or worse) was under way and stopped spending money.

One of the problems facing commercial banks and others was that they didn't have enough liquidity. Normally, a bank that needs short-term funds (overnight money) can borrow from another bank—a product known as federal funds, or "Fed Funds" for short. Banks with more reserves than they need sell them to other banks, usually overnight and unsecured. They charge each other a lower interest rate on Fed Funds than they would pay at the Discount Window. The Federal Reserve knows this and actually sets internal targets on appropriate Fed Funds rates in order to control inflation or spur the economy.

Lowering the discount rate leads to a lower Fed Funds rate and promotes lending and economic growth.

Unfortunately, even though most banks had enough cash, they were reluctant to lend in late 2007 because they were worried that they might suddenly need the money themselves. They were also reluctant to borrow from the Discount Window because they feared it would set off alarms, and people would think that they were in financial trouble.

To try to increase liquidity at the banks, encourage them to begin lending again, and fight off a financial meltdown, the Federal Reserve announced a new and innovative "pilot" loan program, the **Temporary Auction Facility (TAF)**. Under TAF, the Federal Reserve not only allowed banks to bid on loans from the Fed, but accepted a wider variety of collateral to secure the loans too. Banks could bid on any amount they wanted and offer the interest rate they were willing to pay.

The Federal Reserve had a minimum acceptable interest rate and scheduled two auctions in December, one for twenty-eight-day loans and the other for thirty-five-day loans, and each auction had $20 billion allocated. Demand for the money was very high, and ninety-three institutions requested $61.5 billion in the first auction, and seventy-three institutions requested $57.6 billion in the second auction. The Federal Reserve announced on December 21 that it would continue the $20 billion auctions biweekly for "as long as necessary to address elevated pressures in short-term funding markets."[339]

Clearly, Fed Chairman "Helicopter Ben" Bernanke had begun aggressively pumping money into banks to avert an economic meltdown.[340] *Good government is necessary.*

January 2008

Bank of America announced that it was purchasing the troubled mortgage lender Countrywide Financial for $4 billion. By the time the deal closed six months later, Bank of America's stock price had dropped almost 40 percent.

TAF had helped some, but the economy was still weakening, and, in particular, the housing industry was "contracting," and labor markets were "softening." So the Federal Reserve announced on January 22 that it was lowering its discount rate a surprising three-quarters of a point, to 4 percent. Just *one week later*, the Federal Reserve announced that because the financial markets were under stress and because credit had tightened even more for businesses and consumers, it was lowering the discount rate even more, to 3.5 percent.

Put another way, banks had retrenched and were making significantly fewer consumer loans, housing loans, and business loans. Home values were beginning to fall off, and auto lending was down significantly. The economy was in deep, deep trouble.

February 2008

Fannie Mae reported a $3.6 billion loss for the fourth quarter of 2007. The stock price had fallen 59 percent in only five months, from $67.30 at the beginning of October 2007 to $27.65 by the end of February. *Bigger is not always better. It's almost always bad loans.*

The Federal Reserve announced that it would increase its TAF offerings from $20 billion to $30 billion and lower the minimum bid from $10 million to $5 million to try to help smaller community banks.

On February 13, 2008, President George W. Bush signed the **Economic Stimulus Act of 2008** into law. The Economic Stimulus Act provided tax rebate checks to about 130 million taxpayers ranging from $300 to $1,200.[341] The president called it a "booster shot" for the economy, but critics complained that the tax rebates would be saved or used to reduce debts instead of being spent and spurring the economy.

It is reasonable to question whether rebate checks are the most cost-effective way to boost the economy, but in this case, at least, studies showed that consumers spent about 33 percent of their rebate checks and did, in fact, provide a small booster shot to the economy, as expected.[342] Not surprisingly, lower-income households spent more of their rebate checks than higher-income households. You could argue there are better ways to boost the economy, but it's hard to argue this didn't at least help some.

> *"Payback is Hell"*

March 2008

Bear Stearns was forced to choose between filing for bankruptcy and accepting a fire sale buyout from JPMorgan Chase. They sold for $10 a share in a deal that was backed by low-interest Federal Reserve Bank loans totaling $30 billion.

The Federal Reserve also announced a new $200 billion **Term Securities Lending Facility (TSLF)** that allowed commercial, savings, *and investment banks* to temporarily swap their riskier mortgage-backed securities with the Federal Reserve for more stable US Treasury securities. The announcement came shortly after the Federal Reserve and the Treasury helped broker the fire sale of Bear Stearns, leading some to speculate that they intentionally excluded Bear Stearns from the new funding and that it was payback for (Bear Stearns CEO) Jimmy Cayne's refusal to help with the LTCM bailout four years earlier. "Payback is Hell" makes a great headline, but the company was so weak, the Fed wasn't likely to lend them this money anyway.

Where's My Bailout Check?

The Economic Stimulus Act of 2008

In case you were wondering when you would get *your bailout check*, chances are that you have already got it and spent it. In fact, assuming you were one of the over seventy million low- and middle-income taxpayers, you got your checks around the middle of 2008.

The Congressional Budget Office (CBO) projected that it cost about $152 billion to do so, but this spending bill was supposed to revive the weak economy by giving taxpayer "rebates" ranging from about $300 to $600 (or double that for married couples). It gave a special depreciation allowance on tax returns for businesses that purchased certain qualified property (including automobiles) and an increase from $125,000 to $250,000 for property that could be fully expensed in the year it was purchased (what the IRS calls section 179 property). The bill also increased the limits on the number of loans that Fannie Mae, Freddie Mac, and the Federal Housing Authority could purchase or guarantee.

The individual tax rebate checks were specifically directed at the average taxpayer, in part, to avoid a middle-class backlash against other bailout programs that did not include them, and because low- and middle-income taxpayers were more likely than wealthier taxpayers to spend enough of the tax rebate money to boost the economy.

In fact, it helped. The CBO estimates that the rebates added 2.3 percent to economic growth in the second quarter of 2008 and 0.2 percent in the third quarter.

We can argue about the amount. We can argue that it should have gone to more or to fewer taxpayers. We can argue that there are better ways to boost the economy. But in fairness, we can't claim our elected officials totally ignored us.

The Carlyle Group, one of the world's largest private equity firms, was unable to keep its investment fund, Carlyle Capital, afloat, and the fund declared bankruptcy after it defaulted on $16.6 billion of indebtedness. The fund invested heavily in subprime, mortgage-backed securities.

The Federal Reserve was working overtime to get things on track again and made several very aggressive moves in March to increase liquidity at banks and to encourage lending. These actions included:

- Increasing the TAF auction from $20 billion to $100 billion (and in July extending the term to eighty-four days)
- Initiating a $100 billion series of "repurchase transactions," where it would buy mortgage-backed securities (and other securities) from banks and sell them back to them after twenty-eight days
- Increasing the currency swap arrangement with the European Central Bank and the Swiss National Bank from $12 billion to $36 billion and extending it for another six months
- Introducing a **Primary Dealer Credit Facility (PDCF)** to provide overnight loans for the first time to approved *investment* banks
- Lowering the discount rate dramatically, from 3.5 percent to 2.5 percent, and extending the allowable term from thirty days to ninety days

Although Fannie Mae and Freddie Mac both reported big losses for 2007, they held a joint news conference with their regulator (OFHEO) to announce that because the regulator had reduced their capital requirements, they were now able to purchase as much as $200 billion of mortgage-backed securities. Without them, the housing industry and the national economy had no chance of recovering anytime soon, and the very bad economy would have only gotten much worse, adding to job losses and to a deeper and more severe economic meltdown.

Unfortunately, these two GSEs had very little capital to start with, so the weak companies were about to get weaker. Some politicians and conservative commentators complained loudly about their expansion, and under normal circumstances it would be a terrible idea to expand the scope of two huge, undercapitalized companies. But there was nothing normal about the circumstances. Nobody liked the idea, including those who developed it, but their expansion was necessary to fight off a total economic collapse. *We got this way for a reason.*

April 2008

The Federal Reserve lowered the discount rate yet again, to 2.25 percent.

Lehman Brothers, the fourth-largest US investment firm, raised $4 billion from a stock sale. Washington Mutual raised $7 billion from a group led by TPG Inc. Both proved to be really bad investments.

June 2008

Lehman Brothers reported a $2.8 billion loss for the quarter. CEO Dick Fuld said that he "takes responsibility" for the losses, but it was the company president, Joe Gregory, and the chief financial officer, Erin Callan, who were canned. *It's easy to misplace blame.*

The Dow Jones Industrial Average fell over 10 percent in *one month*, from 12,638 at the end of May to only 11,350 by the end of June. The downward spiral continued for the rest of the year, falling 38 percent from its high of 14,121 in October 2007 to only 8,776 by year-end.

July 2008

Both Fannie Mae and Freddie Mac's stock prices fell over 60 percent in *one week* because investors were afraid that subprime mortgage losses would lead to their failure. The Federal Reserve announced that they would lend to both companies if needed, and Treasury Secretary Paulson requested emergency funding to rescue the companies if necessary.

IndyMac faced a run on the bank and failed. Media coverage of the lines forming outside the bank fueled public anxiety about the economy and the strength of the nation's banks. Even comedian Jay Leno got in some jabs when he compared the megahit movie *Batman* with the depositor runs on IndyMac. "The only place with longer lines [than the movie theaters] was customers trying to get their money out of IndyMac Bank."[343] Regulators bristled at the media portrayal of the lines that had formed outside the bank because they felt that the media had failed to effectively report that the FDIC insurance covered almost all of these deposits. Banking is all about confidence, and this was a blow to the collective confidence in the nation's banking system.

Leno had already joked about the government's lack of credibility during the crisis when he said, "Did you see that IndyMac Bank that collapsed here in California? All those poor people waiting in line—my God. But the Feds say not to worry if your money's in a bank, because the government will guarantee it will be there. Remember, they also guaranteed WMDs and guaranteed New Orleans that FEMA would show up. Consider the source!"[344]

Far less amusing was former Senator Phil Gramm, vice chairman of the investment bank division at UBS AG (an international investment banking company based in Switzerland), and chief economic advisor to presidential candidate Senator John McCain, who claimed that the economy was not as bad as it appeared, saying that we had become "a nation of whiners."[345] His comments were not well received. US unemployment had climbed from 4.7 percent to 5.7 percent over the past nine months alone and would continue its devastating climb, exceeding 10 percent only fifteen months later (the highest unemployment rate in twenty-six years). UBS AG would report a $5.1 *billion* loss in 2008 and another $20.9 *billion* loss the next year. *It's easy to misplace blame.*

September 2008

September 2008 proved to be one of the most disastrous months in history for US financial institutions and, as a result, for the US and world economies.

On September 7, the federal government seized control of two government-sponsored enterprises, Fannie Mae (about $895 *billion* in assets) and Freddie Mac (about $804 *billion* in assets), placing them into "conservatorship." Failing to act and, instead, allowing the two GSEs to fail would have been horrific. "If the U.S. government allows Fannie and Freddie to fail and international investors are not compensated adequately, the consequences will be catastrophic," said Yu Yongding, president of the China Society of World Economics. "If it is not the end of the world, it is the end of the current international financial system."[346]

On September 10, Lehman Brothers (total assets of $639 *billion* as of the quarter ending May 2008) announced a $3.9 *billion* loss for the third quarter. Its efforts to convince the Federal Reserve to loan it money had failed. Its attempts to raise more capital came up short. Its losses were mounting. The 158-year-old company filed for the largest bankruptcy in US history on September 15. Treasury Secretary Henry Paulson said, "I never once considered that it was appropriate to put taxpayers' money on the line" to save Lehman Brothers. Many analysts point to this decision as the "event that turned the subprime crisis into a full-blown financial collapse."[347]

***LIBOR**, is the London Interbank Offered Rate, a widely used interest rate upon which other rates are determined. Set by the British Bankers' Association(a trade group),it is a popular benchmark used by bankers around the world to determine the interest rates charged to customers for short-term loans. It's pronounced "li bore," but you should probably add a British accent to make it sound right.*

The panic was on.

On September 15, Bank of America announced plans to buy seriously troubled Merrill Lynch for $50 billion. Bank of America CEO Ken Lewis was criticized for paying too much for the financially distressed company, especially after declaring a year before that "I've had all the fun I can stand in the investment banking business," and "to get bigger in it is not something I want to do."[348] They grew 28 percent, from $1.8 *trillion* in assets to $2.3 *trillion* in assets six months later. *Bigger is not always better.*

The next day, in order to prevent the bankruptcy of the nation's biggest insurer AIG ($1 *trillion* in assets as of June 2008), and as Bloomberg news described the situation, to prevent "the worst financial collapse in history," the Federal Reserve agreed to lend AIG up to $85 *billion* in a two-year loan priced at 8.5 percent *above* the ninety-day LIBOR rate, or roughly 11.5 percent at the time.

These were basically the same pricing terms that a consortium of private lenders did not accept. The terms also stipulated that the Treasury would get a 79.9 percent interest in the company.

Marco Annunziata, an analyst at UniCredit SpA, in a note to clients, says the "punitive" interest rate on the loan "makes it extremely clear that this is not a subsidy extended to keep the company afloat but rather a stranglehold that makes AIG unviable while ensuring that its obligations will be met. This is to all extents and purposes a controlled bankruptcy."[349] *Good government is necessary. Bigger is not always better.*

The AIG bailout was especially expensive, sudden, and disturbing. When Lehman Brothers had been allowed to fail the week before, they had held some 900,000 derivatives and other contracts with banks and other third parties that they could not quickly or fully honor.[350] The credit markets suddenly froze when people realized that not only would Lehman not honor their contracts, but now AIG, which had sold more than $400 billion of credit default swaps, could not come up with the cash to back these products and would have to file for bankruptcy.

The Federal Reserve and Treasury knew that they had to step in because not stepping in would have surely caused a downward spiral and carried the country to the depths of a depression. AIG was simply too big and interconnected to fail. State and local governments, which had loaned to what was once a very sound company, were suddenly looking at $10 billion in losses. Banks were at risk of losing some $50 billion in outstanding loans to AIG.

Businesses that would routinely borrow from AIG (in a product known as commercial paper) were at risk of losing their access to this important credit. In a bankruptcy, any outstanding loans from AIG to those businesses would be sold at about a $20 billion loss.

To make matters worse, retirement plans and 401(k) plans managed by companies such as Fidelity, Vanguard, AT&T, Wal-Mart, DuPont, and others were at risk that $38 billion of insurance they purchased from AIG would not be honored. That insurance was supposed to provide individuals contributing to their individual 401(k) plans a guaranteed minimum return on their investments. It's one thing for employees to see their investments in higher-risk stocks and bonds lose value. They know the value can go up or down. But if their savings were in a conservative, lower-yielding, "guaranteed minimum" investment plan and the guaranteed minimum income wasn't honored, they would likely panic, and large numbers of people would demand their money back.

***Commercial paper** is a type of unsecured short-term loan commonly given to a high-quality corporation. Keeping the term at less than nine months allows the borrowers to avoid certain SEC disclosure regulations. The loan proceeds are used to meet short-term liabilities, such as buying inventory or meeting payroll obligations.*

Furthermore, if AIG defaulted on about $20 billion in loans that they had sold to money market mutual funds and other investors (they were selling commercial paper to these funds), so many of the funds might lose so much value ("breaking the buck" See section below) that the public would rush to remove their cash and cause a run on these funds. In short, Federal Reserve Chairman Bernanke contended that AIG's "failure could have resulted in 1930s-style global financial and economic meltdown, with catastrophic implications for production, income, and jobs."[351]

In a bailout like this, the taxpayers were entitled to earn a very high interest rate on the deal, but like loans to a deadbeat friend, collecting it could be a problem. The Federal Reserve and Treasury would later modify the punitive terms to improve the capital position of the company and its chances of survival, and the bailout would skyrocket from $85 billion to $182 billion. AIG would *hopefully* never be the same again.[352]

On September 17, another shocking event occurred when a highly respected $64.8 billion money market mutual fund, the Primary Fund (established by the Reserve Management Corporation, a private company), "broke the buck." The Federal Reserve was very concerned that if AIG went under, funds like this might break the buck, and a run would occur. They were absolutely right to be concerned. As the *Financial Times* described it, "in the culture of U.S. money market funds, whose shares are supposed to be as safe as cash, 'breaking the buck' is seen as reputational and commercial suicide."[353] They weren't just kidding, either.

Unfortunately, the Primary Fund lost $785 million in commercial paper issued by Lehman Brothers, and, for the first time ever, a public money market mutual fund had "broken the buck" when its net asset value fell to 97 cents a share. Suddenly, everybody wanted their money back because for every buck they had invested, they were only entitled to 97 cents in return. The Primary Fund put a hold on all withdrawal requests, which led to an even bigger panic and a run on accounts like these everywhere. Within a few weeks, investors had withdrawn over $500 *billion* from money market funds! The financial panic was in full swing!

To meet investor demand, money market fund managers began converting more investments to cash and, in particular, stopped buying commercial paper. Suddenly, large commercial customers were losing access to vital short-term loans, and they were going to pay much higher interest rates to get what little money remained. In fact, although the Federal Reserve had been aggressively lowering the discount rate, the cost of issuing commercial paper was climbing to its highest level in eight months, and money market funds had reduced their holdings of the highest rated commercial paper by over $200 billion in the last two weeks of September alone![354]

Companies that routinely used commercial paper to meet short-term funding needs, including their payrolls, such as General Electric, Nestle, Coca-Cola, Johnson & Johnson, Vodaphone, Pfizer, Hertz, and Abbott Laboratories, were about to discover that their access to funding was suddenly more expensive and damn near impossible to find.

Without access to the commercial paper market, even the soundest companies would have struggled to find reasonably priced credit in any form at a time when nobody wanted to lend money. Without access to commercial paper, some of these large companies would have struggled to pay their vendors, ship their products, or even meet their payrolls. Wall Street problems would have smacked Main Street people right in the face. These financial problems would not be limited to a few large companies.

"Breaking the Buck"

If you have an investment portfolio such as an IRA or 401(k), chances are good that the money you have not yet invested has been parked in a short- term money market mutual fund. It's a reasonable place to hold your cash while you ponder longer-term investment opportunities. Fund managers overseeing these accounts are required by law to invest in short-term, low-risk products, such as government securities, bank-issued certificates of deposit, or commercial paper, which is simply a large company's unsecured IOU that comes due in a short time, typically between a few days and nine months.

Sometimes, people confuse money market mutual funds with money market demand accounts (MMDAs) at commercial banks. Here's the difference: an MMDA has FDIC insurance, but a money market mutual fund has no federal guarantees. A money market mutual fund almost never lets the value of an investment fall below $1 a share, and the return on that one buck depends on how well the fund's investments perform. It usually earns more than a commercial bank pays on their MMDA and is considered almost as safe. These funds attracted over $3.5 *trillion* in investments in 2008. Now that's a lot of money!

If the fund value ever falls below $1 a share—highly unusual—it's called "breaking the buck." Investors are likely to panic and rush to withdraw their money. That's why fund managers do everything they can to prevent the value from falling below $1 a share. They invest very conservatively and even contribute their own money if the value declines significantly. In fact, breaking the buck in a public money market mutual fund was *unheard of* until the Primary Fund did so in September 2008.

The shock of that event led to a run on these funds everywhere, and their inability to convert their short-term investments to cash fast enough to meet withdrawal demands would have resulted in more losses and an even larger run on the funds. The result would have been catastrophic had the government not intervened. *Good government is necessary.*

Fortunately, the Treasury and Federal Reserve were able to stop the run on these money market mutual funds and revive the commercial paper market by providing liquidity through the Federal Reserve and a government guarantee through the Treasury. Specifically, the Federal Reserve began allowing mutual funds to sell their commercial paper to banks, and the banks could then use that as collateral to borrow without recourse from the Federal Reserve Bank of Boston. That meant the Federal Reserve was taking the risk—not the banks—that the commercial paper would be repaid. This program quickly provided $150 billion in liquidity and kept that access to credit available for these large corporations.

The Fed also developed a special program to purchase $250 billion of ninety-day commercial paper and, in November, expanded their efforts to provide liquidity to the commercial paper market with a $600 billion "Money Market Investor Funding Facility."[355] Sometimes when we read numbers, it's hard to fully grasp their impact. This one is worth repeating. The Fed developed a $600 billion program to shore up confidence and make sure large, high-quality businesses could meet their short-term borrowing needs. That meant companies across the country could meet their payrolls, pay their vendors, and cover their immediate overhead expenses. It was a very big deal.

More importantly, and somewhat surprisingly, at the same time the Treasury provided a government guarantee to investors (whose money market fund participated in the program) that their net asset value would not fall below a buck. The **Temporary Guarantee Program for Money Market Funds** went into effect on September 19 and eventually guaranteed over $3 trillion in investors' money over the course of one year. By charging the mutual funds a guarantee fee, the taxpayers earned a hefty $1.2 billion in fee income over the program's one-year life span.

This was a stunning development and a high-risk gamble for the taxpayers, who had to guarantee so much investor money to prevent a financial meltdown and to ensure that businesses would not fail because their access to low-cost, commercial paper had suddenly disappeared. Although the Treasury guarantee was clearly communicated to the public, most taxpayers still had no idea that they were on the hook for $3 trillion!

Congressional leaders and the president recognized that it was unfair to offer an unlimited guarantee on money market funds but not on other commercial and thrift bank deposit products. When Congress passed the controversial Emergency Economic Stabilization Act of 2008, two weeks later, the act temporarily raised the basic limit on FDIC coverage from $100,000 to $250,000 per depositor. The increase was later made permanent.

On Sunday, September 20, Goldman Sachs and Morgan Stanley, the last two large investment banks, received unusual and quick (over the weekend) approval to become Federal Reserve-regulated bank holding companies. Because the Federal Reserve Board determined that emergency conditions existed, justifying immediate action on the applications, they waived public notice of the proposals. The move increased their access to Fed borrowings but meant that they had to submit to additional oversight and regulations. Banking analyst Bert Ely declared that "the separation of investment banking and commercial banking has come to an end." Christopher Whalen, managing director of Institutional Risk Analytics, expressed the popular consensus of the time, saying, "They were afraid they'd get killed if they didn't [convert]."[356]

On the twenty-fifth, the largest thrift and tenth-largest depository institution in the country, Washington Mutual Bank (WaMu) failed. Their assets and deposits were sold to JPMorgan Chase & Co. the same day. "This is the big one that everybody was worried about," said Sheila Bair, FDIC chairwomen. "I was worried about it."[357] *Bigger is not always better. It's almost always bad loans. Greed has a price.*

Because it was on the brink of failure, on the twenty-ninth the FDIC brokered a deal for Citigroup to buy the banking subsidiaries of distressed Wachovia Corporation in a deal that paid Wachovia shareholders about $1 a share. They were trading at about $50.15 a share just one year before! The deal was somewhat bizarre because Citigroup was already experiencing a lot of problems on their own. How two huge troubled banks could merge to make one even larger good bank is hard to fathom. But Wachovia was on its deathbed and something had to be done to prevent a huge hit on the deposit insurance fund and a huge impact on the very fragile economy.

The FDIC would help finance the transaction by purchasing $12 billion of Citigroup preferred stock. Citigroup would then have to cover the first $42 billion of Wachovia's mortgage-related losses. The FDIC agreed to cover all other loses over that amount (an exposure to the FDIC of about $270 billion in bad assets). Wachovia's brokerage subsidiaries (AG Edwards and Evergreen) were not part of the deal and would continue to operate under the Wachovia brand name.[358] As it happened, Wells Fargo soon entered the fray and bought Wachovia outright. Thankfully, the FDIC didn't have to offer any extraordinary incentives.

***Economy** is the structured system by which a community creates and sustains wealth for its people.*

The country was in one serious crisis after another. The Federal Reserve and Treasury were working nonstop to address each crisis, but it was nearly impossible to get ahead of the problems. As soon as one fire was extinguished, two larger, more dangerous fires would appear. The country was experiencing widespread panic fueled by uncertainty. Something had to be done to stop the panic cycle and restore the economy.

Good government was necessary. Elected officials, regulators, and taxpayers would have to work as a team, hobble together some shoestrings, and attach it to the throttle of our economic engine. Without somebody carefully pulling the strings, our *economy* would crash hard. Simply put, a massive bailout of some sort was required. Of course, you can imagine the scene as folks hollered at each other: "Slow down!" "Stop!" "Change gears!" No, it wasn't pretty. It wasn't funny. It was necessary.

Merrill Lynch
1914–2008

Some readers might remember the popular Merrill Lynch television commercials from the early 1970s featuring their famous bull mascot. One commercial had a thundering herd of cattle barreling directly at the camera with the tagline "Merrill Lynch: Bullish on America." Another had a full-size bull walking carefully through a china shop as the voice-over proclaims their "sensitivity to your investment goals, and agility in helping you reach them." The commercial tagline was "Merrill Lynch: A breed apart."

The bull was a sign of strength and became one of the most recognized symbols on Wall Street, representing not only the company but, for many people, the industry itself. Unfortunately, after a series of strategic mistakes and bad leadership, Merrill's stated principals of "responsible citizenship" and "integrity" had been called into question.

It wasn't always this way. Founded in 1914 by Charles Merrill and Edmund Lynch, the company earned a good reputation for providing sound financial advice and not only survived the Great Depression but prospered and became a public company in 1971. They had many successes, including their purchase in the 1920s of a controlling interest in Safeway Stores (recently ranked the third-largest grocery chain in the United States), recognition for their work to take Ford Motor Company public in 1956, and arranging the merger of ATT Wireless with Cingular Wireless in 2004. They developed a sound reputation promoting everything from women's employment and investment opportunities, to developing a foundation to support employee financial and educational needs

They lost three good people in the terrorist attacks on the World Trade Center buildings September 11, 2001, and had to evacuate nearly all of the nine thousand employees working in their headquarters across the street. But in spite of the stress and crisis, they survived and by 2006 were managing total assets of $1 trillion. In addition, they owned a 45 percent voting interest in BlackRock Inc., one of the world's largest publicly traded investment management companies with approximately $1.1 trillion in assets under management.

For many years, Merrill had good reason to be proud. Fortune Magazine listed them as the twenty-second largest company in the United States in 2006, making them the second largest securities firm in the country. But things were changing when Stan O'Neal became president and chairman of the board in late 2002, and the changes were not all good.

A report from *NPR* described O'Neal as a "numbers person in what is, at its heart, a people business." The *Financial Times* called his actions "ruthless efficiency" as he fired twenty-four thousand employees (a third of the work force) including nineteen top executives. The *New York Times* quoted him in a 2003 interview as saying, "To the extent that [Merrill Lynch] is paternalistic and materialistic, I don't think that is healthy."[359]

"Mother Merrill's" reputation for taking care of their own was now gone, and, as such, O'Neal generated few friends inside the organization. This was especially true after people found out that while he cut compensation and benefits by 8.12 percent in 2003, Chairman and CEO O'Neal was still paid $28 *million* that year, more than double his pay from the year before!

There is no doubt that O'Neal was aggressive, not only in cutting cost severely, but also in promoting growth. In his 2006 annual report, O'Neal bragged that by "virtually any measure, Merrill Lynch completed the most successful year in its history." Apparently, the measuring stick did not include asset *quality* because although reported earnings reached an all-time high of $7.5 billion, it wouldn't be long before investors discovered that the reported financial results were, shall we say, full of bull.

In early 2007, continuing a trend of risky and unwise investments, Merrill spent $1.3 billion to purchase First Franklin Financial, making Merrill the world's top underwriter of subprime mortgage-backed securities. By the end of the year O'Neal was gone, and the company was reporting an $8.6 billion loss, or, as their annual report sadly proclaimed, the "worst performance in the history of Merrill Lynch." O'Neal's "retirement" on October 30, 2007, occurred because he had not only lost a ton of money from high-risk, asset-backed securities, but he then tried to sell the company to Wachovia Bank (in a deal that would have reportedly paid him personally as much as $274 million!) without first discussing it with his board of directors.[360]

The board had reason to be mad, and earning $274 million by selling a company you drove into the ditch would have been outrageous. But amazingly, in spite of it all, the board still rewarded him with a retirement package valued at an unbelievable $161.5 million.

To be clear, the company loses $8.6 *billion* and still pays their chairman and CEO $161.5 million for his work. What the hell?

Fortune Magazine listed it at #4 in their "101 Dumbest Moments in Business" that year for buying First Franklin, and at #5 for paying O'Neal so much money to retire. It's not clear why Fortune's top three were considered dumber, but for the record, China was rated higher for using lead paint and other dangerous materials in toys and food, Eli Lilly for putting Prozac into dog treats, and Leona Helmsley for leaving $12 million in her will to her dog.

O'Neal was replaced by a new chairman and CEO, John Thain, former head of the New York Stock Exchange and a former chief operating officer of investment bank Goldman Sachs. Merrill then aggressively wrote off or sold over $31 billion of bad securities. But even that wasn't enough to keep the company independent, and when the bad investments continued to erode capital, John Thain announced on September 15, 2008, that Bank of America would pay $50 billion for an all-stock acquisition of Merrill Lynch. Merrill Lynch would no longer exist as an independent company.

AIG
1919–2008

Most taxpayers who have even the slightest knowledge of the Panic of 2008 understand that the government bailed out an insurance company called AIG, but few know they had become owners of the fourth-largest company *in the world* (*Forbes Magazine* 2006).

Cornelius V. Starr founded American International Group Inc. (AIG) in Shanghai, China, in 1919 under the name of American Asiatic Underwriters. His agency offered fire and marine coverage on behalf of several US insurance companies. Seven years later AIG opened its first US office, in New York, which became its headquarters. Under the leadership of Starr's handpicked successor, Chairman and CEO Maurice "Hank" Greenberg, the small insurance agency grew rapidly over the years, primarily through mergers and acquisitions. It became known as AIG in 1967.

Under Greenberg's direction, AIG became the world's leading international insurance organization, operating in over 130 countries. As the owner of a large number of brand-name insurance companies (such as SunAmerica, American General, and American Home Assurance), AIG's product offerings included everything imaginable, from auto insurance to yacht insurance for consumers, and from accident insurance to workers' compensation for businesses. They had their fingers in a variety of businesses and even owned a company that operated a Stowe, Vermont, ski lodge (the Stowe Mountain Resort).

But while general insurance, life insurance, and retirement services dominated their operations and generated growth, it was bad investments and the sale of credit default swaps in a smaller subsidiary they owned that caused a liquidity strain they would not overcome.

Historically, AIG was no stranger to trouble. At the end of Greenberg's reign, they faced a litany of problems related to inaccurate financial reporting. In fact, because of mistakes in their annual reports, they had to refile five years of financial statements (2000–05) with the SEC. AIG even had to refile the first four years a second time because they were still wrong and were overstating earnings by about $3.9 billion. The SEC and the Department of Justice both filed lawsuits against AIG, claiming that AIG "materially falsified its financial statements" in an effort to mislead analysts and investors. AIG paid $825 million to settle the claims.

The New York attorney general and the New York State Department of insurance also sued AIG for not paying enough taxes, among other reasons, and AIG settled those charges for another $818 million.

Chairman and CEO Greenberg was forced to resign in 2005, having led the company for thirty-seven years. He was seventy-nine years old.

Their $1.6 billion in legal fines and penalties for misleading accounting paled in comparison to the $2.1 billion in losses from insurance claims filed after Hurricanes Katrina, Rita, and Wilma hit the southeast United States in 2004. But size has some advantages, and at the end of the day an $853 *billion* company can manage storms like these: in fact, AIG reported a $10.5 *billion* profit in 2005. Wow!

Being aggressive and taking high risks weren't new to the company. In 2001, they advised PNC Financial, a large banking company in Pittsburgh, on (illegally) removing $762 million in bad loans from their books and thus overstating earnings by $155 million (27 percent). The bad advice cost PNC $115 million in federal fines and a shake-up of its executives; it cost AIG $126 million in penalties and fines.

Whether it was intentionally cooking the books or just aggressive bookkeeping is subject to debate, but suspicious activities were not new to the company. After Greenberg left in 2005, AIG executives even admitted to regulators they owned and controlled an offshore insurance company that they had previously claimed wasn't theirs.

And AIG was embroiled in two lawsuits against former CEO Greenberg over an affiliate company that was *oddly* used to provide significant incentive pay to AIG employees. It appears that after Greenberg and former CFO Howard Smith left AIG, the two men acquired control of Starr International Company (SICO) and promptly sold a large number of SICO investments, including $4.3 billion of AIG stock. AIG claims the $4.3 billion in stock was held in "trust" for AIG employees, but there was apparently no documentation to support the claim, and in the first round the federal court judge ruled that the AIG case was "weak." Of course, how a company manages to lose control of $4.3 billion of employee stock is almost beyond words.

In any event, overstating earnings, underpaying taxes, advising a client to illegally hide bad loans, running an undisclosed offshore insurance company, fighting over a company whose only purpose appears to have been to pay AIG bonuses, and losing control of $4.3 billion of stock raise big questions about the competence and integrity of at least some of AIG's management. But although debacles such as this damaged the company's reputation, it didn't cause AIG to fail.

In 1998, AIG's Financial Products subsidiary (AIGFP) began selling a derivative product known as credit default swaps. Ten years later, it was all over.

Credit default swaps were contracts that allowed companies to pay AIGFP a fee in return for covering their losses on loans or investments. It's similar to an insurance policy that pays up if the deal goes bad, and AIGFP was selling these unregulated products all day long. In effect, AIG was betting that the underlying loans and investments they didn't make and didn't own wouldn't go bad. If they did, AIG paid up. If they didn't, AIG made a lot of money ($3.2 billion in 2005 alone)!

AIG kept offering credit default swaps on highly rated securities and other apparently sound investments, and was counting on not having to pay. In small print on page 166 of their 2006 SEC annual report, they stated that "the likelihood of any payment obligation by

AIGFP under each transaction is remote, even in severe recessionary market scenarios."

They were dead wrong. The likelihood of payment obligation was very high after Bear Stearns and Lehman Brothers collapsed. And mark-to-market accounting (what something can sell for if it's put on the market today) required AIG to report huge losses of $11.5 billion in 2007 and $28.6 billion in 2008. AIG then had to put up cash collateral as protection from these losses.

Meanwhile, they had also sold a large number of securities repurchase agreements, called repos. With repos, AIG would sell securities they owned to other investors and then commit to buy them back later. The other investors had extra cash sitting around and liked this deal because they could earn a decent return on a short-term investment. AIG liked it too because they made money by paying the investors 2 percent to 5 percent less than what the securities themselves would pay. It's normally a good deal for everybody.

But the repos that AIG was selling were higher-risk mortgage-backed securities (MBSs) and other collateralized debt obligations (CDOs). A CDO is similar to mortgage-backed securities but could contain other debts too, such as auto loans, business lines of credit, credit cards, etc. When those securities began to lose market value, AIG was required to put up cash collateral to protect the other investors from potential losses.

The combination of lost values in both securities and in credit swap derivatives proved too much. AIG's credit ratings were downgraded, which required them to produce another $20 billion of cash collateral. AIG couldn't convert assets to cash fast enough to survive. They tried to find private financing to save themselves, but given the sheer size of their company and its problems, they couldn't get a large enough consortium of investors to quickly loan them the $85 billion they thought they needed. That amount wouldn't have been enough anyway.

The failure of one of the largest companies in the world would have been devastating. For example, state and local governments were looking at $10 billion in losses on loans they had made to AIG. People who owned 401(k) plans insured by AIG ($40 billion worth) were at risk. And, yes, *people matter.* Nobody wanted to see people's retirement money lost!

Without any doubt, its failure would have caused a devastating international financial panic. The Federal Reserve and US Treasury had to come to the rescue. *Good government is necessary.*

First, on September 18, 2008, the Federal Reserve Bank of New York gave AIG a two-year emergency credit line of up to $85 billion. The interest rate was really high: LIBOR *plus* 8.5 percent on any amount they borrowed (about 11.5 percent). They paid a 2 percent commitment fee (that's $1.7 billion!), and had to pay a fee of 8.5 percent on any outstanding amount they did not borrow. They also had to give taxpayers a 79.9 percent ownership of the company (in the form of preferred stock owned by the US Treasury).

Damn! That was really expensive, or, as they say in the business, "punitive."

But AIG deserved to pay a high price for screwing up so badly. *Greed has a price.* By the end of 2007, AIGFP had grown their portfolio of credit default swaps to unbearable size (supporting over $500 billion of loans, with $62 billion of that tied to subprime mortgages). Their accounting controls were weak. Their public financial statements claiming they had these risks under control were baloney. AIGFP was sloppy and greedy.

AIG quickly used the Fed's $85 billion emergency line of credit to meet its collateral requirements with others, called counterparties. In March 2009, the Federal Reserve Board and US Treasury gave in to public pressure and released the names of these counterparties. It's easy to see why the Fed and Treasury were reluctant to do so. It was one thing for so many states, such as California, Virginia, Hawaii, Ohio, Georgia, and Colorado, to get substantial money. But a loud public backlash occurred when they revealed mega companies like Goldman Sachs got $2.5 billion in the deal. People were especially suspicious about Goldman Sachs because the US Treasury secretary was once Goldman's CEO. They were equally incensed that foreign banks like the French bank Societe Generale ($4.1 billion) and the German bank Deutsche Bank ($2.6 billion) also got a US taxpayer bailout.

In any event, the $85 billion line would not be enough, and a new bailout package was cobbled together. In April 2009, the Government Accountability Office (Congress's auditors) valued AIG's bailout package from the Federal Reserve and US Treasury at $182 billion! That's a whole lotta money! It included a new Fed line of credit for $60 billion (down from the $85 billion) and Fed loans to two new companies totaling $52.5 billion. The companies were set up to buy and eventually sell off the high-risk securities (toxic assets) owned by AIG. The US Treasury provided the rest—$70 billion, when they bought AIG preferred stock. By the beginning of 2011, the Fed line had been fully repaid with interest, and the two loans were performing as agreed. The US Treasury preferred stock had been converted to common stock, meaning taxpayers owned 92 percent of AIG.

It isn't clear if the Federal Reserve Bank of New York will collect everything the Fed is owed on their AIG loans. It's hard to believe they won't. They have a certain amount of expertise in financial matters such as these.

On the other hand, US taxpayers certainly will be repaid from the sale of AIG common stock, and there's a very good chance we will have earned a nice profit in the process. We should. It's a well-deserved profit for such a high-risk venture.

Chapter 10
The Bailout

LASIK surgery is awesome. Somewhere around twelve million patients in the United States have undergone this eye procedure to correct their vision, and many readers have undoubtedly considered it. I had horrible vision before having the surgery, and now I can see through walls. It's incredible.

It was soon after the surgery that a buddy of mine and his dad took me to a dirt track at Eldora Speedway in Rossburg, Ohio, to watch a World of Outlaws winged sprint car race. I had never been to a dirt track before, and the experience activated deep within me a redneck gene I didn't know I possessed. I hadn't seen that many beer guts and tube tops since a Charlie Daniels concert in the 1970s. I became an instant fan of the people, the venue, the drivers, and the culture. It was one of those eye-popping events that I had not even considered before, and, now, I'm glad I did. Being able to see so clearly even while the mud was flying off those cars and covering the fans in dust was exhilarating. When it was over, I felt dirty but satisfied.

It seems odd, but this is how Treasury Secretary Henry Paulson may have felt when he had to approach the president, Congress, and the American people to ask them to bail out the financial system. Like my experience at the race track, it was one of those eye-popping events that he had not seriously considered before the Panic of 2008. Eventually, he could see clearly what had to be done. It went against his own ideology and against his political party's principles. But it had to be done. He ended up covered in mud, and I suspect when it was over he felt dirty.

Secretary Paulson had been dealing with his own World of Outlaws, only these were people whose actions caused tremendous harm to the country. Unlike the awesome drivers at Eldora Speedway spewing dirt on their delighted fans as they sped around the track, these bankers had driven the country to the edge of disaster and were now thrusting out their dirty hands looking for help. I am certain he felt quite sick when he had to make a request to bail out the financial system.

Panics occur amid a lot of uncertainty. The US and world economies were in such perilous shape that the US Treasury secretary, Federal Reserve chairman, and SEC chairman were forced to hold emergency meetings with congressional leaders in September 2008 to develop a plan to bring stability to the markets and the country. Their efforts so far had prevented a complete meltdown, but they would need help. "We can't keep doing this," Fed Chairman Bernanke was said to have told Treasury Secretary Paulson. "Both because we at the Fed don't have the necessary resources and for reasons of democratic legitimacy, it's important that the Congress come in and take control of the situation."[361]

At this point, although the Federal Reserve had been very aggressive in its actions, the average citizen didn't understand the Fed's tools and techniques at all. Perhaps folks understood the discount rate changes. But the Fed had also implemented new programs that the average Joe would never understand or come to appreciate. TAF, TSLF, PDCF, AMLF, CPFF, and others provided billions and billions in liquidity—providing more than enough funds for businesses to borrow and ensuring that folks could withdraw money from investment products as normal.[362] While the general public may have known little about these programs, financial analysts, economists, and others were well aware of these drastic and dramatic actions.

As Fed Chair Ben Bernanke later explained, he was forced to act, and although pumping so much money into the economy may have been controversial, he "was not going to be the Federal Reserve chairman who presided over the second Great Depression."[363] Helicopter Ben may have been pumping money into the economy, but, to be clear, these were precision strikes designed to address specific liquidity needs. It's not like he had a printing press in his office cranking out cash.

The Treasury, the FDIC, and the SEC were also every bit as engaged in preventing a financial meltdown, and the Treasury in particular was very aggressive.[364] These were incredibly challenging times in uncharted waters. There would be plenty of time later to assess how a panic like this could occur. But that conversation would have to wait. For now, somehow, the regulators had to reposition themselves from being the institutions that put out fires, to their original purpose: being the ones that prevent them.

The problems were mounting because everybody wanted—*needed*—to be rid of the toxic mortgages or other debts they held directly or in the form of securities. But nobody wanted to buy them, mainly because there was no way to put a realistic value on them. With the value of these assets falling every minute, banks were required to raise more capital to cover the losses, which was nearly impossible in this environment.

If a bank can't raise capital, it tries to "shrink its balance sheet" to meet the capital ratios that the regulators require, because the ratio increases with either more capital or with fewer assets. But capital was in limited supply, and nobody would buy the mortgages to help reduce assets. Once this downward financial spiral had begun, it was impossible to stop it without drastic measures.

Thrifts, commercial banks, and investment banks were all overwhelmed with bad loans and investments: their losses were mounting, shareholder wealth was getting wiped out, and credit was drying up. Only the absolute best new business loans were getting booked, and banks were either turning down loans outright or were pricing them so high that borrowers wouldn't take them. An FDIC report showed the number of bank and thrift loans secured by business properties had fallen 25 percent in one year. The "mom and pop" business loans between $100,000 and $250,000 were especially hard hit and had declined by 54 percent.[365]

But it wasn't just small-business loans that were getting harder to get; consumer lending was drying up too. Lenders were beginning to reduce the amount available under their home equity lines of credit and credit cards and were refusing to give any meaningful number of loans to build or buy a home. Given the issues with bad loans and investments, lenders were understandably focused to collect, not originate, new loans.

The problems may have started on Wall Street, economists and politicians argued, but it was definitely spreading to Main Street, and it was going to quickly get a lot worse if the government didn't implement an emergency plan. It happened in a tumultuous way only five weeks before the US presidential election. Nobody liked the idea of a bailout package, but without a way to remove the troubled assets from the lenders' books and help them regain their footing, the lenders sure as heck weren't going to be able to make new loans. And without access to business and consumer loans, the economy would completely collapse. It was a very sobering time, and the thought of reliving another Great Depression (or worse) was unacceptable to everybody except the extremists.

At this point, only the taxpayers had enough resources to bail out the financial system. It had been done successfully before with the $2 billion Home Owners' Loan Corporation (HOLC) following the Great Depression seventy-five years ago.[366] Now the Treasury secretary was working very hard with the Congress and the president to create a $700 billion program to do something similar.

It was so important that President Bush made a twelve-minute, prime-time address to the nation explaining that "we're in the midst of a serious financial crisis" and that "our entire economy is in danger." He announced his full support for the Treasury's rescue plan and lobbied members of his own party for support. The original proposal from Treasury was three pages long and gave them incredible authority to do as they saw necessary. Of course that would be ridiculous, even in a crisis like this. So congressional leadership of both parties went about the urgent business of developing the bailout bill while simultaneously trying to get public and political support.

People still didn't understand how bad things had become even though the terrible news continued. Businesses' inventories declined another 37 percent in the third quarter, following a 49 percent decline the quarter before. It didn't matter. The thought of bailing out big businesses was contrary to everything most Americans had come to believe about our free enterprise system. Conservatives especially objected to the idea of a massive government intervention, believing that businesses should be allowed to succeed or fail on their own without government influence. Less government is always better, they said. Liberals objected that the bill contained too much for Wall Street companies without placing any limits on their activities and especially on their compensation. They also thought there was insufficient relief for homeowners facing foreclosure.

Finally, on Monday, September 29, 2008, Alabama Congressman Spencer Bachus, the ranking Republican on the House Financial Services Committee, declared, "Our time has run out. We're going to make a decision. There are no other choices, no other alternatives."[367]

It was September 2008.
$895 billion Fannie **failed.**
$804 billion Freddie **failed.**
$639 billion Lehman **failed.**
$1 trillion Merrill was suddenly **sold.**
$1 trillion AIG **failed.**
$500 billion in money market funds **disappeared.**
$1.1 trillion Goldman's charter suddenly **changed.**
$987 billion Morgan's charter suddenly **changed.**
$307 billion WaMu **failed.**
$812 billion Wachovia was suddenly **sold.**
159,000 jobs in one month were **lost.**
760,000 jobs in nine months were **lost.**
Auto manufacturers were facing **bankruptcy.**
Businesses' inventories were **falling.**
Small businesses were **failing.**

With the fate of our financial system on the line and the world watching closely, the House of Representatives debated a bill whose passage was needed to save the country from financial ruin.

In the end, 95 Democrats and 133 Republicans out of 433 elected officials provided just enough votes—13—to kill the bill.

With the fate of our financial system on the line and the world watching closely, the House of Representatives debated a bill whose passage was needed to save the country from financial ruin. In the end, 95 Democrats and 133 Republicans out of 433 elected officials provided just enough votes—13—to *kill* the bill. The *New York Times* called it a "catastrophic defeat" for President George W. Bush, who intensely lobbied the public and his party to support the failed measure.[368] But the collapse in the president's political fortune was nothing compared to the collapse of the public's financial fortune.

The Dow Jones dropped 778 points that day, the biggest single-day point loss in history, and the first ever $1 trillion + loss in one day.

Finally, politicians and the public began to better understand the unfortunate reality of the situation. On Wednesday, the Senate quickly amended an unrelated and completely different bill (ironically related to mental health) that had already passed the House and was awaiting Senate action.[369] They kept most of the provisions from the defeated House bill, but added some new and expensive features to make it more palatable to both liberals and conservatives. The new features, which had nothing to do with the financial bailout, were estimated to cost about $150 billion and included adding a number of energy tax breaks (such as deductions for buying solar panels) and extending some expiring tax breaks (such as allowing state and local sales tax deductions on federal tax returns).

Emergency Economic Stabilization Act

Bailing out the banks

The Senate passed the Emergency Economic Stabilization Act that day with seventy-four votes in favor and twenty-five opposed; the House agreed two days later by a vote of 263 in favor and 171 opposed. Although the bill failed in the House by thirteen votes that Monday, it passed by fifty-eight more than necessary on October 3, 2008. President George W. Bush immediately signed it into law.

The bailout bill itself is divided into three parts. Division A is the focus of the bill. Division B has numerous tax provisions related to energy production, transportation, and conservation. Division C extends various expiring tax provisions such as alternative minimum tax relief, and it includes the original purpose of the House bill addressing mental health and addiction that the

Senate co-opted in a procedural maneuver in order to rush the bailout bill through.

Funding is divided into three pieces: $250 billion is immediately available; $100 billion is available when the president approves it; and $350 billion is available if the president sends notice to the Senate of the need, and they do not disapprove of the request within fifteen days. In a show of bipartisanship politics, President Bush made the official request for that $350 billion of additional funding, and President-elect Obama lobbied in favor of it. The Senate defeated a resolution of disapproval 52–42 on January 16, 2009.

The first piece of the funding is Division A. It created the now well-known Troubled Assets Relief Program (TARP), which allows the Treasury secretary to remove toxic assets from banks (more technically, to purchase, insure, hold, and sell them), particularly those related to residential or commercial mortgages that led to the economic crisis.

In effect, TARP was a way to remove bad loans from the lenders who made them so they could start over by making new, improved loans. If you could replace the bad loans with cash, lenders might still be cautious in their lending because they had been burned so badly before, but at least they would begin lending again. The bailout bill was sold to the taxpayers as a way to buy toxic mortgages from banks similar to what the Homeowners Loan Corporation (HOLC) did in 1934, but, somewhat surprisingly, Treasury Secretary Henry Paulson tabled the idea after the bill passed and instead forged ahead first with a plan to buy stock in the banks under a Capital Purchase Program (CPP).

The Capital Purchase Program

Although it may have surprised taxpayers that a bill sold as a means to remove bad loans from banks was instead being used to buy stock in the banks, it wasn't a bad idea, and it was clearly allowed by law (although it was buried in the legislation and went unnoticed by most people). It's hard not to be cynical here. The bill was called the Troubled Assets Relief Program, TARP, and was promoted as a way to remove toxic assets from the banks' books. You can imagine the uproar from voters if the bill was instead promoted as a way to buy stock in failing banks. It probably wouldn't have passed. Even though the stock idea was the better idea, the sales job sure leaves a bad taste.

We weren't the first country to buy troubled bank stock. The British had already announced their own £500 billion bailout package (about $865 billion) that included buying up to £50 billion (about $87 billion) of preferred stock in banks.[370] The eight largest British banks quickly participated in the plan, and similar programs were soon implemented in France, Germany, the Netherlands, Spain, Italy, Austria, Portugal, and Norway.

The British plan came with significant strings attached, including a requirement that banks keep lending at the same levels for three years as they had in 2007. This move would restrict their ability to "shrink the balance sheets" but should help ensure continued access to credit. Among other things, the plan also required government approval of dividend payments, of certain board members, and of certain compensation programs.

The US Capital Purchase Program was similar but generated a lot of consternation in the United States. First, to kick off the program and restore public confidence in the banking system, the Treasury secretary held a closed-door meeting where he reportedly strong-armed the top nine US banks into agreeing to sell preferred stock to the Treasury. Along with Fed Chairman Ben Bernanke, New York Federal Reserve President (and future Treasury Secretary) Tim Geithner, and FDIC Chair Sheila Bair sitting at the table, Henry Paulson explained to the leaders of the nine large banking companies that the Treasury was unveiling the capital purchase program, and it would be a bad idea if they didn't participate.[371] An internal talking points document Paulson used at the October 13, 2008, meeting set the tone with suggested language that included comments such as, "We don't believe it is tenable to opt out [of the program] because doing so would leave you vulnerable and exposed," and "If a capital plan is not appealing, you should be aware that your regulator will require it in any circumstance."[372]

Clearly, the Treasury was not interested in bankers refusing the deal because if they did, it would make the others look like they were in trouble. The program to restore confidence by pumping capital into banks wouldn't work if it raised more suspicion rather than calm investors' fears. But you can imagine that the bankers at the table felt blindsided by the "request" and guessed that the Treasury secretary would have regulators in their bank the next day if they didn't participate.

Wells Fargo Chairman Richard Kovacevich objected that his bank wasn't in as bad shape as the others and shouldn't participate. A *New York Times* article reported that he was concerned that the government program would restrict executive compensation. The article noted that his own retirement package was worth about $43 million and that he had amassed about $140 million in accumulated stock and options at Wells.[373] Bank of America Chairman Ken Lewis was also reluctant because his bank had just raised $10 billion, and he didn't think he needed more capital. In the end they both relented. Wells Fargo sold to the Treasury $25 billion of preferred stock (the largest investment amount in the program), and Bank of America sold $15 billion. Ironically, although allowed to do so, neither bank had repaid the money one year after receiving the funds.

The nine bankers in the room surely did not see it this way, but the Capital Purchase Program for banks was deemed a *voluntary* program. Other than these nine banks, at this point there is no real evidence that other banks were *forced* to participate, and, in fact, the terms made it quite beneficial for most banks to sign up. The Treasury reports that one year after unrolling the program, 690 banks had participated in the capital purchase program; the taxpayers had invested $205 billion (of the $250 billion available); and forty-two of those participants had already paid back $71 billion of the investments.[374] In the first year of the program, it has earned taxpayers $6.79 billion in dividends, interest, and fees and another $2.9 billion in stock warrants.

For bankers, the terms of the deal were far from punitive and were better than they could get elsewhere. The nonvoting preferred stock pays 5 percent dividends, which increases to 9 percent after five years. The increase was designed to encourage banks to improve capital and pay back the taxpayers after the crisis was over. The program also gives the Treasury the right for ten years to purchase the bank's common stock (called *warrants*) in an amount equal to 15 percent of the preferred stock investment and at a price that was basically the average market price of the stock just before the deal was made.[375]

As a practical matter, most banks will repurchase these warrants from the Treasury when they repay their preferred stock. The bank offers to repurchase the warrants at a price they deem fair, and Treasury, which uses the same formula with all banks to value the warrants, may accept or reject it. If they don't accept the price, the warrants are sold at an auction, and the Treasury gets the proceeds.

A deal like this wasn't all bad for taxpayers, and in many cases it generates a very good return on investment. For example, Goldman Sachs sold the Treasury $10 billion of preferred stock on October 28, 2008. They paid it back on June 17, 2009. Taxpayers received $318 million in dividends on it, and when Goldman Sachs bought back the warrants, they paid the Treasury a solid $1.1 billion on July 22, 2009. So the taxpayers earned over $1.4 billion in nine months, about a 23 percent annualized return on investment. That's not too shabby.

But the whole bailout deal was done with a gun to the taxpayers' heads, and nobody likes to do business that way. Bankers were unhappy too, not so much with the preferred stock as with the warrants. Diane Casey-Landry, a senior official with the American Bankers Association (the largest bank advocacy group), wrote to Treasury Secretary Geithner complaining that "many banks participated in the CPP reluctantly and at the urging of their primary regulator," and the resulting public backlash at the program has caused them to want out now. However, paying the warrants amounts to an "onerous exit fee, not a proper return on investment."[376]

Taxpayers would surely disagree.

Executive Compensation

By December 2008, the economy was in serious trouble, and the public was very concerned. In one poll conducted by the American Research Group, 86 percent of Americans rated the economy as bad, very bad, or terrible, and 41 percent said their household financial situation was getting worse.[377] The problems on Wall Street were rolling onto Main Street with a vengeance. The Fed's December 3 Beige Book, a publication of anecdotal information from the District Reserve Banks on current economic conditions, affirmed a very gloomy outlook. Overall economic activity was weakening nationwide with problems in retail and vehicle sales, tourism, manufacturing, housing, commercial real estate, agriculture, mining, and energy. Labor market conditions were weakening everywhere, and the national unemployment rate had reached 7.2 percent, its highest level in almost sixteen years. Most economists were predicting it would climb to double digits within the year (which it did, reaching 10.2 percent in October 2009).[378]

Although the Treasury Department called the $250 billion Capital Purchase Program (CPP) an investment and not a bailout, few people viewed it that way. FDIC Chairperson Sheila Bair, who sat at the table with the Federal Reserve and Treasury when the plan was revealed, would later say that "at the time it sounded like the right thing to do. It was part of an international effort. But I just see all the problems it's created now. It's had a terrible, terrible impact on public attitudes toward the financial system, toward the regulatory community, and it's created all sorts of issues about government ownership of these institutions."[379]

The FDIC chairperson was probably just positioning her agency more favorably with community banks when she made these comments (to try to fend off proposed congressional changes to the FDIC), but one thing she was right about: the public was angry with bankers. But not because of the CPP. Let's face it: the average Joe couldn't tell the CPP from a CPA. But he sure as hell knew how much money he was earning for his hard work, and he was understandably angry about the incredible paychecks the executives of these failed or bailed-out companies were getting.

To make matters worse, incomes for average households were falling. The US Census Bureau reported that the average household income in 2008 was $50,303, down 3.6 percent from the year before.[380] And yet, people who were perceived as being at least partially responsible for taking down the economy were raking in the dough. It's bad enough that both Jimmy Cayne at failed Bear Stearns and CEO Dick Fuld at bankrupt Lehman Brothers made over $34 million in 2007 and that CEO Stan O'Neal at Merrill Lynch was forced to retire (fired) but still received $161.5 million as a going away present. But the nerve of Merrill's new CEO John Thain authorizing ***$3.6 billion*** in bonuses to his employees at the same time his failed company was being acquired by Bank of America *with $25 billion of taxpayer money*, and AIG's planned **$1.2 *billion*** bonus program with what amounted to *$182 billion in bailout money* proved to be watershed moments. *Greed has a price.*

AIG Arrogance

Merrill's CEO, John Thain, got fired, but AIG was different from Merrill. AIG was not a privately owned company spending taxpayer money. It was now a government-owned company using a lot of taxpayer money to pay huge bonuses!

Nobody was happy with the idea of AIG's bailout, including the people who worked there who had nothing to do with its failure. In fact, most of this huge company was performing quite well financially and would have continued to earn a nice return for its shareholders and great paychecks for its employees had it not been for the Financial Products subsidiary run by Joe Cassano.

CEO Cassano reportedly ran the division with an iron fist. While he was driving AIGFP deeper and deeper into high-risk products that caused the company to fail, he raked in an astonishing $315 million. "It is hard for us, without being flippant, to even see a scenario within any kind of [rhyme] or reason that would see us losing one dollar in any of those transactions," he told investors before the company failed.[381] Seriously? At $315 million in compensation, most people would expect the CEO not only to see potential risks but to prevent them. The combination of personal arrogance, compensation that was over the top, and financial devastation made him an easy target, and the media portrayed him in a very unfavorable light.

Vanity Fair magazine ran a feature article on him entitled "The Man Who Crashed the World." *Time* magazine listed him at #7 on their "25 People to Blame for the Financial Crisis," and CNN's Anderson Cooper ranked him at #10 on their series entitled "Ten Most Wanted: Culprits of the Collapse." But Matt Taibbi went even further in *Rolling Stone* magazine, calling him "Patient Zero of the global economic meltdown" and describing him as a "pudgy, balding Brooklyn College grad with beady eyes and way too much forehead" and a "greedy little turd with a knack for selective accounting."[382]

AIG had more than their share of corporate and individual arrogance. Less than a week after the Federal Reserve announced its initial $85 billion bailout, AIG executives were jetting off to the St. Regis Resort in Monarch Beach, California, for a week-long retreat at the luxury resort and spa—at a cost of over $440,000 (including $23,000 in spa charges). "They're getting their pedicures and their manicures, and the American people are paying for that," said Congressman Elijah Cummings (D-MD).[383] A second conference for 150 AIG insurance agents at the Ritz Carlton in Half Moon Bay (where the cheapest rooms go for $400 a night) near San Francisco, California, was reluctantly cancelled after the public outcry. AIG officials actually considered an advertising campaign to explain why these junkets were important. As one with a strong grasp of the obvious, their PR consultant George Sard advised otherwise, calling it a "really bad idea" and explaining to the clueless that "to spend the taxpayer's money on an expensive ad campaign to apologize for how you used taxpayer money leaves you open to further attacks."[384]

Naturally, the biggest outcry occurred when word got out that the taxpayer-owned company was paying huge bonuses and retention awards. In January 2009, AIG revealed that it was paying $619 million in bonuses. Two weeks later, they disclosed that about four hundred workers in AIGFP—the subsidiary that caused the company's collapse—were being offered $450 million in retention pay. Unbelievably, the total planned company bonus and retention plans exceeded $1 billion![385]

Outside of cussing, there are no words in the English language to describe the public outrage. Although Treasury Secretary Geithner tried to have the bonuses changed (and did get them scaled back by about 30 percent), new AIG CEO Edward Liddy reported that these contracts were in place to keep executives from jumping ship and that they had been arranged before the government takeover. Furthermore, the bonuses had been promised before he had agreed to accept the AIG CEO position (at a $1 a year salary) after the government bailout. Liddy claimed that his "hands were tied." The president's chief economic adviser, Larry Summers, would say, "The easy thing would be to just say, 'off with their heads, violate the contracts.' But we are a country of law. The government cannot just abrogate contracts."[386]

Summers was definitely out of touch with the public mood. This was not good enough for taxpayers. Some reports had the average salary of AIGFP employees at $270,000 a year—without the bonuses. People were furious. At a congressional hearing, CEO Edward Liddy read one of the many death threats company officials had received that said, "All the executives and their families should be executed with piano wires around their necks." Liddy was under considerable pressure and asked employees getting more than $100,000 in bonuses to voluntarily return half. AIGFP employees did agree to return $45 million of their bonuses—but five months later, only $19 million had been returned.

New York Attorney General Andrew Cuomo conducted an investigation of the company and got commitments from nine of the top ten executives and fifteen of the top twenty to return the money. Despite calls to make the names of AIG bonus recipients public, investigators and company officials didn't do so because they were concerned about the safety of managers and executives.

Clearly, not all AIG executives were moved by the outcry. In a widely read *New York Times* opinion piece, "Dear A.I.G., I Quit," Jack DeSantis, an executive vice president in the failed Financial Products Division, attributed the failure to a handful of people and expressed dismay that he and the others at the company were vilified for the actions of a few. DeSantis said he would donate his after-tax bonus to a charity of his choice rather than see the money go back into the obscurity of AIG's or the federal government's budget. His self-righteous letter did not get much sympathy except from some coworkers.

> "He acts like he's a victim because he didn't get to keep his after-tax bonus of $742,006.40 in the middle of a global depression," responded Matt Taibbi. "Out in the real world, when your company burns a house down, you're not getting paid by that client. It's only on Wall Street, where the every-man-for-himself ethos is built into an insanely selfish and greed-addled compensation system, that people like you expect to get paid in a bubble—only there do people expect their performance bonuses no matter how much money the shareholders lose overall, no

matter how many people get laid off after the hostile takeover, no matter how ill-considered the mortgages lent out by your division were."

"Hey Jake, it's not like you were curing cancer. You were a [expletive] commodities trader. But your company went belly-up and broke, almost certainly thanks in part to you, and now you don't get your bonus.

"So be a man and deal with it. The rest of us do, when we get bad breaks, and we've had a lot more of them than you."[387]

Recognizing the importance of responding to their constituents' fury, the House of Representatives passed a law imposing a 90 percent tax on the bonuses paid to AIG executives, or any other company that received more than $5 billion in bailout money. The Senate didn't act on the bill, and it died in committee, but congressional hearings were held on everything from specific pay packages at AIG, Bear Stearns, Countrywide, Lehman Brothers, and others, to conflicts of interest by executive compensation consulting firms.

In 2009, the SEC began questioning large firms about their disclosed compensation strategies, although it was focused more on how the firm disclosed their compensation decisions, not on how much they paid. The IRS issued a ruling that put limits on business tax deductions for compensation exceeding $1 million if it was part of an involuntary termination.[388]

During the crisis, Congress considered several bills that at least require nonbinding shareholder votes on executive pay packages.[389] One bill in particular, the Corporate and Financial Institution Compensation Fairness Bill, passed the House on July 31, 2009, that would have given shareholders nonbinding votes on pay packages. It would also allow regulators to consider whether pay packages at institutions with over $1 billion in assets encouraged taking excessive risk. A similar law has been in effect in Great Britain since 2002, but shareholders there rarely vote against the pay packages, and when they do, it is only an advisory vote and can be ignored. The bill died in the Senate.

The highest profile response came when the second round of TARP funds was released in January 2009. While seventy-four senators voted to approve the rescue bill in September 2008, only fifty-two would support the second round of funding just over one hundred days later. Their opposition reflected public outrage over a number of issues, and the Obama administration helped win votes and ensure that funds were released by promising to implement more oversight and transparency and by placing executive pay limits at companies receiving bailout money.

The next month, the administration rolled out a plan that would cap the salaries of top executives who received bailout money at $500,000, although stock incentives would still be allowed. But the effort wasn't good enough for taxpayers or Congress and, instead, a provision was inserted into a $787 billion economic stimulus bill requiring the Treasury to develop rules restricting compensation for the five top officers and the twenty highest-paid executives at the largest bailout recipients.

In December 2008, the National Bureau of Economic Research officially declared the obvious: the United States had been in a recession since December 2007. Two months later, the controversial and partisan $787 billion economic stimulus bill, more formally known as the American Recovery and Reinvestment Act of 2009 (ARRA), was signed into law. ARRA contains substantial spending programs, provides numerous tax cuts or credits (that add about 34 percent to its total costs), and, most significantly, places limits on executive compensation (Title VII).[390] Specifically, this stimulus bill amends the Emergency Economic Stabilization Act of 2008 (the bank bailout bill) and subjects any institution that has TARP funds to new compensation standards established by the Treasury.

The Treasury Department must establish standards to ensure that the recipient has not engaged in excessive risk that could hurt their company. These standards must also include "claw-back" provisions to recover bonuses, retention pay, or awards to senior executives and the next twenty most highly paid employees when financial statements are notably inaccurate. These standards also restrict golden parachutes (significant compensation if employment is terminated) to a senior executive officer or to any of the next five most highly paid executives. Long-term restricted stock is allowed under this bill, but with restrictions.[391] The law also places limits on luxury items, such as company jets. And the law specifically directs the US Treasury to review compensation paid to the senior executives and top twenty most highly paid employees whose company received TARP money before this law was passed. Treasury also must determine if executives' compensation is inconsistent with this law, TARP, or "otherwise contrary to the public interest." That means the Treasury could negotiate with these folks for repayment.

To help implement this law, on June 10, 2009, the Treasury secretary appointed Kenneth R. Feinberg as Special Master on Executive Compensation, or as the media would call it, the pay czar, to specifically review the compensation strategies of five senior executives and the next twenty highly paid people at the seven largest recipients of TARP money: AIG, Citigroup, Bank of America, General Motors and GMAC, Chrysler and Chrysler Financial. "He has a lot of authority with respect to not just the seven but with respect to all TARP firms," said Stephen Bainbridge, law professor at UCLA. "It's an enormous expansion of federal power over corporations."[392]

Bainbridge may be correct that the legal authority of the Treasury secretary represents an expansion of federal power over corporations, but the power is less absolute than it is moral suasion. According to Mr. Feinberg's congressional testimony, his "jurisdiction under the regulations is limited to the senior executives of these seven companies, and *only* these seven companies." Although he has the authority to make recommendations on compensation packages at other TARP-recipient companies, those recommendations are nonbinding, and the pay czar has stated that he does not support going beyond the seven companies. "I do not believe it necessary or wise to broaden my jurisdiction or make my legal authority more pervasive."[393]

But that's not to say he failed to make a statement. Feinberg reduced proposed payouts at six of the seven companies by half and reined in company perks, such as excessive use of private planes. He did not go after employment agreements or other contracts made before the law was passed but said he considered them when he was looking at future payouts. And he made an important statement when he reduced cash compensation for AIG employees 91 percent from 2008 levels. He also made important changes in their stock incentive programs that when combined with the cash reductions, decreased their total compensation by 58 percent from the year before. At Bank of America, cash compensation was reduced 94 percent and total compensation 62 percent. At Citigroup, cash compensation was reduced 96 percent and total compensation 70 percent. *Greed has a price.*

Needless to say, companies that were subject to Treasury oversight became very anxious to repay their bailout money and remove themselves from pay restrictions. By mid-November 2009, forty-seven companies had repaid and were no longer subject to potential Treasury compensation oversight. The ten largest amounts that were returned were from JPMorgan Chase & Co.($25 billion), Goldman Sachs ($10 billion), Morgan Stanley ($10 billion), U.S. Bancorp ($6.6 billion), Capital One Financial Corp. ($3.6 billion), American Express ($3.4 billion), BB&T ($3.1 billion), Bank of New York Mellon ($3 billion), State Street ($2 billion), and Northern Trust ($1.6 billion).

On October 22, 2009, the Federal Reserve Board also announced a proposal to begin reviewing institutions under its regulatory oversight "to ensure that the incentive compensation policies of banking organizations do not undermine the safety and soundness of their organizations."[394] Although the Federal Reserve was unlikely to adjust specific individual compensation packages, it would review *the process* that sets those pay packages and could force changes to the method used.

In spite of all the attention, it isn't entirely clear whether Wall Street's senior executives fully grasped the public anger about compensation packages that companies receiving bailout money paid to their executives. Goldman Sachs, for example, received $10 billion in bailout money and, more importantly, was a major beneficiary of the AIG bailout. When the Federal Reserve honored AIG's credit default swaps in full instead of negotiating a lesser amount as part of their bailout package, Goldman was the biggest recipient, receiving $13 billion from the government. If the Federal Reserve had not bailed out AIG, some contend, Goldman would have failed as well (although at that point, just about all major brokerage firms would have gone under). Many people complained that it was a "backdoor bailout" and a sweetheart deal from then New York Federal Reserve President Timothy Geithner. When the Federal Reserve gave its weekend approval for the investment bank to convert to a bank holding company and get access to Reserve Bank lending programs, it raised even more suspicions.

> *[Goldman Sachs is] a great vampire squid wrapped around the face of humanity, relentlessly jamming its blood funnel into anything that smells like money.*

None of these government bailout programs or the perceptions of favoritism would deter Goldman from paying its people generously. According to an analysis by the *Wall Street Journal*, Goldman Sachs was on track to pay $20 *billion* in compensation packages in 2009 (amounting to roughly $700,000 per employee). The public backlash against Goldman was very strong.

Matt Taibbi penned the most quotable quote of all when he described the "world's most powerful investment bank" as "a great vampire squid wrapped around the face of humanity, relentlessly jamming its blood funnel into anything that smells like money."[395]

With press like that, Goldman Chief Executive Lloyd Blankfein, who received $70 million in 2007 compensation, went on the offensive to soften Goldman's image, promote their charitable giving, and explain their business model.[396] It wasn't easy.

In an extensive interview with John Arlidge of the *Sunday Times* (London), Blankfein comes across terribly.[397] Here are some excerpts from his article, entitled "I'm doing 'God's work.' Meet Mr. Goldman Sachs":

> Whatever the truth behind the bail-out, not even the smartest Goldmanite can deny that it is only thanks to government aid that the bank still has a financial system to work with. Washington has bolstered the U.S. economy and banks to the tune of $12 trillion. Does Blankfein not acknowledge that it is maddening for most of us to watch Goldman gobble up so much cash while we struggle? Quite the opposite. He insists we should be celebrating his bank's success, not condemning it. "Everybody should be, frankly, happy," he says. Can he be serious? Deadly.
>
> So, it's business as usual, then, regardless of whether it makes most people howl at the moon with rage? Goldman Sachs, this pillar of the free market, breeder of super-citizens, object of envy and awe will go on raking it in, getting richer than God? An impish grin spreads across Blankfein's face. Call him a fat cat who mocks the public. Call him wicked. Call him what you will. He is, he says, just a banker "doing God's work."

Apparently, Goldman has a long way to go to improve their image. At least Stephen Colbert, host and executive producer of television's The Colbert Report on Comedy Central, came to his defense, saying, "It's all the rage out there to be all the enraged at bank CEOs" and pointing out that even though unemployment is high, at least bank CEOs have jobs. "They must be doing something right." The always clever Colbert mockingly praised Blankfein for his "humility" and as one who, despite his $68 million a year pay, never forgets he is a "blue collar guy" as he said in the *Times* interview.

> *"... God's work no longer includes punishing pride, greed, vanity, or gluttony."*

"Bravo," Colbert says of Goldman Sachs. "Keep doing God's work. And it is nice to see that God's work no longer includes punishing pride, greed, vanity, or gluttony."[398]

Changing the Accounting Rules

An accounting rule known as *mark-to-market* is a very big problem in dealing with falling asset values. Mark-to-market requires banks to use the *current* market values of investments on their financial statements unless they intend to hold those investments for a long time, typically until they mature. If investments are held for a shorter term, they must use the current market values unless those investments are just *temporarily impaired*, i.e., they haven't lost their value permanently. If the security was intended to be held short term and was "other than temporarily impaired," i.e., its value was down, and it wasn't just a temporary glitch, banks had to report the losses on their balance sheets and income statements. The idea behind this generally accepted accounting principle (GAAP) was to allow investors to know how well a bank's investments were doing today, rather than the day they were purchased.

Most of the troubled mortgage-backed securities were held for short terms, and it was difficult to know their value during the crisis. After all, nobody was buying the securities at anything other than fire-sale prices, if at all. It seemed especially unfair for banks to write down their values so drastically because in most cases the underlying loans themselves were still performing; it was the mortgage-backed security that *on paper* was losing market value. To them, the accounting rule itself made matters worse.

The mark-to-market accounting rule was implemented after the savings and loan crisis in the early 1980s when companies could report asset values based on historic cost rather than on current values. By not reporting the true value of their investments, the S&Ls were allowed to continue to grow when they didn't have enough capital, leading to a huge government bailout later. S&Ls were also allowed many other accounting breaks, such as being allowed to operate with less capital when times got tough and being allowed to follow more liberal regulatory accounting procedures (RAP) instead of GAAP.

In any case, in the current crisis, banks were getting killed with the GAAP accounting rule. Bank of America, for example, had about $3.5 billion in reported losses because of the rule.[399] Larger and larger losses were requiring more and more capital, and bankers everywhere were in a bind. To eliminate losses, they had to eliminate the toxic mortgages. But selling so many mortgage-backed securities would drive the securities' values lower and lower, thus requiring even more capital, and the downward spiral gets worse. (It's an effect known as "cumulative causation," but my editor thinks that's too much information, and I shouldn't mention it.)

From a banker's perspective, the best solution is to change the accounting rules. Because everybody from the Atlanta Federal Home Loan Bank to Zions Bank in Utah was affected, industry lobbyists began working overtime to change the mark-to-market accounting rules.

The Financial Accounting Standards Board, a private and independent agency responsible for establishing accounting rules, finally gave in to industry and political pressure and changed two things. The first change allowed banks to report the value of assets at a price they would receive in an *orderly* transaction, rather than at a fire sale. The second allowed them to avoid reporting the lost values (write-downs) if they claimed that it was *more likely than not* that they would hold an asset long term.[400]

In effect, the two changes gave bank management much more leeway in reporting losses in their portfolio. Not surprisingly, bankers and investors liked the rule, and the KBW Bank Index (that tracks bank stock prices) jumped over 20 percent in less than two weeks.[401] It brought a lot of short-term relief to bank profits and capital positions.

Under the best of circumstances, mark-to-market accounting is hard to implement. But under the new standards, accounting transparency became much more clouded. Not everybody was pleased. "Most of these assets are still losing value at a rapid clip. The fact that banks will not have to reflect that loss from an accounting point of view doesn't change the reality," claimed tax and accounting analyst Robert Willens. "Shenanigans such as this do nothing to resolve the many problems facing the financial system; indeed this decision is more likely to delay necessary reform and restructuring than it is to create a positive outcome," said economist Joshua Shapiro. "This is bull%#@$," said my friend Toby.[402]

Whether opponents are correct remains to be seen. But public confidence rarely improves when you change the rules in the middle of a crisis just to make things look better. *Accounting is not a game.*

Toxic Assets

When Treasury Secretary Timothy Geithner replaced Henry Paulson in 2009, he changed course and announced a **Public-Private Investment Program for Legacy Assets (PPIP).** PPIP would use up to $100 billion from the bailout bill along with money from private investors to purchase bad loans and securities (toxic assets) from banks. By bringing private investors into the mix, the Treasury Department believed that the purchasing power of the partnership would remove $500 billion of bad loans and securities from the market quickly and up to $1 trillion over time. If things went badly, taxpayers would not have to bear the losses alone—the private sector would bear some loss too. And the upside would work the same way—shared profits.

Because there had been a profit in the HOLC some seventy-five years earlier, regulators were hopeful that private investors would be willing to invest in this program too, and they were right. But the problem here was determining how much to pay for the bad assets. The HOLC had refinanced loans directly with the home owner at low 5 percent fixed-interest rates, with fifteen-year maturities, and in amounts up to 80 percent of the property's appraised value. But unlike HOLC, the Treasury Department wasn't refinancing the loans directly with borrowers, so how could they determine a fair price to pay for the loans?

Apparently, by letting the markets decide. Lenders would establish a pool of bad assets they wanted to sell at auction to the highest bidder. Bidders would be investment companies, and the winning bids would determine the market value of these toxic assets.

To encourage investors to bid on toxic loans—something they had stopped doing on any scale after Bear Stearns failed—the Treasury would encourage private investors (individuals, pension plans, insurance companies, and others) to invest in a "fund" that would buy the assets at the auction. If the fund was approved for the program, the Treasury would match every dollar fund managers raised from private investors with TARP money. So half of the money to buy toxic assets was private; the other half was public. For example, a fund with $5 million from private investors could then get $5 million in equity from taxpayers (TARP funds). If things went well, taxpayers and private investors made a profit. If they didn't go well, both would suffer a loss.

With the money in place, these privately managed funds would bid at an FDIC-sponsored auction on toxic loans being sold by participant banks. As part of the deal, the participant banks would loan the money needed to buy the toxic loans to the fund. They were willing to do this because the FDIC would guarantee the loans. Everybody knows making a new loan with an FDIC guarantee is a whole lot better than a living with a toxic loan from a subprime borrower. The FDIC set certain limits, but you get the idea.

The initial reaction to the program was generally favorable both at home and abroad. The (often negative) *Wall Street Journal* editorial said, "This isn't the worst idea the federal government has ever had, and if it works it will help banks take their losses and burn down debt." Richard Beales of the British daily newspaper the *Telegraph* claimed, "Tim Geithner needed a credible and detailed 'bad bank' plan this time round. The besieged U.S. Treasury secretary has delivered. There are some niggling problems. But it appears more feasible than anything previously announced." James Surowiecki wrote in the *New Yorker* magazine that "the people who came up with this plan—Geithner, Larry Summers, and Ben Bernanke—are well-versed in the problems of the banking system and serious about trying to solve them, rather than being either oblivious or corrupt."[403]

TARP was sold to the American public (taxpayers) as a way to remove toxic loans from the lenders who made them so they could start over by making new, improved loans. It took a long time to get there, but the PPIP would have satisfied that promise. As it turned out, the program failed to get off the ground for several reasons. For one, mark-to-market accounting flexibility limited the amount of losses that banks were forced to recognize. For some banks, it was better to keep these bad assets on the books at the value they thought was reasonable than to put the assets up for sale and find out if they were right! Besides, the large banks managed to raise enough capital—through the private sector and TARP's Capital Purchase Program (CPP)—to eliminate the need to unload these loans at a loss. And smaller banks faced other barriers, such as not having enough bad assets to package and sell (an economy of scale issue) and concerns that the losses on their sale would be too much. Some participants were even concerned that if the program was highly successful and they generated good profits, public anger could erupt again as it had with executive compensation issues.

In June, the FDIC announced that while it would continue to develop the PPIP program (their part was called the Legacy Loans Program, or LLP) in case it was needed later, it was suspending the plan for now. Chairman Blair stated, "Banks have been able to raise capital without having to sell bad assets through the LLP, which reflects renewed investor confidence in our banking system. As a consequence, banks and their supervisors will take additional time to assess the magnitude and timing of troubled assets sales as part of our larger efforts to strengthen the banking sector."[404] The Treasury also had a similar plan to remove bad securities backed by residential and commercial properties from the banks, but it too was not implemented.

Until a program is actually implemented, it is hard to gauge its success. On the other hand, just having these plans available has been helpful because investors know that there is a way to remove toxic loans from the bank's books in case of emergency. As Scott Romanoff of Goldman Sachs said, this is "the greatest program that never occurred."[405]

Bank of America

Acquires Merrill Lynch, a Government Bailout, Public Outrage and Shareholder Anger

When CEO Ken Lewis announced that Bank of America (BofA) had struck the $50 billion deal to buy Merrill Lynch, he called it a "great opportunity" for the shareholders. The acquisition would make BofA the largest brokerage company in the world, with more than twenty thousand financial advisors and $2.5 trillion in client assets. But investors were less than impressed with the deal—they were paying about $29 a share for a troubled company whose stock was trading at less than $16 a share —and the BofA stock price fell 21 percent when the announcement was made in September 2008.

But a deal's a deal, and the Federal Reserve approved it in November. In spite of the price, BofA shareholders approved it on December 5. Closing was scheduled for New Years Day 2009, and according to Lewis, it was all planned "*without any promise or expectation of government support.*"

It didn't take long for the deal to turn sour. According to Ken Lewis, he discovered nine days after shareholder approval that Merrill would report a $12 *billion* loss for the quarter (it was actually a $15.31 *billion* loss and a $27.6 *billion* loss for the year). BofA's failure to uncover this in their due diligence process earlier certainly reflected poorly on their management team, and Merrill's failure to disclose the losses sooner raises questions about their self-proclaimed "responsible citizenship" and "integrity," or perhaps just their competence. But regardless of their motives, a deal's a deal.

Or was it? BofA senior management called the Federal Reserve and US Treasury in mid-December to report that they were considering walking away from the deal by invoking a "material adverse event" clause in the contract (commonly called a MAC clause). Successful or not, simply invoking the MAC clause would have resulted in lengthy litigation and would have surely thrown the economy into an even deeper downward spiral. These were horrendous times—Fannie Mae and Freddie Mac had been "nationalized" the week before, and Bear Stearns was no more. Lehman Brothers had gone bankrupt, and now Merrill, one of the largest securities firms in the world, would have a very hard time surviving if BofA walked.

Federal Reserve Board Chair Bernanke told BofA officials that walking away would cause great systemic risk to the economy, as not only would Merrill be destabilized, but so would BofA. After all, who would have confidence in a company that spent three months telling everybody what a great deal they had made only to then turn around and admit they didn't see a $27 billion loss heading their way! In any event, Fed lawyers didn't think invoking this MAC clause was legal. They believed that the merger contract was binding. An internal memo from a Federal Reserve senior advisor (Tim P. Clark) noted that a general consensus was forming among several senior Fed officials that Ken Lewis's "claim that they were surprised" by the increasingly large losses "seems somewhat suspect."

Was it possible that Lewis was just using the threat of walking as a bargaining chip to get a "deal" from the Treasury and Fed? Of course it was. After all, they didn't approach Merrill to restructure the deal—they approached the government to get a deal. But the reality was that BofA was not on solid financial ground. Some government assistance would be needed anyway.

Did Treasury Secretary Paulson tell Lewis that if they walked from the deal and caused Merrill, BofA, and the economy to tank, thus requiring an even larger government bailout, they would lose their jobs? Yep.

Paulson told him the obvious. If senior management made bad decisions and showed a "colossal lack of judgment" by trying to invoke the MAC clause to walk from the Merrill deal, and those decisions ruin Merrill, their own bank, and the US economy, senior management would certainly be replaced. They sure as hell should have been.

By the middle of 2008, the entire financial system was in jeopardy, and, much like other large financial institutions, BofA was not exempt. That's why they "accepted" $15 billion from the Capital Purchase Program allowed under the Troubled Asset Relief Program (TARP). In spite of public outrage that any financial institution should get a taxpayer bailout, BofA was in no position financially or politically to turn it down. The Treasury was using taxpayer money to purchase (nonvoting) preferred stock in US banks under the same terms for everybody: 5 percent interest for five years and then 9 percent interest after that. Merrill Lynch was also eligible for some taxpayer TARP money and received $10 billion. That made BofA, Merrill's new owner, responsible for repaying the combined $25 billion in taxpayer bailout funds.

Although BofA had just received $25 billion in taxpayer money, it wasn't enough to keep their management team from seeking even more government help with the Merrill deal. They got it on January 16, 2009, when the Treasury invested *another $20 billion* under their "Targeted Investment Program" to buy preferred stock. This preferred stock paid taxpayers 8 percent interest.

It was possible that taxpayers could make a nice return on investments like these, or they could lose a ton of money. But the financial merits got lost in the debate because taxpayers were outraged that in their view, bank deals like these were made under duress with very rich company executives who contributed to—if not caused—the problems in the first place. The national debt was skyrocketing as the country struggled to finance domestic programs and the wars in Iraq and Afghanistan. Bank bailouts left a very bitter taste.

To make matters worse, three days after shareholders approved the deal and before the year-end financial statements were even finalized, Merrill Chairman and CEO John Thain authorized bonus payments to his company employees of about $3.6 *billion*, including $1 million or more to at least 696 employees. This was on top of the $1.2 million the company had paid to renovate Thain's office the year before. Public shame forced Thain to repay the office renovations, but that was nothing compared to the public anger that came when the company insisted on paying the huge bonuses and was using taxpayers' bailout money to do so!

Thain was fired soon after. *Greed has a price.*

Lewis initially denied having anything to do with the bonuses, claiming it was Thain's decision because the company was not part of BofA until the deal was officially consummated January 1, 2009. But the merger agreement specifically addressed bonus payments, and BofA was clearly aware of them even if they were unaware of the specific allocations.

Shareholders were mad about the deals and their declining stock values. Because BofA management did not reveal these bonus plans and the mounting losses at Merrill before the shareholders voted in early December, several BofA shareholders filed suit against the company for misleading them. The New York Attorney General's Office, Congress, and the SEC have all investigated, and the matter may not be settled for several years.

The SEC proposed a $33 million settlement with BofA that did not require them to admit or deny accusations that they mislead shareholders. However, a federal judge refused to allow the settlement, saying that if the companies had lied to their shareholders, the settlement was too weak.

Lewis was removed by the shareholders as BofA board chairman in April and announced his retirement as CEO of the company at year-end 2009.

Chapter 11

The Conclusions

We have all been here before ...
Crosby, Stills, Nash & Young

I don't normally get caught up in these things, but as New Year's Day came around, I decided that my goal for the next year was to be 10 percent less of an ass than I was the year before. I'm sure that if I just cleaned up my language I would probably shave a point or two off the goal but, c'mon, 10 percent less "jerk" just doesn't have the same effect, now does it?

Okay, so here I am trying to be 10 percent less of an ass, which, by the way, is not as easy as you think, when my funniest friend Johnny piped-in with his senior executive sales management query.

"How are you going to benchmark this," he asked?

"Huh? What are you talking about," I replied.

"How will you measure the success of your goal? Have you established clear benchmarks to compare year over year?"

"What on earth ..." I began to stutter. "How the hell would I do that?"

"Well, maybe you should send out a survey to all of your friends. You know, have them rate you. Like on a scale of one to ten, where one is a total ass and ten is a real nice guy. You could have categories for social settings, sporting events, business meetings ..."

"Aw, shuddup," I interrupted. I was pretty sure I didn't want to see any survey results.

That New Year's resolution presented a challenge for this final chapter because it's hard not to come across harshly. These lessons seem so obvious, so simple, and yet so frequently they are ignored or forgotten. Readers may be inclined to quickly glance at them and then dismiss the chapter as too basic or superficial, but, honestly, these are some of the most important fundamentals of the game. In sports, the losing coaches will often talk about a breakdown in the fundamentals, such as the failure to block and tackle that cost them a victory. In banking, it's the same thing. We fail to remember the fundamentals, the lessons that every banking school in the country should teach.

For years, when I was consulting with banks about more effective loan-pricing strategies, one of my standard suggestions at a typical community bank was to have lenders price their loans in smaller increments. If they charged an extra 1/8 percent on a loan (or reduced it by only 1/8 instead of 1/4 percent when negotiating), they could generate significant income for the bank— usually between $25,000 and $100,000 on their typical annual loan production.

Management often thought that everybody knew this already, and that lenders were routinely pricing in small increments. The suggestion appeared to have little merit because it was so obvious. Then I would point out the problem. An analysis of loan production at their own bank would frequently show that over 90 percent of their commercial, commercial real estate, and construction loans and lines of credit were priced in quarters and halves. Sure, everybody said they knew the strategy, but they failed to implement it.

That's why this chapter is so important. We have all been here before. We know these lessons. We just choose to ignore them sometimes. There are more, of course, but my New Year's resolution is at stake so I'm leaving those out. Perhaps they will be featured in my next book, tentatively titled, *Listen Up! I'm Done with Resolutions*.

1. We got this way for a reason.

Things happen for a reason. We stopped exchanging bushels of corn for live chickens because it was cumbersome. We tried exchanging other items of value instead, like wampum, tobacco, and eventually Spanish coins and bank-issued currencies, but all had shortcomings, including not having enough of whatever it was on hand to represent our collective value. We tried multiple currencies and coins, but counterfeiting and fraud caused big losses to individuals and businesses. We tried a national currency, but until we fought a war over the role of the federal government, we couldn't agree about using it. We tried backing our currency with gold and silver, but it unnecessarily limited growth and painfully contributed to economic downturns.

We have now developed a more complex system, and while it might be confusing to the average person (if they even notice), it works better than anything we have tried before. Folks clamor for going back to a simpler system like the gold standard. But we forget that a lot of people suffered unnecessarily from that system. We found that we could do better. We got this way for a reason. Going back would be worse.

Not just in the United States, but around the world we are a creative people and, over thousands of years, have developed and refined a system, an economy, that allows access to credit and opportunities to create wealth. By combining our desire to safely store our valuable commodities (currencies and coins) we found a way to share our wealth with others and to benefit personally in the process.

We created a banking system that offered both loans and investments, and it has proven to be a remarkable way to safely share wealth. No longer is wealth limited to the chosen few who by birth or luck owned land or the means of production. Now, anybody with the motivation, work ethic, and ability to create their own wealth can get in on acquiring it. There are no guarantees, but there are opportunities. There are fewer reasons for revolutions when everybody has an equal opportunity. We got this way for a reason. The alternatives are worse.

Our system has flaws. Capitalism is not perfect, and it would be silly to assume otherwise. For example, it has not always served low- and moderate-income families especially well. We are not immune to uprisings when economic injustices arise. Today we almost expect to see protests outside large-scale meetings of our political parties, or of the World Bank, IMF, or Group of Twenty (G-20) finance ministers and Central Bank governors when their summits are held in the United States. We have a long history of violent economic protests. The Boston Bread Riot of 1713, the Haymarket Riot (Chicago) in 1886, the May Day Riots of 1894 (Cleveland), the Columbine (Colorado) Mine massacre in 1927, and, most notably, the Hunger March (Detroit) in 1932 are just a few examples of violent protests against economic injustice.

During the Great Depression, economic injustice wasn't unique to the United States. While many other countries were responding to economic injustices by removing the means of production (factories, machines, land, tools, etc.) from the few and concentrating it instead in the hands of the governing through communism, totalitarianism, and other dictatorships, the United States kept its capitalist approach. Then and now, when confronted with deficiencies in our system we adapt and respond in reasonable if imperfect ways. One such response following the economic collapse with the Great Depression was to turn away from the allure of communism and instead strike a "New Deal with America," one that featured homeownership as a pillar of its foundation.

Our country believes that safe, decent, affordable housing is a human right and a smart idea because it helps generate wealth that can be used for retirement and other purposes; it helps reduce crime, improves citizenship, strengthens self-esteem, and provides many other social and economic benefits. We developed an entire financial system to encourage affordable housing for everybody and, in the process, create jobs and wealth. It was the way out of the Great Depression, away from communism, and toward greater prosperity. Until now, it worked pretty damn well. We got this way for a reason.

We developed savings banks (and credit unions) and other institutions to help the working poor; we developed loan programs that met the needs of our middle class better; we implemented regulations and controls to limit fraud and excessive risk; we created a Farm Credit System, Federal Home Loan Bank System, and other government-sponsored enterprises to promote healthy food and quality housing. We passed laws to prevent discrimination to ensure fair housing.

We are a better nation because of these programs, laws, and regulations. None of these actions were especially easy or without controversy; all have issues. Even so, totally eliminating the programs and laws that have served us so well is a very bad idea. We got this way for a damn good reason.

We have seen that real estate booms and busts over the past several hundred years, but, in each case, we adapted with both more liberal programs to jump start the housing industry (such as FHA and GSE programs), with more government regulations to limit abuse (such as predatory and usury interest rate limitations), and with more conservative actions to prevent excess (such as tighter loan underwriting standards). We have seen taking excessive risk hurt our national interests, and we usually respond with appropriate industry and government regulations. They aren't perfect, don't always work, and are continuously evolving, but we got this way for a reason, and going back without first specifically addressing the previous shortcomings would be worse.

We have developed an extensive financial system in this country that includes a large number of commercial banks, thrifts, investment banks, government-sponsored and government-owned enterprises, and regulators. Some are small, some are large, and all are flawed in one way or another. They all provide good jobs and benefits. They serve our economy well. Fortunately, all have attended the school of hard knocks, and we the people have time and again risen to the challenge of changing, creating, and adapting our financial system for the better.

The process will never stop, nor should it. As long as we ignore simple ideological slogans when we contemplate changes and instead focus on smarter and better solutions than before, we prosper. Financial institutions and regulators operate the way they do for good reason.

And it has been for the better.

2. Good government is necessary.

Political battles have been waged over everything imaginable, and almost all of them are, in one way or another, over money. Describing the political theater that has molded our economy and our country would take forever and would surely include the battles to develop a sound national currency; the development of a gold *and silver* standard to protect mining interests out West; the desire to increase fiat currency with pressure from the Greenback Party after the Civil War; changes to chartering authorities and oversight for banks and thrifts; creation of the Farm Credit System, the Federal Reserve System, the Federal Home Loan Bank System, Fannie Mae, Freddie Mac, Ginnie Mae, and other government-sponsored or -owned enterprises; creation of Farmer Mac, the FHA, and the SEC; and the numerous industry bailouts. And these are just a few examples of political events that led to the financial system we have today.

Good Government

For the most part, the programs and systems we have developed have proved tremendously beneficial. Some might brag that we are the envy of the world. Our prosperity is noteworthy, and opportunities abound. Large numbers of people are migrating here seeking wealth and opportunity. We sometimes fail to recognize that every one of the government's economic and financial agencies and institutions and virtually every law and regulation associated with them were developed methodically and meticulously (although occasionally very quickly) to encourage or repair a part of the economic system.

Everybody knows that government intervention has side effects, but when done right it's normally worth it. Counterfeiting currency was a horrible problem before we established a national currency, the US Bureau of Printing and Engraving, and the Secret Service.

FDIC insurance is a government-mandated program with side effects. It costs the industry money to provide deposit insurance, and it can have the effect of allowing more money to flow to the worst bankers in the country, who pay crazy interest rates for deposits in a last-ditch effort to survive. Even so, the insurance is critically important, has prevented depositors from losing money, and has virtually eliminated large-scale runs on banks and thrifts that previously devastated the industry and destroyed individual and business savings.

FHA insurance has done a remarkable job of giving housing opportunities to the middle class and of covering its own expenses—indeed, generating billions in taxpayer profits along the way. FHA isn't perfect, but the program has been well worth it.

Government programs can pay their own way. The HOLC, Federal Reserve System, Federal Home Loan Bank System, Farm Credit System, FDIC, FHA, and many others are self-funded, and some return profits to the government.

People argue for less government, but we live in a complex country. Less government can prove very costly. When it gets right down to it, few people seriously advocate for less government oversight of food, medicine, transportation, building construction, industrial pollution, or banking and finance. A better argument is for less expensive government and less personally intrusive government. Good government is necessary.

Bad Government

Government bailouts are a fact of life, and anybody who advocates otherwise because bailouts present a *moral hazard* (taking more risk because they know they are covered for any loss) is absolutely right to do so but is wrong to think it will happen. We have bailed out industries again and again. It's done in a bipartisan manner. President Hoover adamantly opposed government economic intervention, but his administration established the Reconstruction Finance Corporation in 1932, which loaned money to troubled banks, railroads, savings and loans, and life insurance companies. President Carter's administration gave loan guarantees to Lee Iacocca's Chrysler in 1979. President George H. Bush's administration bailed out the savings and loan industry in 1989. President George W. Bush helped the airline industry after September 11, 2001, to name just a few.

Some people think that we should have let these businesses and industries fail because the financial cost is so high and any government intervention is inherently bad. However, it's not just "the industry" that pays the price. *People* suffer with increased rates of unemployment, depression, suicide, divorce, bankruptcy, homelessness, crime, stress, and hunger, to name just a few. Today, many people have been sheltered from the harsh side effects of economic disasters precisely because we have systems to help prevent them or reduce their severity. Most of us have never witnessed the soup lines and shantytowns that appeared during the Great Depression and that led US citizens to demand government intervention. Fortunately, as a nation we have proven to be better than to allow this kind of large-scale human suffering to occur, and our government intervention has been reasonably successful in preventing it.

That's not to say that all government actions have been good. Just as we have seen failings in our own businesses and even in our own families, everybody screws up at one time or another, and governments are no different. When the federal government sold Fannie Mae to raise money to fight the Vietnam War, for example, it seemed like a good idea but eventually came back to haunt us because we failed to establish appropriate limits on Fannie's size and capital base. Even worse, we let politics dictate Fannie's destiny because we were swayed by their heavy lobbying and by their significant contributions to both major political parties and a large number of nonprofits. In the process, we ignored their excesses, weakened their regulatory oversight, and aggressively attacked their opponents for any critical comments they uttered.

At one time, these GSEs provided an exceptional product and service from which we all benefitted and should all be proud. However, by not paying attention to the politics and policies around Fannie Mae and Freddie Mac, we allowed these two extremely important institutions to self-destruct. It will cost us a fortune to recover our losses and rebuild the secondary market they were allowed to dominate. As a nation, we should do better than that. Good government is necessary.

Worse yet, time and again we allowed our politicians to interfere with the regulators. That's not to say that congressional oversight isn't important—it's actually critical to the system. But intervening on behalf of a specific company in the middle of an audit or examination is terrible political judgment, or worse. Whether it was the five US senators (Keating Five) who improperly intervened to disrupt the Federal Home Loan Bank Board's investigation of Lincoln Savings and Loan in 1987, or it was Senator Christopher Bond going after the OFHEO in 2004 while they were in the middle of investigating Fannie Mae for accounting fraud, this interference should never have occurred.[406] The politicians should be held accountable. After all, the reputational damage they caused carried over to the entire industry and to all elected officials.

Politicians aren't experts in every industry. That's why vigilance is especially critical when politicians appoint industry experts to regulatory roles.

These appointments matter. If we support appointments of individuals who want to dismantle, downsize, or otherwise weaken the regulator's role, we must be prepared for the consequences. It is not acceptable to buy into the slogans of "less government" if we don't also understand what it really means. History has shown that self-regulation and self-control properly goes along with government regulation. It's not a substitute. It is incredibly naïve and dangerous to assume that self-regulation alone is a good alternative to government regulation.

After the financial panic led to the collapse of the US economy in 2008, FDIC Chairman Sheila Bair said, "Not only did market discipline fail to prevent the excesses of the last few years, but the regulatory system also failed in its responsibilities." After the improper and largely unregulated use of derivatives contributed to large-scale failures and made the government bailout of AIG and others necessary, former Federal Reserve Chairman Alan Greenspan said, "those of us who have looked to the self-interest of lending institutions to protect shareholders' equity (myself especially) are in a state of shocked disbelief." Morgan Stanley CEO John Mack said of Wall Street's investment banks, "Regulators have to be much more involved. We cannot control ourselves." After the top three investment banks under their supervision failed, SEC Chairman Christopher Cox said in September 2008, "The last six months have made it abundantly clear that voluntary regulation does not work."[407]

Why did we ever assume otherwise?

3. Don't sleep with each other.

It seems so obvious, and yet it happens. Regulators are aware of the risk of regulatory capture and all have policies that try to minimize the risk. Often, it's simple things, like rotating examiners every so often so the same people are not examining the same company for more than a few years at a time. It's not always easy to strike the perfect balance because you want people who have been examining an institution long enough to have become experts in its operations and risk-management practices and thus better at identifying fraud or mismanagement. On the other hand, there is a very real risk that people can become too close or too trusting.

Exhibit A: Bernard Lawrence Madoff.

Bernie Madoff was a lying, manipulating, callous crook; a detestable man; and a *schmuck*. He was also the former chairman of the NASDQ stock exchange, a highly regarded investment advisor for thousands of wealthy people and organizations, and a philanthropist who gave hundreds of thousands of dollars a year to charities.

Unfortunately, his wealth and investment abilities were all a fraud. He ran the largest *Ponzi scheme* in world history. His *affinity fraud* likely cost investors somewhere between $10 billion and $20 billion in losses. On March 12, 2009, he pled guilty to eleven felony counts of securities fraud, investment advisor fraud, mail fraud, wire fraud, money laundering, perjury, and theft, and was sentenced to the maximum 150 years in federal prison. He was seventy-one.

The government agency responsible for preventing Madoff's Ponzi scheme was the SEC, and they failed miserably. A 457-page report by the SEC's Office of Inspector General (OIG) found that the "SEC received numerous substantive complaints since 1992 that raised significant red flags concerning Madoff's hedge fund operations and should have led ... to a thorough examination and/or investigation of the possibility that Madoff was operating a Ponzi Scheme." The report concluded that the SEC "never took the necessary and basic steps" to uncover the illegal activities. The OIG report blamed inexperienced personnel who conducted their work with inadequate planning and insufficient scope. "While the examiners and investigators discovered suspicious information and evidence and caught Madoff in contradictions and inconsistencies, they either disregarded these concerns or relied inappropriately upon Madoff's representations and documentation in dismissing them."

The report identified a long list of deficiencies at the SEC, showing just how badly the staff was outmatched by the industry. At all levels of the SEC, they had become a victim of regulatory capture, believing the crap fed to them by a smooth-talking crook—some would say a psychopath—because of his perceived stature and prominence.

Ponzi scheme *was named after a famous swindler, Charles Ponzi (1882–1949). It describes an illegal scam that uses money from newer investors to pay off the earlier investors. Swindlers like Ponzi can never sustain their promised returns, and their pyramid schemes eventually collapse, leaving later investors with big losses. The crooks who are behind these scams, like Ponzi and Madoff, often pocket large sums and live lavishly until everything collapses.*

Affinity frauds *are investment scams against members of similar groups, such as religious or ethnic communities, professional organizations, the elderly, etc. The fraudsters are often members of the group, who then exploit the trust and friendships they have developed to convince group members to invest money with them.*

Schmuck *is a contemptible person. The insulting term is derived from the Yiddish word shmok.*

As the OIG would report, "in light of Madoff's reputation, the examiners did not think it necessary" to look into Madoff's operation any further than absolutely necessary. "Madoff was able to use his stature and perceived connections to push back against the inexperienced junior examiners, who did not feel confident [enough] to be more aggressive and who were informed by senior officials in Washington DC, as they were conducting the examination, of Madoff's [good] reputation in the industry." The OIG stated that Madoff's "prominence made it less likely for the SEC investigators to believe that he could be running a Ponzi scheme."[408]

Former SEC Chairman Christopher Cox claimed in a 2008 interview that "the SEC is not a safety and soundness regulator." If that were the case, it is unclear why they would agree to become the umbrella supervisor for the largest investment banks in the country under the Consolidated Supervised Entity (CSE) program. Allowing these banks to use Basel II capital standards and foolishly high leverage ratios with so few skilled staff to oversee the operations was another instance of putting too much trust in the institutions they were regulating.

Regulatory capture happens at other agencies too. The FHLB was too close to the savings and loan industry they regulated and was stripped of their authority following the S&L crisis in 1989. The leadership at their successor, the OTS, turned out to be even worse.

At one point the OTS was reducing staff while the thrifts under their watch were growing in number, size, and complexity. They *unilaterally* reduced their thrifts' Community Reinvestment Act (CRA) examination process beyond that of any other federal regulator in spite of over four thousand public opposition letters (including twenty-eight from members of Congress and forty-five from US mayors). They opposed OCC efforts to crack down on high-risk Option ARM products, an action that led to the failure of IndyMac and Washington Mutual. They allowed IndyMac and BankUnited of Coral Gables, Florida, to illegally backdate capital, thus permitting the thrifts to avoid harsh public scrutiny and additional regulatory oversight. They allowed Countrywide to change charters even though it was very clear that it was in bad financial shape and was changing charters to avoid the inevitable OCC crackdown. These are not trivial matters. They show a pattern: the OTS was falling victim to regulatory capture.

Every regulatory agency should be diligent in guarding against even the perception of regulatory capture. It isn't unreasonable to present the industries in which you have supervisory and regulatory authority in a favorable light.

They overwhelmingly have good people working to do what they perceive as right for their shareholders, employees, and customers. However, it's a bad idea to become their advocate. Regulators have to be neutral third parties and should be fully attuned to outside perceptions. Whether it is the Farm Credit Administration's willingness to let associations like CoBank and AgriBank become so large so quickly, or the Federal Reserve's opposition to regulating derivatives, or FINRA's (the largest independent securities firm regulator) uninspiring response to the 2008 industry debacle, history shows that real or perceived bias will eventually hurt both the agency and the industry.

Closely related to regulatory capture and equally dangerous is regulatory interference. The debacles with Fannie Mae and Freddie Mac will, we hope, give rise to many books and investigations, and all of them will have to include the unbelievable interference by both Democrats and Republicans. Our elected officials share responsibility for ensuring proper oversight of government-sponsored enterprises, but in far too many cases, they were in bed with the industry too.

Our regulators got too cozy with the investment banking industry and allowed them to take too many high risks, especially in derivatives. We gave favored status to three credit rating agencies and then let them laugh all the way to the bank. We had the notion that the industry could self-regulate. We bought into the argument that less regulation is better for everybody, but there should have been limits.

Regulators should know not to get in bed with the ones they regulate. The industries should know better too. *Don't sleep with each other.* Just the perception that the regulators were sleeping with the regulated has forced our elected officials to aggressively intervene. Getting too close to the fire can leave everybody burned.

4. Greed has a price.

America is the land of the free and the home of the brave, and all that stuff, and we do celebrate the success of our entrepreneurial heroes, such as Bill Gates (Microsoft), Steve Jobs (Apple), Warren Buffett (Berkshire Hathaway), and Ted Turner (CNN). We haven't made a stink about their paychecks because they appear to have done things honestly and fairly and have earned their rewards. We are proud of their success, and they serve as excellent reminders that the United States really is a land of opportunity.

But cross that line of honesty and fairness, and the public can turn against you. This isn't news, and it isn't new.

Michael Milken was known as the "junk bond king." Large companies that want to engage in higher-risk projects or have weak credit will issue their own debt securities (nicknamed junk bonds) that pay a higher interest rate to compensate for the risk. Milken was the star trader at Drexel Burnham Lambert, a firm best known for its junk-bond trading in the 1980s.

At the time, junk bonds got a bad reputation because of the callous nature of some of the corporate takeovers they financed. Not only was Milken financing unpopular hostile takeovers to benefit people like T. Boone Pickens, Carl Ichan, and Ronald Perlman, but the successful takeovers he financed resulted in large-scale layoffs, asset stripping (acquiring a business with the intent of tearing it apart to sell off all its assets at a profit), and raids on the company's pension funds to remove "excess" contributions to pay for the merger. Some argue that the mergers were beneficial and the layoffs temporary; the new companies would eventually create more jobs than they lost. But that wouldn't matter. More people thought it was unfair that dedicated employees were getting screwed while Michael Milken earned over $200 million *a year* putting together deals that reduced employees' future pensions and got them fired. He had a reputation for being an arrogant and greedy man who cared little for anybody but himself. He was the epitome of Wall Street greed.

It didn't take long before he was investigated for violating securities laws, and after being indicted on ninety-eight counts of racketeering and securities fraud by Rudy Giuliani, the United States attorney for the Southern District of New York (and later the mayor of New York City and an unsuccessful US presidential candidate), he pled guilty to six securities and reporting violations. He served twenty-two months in jail and paid about $900 million to settle claims with the government, litigators, and creditors. Drexel Burnham Lambert was forced to file bankruptcy on February 13, 1990. For the record, Milken went to jail for six technical securities and reporting violations. In reality, he went to jail for his perceived greed.

In another infamous case, Dennis Kozlowski, the former chairman and chief executive of industrial conglomerate Tyco International, was found guilty of twenty-two counts of grand larceny, fraud, and conspiracy. "Deal a Day Dennis" became CEO of Tyco International in 1992 and went on a rampage, buying several hundred diverse companies around the world from financial services firms to electronic securities companies. He had a reputation for tossing out the management of firms he bought, firing workers, and closing factories "without sentiment."[409]

He also paid himself generously, using company funds to purchase more than $10 million in artwork (including a $4 million Monet painting) and to buy an $18 million apartment on New York's Fifth Avenue that he charged Tyco to renovate and furnish for over $15 million (including a $6,000 shower curtain). He had the company pay for half of his $2.2 million "toga" birthday party for his wife on the Italian Island of Sardinia (where Jimmy Buffet performed and waitstaff were dressed as nymphs and gladiators). He helped drive the company's stock price from around $32 a share when he became CEO to over $105 a share in 1999, only to have it collapse under the weight of his criminal indictments to $8.25 in June 2002.

The company's accounting scandals, excessive expenditures, and high salaries (he was paid over $170 million in 1999 alone) were well known and eventually proved to be unacceptable. Along with his chief financial officer, Mark H. Swartz, he was convicted of looting the company. Because of his greed, he was sentenced to serve from eight and one-third years to twenty-five years in a New York state prison.

Cases like Milken and Kozlowski are just the tip of the iceberg. Many high-profile, greedy CEOs have faced similar plights. Fraud has caused their company failures and their own demise as corporate pigs. Bernie Ebbers got twenty-five years in jail for his role in the collapse of WorldCom (now Verizon); John Rigas of Adelphia (at the time the fifth-largest cable company) got fifteen years, and his son Timothy, the former CFO, got twenty years; Jeffrey Skilling at gas-providing and energy-trading giant Enron got twenty-five years (convicted chairman Ken Lay died of heart disease before he was sentenced); Joe Nacchio at telecommunications giant Qwest International got six years (for insider trading); Sam Waksal at ImClone, a biotech firm that invented a promising cancer-fighting drug, got eighty-seven months (for insider trading). Even entrepreneur Martha Stewart got caught for using insider knowledge from her broker (who was aware of Waksal's pending stock sales) to dump ImClone stock and avoid a potential $46,000 loss. She had to serve five months in the slammer.

The DeVito Line

Where is that line in the sand where the money you make isn't worth the actions you take?

It's hard to know how the recent controversies over executive pay will end, but if it does end—and that's a big *if*—it will not be soon, and its resolution will satisfy few. Executive pay has always been an issue, but especially today because of the staggering compensation packages paid to executives of failed or taxpayer-rescued companies. It sure looks greedy.

Recipients of excessive pay may have an incentive to cross the lines of good business, good judgment, and strong ethics because the math works even after factoring in lawsuits and jail time. Mike Milken was reported to still have a billion-dollar net worth after his jail term, and he was apparently willing and able to spend fortunes to improve his reputation after he got out of jail. Just go to his website, www.mikemilken.com, for a flavor of his propaganda. In early 2010, the second sentence on his home page touted his success in "creating value, whether measured in lives saved … students inspired, or jobs created." His charity work and commitment to worthy causes is truly commendable. But who the hell brags about "creating value" by saving lives?

Joe Cassano (born in 1955) worked with Mike Milken at Drexel Burnham Lambert before it failed. After the company went bankrupt, he landed with some of his coworkers at AIG, where he established and led their Financial Products division that engaged in risky credit default swaps that took down the company.

Cassano, dubbed a "greedy little turd" in *Rolling Stone* magazine, was paid $315 million for his work. In early 2010, he was reportedly under investigation by the US Department of Justice and the SEC, the IRS, and Britain's Serious Fraud Office, and was facing at least one lawsuit (by the Jacksonville Police and Fire Pension Fund) for misleading investors. Assuming that several lawsuits are filed against him that his insurance policies don't cover, and even if he does go to jail for some reason (it isn't likely), you have to wonder if those costs would be a deterrent. How expensive would these out-of-pocket settlements have to be, and how much time would he have to serve to make an arrangement like this "unprofitable"? An hour-long appearance before a congressional hearing is surely not enough. At $315 million in compensation, the DeVito Line is far, far away.

The same question holds true with Jimmy Cayne at failed Bear Stearns and Dick Fuld at bankrupt Lehman Brothers. Each of them made over $34 million in the year that their companies collapsed. Stan O'Neal at Merrill Lynch was forced to retire when his company tanked, but he still received $161.5 million to go away. Angelo R. Mozilo at Countrywide was paid $51.8 million in 2006 and another $11.9 million the next year when his company collapsed. Fannie Mae's

Frank Raines battled with the SEC over 101 charges against himself and two others for fraudulently manipulating earnings. He was paid over $90 million over five years and ended up returning $27 million to settle the suits while admitting no wrongdoing.

Did they even get near the DeVito Line? Even if all of these individuals were found guilty of illegal activities, would their punishments ever exceed their compensation?

Would you be willing to serve a couple of years in jail if you could walk away later with millions of dollars in your bank account? It isn't likely that you would have crossed the DeVito Line where the punishment exceeds the financial gain. If you think about the amazing things you could do with millions of dollars, your ability to justify the action gets a lot easier. Justifying the wrong business ethics may not be as hard as you think.

Until white-collar punishments exceed the bad judgments, lack of ethics, greed, or the crimes, there is no incentive to change behavior. Without some constraints, executives will almost always take maximum risk to get the maximum personal reward.

Greed has a price. Is it high enough?

Blame the game, not the players

Comedian Chris Rock was talking about becoming rich and earning a lot of money when he slyly noted to the audience that we should "blame the game not the players." He's right. We may be pleased to see high-profile CEOs go to jail for fraud when their companies collapse, or folks like Goldman Sach's CEO Lloyd Blankfein have their paychecks reduced for one year because of public outrage, but if the rules of the game do not change, the problem won't go away. This is bad for everybody.

Americans don't mind big paydays. Most people are proud that successful entrepreneurs make a killing. It's what the free enterprise system is all about, and everybody hopes to be one of the winners. Problems arise and tempers flare, however, when taxpayers are called on to bail out industries that won't rein in excessive compensation. When people get mad enough, the pendulum can swing wide and hard in the opposite direction.

When word got out that former bank Chairman and President Bert Lance, head of the US Office of Management and Budget during the Carter administration, had previously arranged sweetheart loans to other bankers and himself that were not available to the public (in the early 1970s), Congress outlawed the practices and began requiring additional personal financial reports from executive officers and directors (Regulation O). Responding to public anger over corporate and accounting scandals in companies like Enron, Adelphia, and WorldCom, Congress passed the Sarbanes-Oxley Act of 2002 that places extensive and expensive constraints on public companies' accounting standards and controls. The cost to comply with these laws is high. It may be an overreaction, but that's the nature of the game. *Greed has a price.*

As it stands now, far too many public companies have been unable or unwilling to properly match compensation strategies with performance. It's even more offensive when it appears that the investment bankers benefitting from the taxpayer bailout in 2008 made no real effort to do anything other than justify existing compensation.

The industry could have implemented a variety of self-help measures, such as having FINRA (their own regulators) specifically prohibit compensation consultants from doing other business with the firm, a rule that helps prevent the consultants from trying to keep the top executives happy in order to generate more consulting business for themselves. A company's board of directors should hire compensation consultants who report only to the board, and the consultants should be changed periodically to prevent "capture" by the company executives. Claw-back provisions (that allow companies to recover bonuses paid under false pretense) could be clearly defined and strengthened. Delaying the payment of annual bonuses would help uncover fraud and excessive risk before the money leaves the company. Requiring executives to hold stock for longer periods would mitigate excessive short-term thinking. There are dozens of sound measures the industry executives could take to strengthen these public companies while still rewarding employees and shareholders fairly.

It is another lesson we never seem to learn: any industry that doesn't exercise self-control will probably be subjected to political intervention. From specific wage and price controls, such as those imposed during the Nixon administration, to Regulation O, to Sarbanes-Oxley, to proposals that levy a tax on specific pay packages at AIG, to appointing a pay czar to oversee bonuses paid at select companies, politicians are not afraid to get involved. The public demands it. It's not just an issue in the United States of America either. In England, the government's response to public anger over executive pay at bailed-out companies was to place a 50 percent tax on all bonuses over $50,000. Greed does have a price. It's just a matter of when the bill comes due.

In the United States, the Obama administration has talked loudly but so far has carried a relatively small stick. The president referred to the industry executives as "fat cat bankers," but in 2009 had imposed only modest pay restrictions on companies that hadn't yet repaid their Troubled Assets Relief Program (TARP) funds. In 2010, however, he proposed a "Financial Crisis Responsibility Fee" to tax investment banks and others with assets of more than $50 billion and clearly set the tone when he suggested that the industry not fight the proposal.

"Instead of sending a phalanx of lobbyists to fight this proposal or employing an army of lawyers and accountants to help evade the fee, I'd suggest you might want to consider simply meeting your responsibilities," he said. "I'd urge you to cover the costs of the rescue not by sticking it to your shareholders or your customers or fellow citizens with the bill, but by rolling back bonuses for top earners and executives."[410]

It behooves the industry to take note. It pays to watch the paychecks. There is a fine line between success and greed.

5. Accounting is not a game.

Timely, accurate, and complete financial disclosures are critical if our economy is to function properly. They give investors, depositors, and others the basis from which to make sound decisions about their money. Regulators place strict reporting requirements on public companies because the regulators rely heavily on these disclosures to monitor the level and trend of risk at the companies and in the industry and to determine the scope of their examinations and oversight. Proper disclosure reduces the need for excessive government intervention. Company executives and accountants understand this as well, and although it happens occasionally, very rarely do they fraudulently mislead the public about the financial condition of their company. Unfortunately, we can't rely too heavily on their financial disclosures because, even under the best of circumstances, the public financial statements are rarely *timely, accurate, and complete.*

Timely

Balance sheets and income statements are a snapshot of a particular point in time. Public companies usually generate these reports quarterly, and publish them thirty days later. Unfortunately, by the time this information is published, it could be too late. It's nobody's fault. It's just the nature of the beast. Expecting people to consistently make sound decisions based only on timely financial reporting is probably asking too much.

The liquidity crisis at Bear Stearns presents just one example of the problem.

Bear appeared to have had more than enough liquidity when it filed its annual financial statements with the SEC in 2008, and there was little cause for alarm. If you read their 10-K form as of November 30, 2007, on page 45 you would have discovered that the firm's policy was to maintain a liquidity ratio at 110 percent or more and that it was actually well beyond that at 171 percent.[411] In addition, the report stated that the parent company also maintained a $17 billion liquidity pool for "company-specific stressed liquidity events that the firm could face over the next 12 months." There was no indication of insufficient liquidity. The SEC would later reveal that Bear's liquidity pool had climbed even higher, to $21 billion on March 6, 2008. But Bear Stearns saw this huge pool get wiped out *in one week*, declining to only $2 billion by March 13. The company was then quickly sold under duress in a deal arranged by the regulators.

There is no way that published financial statements could have presented this information in a timely manner. While insiders and regulators were aware of these details, the company's public financial reporting could not reveal this data fast enough to be worthwhile to investors.

Accurate

Recent events have shown that with some large commercial bank failures, management at the bad banks may have misled investors by not fully recognizing loan losses on their books. When BB&T (Winston-Salem, North Carolina) acquired failed Colonial BancGroup (Montgomery, Alabama), they wrote down the value of their assets an average 37 percent. When JPMorgan Chase acquired failed WaMu, they wrote down those residential mortgages by 16 percent and home equity loans by about 20 percent. While it isn't uncommon for acquiring banks to place a more conservative value on the bad loans they purchased, it is also clear that bankers have a lot of leeway in valuing their assets and in covering their asses.

In a commentary for *Bloomberg News*, Analyst David Reilly astutely noted, "This means that the collapsed banks hadn't created adequate reserves for possible losses, leading their loans to be wildly overvalued."[412] He may be right. It also means that shareholders are not getting an accurate picture from the bad bank, the acquiring bank, or both. Either the failed bank was too generous in their valuations or the buying bank was too conservative. This isn't new. We saw the same problem of properly valuing assets during the S&L crisis of the 1980s.

With mark-to-market accounting, it's even more difficult to evaluate the accuracy of financial statements or to compare companies. At one time, mark-to-market required banks to reflect the *current* market values of investments on their financial statements unless they intended to hold them until they matured (or if banks held them for a shorter term, unless the investments were just *temporarily impaired*). This would have allowed analysts to know how well a bank's investments were doing today, rather than the day it was purchased.

But now, banks can report the value of assets at a price they would receive in an *orderly* transaction, rather than at a fire sale. They can avoid reporting the lost values today (write-downs) if they claim that it is *more likely than not* that the bank will hold an asset for the long term. It gives bank management much more leeway in reporting losses in their portfolio. The accounting has become as clear as mud, and accuracy is in the eye of the beholder, not the outside analysts.

Once again, that isn't to argue that the rule is wrong. It just points out that ensuring accuracy is not as easy as it sounds. Under the best of circumstances, mark-to-market accounting is hard to do. But under the new standards, accounting transparency has become much more clouded. We can say the same thing about derivatives accounting. Company management sometimes argues that they are not misrepresenting financial information but are interpreting the financial reporting requirements differently than the regulators later demanded. Of course, these were the weak arguments used by management at Enron, AIG, Fannie Mae, and Freddie Mac after they were accused of fraud.

Complete

Financial statements presented to the public are great, but they can never give a complete picture of a company's financial condition. You have to go beyond the numbers and actually talk to company management. That's why the larger companies host conference calls with analysts and the public, and why annual meetings are so important. Even then, as we discovered with Enron, Lehman Brothers, Bear Stearns, AIG, and so many others, sometimes companies hide information from the public, for instance, shuffling substantial assets worth untold amounts of money off their books. Enron was using its derivatives activities and a variety of accounting tricks to hide some very unprofitable offshore businesses. AIG owned an offshore insurance company that they previously were claiming was an independent company. When Lehman Brothers was under intense scrutiny for their concentration of high-risk, mortgage-backed securities, they were mysteriously selling about $4.5 billion of assets to a hedge fund run out of their offices by seven *former* Lehman executives, and Lehman was a "significant" investor in the deal. It was nearly impossible for anybody outside the companies to truly understand the implications of these multibillion dollar, off-balance-sheet deals.

It isn't uncommon to move assets off company books, and it isn't always illegal even if it is hard to monitor. How many people really understood the implications of QSPEs, those qualified special purpose entities that allowed investment banks to remove securitized assets such as subprime mortgage-backed securities from their balance sheets? Yeah, I know. Just the name is enough to make you sleepy.

By removing these investments from their balance sheets, the companies could avoid extensive disclosures and limit the amount of capital required to support them. With transactions such as these, or with others like credit default swap derivatives, it is nearly impossible for the average American to know about some of the potential risks and to even remotely understand the complex financial information publicly presented. Having the average American hire financial experts to help manage personal investments is not unreasonable, but it is costly and has its own risk.

Companies like Morningstar Inc. (an independent investment research website) or Moody's, Standard & Poor's, and Fitch, all screw up. Morningstar's analyst report on January 1, 2008, for example, said Wachovia was "a compelling business" and "will be one of the survivors of the housing and economic turmoil."[413] They gave it a five-star rating. It failed nine months later. The credit rating agencies were even worse.

Commercial banks and thrifts are required to use very structured forms when they submit their Reports of Condition and Income to the regulators. These reports can then be used to develop exceptional Uniform Bank Performance Reports, which allow comparisons of institutions by size, type, geography, etc. On the other hand, investment banks and others who report to the SEC are allowed much more leeway, which makes it far more difficult to get an accurate and detailed view of their condition or to compare their performance with similar companies in the industry. The contrast is very telling.

Author and analyst Naomi Prins noted in her blog that "the nation's biggest [investment] banks, plumped up on government capital and risk-infused trading profits, have been moving stuff around their balance sheets like a multi-billion dollar musical chairs game." In one example, she accurately noted that Bank of America wasn't breaking down the trading versus investment banking revenues of its Merrill Lynch subsidiary, which "makes it a lot harder for regulators, shareholders, or we, taxpaying subsidizers, to know whether the merger was a success or not." In another example, she noted that Wells Fargo filings themselves claim their accounting process is "dynamic" and, not "necessarily comparable with similar information for other financial services companies."

"This statement should give lawmakers pause," she says. "If banks are so complex as to constantly fluctuate their own reporting, deciphering figures just before a crisis won't exactly be a walk in the park."[414]

Relying on credit rating agencies and other paid analysts to decipher the information is a good thing if we have some assurance that they aren't in bed with these companies and that the information they present is timely, accurate, and complete. Unfortunately, this has clearly not been the case.

When multitrillion dollar industries made up of huge companies present financial information that cannot be easily deciphered and compared, and that is not timely, accurate, and complete enough, then it's up to the government to increase its oversight and force changes.

Accounting is not a game. It is serious business.

6. Bigger is not always better.

It's simple, really. If the pie keeps getting bigger, your slice will too. Grow your institution, and your wealth grows with it. Growth is generally a very good thing for everybody. But we sometimes forget the risk of growing too fast or too large. Without *quality* growth and without *controlled* growth, the risk will almost always exceed the rewards. As a shareholder, your company can get too big to succeed. As a taxpayer, these companies can get *too big to fail.*

The list of companies with poor quality and uncontrolled growth that led to their failures is long. Countrywide growth rates ranged from 513 percent in 2002 to 111 percent in 2004 before it collapsed under the weight of bad subprime and Option ARM loans that had fueled its growth. Fannie Mae had grown from a $575 billion company in 2000 to over $1.02 trillion by the end of 2004. Freddie Mac had grown from a $386 billion company in 2000 to a $617 billion company two years later. Both grew with thin capital margins and low-quality assets. Bear Stearns, Lehman Brothers, and Merrill Lynch all grew too fast, especially with high-risk, off-balance-sheet assets that were marketed to outside investors and managed by their own company-run hedge funds. They failed or were sold under duress as a result.

Shareholders often win when companies grow. Wouldn't you have loved to have bought stock in Coca-Cola, Microsoft, Apple, or any one of hundreds of successful companies when they were just starting out? As they grew and prospered, you would have too. Unfortunately, size alone is no guarantee of success. There are plenty of examples of companies that grew tremendously, but shareholder value did not. Investors in banks such as Lincoln Savings and Loan (Irvine, California), Continental, IndyMac, and many others lost significantly as the companies grew beyond their financial and managerial expertise.

Wachovia is a good example of a company that struggled terribly to manage its rapid growth from $341 billion in 2002 to almost $800 billion in only five years. Their downfall happened after a series of internal control problems: misleading investors on their auction-rate securities sales, miscalculating taxes on lease transactions, and allowing an illegal telemarketing program. Worst of all was the terrible job evaluating the loans at Golden West Financial Corporation, owners of World Savings Bank, before buying the bank for $25 billion in 2006. These combinations—a rapid growth rate that they struggled to digest, and one fueled by poor quality assets—would lead to disaster. Their stock price would rise from $31 in 2001 to $57 in 2006, only to collapse to $6.50 in 2008 when these problems came to light.

Shareholders aren't the only ones who suffer from rapid growth rates and excessive size. As noted before, systemic risk is where some event causes a big loss of confidence in part of our nation's financial system, and this loss of confidence becomes contagious and affects other parts of the financial system. When Continental Bank, the seventh-largest bank in the country, became insolvent in 1984, regulators and policymakers were very concerned that the bank was "too big to fail" and would cause so much panic that the entire industry would be in danger. They couldn't take the risk, and the government ended up running it themselves for a few years until it could be sold. When the large hedge fund known as Long-Term Credit Management (LTCM) faced financial ruin in 2000, the same systemic risk issue arose, and the regulators helped form an industry consortium to bail them out. *Bigger was not better.*

When so many tremendously large investment banks faced a bad asset quality and liquidity crunch that put them on the brink of failure in 2008, the government was forced to respond again to protect us all from systemic risk. Only this time, the risk was not confined to one entity—it had spread rapidly and uncontrollably. It was one thing to run Continental Bank for a few years or to arrange a bailout for a large hedge fund, but having to respond suddenly when the entire financial systems is collapsing is an entirely different matter.

Over ten months in 2008, the huge behemoths Countrywide, IndyMac, Fannie Mae, Freddie Mac, Bear Stearns, Lehman Brothers, Merrill Lynch, AIG, and Wachovia all collapsed. They had each grown so quickly and to such mammoth size that their failures would devastate the economy. Money market funds saw billions pour out in a matter of days, choking off loans (commercial paper) to businesses nationwide. Unemployment was beginning to skyrocket as companies shed payrolls as fast as they could. Consumers stopped spending money. Automobile manufacturers and others generated so few sales that their industries began to collapse. Banks couldn't raise capital to cover bad loans and began to shrink their balance sheets to protect themselves from the pending crisis, thus choking off loans to businesses and consumers. Once this downward financial spiral had begun, it was impossible to stop it without drastic measures.

Everybody recognized that the commercial, thrift, investment, and insurance businesses were so interrelated that a domino effect was under way where one company's failure caused another to fail and so forth. Given the size and dominance of these businesses, a financial meltdown was under way and causing a tremendous shock both in the United States and around the world. A small group of people might argue that the economy could have withstood the impending shock and that a regulatory and taxpayer bailout was both unnecessary and unwise, but you would be hard pressed to find any credible economists in the country or any officials at the US Treasury or the Federal Reserve System who agreed with this view. At this point, it would have been far too dangerous and irresponsible to gamble with inaction. Nobody in their right mind was willing to stand by and do nothing as the entire economy collapsed around them. These companies had become so large that their individual failures were leading to industry failures and then on to entire economic failures. They had become too large to let them die. *Bigger was not better.*

We were placed in the unenviable position of having to resolve the nationalization of AIG, Fannie Mae, and Freddie Mac. As a nation, we are now forced to face this issue more diligently, which is why the regulators must closely monitor their industries. We would all hope, for example, that the Farm Credit Association closely monitors companies like CoBank, which nearly doubled in size over five years to $61 billion in 2008 (98 percent growth rate) and AgriBank, which grew from $42 billion to $70 billion (69 percent growth rate) with only a moderate amount of capital to support their rapid growth.

Several solutions have been offered to address the problem of institutions becoming too big to fail. Some have suggested we do nothing. If the company fails, so be it. There should never be a bailout. If company managers know they won't get a bailout, they will behave better. Unfortunately that view is really naïve because most companies growing to such large size never thought they would fail to start with. The idea that managers were taking more risk because they knew they were covered for any major loss (moral hazard) is overstated. Arrogance, bravado, and profits were driving their growth. The thought of failing (with or without a bailout) wouldn't stop it.

Some people suggest that we restrict the size of banks by imposing more firewalls, such as preventing commercial banks from engaging in hedge-fund investing. In fact, the Dodd-Frank Act includes something called the Volcker Rule (named after former Federal Reserve Chairman Paul Volcker) that specifically restricts bank ownership of, investment in, or sponsorship of hedge funds. Some people think we should be even more extreme and limit the commercial banks and thrifts to a very narrow business of only accepting deposits and making loans. Others want really high taxes after they reach a certain size.

Former Federal Reserve Chairman Alan Greenspan says US regulators should just break up companies when they reach a certain size. "If they're too big to fail, they're too big," he said.[415] Greenspan points to the government's breakup of Standard Oil in 1911 as an example where it served the country very well.

The Dodd-Frank Act contains provisions not too far removed from that suggestion. A Financial Stability Oversight Council was created with a lot of power. Comprised of fifteen members (ten voting), they are charged with watching and responding to emerging risks. The council will be chaired by the Treasury secretary and include as voting members the Federal Reserve Board, SEC, Commodity Futures Trading Commission (CFTC), OCC, FDIC, Federal Housing Finance Agency (FHFA), NCUA, the new Consumer Financial Protection Bureau, and an independent appointee with insurance expertise.

The council can force large, complex financial companies to divest themselves of some of their holdings if they pose too much risk. They can require the largest institutions to hold significantly more capital, or they can impose really high taxes on them when they reach certain sizes. They will require large institutions to submit for approval a detailed bankruptcy plan that won't cause systemic risk. If the plan isn't good enough, the council can require more capital, more liquidity, or both.

Most importantly, if things look bad enough and the Treasury, Fed, and FDIC all agree, they can force a company into liquidation. That's a lot of power given to those three agencies (dubbed the Death Panel), but the alternative is to leave the power—unchecked—with Wall Street. The existing structure of bankruptcy proceedings and other legal challenges can delay action to the point that the company assets become worthless, and the systemic risk is too much to manage. Without a clearly defined structure like this to quickly close large failing companies, we continue to face economic disaster. Will the regulators have the confidence to impose such an extreme measure on a company like Goldman Sachs, or Citigroup, or any other financial giant? That's open to lively debate. Let's hope we don't have to find out.

No matter the solution, we always have a hard time convincing aggressive managers that getting bigger is not always better—for their company or the country. It's a lesson so hard to learn that strong supervision and regulation of large companies will always be necessary.

7. It's almost always bad loans.

It's a lesson we all know, but it still haunts us. Since the Civil War, the overwhelming majority of US financial institutions that failed did so because they had to confront a bunch of bad loans. It's almost always bad loans that bring financial institutions to their knees.

Regulators take a series of actions before closing a commercial bank or thrift. They require board resolutions, they demand written agreements, and they impose cease-and-desist orders. Each action requires improvements in internal controls, loan reviews, liquidity positions, and capital levels. All are important, and when banks do fail, they are usually closed because they had insufficient capital or liquidity to continue. But those are the symptoms, not the cause of failure. Banks usually fail because of bad loans.

When the regulators closed Southeast Bank, NA, of Miami on September 19, 1991, for example, it was widely reported that the $10.4 billion bank had reached a liquidity crisis and was unable to repay borrowings from the Federal Reserve Bank of Atlanta's Discount Window. Attempts by the "Morgan of the South" bank to obtain additional loans to stay afloat were unsuccessful, and deposits were pouring out of the bank (from $11.2 billion at year-end 1990 to $8 billion eight months later). Liquidity problems would cause the bank to be shut down, but that was only the symptom. The cause was the concentration of bad loans.

In 1991, the bank was caught in Florida's bad economy and distressed commercial real estate market. Nonperforming assets equaled 10 percent of their loan portfolio, and real estate loans were 45 percent of their total loan portfolio. This concentration of nonperforming commercial real estate loans scared potential investors and depositors away. Investors declined to buy more stock in the bank, and depositors began pulling money out. Surprisingly, the loans were not as bad as it may have seemed at the time. When the dust settled and the assets were liquidated, the FDIC had received $221.4 million more than their expenses.[416] That wouldn't matter. The perception of bad loans was enough to kill the bank.

The problems of liquidity would haunt others, such as Bear Stearns, as well. A high concentration of subprime and Alt-A loans made investors so nervous that they tried to cash out their investments in the hedge funds that had purchased these loans, and a liquidity crisis ensued. Liquidity was the symptom; bad loans were the cause.

In many cases, lending institutions do not fail simply because their local economies go bad. They fail because they have a concentration of loans to a particular industry or with a specific product line. In 1873, Jay Cooke & Co. had a concentration of railroad loans (bonds). In the 1980s, fraud, regulatory failures, oil price declines, an agricultural recession, and a crash in real estate values dominated the headlines as over sixteen hundred thrifts and banks failed in just twenty-five years. All were significant factors, but the majority of bank failures were due to excessive growth (Lesson #6), and significantly higher levels of risky loans. Concentrations of commercial real estate and agricultural loans were proving especially harmful.[417]

In 1991, Southeast Bank failed because they had a concentration of commercial real estate loans. In 2007, Bear Stearns and Lehman Brothers had concentrations of subprime and Alt-A loans. Wachovia had a concentration of Option ARM loans. It was either Mark Twain or Andrew Carnegie (it's been attributed to both) who once said, "Put all your eggs in the one basket and watch that basket." With lending, however, concentrating your loans in one product is a bad idea. It's one reason the thrift charter is a risky charter: it requires a concentration of mortgage-loan products.

Understandably, when you have a loan product in high demand that is performing as agreed and earns good profits, it's hard to hold back. Consider the thirty-one banks that failed in Georgia from 2008 to January 2010. This was an astounding number of failures for one state. In fact, Georgia led the country in failures (followed by California and Illinois, which each had twenty-three failures, and Florida, with eighteen failures) at the time. In all Georgia cases, the banks had been operating with enough liquidity, and their capital had met minimum regulatory requirements, but it was not enough to cover the concentration of nonperforming construction loans that took them down.

The Georgia banks didn't have high levels of subprime lending, Alt-A loans, Option ARMs, or other high-risk mortgage loans that destroyed the larger commercial, thrift, and investment banks. They did not engage in excessive derivatives activity with intraparty risks that could not be managed. Only one, Omni National Bank, had specialized in urban renewal and the Community Reinvestment Act (CRA) lending, but their demise was a result of fraud (the bank's cofounder has already pled guilty), not CRA lending.

The other thirty Georgia banks were making highly profitable construction loans. While commercial banks nationwide held about 4.8 percent of their assets in construction and land-development loans, these Georgia banks held an average 40.7 percent of their assets in these products.[418] It's easy to see why they concentrated on these loans because construction lending is one of a bank's most profitable products. It can quickly become a banker's crack cocaine, and addiction has a price.

Integrity Bank in Alpharetta, Georgia, for example, was chartered in November 2000, grew rapidly, and reached a billion dollars in assets before failing eight years later. Their construction and development loans climbed from a very high 57 percent of their loan portfolio in 2005 (the average bank like theirs had less than a 13 percent concentration) to 74.5 percent in 2007. Much like the other failed banks in Georgia, they sought rapid growth associated with a booming real estate market, but when the loans turned sour, they crashed.

We can blame management for rapid growth, board members for insufficient oversight, lenders for excessive risk, or regulators for insufficient action when problems were first noted. Frankly, everybody could have done a better job. But at the end of the day, Georgia banks and most other financial institutions nationwide don't fail as much from corruption, competition, capital, liquidity, insufficient oversight, or weak regulators as they did for one simple reason. They made bad loans. It's almost always bad loans.

8. We should have seen it coming.

Panics happen. They always have and always will, although we hope less frequently and with less severity as we develop better systemic-risk controls. More often than not, there are plenty of red flags warning us of trouble ahead, but too many times we fail to take note. Understandably, it's hard to see the hangover coming when the wine tastes so darn good, but somebody has to stay sober enough to keep the party from getting out of hand. After all, turning down the stereo, cutting back on the booze, and removing the lampshades from our heads is far better than dealing with the police and winding up in jail. In banking, it's called risk management, and, as an industry, we should always be ready for the worst because bad things can happen really fast. Chances are good that if we pay close enough attention, we can see it coming and reduce its damaging impact.

Red flags indicating important business and economic trends are everywhere. Economists, analysts, and other experts closely track these warning signals, and the information is readily available to anybody who cares. For example, consumer spending comprises two-thirds of our national economy—our GDP to be more precise—and monitoring the level and trend of consumer confidence and spending provides very important information. The Consumer Confidence Survey prepared by the Conference Board (www.conference-board.org) and the University of Michigan Consumer Sentiment Index, run by University of Michigan's Institute for Social Research (http://www.sca.isr.umich.edu/) are two great sources of information about consumer attitudes and spending patterns. Information such as this gives us clues about upcoming risks. For example, when consumer confidence is falling, it's *possible* that their spending will soon fall with it, unless something such as government incentives or other economic stimulus changes the behavior. A slowing economy should make lenders more cautious about business loans because repaying those loans is based on consumers spending more. The red flags are there.

Every industry has clues, and bankers providing credit to those industries must pay attention to them. Construction lenders, for example, can track building permits and vacancy rates. Increasing vacancy rates, slow housing sales, high levels of building permits, and other data from local governments and the US Census Bureau (http://www.census.gov/mcd/) are very important red flags that a market might be overbuilt. This isn't news to good lenders, but even good lenders fall into the trap of ignoring the clues. It's just hard to see them when things are going so well.

Alpharetta, Georgia, is a good example. In 1981, they had approximately three thousand residents, but by mid-2007 had grown to over fifty-one thousand. The number of housing units increased by more than 1,000 percent during that time, and it seemed it would never end. In 2000, the city issued 399 building permits for everything from minor renovation projects to major housing developments, including fifty-two permits for constructing new single-family homes. Five years later, they were issuing 214 permits for new single-family-home construction *in that one year*. Business was booming, but how long did people really expect that trend to continue at such a high level? Growth like that doesn't go on forever. By 2008, the market had collapsed, and the number of housing permits the next year declined to only thirty-six. If you had been a construction lender in Alpharetta, you might have been left with a lot of unsold homes and unpaid loans.

Just ask the former officers of Alpha Bank & Trust, a $383 million bank. The bank was chartered in May 2006 with a really high $35 million of shareholder money. Sixteen months later they were growing like crazy and had a ton of construction loans and a nice $429,000 profit. But the red flags were there. They had grown too fast, and, most importantly, construction loans comprised almost 80 percent of their entire loan portfolio. That's a whole lot of construction and development loans. If real estate took a downturn, it could kill the bank. It did, and it did. The bank failed in October 2008, less than thirty months after it opened!

The red flags were there. We should have seen it coming.

It's hard to believe that thrifts like Countrywide and investment banks like Bear Stearns failed to see the full extent of risks when they began packaging subprime, Alt-A, and Option ARM loans into securities. Red flags were all over the place, but credit agencies were giving the securities their blessings within days of receiving the security details. Wouldn't you expect the credit agencies to at least look at some loan files, even just to spot-check them for accuracy? How could they analyze such a massive amount of securities in such a short time? Sure, computer-generated risk models developed by young, talented analysts are nifty, but doesn't it seem incredibly risky to ignore their lack of experience and bet the bank on the relatively new, untested systems? Investment banks were borrowing outrageous amounts to invest in new mortgage-dominated securities, but wouldn't putting so many eggs in one basket—any basket—seem like a really bad idea? The financial disaster that ensued should not have been a surprise. In fact, there are almost always people speaking out against excessive risks, but most of us ignore them or fail to act. We don't always listen well.

Red flags are always there. In almost every case, we should have seen it coming.

9. People matter.

Bankers have responsibilities to three groups: shareholders, employees, and communities. You may not especially like one or more of the stakeholders, but they matter just the same. Shareholders expect fair accounting and reasonable returns. Screw that up, and they can fire you. Employees expect fair salaries. Screw that up, and they can leave you. Communities (consumers and businesses) expect fair treatment and fair business practices. Screw that up, and they can sue you, or even worse, send their elected officials after you. Fortunately, the majority of the banking industry is made up of ethical, moral people who consistently try to do the right thing, and these folks are rarely the problems. Quite the contrary. They earn our respect.

Unfortunately, sometimes bankers get caught in problems that they failed to recognize were important. When investigative reporter Bill Dedman's "Color of Money" series was published in 1988 in the *Atlanta Journal Constitution* newspaper showing that minorities were denied loans two and a half times more frequently than whites with the same income, it pissed people off and set off an avalanche of activity. There was clearly no overt lending discrimination, but as an industry at that time, bankers didn't fully recognize the barriers that minorities faced when trying to get credit. Just the perception of lending discrimination caused the industry to pay a high price. Protests, hearings, new laws, and additional reporting and disclosure requirements were implemented in response to lending disparities. There was no malice on the part of bankers, but they were so focused on providing service and generating profits with existing customer relationships that they forgot that *all* people matter.

Around the world, commercial and thrift bank owners may want their business to be treated like other industries, but that simply is not going to be the case. They are the main source of credit for everything from running a successful small business to owning a home. As a nation, this industry is important because small businesses employ the most people, and homeownership provides savings and security. Access to credit, and by extension, a safe and sound banking system, is a matter of national interest. In some countries, it's as important as a strong national defense. That's one reason why it's such a heavily regulated industry.

A less regulated industry, such as during the free banking period (1837–1863), proved once again that self-interest can be self-destructive. It was bad news to discover that some bankers had lied about the amount of specie (gold and silver) backing their currency and that the bills folks were holding had lower or no value. When it became evident that roughly one-third of the industry's currency was counterfeit, people complained, Congress responded, and local bank currency was taxed out of existence. The people mattered too much to leave them with unstable currency.

The gold (and silver standard) did not work well. Eliminating the gold standard and implementing a fiat currency didn't occur because an evil government wanted to make bankers rich and destroy the integrity of our financial system, as some extremists might contend. The gold standard had serious limitations, most notably for farmers and people settling in the western United States who found the severe shortage of currency devastating. The people mattered too much to leave them without enough currency to grow their business and improve their plight. People complained. Congress responded. The greenback currencies were back.

Our government does respond, if in imperfect ways. When a small number of banks in the southeast United States began paying less than their advertised interest rates on savings accounts because they were first deducting the amount of their reserve requirements (needed to meet withdrawal demands), it came across as sinister and designed to rip off depositors. For example, an unscrupulous banker advertising a 4 percent interest rate was actually only paying about 3.5 percent on the account balance after subtracting the reserve requirements. Although legal, most consumers, regulators, and bankers found this practice to be deceitful. People matter, and the result was a new law that imposed additional reporting and disclosure requirements on *all* banks and thrifts. The Truth in Savings Act, in 1991, was passed because a few bankers cared less about the industry than about themselves. "A lot of us are doing this [paying on the full deposit amount] already, but it will bring consistency to the industry," Henry C. Riley, Bay Bank in Boston EVP said tactfully. "It provides what a consumer should expect and deserve."[419] He was being too kind to the offending bankers. Everybody should have been mad that a handful of arrogant bankers caused a regulatory burden on the rest.

In the most recent financial crisis, the Federal Reserve got a black eye. Many people criticize the Federal Reserve for causing the crisis by leaving interest rates too low for too long, and for poorly regulating the largest banks. When the crisis unfolded, people perceived the Federal Reserve as being more concerned about saving Wall Street than caring about Main Street. Everybody knew the Federal Reserve was lending huge sums of money to commercial and investment banks, and to AIG and other nonbanks. But the thousands of families whose jobs and homes were at risk were not convinced these actions would benefit them. Far from it. People matter, and the Federal Reserve wasn't making a lot of friends with people outside of Wall Street. The voters demanded accountability.

The Dodd-Frank Bill answered the cry by, among other things, authorizing a study on the system for appointing Federal Reserve Bank directors, requiring an audit of the Federal Reserve emergency loans during the recent crisis, and restricting the Fed's emergency lending powers. As if to drive home the point that the Federal Reserve should be more accountable to the people, the law also required the Federal Reserve to pay the bills for a new, large, potent, and *independent* agency, the Bureau of Consumer Protection, which will assume responsibility for enforcing federal consumer protection laws.

In the United States, a safe and sound commercial and thrift banking system means a profitable banking system because without profits there is nothing safe or sound about it. To help ensure that it's in good shape, the government specifically charters the banks and thrifts, and works to ensure that the owners and management are honest, ethical, and capable (or at least not criminal); they specifically limit competition to ensure that markets are not overloaded with competitors, which could lead to the bankers taking excessive risk to get market share; and they provide federal deposit insurance that not only protects the company's customers but gives this industry an advantage in getting money to grow and prosper.

In return for their charter, for limited competition, and for federal deposit insurance, the commercial and thrift banking industry has *an obligation* to meet the credit needs of *all their communities* while at the same time sticking to safe and sound banking principals. They are *not* like other industries. Nor should they be.

10. It's easy to misplace blame.

Clearly and unequivocally, we can identify specific bankers with power and influence who made mistakes, used terrible judgment, were unethical and greedy, or were outright liars and criminals. Their actions hurt people and in some cases caused a lot of harm to our country.

Andrew Dexter was a liar and a crooked banker who issued far more currency from his Farmers Exchange Bank of Gloucester, Rhode Island, than he ever had in gold or silver backing it. After acquiring control of the bank in February 1808, he issued over $760,000 in currency (the equivalent of about $10 million today), a great deal of which he exchanged for sound currency from other banks for himself. When it all collapsed two years later, the bank had only $86 of gold and silver on hand (about $1,200 today). Anybody holding the currency was holding worthless paper. Dexter sneaked off to Nova Scotia and eventually worked his way to Alabama as a real-estate developer. They named a street after him (Dexter Avenue, leading to the state capitol in Montgomery). They should have thrown him in jail for bank fraud. He should have been held accountable for his crimes.

We should know the truth about Dexter. We should also learn from the criminal actions of Jake Butcher, who, along with his brother Cecil H. Butcher (C. H.), used forged documents and fraudulent loans in the early 1980s to gain banking dominance in Tennessee and parts of Kentucky.

The Butchers owned and controlled the City and County Bank of Knox County, and the flagship United American Bank of Knoxville. These crooked bankers would cleverly shuffle bad and illegal loans between their banks before their annual bank examinations so that they were out of the regulators' view. Their system failed when over 150 bank examiners conducted a surprise visit to the banks the day after the World's Fair in Knoxville ended. Ironically, Jake Butcher had served as a driving force to bring the high-profile fair to Knoxville, and this proved to be his last hurrah. With no advance notice, the Butchers couldn't effectively hide their fraudulent activities from the examiners, and both went to jail in 1985. Jake was paroled in 1992 and C. H. in 1993. It's good they were held accountable for their crimes.

Our media have historically called out bankers for their criminal, unethical, immoral, and arrogant behavior, and although they occasionally let the mob mentality get the best of them, naming names is usually a good thing. Whether it was Jay Cooke for overinvesting in railroad bonds or Bernie Madoff for his Ponzi scheme, the media coverage and our disappointment and anger are warranted. More recently, just about every major newspaper, magazine, and television network had Top 10 or Top 25 lists of people contributing to the Panic of 2008, and that's a good thing. People responsible for causing financial havoc should be accountable for their actions.

Even so, it's far too easy to name the obvious culprits, and then do nothing more. Every time a financial problem arises, whether it is a teller stealing from the cash drawer or a CEO stealing from the shareholders, we must ask and answer the right questions. Sure, it's interesting to know that seventy-three-year-old Bear Stearns CEO Jimmy Cayne smoked pot.[420] But unless he was high on the job (he wasn't), does it really matter? Far more important questions must be answered. Where were the internal and accounting controls? Where were the auditors? Where were the board members? Where were the regulators? Where are the penalties?

Many of the answers are clear. Most recently, the financial industry did not implement enough self-control. Many auditors were in over their heads or were inept. A lot of board members failed to do their job. The regulators were, by design, largely absent, and they relied on the markets to regulate themselves. The market participants, from credit rating agencies to hedge fund managers, were raking in the dough and didn't care enough about the consequences. The rest of us turned a blind eye to it all because we were thrilled to see our net worths rise with increased housing values and a strong stock market. Ignorance is bliss. Today, as in the past, we all have some responsibility for the financial crisis.

It's easy to assess blame but much harder to recognize our own responsibilities. When we do, the answers are often hard to swallow because they challenge so much of our belief system. Consider Fed Chairman Alan Greenspan's testimony before Congress following the Panic of 2008, when he admitted that limited government oversight and regulation does not work. When Congressman Henry Waxman asked Greenspan, "You found your view of the world, your [free-market] ideology, was not right, it was not working?" his answer was astounding and the look of devastation on his face was haunting. "Absolutely, precisely," he said. "You know, that's precisely the reason I was shocked, because I have been going more than forty years or more with very considerable evidence that it was working considerably well."

When people blame financial crises on others, they need a scapegoat, but blaming a scapegoat can also be intellectually dishonest. Blaming twenty-six-year-old MBA graduates for developing shoddy investment models misses the point if it also ignores the inadequate system of controls that senior management should have put in place to prevent or limit mistakes by inexperienced staff.

Blaming the Panic of 2008 on the poor and minorities is easy, and it's offensive. The poor didn't own the gold and make the rules, and the fact is, they weren't the ones who got the subprime and Alt-A loans that took down the large investment banks either. Further, lending to minorities occurred because that's where the opportunities were and where money was to be made. When wealthy individuals and their private banking agents blame the poor, minorities, and a thirty-year-old community reinvestment law for their own failures, it's despicable and dishonorable.

Lending in these markets presents risks and challenges, yes, but banks failed because they ignored underwriting fundamentals, not because poor people or minorities beat them out of their money.

Sound underwriting has been developed over hundreds of years as we learn from our mistakes and cautiously develop new safe, sound, and profitable lending and investing criteria. Constantly challenging and continually tweaking underwriting standards is healthy. But the sudden and rapid expansion of poorly analyzed, haphazardly underwritten, and unverified subprime and Alt-A loans was foolish. It's almost always bad loans, and when the system of checks and balances fails, you can also blame those responsible for managing that system.

Pointing fingers at the leadership of these failed and troubled financial institutions is appropriate. They were seriously overpaid for the sorry job they performed. They should pay a high price, and when looking at the recent *or any other significant* financial panics, we should start with them. But *only* pointing the finger at these obvious culprits is not enough. There is plenty of blame to go around.

Conclusion

When we let the banking industry self-regulate and stopped believing that our government was made up of good people who were doing the right thing, we set ourselves up for disaster. Good government is necessary.

When we began to trust but failed to verify, we found ourselves in bed with the ones we should have been regulating, and we ended up getting hurt. Bankers and regulators should never sleep in the same bed.

It is entirely unacceptable to allow the greed of so few people to damage or destroy the wealth of a nation. Greed has a price, and it needs to be very high.

The only way to ensure that capitalism can thrive and that government intervention can be limited is to have complete, accurate, and timely financial disclosures. Accounting integrity really does matter. It is not a game.

Getting bigger is fine, but doing so too quickly and recklessly is not. When public companies or government-sponsored enterprises grow rapidly, excessively, and recklessly, we all get burned.

Financial institutions fail when they don't have enough capital or liquidity, or when management doesn't implement good internal controls, is incompetent, or commits fraud. But mostly, financial institutions fail because they made bad loans. It's almost always bad loans.

There are plenty of red flags warning us of the danger ahead, but we are often too caught up in the euphoria to notice. We should pay attention. We can see trouble coming if we pay attention.

We need each other. We all matter. The commercial, thrift, and investment banking industries are all made up of really good people trying to do the right thing. They help us in ways we can hardly imagine when they provide access to the credit and capital that serve as the lifeblood of our economy. Many of these outstanding people serve in leadership positions on our own company or community boards of directors. Many volunteer their time and energy in support of local community programs and initiatives. Their auditors and regulators take their jobs and responsibilities seriously, and the consumers and citizens, many of whom are also shareholders, revel in their success and benefit from their products and services. We are all in this together, creating, controlling, refining, and growing an exceptional financial system. We all matter. And when we fail to appreciate each other, we fail.

It's easy to misplace blame. In reality, there is plenty to go around.

We occasionally forget the basics, and when we do, the repercussions can be severe. Fortunately, we always manage to figure it out, fix the problems, and rise up again.

We got this way for a reason. A good bit scarred but a whole lot smarter.

Chapter Notes

1. Timothy Curry and Lynn Shibut, "The Cost of the Savings and Loan Crisis: Truth and Consequences," *FDIC Banking Review*, Vol. 13, No. 2, Dec. 2000, <http://www.fdic.gov/bank/analytical/banking/2000dec/brv13n2_2.pdf>, accessed March 2010.
2. PricewaterhouseCoopers' restated financial results (Nov. 21, 2003) reported net income of $3.66 billion in 2000 compared to the $2.55 billion previously reported; $3.16 billion in 2001 compared to the $4.15 billion previously reported; and $10.09 billion in 2002 compared to the $5.76 billion previously reported. That means they *understated* earnings by $1.19 billion in 2000, *overstated* them by $989 million in 2001, and *understated* them again by $4.3 billion in 2002. In all, the mistakes resulted in understating earnings by $4.45 billion over three years! The details are contained in Freddie Mac's 2002 annual report, p. 28.
3. Important disclosure: Before writing this book, I had a small financial interest in AIG preferred stock and in Citibank preferred stock. They have since been sold. I also maintain loan and deposit accounts with Wells Fargo Bank and a brokerage account with Wells Fargo securities. I have no other direct financial interest (outside of mutual funds) in any other company discussed in this book.
4. The McFadden Act prevented banks from opening full-service offices across state lines until the US Supreme Court allowed in their ruling on NORTHEAST BANCORP v. BOARD OF GOVERNORS, FRS, 472 U.S. 159 (1985) , 472 U.S. 159, argued April 15, 1985, and decided June 10, 1985.
5. Number 2 and very close behind is JPMorgan Chase Bank, NA, with total assets of $1.2 trillion. Number 3 is Citibank, NA, at $1.1 trillion. Data, as of June 30, 2007, were obtained from the FDIC Institution Directory,< http://www2.fdic.gov/idasp/main.asp>, accessed March 2010.
6. FDIC Statistics on Depository Institutions database as of 9-30-09, and the Federal Reserve Bank of St. Louis Archival System for Economic Research (FRASER), Annual Statistical Digest 2, <http://fraser.stlouisfed.org/publications/astatdig/>, accessed March 2010.
7. FDIC Statistics on Depository Institutions database as of 9-30-09. Industry assets have grown from $7 trillion in 2000 to $13.2 trillion as of September 2009. At year-end 2008, Bank of America NA reported $1.47 trillion in assets; JPMorgan Chase NA reported $1.7 trillion. Year-end 2008 depository institution assets totaled $13.8 trillion.
8. President George W. Bush's attorney general was required to appoint a "Special Master" to implement the program. In 2008, Bush would again call for a federal bailout—this time for the banking industry. His successor, President Obama, would

also appoint a Special Master to oversee executive compensation at companies receiving money.

9. I was one of a large number of examiners charged with reviewing loan files to be sure that the necessary documentation was there. We put those loan docs in filing cabinets that we sealed with special stickers over the drawers. Those stickers signified that the files were acceptable collateral and not to be disturbed.
10. "A Mortgage Fable," The Wall Street Journal, Opinion Journal, Sept. 22, 2008, < http://online.wsj.com/article/SB122204078161261183.html?mod=googlenews_wsj >, accessed Apr. 2010.
11. "Villain Phil," *National Review Online*, The Editors, Sept. 22, 2008, < http://article.nationalreview.com/371921/villain-phil/the-editors >, accessed Apr. 2010.
12. "CRA Defenses Sound More Like CYA," Investors.com, Powered by *Investor's Business Daily*, Dec. 9, 2008, <http://www.investors.com/NewsAndAnalysis-/Article.aspx?id=490737&Ntt=triggered+the+subprime+crisis> accessed Apr. 2010.
13. Glyn Davies, *A History of Money: From Ancient Times to the Present Day* (University of Wales Press, Cardiff, Wales, 2002), 36–46.
14. William J. Baumol and Alan S. Blinder, *Economics Principles and Policy* (Harcourt Brace Jovanovich Inc., 1979), 204–205.
15. Arthur Crump, *The English Manual of Banking*, 4 ed. (Longmans, Green, & Company, 1879), chap. 1.
16. Margaret G. Myers, *A Financial History of the United States* (New York: Columbia University Press, 1970).
17. Clarence L. Ver Steeg, *Robert Morris* (Philadelphia: University of Pennsylvania Press, 1954). Reprint, New York: Hippocrene Books, 1970.
18. Q. David Bowers, *Obsolete Paper Money: Issued by Banks in the United States, 1782–1866, a Study and Appreciation for the Numismatist and Historian* (Whitman Publishing Company LLC, 2006), 20.
19. John J. Klein, *Money and the Economy*, 4th ed. (Harcourt Brace Jovanovich Inc., 1978), 165.
20. Ibid., 167.
21. Kevin Dowd, ed., *The Experience of Free Banking* (New York: Routledge, 1992), 210.
22. *"Federal Reserve Bank of San Francisco's American Currency Exhibit, Westward Expansion,"* <http://www.frbsf.org/currency/expansion/history/index.html>, accessed March 2010
23. Stephen Mihm, *A Nation of Counterfeiters: Capitalists, Con Men, and the Making of the United States* (Harvard University Press, 2007) 235–241.
24. Ibid., 48.
25. Mihm, 51.
26. Given its banking history and its close association with the word Dixie, this obsolete

currency is quite valuable today, with collectors paying around $1,500 for a single quality bill.

27. Estimates of the number of Irishmen buried along the New Basin Canal range from three thousand to thirty thousand. People at that time sang a popular song of unknown origin with the lyrics:

    Ten thousand Micks, they swung their picks,
    To dig the New Canal.
    But the cholera(y) was stronger than they,
    An twice it killed them awl.

    Source: Louisiana State Museum, <http://lsm.crt.state.la.us/education/education_old/irish3.htm>, accessed Mar 2010.
28. *The Louisiana Weekly*, New Orleans, Feb. 14–20, 2005, Sec. A, p. 1.
29. I'm kidding. We stopped dressing that way in the late 1960s. In the 1970s we began dressing like John Travolta from *Saturday Night Fever.* Yes, that's me on the right.
30. Myers, 165.
31. "About the OCC," Office of the Comptroller of the Currency website, <http://www.occ.treas.gov/exhibits/histor3.htm>, accessed March 2010.
32. The landmark Supreme Court case was Veazie Bank vs. Fenno, 8 Wall (75 U.S.) 533 (1869), and was decided on Dec. 13, 1869, by a vote of 7–2.
33. It's been reported that there were $207 million worth of state currencies in circulation in 1860, but by 1867, the amount had declined by over 98 percent to only $4 million. *Historical Statistics of the United States* (New York: Horizon Press, 1965), 649.
34. "Statement of Assets and Liabilities," *New York Times*, Sept. 27, 1873, <http://query.nytimes.com- /mem/archivefree/pdf?res=9404EED71239EF34BC4F51DFBF668388669FDE>, accessed March 2010.
35. G. Patrick Lynch, "U.S. Presidential Elections in the Nineteenth Century: Why Culture and the Economy Both Mattered," *Polity* 35, no. 1 (Autumn 2002): 29–50.
36. Klein, 161. Silver purchase acts were passed in 1878, 1879, 1890, 1893, 1918, 1934, 1939, and 1946.
37. A new gold certificate issue in 1934 was never released into circulation.
38. National Bureau of Economic Research, Business Cycle Expansions and Contractions, December 16, 2009,< http://www.nber.org/cycles.html> , accessed March 2010.
39. Bradford DeLong, "Why Not the Gold Standard? Talking Points on the Likely Consequences of Re-Establishment of a Gold Standard," <http://www.j-bradford-delong.net/politics/whynotthegoldstandard.html>, accessed March 2010.
40. "Quarterly Banking Profile, Fourth Quarter 2008," *FDIC Quarterly* 3, no. 1 (2009), <http://www2.fdic.gov/qbp/2008dec/qbp.pdf> accessed March 2010.
41. "The Small Business Economy: A Report to the President," SBA Office of Advocacy, US Government Printing Office, Washington, 2009.

42. FDIC Learning Bank, The Great Depression: 1929–1939, <http://www.fdic.gov/about/learn/learning/when/1930s.html> accessed March 2010. I specifically chose this reference because the FDIC has an exceptional website that provides almost anything you want to know about banks. This particular page is designed for kids who want to learn about banking, but you might like to wander to the FDIC home page and explore their site.
43. *Time* magazine, March 27, 1933, <http://www.time.com/time/magazine/article/0,9171,745426-2,00.html> accessed March 2010. Note also that $160 million in deposits in 1933 was the equivalent of $2.5 billion in 2007.
44. Certain corporate forms of ownership are required to protect the bank itself from the investment. If the investment goes bad, the corporation might fail, but the assets of the bank itself can't be touched.
45. The investment banking firm was originally called Drexel, Morgan & Company, but changed its name to J.P. Morgan & Company when one of the founders, Toney Drexel, died in 1893. Today the investment banking firm is called J.P. Morgan Securities LLC, and is a subsidiary of JPMorgan Chase & Co. (a financial holding company).
46. To keep it simple for the reader, the ratios presented in this analysis were calculated with data obtained from the FDIC—Statistics on Financial Institutions for all commercial banks in the US, as of year-end 2006, < http://www2.fdic.gov/sdi/>, Jan. 2011. Analysts may prefer the FFIEC Peer Group Average Report for all insured commercial banks, also as of year-end 2006, <https://cdr.ffiec.gov/public/Reports/UbprReport.aspx?rptCycleIds=43,37,26,28,4&rptid=284&peergroupid=3>, Jan. 2011. Using this database, Interest Income(TE)/Average Earning Assets was 7.15 percent; Interest Expense/Average Earning Assets was 2.93 percent; Noninterest Income/Average Assets was 0.70 percent; Personnel Expense/Average Assets was 1.74 percent; and the Provision for Loan and Lease Losses/Average Assets was 0.16 percent.
47. Analysts prefer to use *average* assets because it prevents the ratios from getting out of whack if assets jump or decline suddenly. Let's say that a really large company deposits a chunk of money in the bank but withdraws it in a day or two. You'd need to average the amount of assets to keep that unusual deposit from misleading everybody.
48. FFIEC Uniform Bank Performance Reports.
49. This data was provided by ICLUBcentral, a company that provides stock market and investing information to individual investors. It was compiled using data from Better Investing's Standard & Poor's Stock Data Service. <http://www.iclub.com/investing/stock_watch_list_industry.asp> accessed March 2010.
50. In his article published by Thornburg Investment Management, Brad Kinkelaar, co-portfolio manager and managing director, cites these studies as examples: *CSFB Equity Quantitative Strategy*, "Analyze Those Dividends," December 16, 2002;

Smith Barney and Frank Russell Company, *Portfolio Strategist,* "Dividends: Be Careful What You Screen For," and "The 'D' Word," July 3, 2003; *Smith Barney, Quantitative Strategy,* "Historical Performance of Dividend Yield Strategies," Jan. 31, 2003; *ING Financial Markets, Equity Markets Strategy,* "Dividends = Outperformance" Jan. 13, 2003.

51. John S. Howe and K. Stephen Haggard, "Bank Dividends: Increasing, Decreasing, and Unresponsive," *Journal of Applied Financial Research* 2 (Fall 2008): 1–32.
52. The acronym is ***r***isk management, the company's ***f***inancial condition, the ***i***mpact the BHC and nonbank subsidiaries could have on the bank, and it provides a ***c***omposite rating on the BHC, and a rating on the ***d***epository ***i***nstitution. It's also a crummy acronym, which makes regulators look a little less cool—as if they can afford that.
53. FDIC.
54. Federal Reserve Board, Share Data for US Offices of Foreign Banks, Table 1. The data cover "foreign-bank branches and agencies in the 50 states and the District of Columbia, New York investment companies (through September 1996), and U.S. commercial banks that are at least 25 percent owned by foreign entities, including International Banking Facilities in each category. The data exclude Edge Act and agreement corporations; U.S. offices of banks in Puerto Rico, the U.S. Virgin Islands, and other U.S.-affiliated insular areas; and foreign-bank offices in U.S. affiliated insular areas. Foreign entities are those owned by institutions located outside of the United States and its affiliated insular areas. From 1997 forward data include U.S. chartered entities that are completely or partially owned by foreign companies that are not banks themselves."
55. The MSN site could be found at <http://moneycentral.msn.com/ownership>, accessed March 2010.
56. "OCC, Wachovia Enter Revised Agreement to Reimburse Consumers Directly," OCC press release, Dec. 11, 2008, <http://www.occ.gov/news-issuances/news-releases/2008/nr-occ-2008-143.html>, accessed Jan. 2011.
57. "Wachovia Details 2nd Quarter Loss; Outlines Initiatives to Preserve and Generate Capital, Protect Strong Liquidity and Reduce Risk," Wachovia press release, July 22, 2008, <https://www.wachovia.com/foundation/v/index.jsp?vgnextoid=c9956c772350f110VgnVCM200000627d6fa2RCRD&vgnextfmt=default&key_guid=69817798ebbdc110VgnVCM100000127d6fa2RCRD#wealth>, accessed Jan. 2011.
58. Carey Gillam, "Wachovia settles acution rate securities probe," *Reuters*, Aug. 15, 2008, < http://www.reuters.com/article/2008/08/15/us-auctionrate-wachovia-idUSN1529836120080815,>, accessed Mar 2011.
59. Peter Lester Payne and Lance Edwin Davis, *The Savings Bank of Baltimore, 1818–1866: A Historical and Analytical Study* (Baltimore: The Johns Hopkins Press, 1956), and E. W. Brabrook, *Provident Societies and Industrial Welfare* (London: Blackie and Sons, 1898), 165.
60. Priscilla Wakefield, "Extract From an Account of a Female Benefit Club at

Tottenham," *The Reports of the Society for Bettering the Condition and Increasing the Comforts of the Poor*, vol. III (London: W. Bulmer and Co., 1802), 186–191.

61. David L. Mason, *From Buildings and Loans to Bailouts* (New York: Cambridge University Press, 2004), 15.
62. Before 1971, in the United Kingdom twelve pennies was equal to one shilling, and twenty shillings equaled one pound. In July 2008, one UK pound equaled about two US dollars.
63. H. Oliver Horne, *A History of Savings Banks* (London: Oxford University Press, 1947), 3. Defoe also wrote the tremendously popular novel *Robinson Crusoe* in 1719.
64. Daniel Defoe, "Giving Alms No Charity," *Great Literature Online, 1997–2010* <http://www.classicauthors.net/defoe/almsnocharity/>, accessed March 8, 2010.
65. David M. Tucker, *The Decline of Thrift in America: Our Cultural Shift from Saving to Spending* (New York: Praeger Publishers, 1991), 40.
66. Rev. Henry Duncan, *ESSAY ON THE NATURE AND ADVANTAGES OF PARISH BANKS FOR THE SAVINGS OF THE INDUSTRIOUS*, (Edinburgh, Scotland: Oliphant, Waugh & Innes, 1816), 7, <http://www.archive.org/stream/essayonnatureadv15dunc#page/n5/mode/2up>, accessed Jan. 2010.
67. Peter Lester Payne and Lance Edwin Davis, *The Savings Bank of Baltimore, 1818–1866: A Historical and Analytical Study* (The Johns Hopkins Press, 1956).
68. *History of the 1980's—Lessons for the Future: Volume 1: An Examination of the Banking Crisis of the 1980s and Early 1990s*, FDIC Division of Research and Statistics (December 1997): 212, <http://www.fdic.gov/bank/historical/history/3_85.pdf>, accessed March 2010
69. Mason, 16.
70. Joesph A. Montagna, *An Interdisciplinary Approach to British Studies*, vol. II, chapter 6, "The Industrial Revolution," Yale-New Haven Teachers Institute, New Haven, CT, <http://www.yale.edu/ynhti/curriculum/units/1981/2/81.02.06.x.html>, accessed March 2010.
71. Issac Merritt Singer patented a different sewing machine in 1850 and within two years was the leading manufacturer of sewing machines in the United States. In 1856, the Singer Sewing Company began offering one of the first installment payment plans in the United States, which allowed low-income individuals a chance to buy the machines and increase their self-employment income.
72. Robert E. Wright, *The First Wall Street: Chestnut Street, Philadelphia & The Birth of American Finance* (University of Chicago Press, 2005), 114.
73. Alan Teck, *Mutual Saving Banks and Savings and Loan Associations* (New York: Columbia University Press, 1968), 19–32; Lintner, *Mutual Savings Banks*, 473.
74. Thirty-four men subscribed to one share, and two men subscribed to two shares of stock.
75. Details on the Oxford Provident membership and loan program were obtained

from Gerard Caprio and Dimitri Vitta, "Reforming financial systems: historical implications for policy" (New York: Cambridge University Press, 1997), 164.

76. The Farm Credit System has a similar program today where borrowers must own stock to qualify for the loan, but the stock purchase is included in the loan amount.
77. Mason, 32.
78. David Whitten, "Depression of 1893," edited by Robert Whaples, EH.Net Encyclopedia, August 14, 2001, < http://eh.net/encyclopedia/article/whitten.panic.1893>, accessed Dec. 2010.
79. *Savings and Loan Fact Book* (Chicago: United States Savings and Loan League, (1955), 39, as reported in *From Buildings and Loans to Bailouts*, 121.
80. Thrifts can choose one of two ways to a be qualified lender and avoid the higher federal taxes. They can (1) pass a qualified thrift lender test (QTL) or they (2) can pass a similar Domestic Building and Loan Association (DBLA) test in the IRS tax code. Generally speaking, the QTL test requires them to keep investments equal to 65 percent of their assets in loans for real estate, education, small businesses, credit cards or similar securities, and FHLB stock. The DBLA test requires that 75 percent of deposits must come from the public, that 75 percent of its income must comes from loans and government securities, and that 60 percent of assets must come from normal thrift assets, such as real estate, loans, and similar securities and FHLB stock.
81. Charles J Woelfel, *Encyclopedia of Banking and Finance*, 10th ed. (Chicago: Probus Publishing Company, 1994), 292.
82. U.S. Department of Labor, Bureau of Labor Statistics Database, <http://www.bls.gov/data/#prices>, accessed Jan. 2011.
83. You knew how much interest could be paid on the account by looking at the short-term borrowings to finance the national debt (the weekly average of six-month US Treasury bills).
84. This product was first offered at the Consumer Savings Bank in Worcester, Massachusetts, in 1972, but was confined to savings banks in Massachusetts and New Hampshire until 1980.
85. Musician Kid Rock was arrested on October 21, 2007, for his involvement in a fight at a Waffle House restaurant near Atlanta. He was eventually sentenced to one-year probation and anger-management counseling. To his credit, he tried to turn the negative publicity into a more positive cause when he later hosted a homeless shelter charity event at another area Waffle House.
86. "America's Wars" pamphlet, US Department of Veterans Affairs, Office of Public Affairs, November 2008.
87. *Current Population Survey/Housing Vacancy Survey*, Series H-111 Reports, Bureau of the Census, Washington DC, and *Buildings and Loan*, 145. The homeownership rate peaked at 69 percent in 2006, and measured 67 percent at year-end 2008.
88. Mason, 264.

89. Unless otherwise noted, financial information in this sidebar story was obtained from SEC Form 10-K, IndyMac Bancorp Inc., December 31, 2007.
90. Remarks by John F. Bovenzi, chief operating officer, FDIC, on "The Role of Deposit Insurance in Financial Crises: Past and Present," at the International Association of Deposit Insurers (IADI) 7th Annual Conference; Arlington, VA, October 29, 2008, http://www.fdic.gov/news/news/speeches/archives/2008/chairman/spoct2908.html, accessed March, 2011.
91. "FDIC Establishes IndyMac Federal Bank, FSB as Successor to IndyMac Bank, F.S.B., Pasadena, California," FDIC press release, July 11, 2008, http://www.fdic.gov/news/news/press/2008/pr08056.html, accessed March, 2011.
92. Unless otherwise noted, financial information in this sidebar story was obtained from SEC Form 10-K reports filed by Countrywide Financial Corp.
93. Unless otherwise noted, financial information in this sidebar story was obtained from SEC Form 10-K reports filed by Washington Mutual Inc.
94. Kelly Holman, "TPG Loses $1.3B From WaMu Failure," *Investment Dealers' Digest*, Sept. 26, 2008, http://www.iddmagazine.com/news/185936-1.html, accessed March 2011.
95. *The Simpsons*, "Trash of the Titans" episode, 1998, <http://www.imdb.com/title/tt0701277/quotes>, accessed Jan. 2011.
96. Susanne Craig, "Goldman's Soft Sell: Its Warm, Fuzzy Side," *Wall Street Journal*, October 15, 2009, <http://online.wsj.com/article/SB125556536458586219.html>, accessed Dec. 2010.
97. James B. Stewart, *Den of Thieves* (New York: Simon & Schuster Paperbacks, 1992), 261.
98. Commercial banks, savings banks, savings institutions, and credit unions total assets obtained from SNL Financial, LLC database, which was derived from financial institution call reports and thrift reports. Investment banks total assets obtained from the Investment Company Institute's "2009 Investment Company Fact Book," whose sources also included the Strategic Insight Mutual Fund Research and Consulting LLC.
99. "2009 Investment Company Fact Book," Investment Company Institute, <http://www.icifactbook.org/fb_sec1.html>, accessed Mar 2010.
100. Ibid.
101. Charles R. Geisst, *Wall Street: A History* (Oxford University Press, 1999), 13
102. Geisst, 12.
103. The Treaty of 1783 with England decided that the territory between the Allegheny Mountains and the Mississippi River was to be part of the United States, leaving a huge tract of land in the hands of the US Treasury for disposal.
104. Data obtained from the World Federation of Exchanges, as of August 2008. Domestic market capitalization is defined by the federation as, "The market capitalization of a stock exchange is the total number of issued shares of domestic companies,

including their several classes, multiplied by their respective prices at a given time. This figure reflects the comprehensive value of the market at that time."

105. NYSE Euronext History from their website, <http://www.nyse.com/about/history/timeline_2000_Today_index.html>, accessed March 2010.

106. US Department of Labor, Bureau of Labor Statistics, Occupational Employment Statistics, May 2007, National Industry-Specific Occupational Employment and Wage Estimates for NAICSA 52300—Securities, Commodities Contracts, and Other Financial Investments and Related Activities, <http://www.bls.gov/oes/current/naics3_523000.htm#b00-0000>, accessed March 2010.

107. Ibid. National Industry-Specific Occupational Employment and Wage Estimates for NAICSA 52200—Credit Intermediation and Related Activities.

108. Tim Gaynor, "Americans query CEO pay scales as crisis deepens," Oct. 3, 2008, <http://www.reuters.com/article/domesticNews/idUSTRE4924G420081003>, accessed March 2010.

109. Anthony Saunders and Marcia Cornett, *Financial Institutions Management: A Risk Management Approach*, 6th ed. (McGraw-Hill Higher Education, 2008), 95.

110. Joseph M. Anderson, "The Wealth of U.S. Families: Analysis of Recent Census Data, No. 233," US Department of Commerce, Bureau of the Census, November 10, 1999, <http://www.census.gov/sipp/workpapr/wp233.pdf >, accessed Sept. 2010.

111. Taken from his letter to the SEC, dated January 22, 2004, and available at url <http://www.sec.gov/rules/proposed/s72103/s72103-9.pdf>, accessed Dec. 2010.

112. The commission was comprised of three Republicans and two Democrats. They were Republicans William H. Donaldson (chairman), Cynthia A. Glassman, and Paul S. Atkins, and Democrats Harvey J. Goldschmid and Roel C. Campos. All were appointed by President George W. Bush.

113. Vanessa Drucker, "The SEC Killed Wall Street on April 28, 2004," RealClearMarkets.com, Feb. 18, 2009, <http://www.realclearmarkets.com/articles/2009/02/the_sec_killed_wall_street_on.html>, accessed December 2010.

114. "Chairman Cox Announces End of Consolidated Supervised Entities Program," SEC press release, Sept. 26, 2008, < http://www.sec.gov/news/press/2008/2008-230.htm>, accessed January 2011.

115. Brian L. Rubin and Christian J. Cannon, "Litigating Disciplinary Charges Against the SEC and FINRA: It Sometimes Pays," <http://www.sutherland.com/files/Publication/6962e6c4-9b3d-4c3a-9fc7-de222819176f/Presentation/PublicationAttachment/14941565-96f4-49ab-b045-de4279cbbf38/April2009CannonSutherlandMarked.pdf> accessed March 2010.

116. Carol E. Curtis "FINRA Lays Off Five Enforcement Officials," *Securities Industry News*, Jan., 22, 2010, <http://www.securitiesindustry.com/news/-24553-1.html>, accessed March 2010.

117. Jon Birger, "The woman who called Wall Street's meltdown," *Fortune Magazine*,

August 6, 2008, <http://money.cnn.com/2008/08/04/magazines/fortune/whitney_feature.fortune/index3.htm>, accessed March 2011.

118. Fitch Credit Agency report, < http://www.fitchratings.com/creditdesk/reports/report_frame.cfm>, accessed March 2010.

119. Roger Lowenstein, "Triple-A Failure," *New York Times Magazine*, Apr. 27, 2008, <http://query.nytimes.com/gst/fullpage.html?res=9900EFDE143DF934A15757C0A96E9C8B63&scp=2&sq=roger lowenstein Triple A Failure&st=cse&pagewanted=7>, accessed March 2011.

120. William D. Cohan, "Rating McGraw-Hill," *Fortune Magazine*, April 23, 2009, http://money.cnn.com/2009/04/16/news/companies/cohan_mcgraw.fortune/, accessed March 2011.

121. Some of the factual information contained in this summary was derived from an exceptional Congressional Research Service Report for Congress entitled, "Bear Stearns: Crisis and 'Rescue' for a Major Provider of Mortgage-Related Products," prepared by Gary Shorter, specialist in business and government relations, Government and Finance Division, March 26, 2008.

122. Cynthia Crossen, "We Worship Jefferson, But We Have Become Hamilton's America," *Wall Street Journal*, February 4, 2004, <http://www.freerepublic.com/focus/f-news/1071513/posts,>, accessed March 2010.

123. The guy whose job he took as ambassador was former Vice President Charles Dawes (he served with President Calvin Coolidge), who was then appointed to head the Reconstruction Finance Corporation. Charles Dawes was the comptroller of the currency from 1898 to 1901. He also won a Nobel Peace Prize in 1925. He left the Reconstruction Finance Corporation (RFC) post after only a few months, reportedly to help rescue the City National Bank of Chicago, where he was named chairman of the board. (There were also some rumors that Dawes had been improperly funneling money to City National from the RFC before he left the job.)

124. Speaking at a White House press conference on March 18, 2009.

125. "Policy and Supporting Positions (Plum Book)," U.S. Senate Committee on Homeland Security and Governmental Affairs, November 2008, <http://www.gpoaccess.gov/plumbook/2008/2008_plum_book.pdf >, accessed March 2010.

126. Wells Fargo & Company proxy statement schedule 14A filed with the SEC on March 18, 2009, reports Mr. Stumpf's total compensation in 2008 at $13,782,433.

127. *The American Heritage Dictionary of the English Language*, 4th ed., 2000.

128. *BusinessWeek* , < http://www.businessweek.com/careers/bplc/companies_48.htm>, accessed March 2010.

129. "Annual Report of the Comptroller of the Currency to the First Session of the Forty-Seventh Congress of the United States," December 5, 1881, Washington: Government Printing Office, 37–38. Italics were those of the comptroller, not this author.

130. Robert Cyran, "The Downfall of a Regulator," *New York Times*, April 8, 2009, <http://www.nytimes.com/2009/04/09/business/09views.html>, accessed March 2010.

131. Binyamin Appelbaum and Ellen Nakashima, "Banking Regulator Played Advocate Over Enforcer," *Washington Post*, November 23, 2008, A01.

132. Staff addition obtained from OTS OMB FY 2006 Performance/Budget Plan Submission, 16. Thrift number and asset size obtained from SNL Financial and FDIC.

133. "NCRC Calls for OTS' Director Gilleran's Resignation," press release, February 28, 2005.

134. Bruce Feirstein, "100 to Blame: Ralph Nader, Ninja Loans, and More," *Vanity Fair*, September 23, 2009, <http://www.vanityfair.com/online/daily/2009/09/100-to-blame-ralph-nader-ninja-loans-and-more.html>, accessed December 2010.

135. Press release, as noted in ICBA *Washington Report* newsletter, <www.icba.org/publications/NewsletterDetailWWR.cfm?ItemNumber=8953&sn.ItemNumber=13783>, accessed March 2010.

136. Extracted from the OTS mission statement, April 2009.

137. SNL Financial and FDIC. The chart is a reasonable representation of the issue, but is not precise because it excludes the bank and thrift holding companies, and it looks at agency assets and numbers at year-end 2008 (plus failed institution assets) while the failures occurred over eleven years.

138. If you are unaware of Bonnaroo, an annual four-day music festival in Manchester, Tennessee, that typically draws over eighty thousand people, then think of the 1969 Woodstock festival but with fewer drugs and a better sound system.

139. US Geological Survey.

140. Abigal Tucker, "The Financial Panic of 1907: Running from History," Smithsonian.com, October 10, 2008, interview with Robert F. Bruner, coauthor of *The Panic of 1907: Lessons Learned from the Market's Perfect Storm*."

141. Thomas P. Kane, *The Romance and Tragedy of Banking* (The Bankers Publishing Company, 1922). Kane was previously the deputy comptroller of the currency.

142. "Bigelow Gets Ten Years: Bank Wrecker Sentenced by His Friend Starts at Once for Prison," *New York Times*, June 11, 1905.

143. William Greider, *Secrets of the Temple: How the Federal Reserve Runs the Country* (New York: Simon & Shuster Inc., 1987), 268.

144. Klein, 177.

145. Representative Glass later served a short term as Treasury secretary under Woodrow Wilson before being elected to the US Senate.

146. Greider, 292.

147. Michael R. McAvoy, "How Were the Federal Reserve Bank Locations Selected?" <http://eh.net/Clio/ASSAPapers/McAvoy.pdf.>, accessed March 2010. See also Kerry Odell and David F Weiman, "Metropolitan Development, Regional Banking

Centers, and the Founding of the Fed in the Lower South, 1860 to 1920," *Journal of Economic History* 58, no. 1 (Mar. 1998): 102–25

148. The law required the Fed to pay interest beginning October 1, 2011, but that wasn't considered soon enough so another law, the Emergency Economic Stabilization Act of 2008, made the effective date October 1, 2008. The rate is set by formula and is determined by the FOMC.

149. The requirements were established in the Dodd-Frank Wall Street Reform and Consumer Protection Act (Dodd-Frank Act), signed into law on July 21, 2010.

150. Copies of the Beige Book are available from the Federal Reserve Board of Governors, <http://www.federalreserve.gov/FOMC/BeigeBook/2010/ >, accessed December 2010. In an effort to ensure full disclosure, and perhaps to brag a bit, when I served as assistant corporate secretary to the Atlanta Reserve Bank's board, I would occasionally help edit the Beige Book. It wasn't all that exciting, but it sure was interesting!

151. The Eccles Coliseum at Southern Utah University in Cedar City is named after Marriner Eccles's younger brother and sister-in-law, George and Delores Eccles. Go, Thunderbirds!

152. The speech was delivered in Washington DC, on November 21, 2002, and can be found at the Federal Reserve Board website, <http://www.federalreserve.gov/boardDocs/speeches/2002/20021121/default.htm#f18>, accessed December 2010.

153. The Fed's right to offer emergency credit is provided under Section 13(3) of the Federal Reserve Act.

154. It was known as Governor's Committee on Centralized Execution of Purchases and Sales of Government Securities.

155. The sixteen dealers as of April 2009 were: BNP Paribas Securities Corp.; Banc of America Securities LLC; Barclays Capital Inc.; Cantor Fitzgerald & Co.; Citigroup Global Markets Inc.; Credit Suisse Securities (USA) LLC; Daiwa Securities America Inc.; Deutsche Bank Securities Inc.; Dresdner Kleinwort Securities LLC; Goldman, Sachs & Co.; HSBC Securities (USA) Inc.; J. P. Morgan Securities Inc.; Mizuho Securities USA Inc.; Morgan Stanley & Co. Incorporated; RBS Securities Inc.; and UBS Securities LLC. For more information, see the Fed New York website, at < http://www.newyorkfed.org/markets/pdcf.html>, accessed December 2010.

156. Allan H Meltzer, *A History of the Federal Reserve: 1913–1951* (University of Chicago Press, 2003), 190–195.

157. Excerpts from the Minutes of the Governors Conference, May 2–4, 1922, subsection c, "Policy as to amounts of investments," <http://fraser.stlouisfed.org/docs/meltzer/bogsub0502_0422.pdf>, accessed December 2010.

158. Martin served as Fed chairman from April 2, 1951, until Jan. 30, 1970 (6,879 days). Fed Chairman Alan Greenspan served the second longest term (6,749 days) from August 11, 1987, until January 31, 2006.

159. *The Federal Reserve System Purposes and Functions*, Board of Governors of the Federal Reserve System, 9th ed., Washington DC, June 2005.
160. The Gramm-Leach-Bliley Financial Services Modernization Act was enacted on November 12, 1999.
161. Remarks by Governor Laurence H. Meyer before the spring 1998 Banking and Finance Lecture at Widener University, Chester, Pennsylvania, on April 16, 1998. The full speech can be found at the Federal Reserve Board website, <http://www.federalreserve.gov/boarddocs/speeches/1998/199804162.htm>, accessed December 2010.
162. Gregg Allman wrote the song "Whipping Post" in 1969. It appeared on the Allman Brothers Band debut album the same year. It has nothing to do with banking because it's about love. It contains the lyrics:

    Sometimes I feel
    Like I been *tied* to the whipping post!
    TIED to the whipping post!
    TIED to the whipping post!
    Good Lord, I feel like I'm dyin'...

163. The Financial Stability Oversight Council has ten voting members. They are: (1) the secretary of the Treasury, (2) chairman of the Federal Reserve, (3) comptroller of the currency, (4) director of the Bureau of Consumer Financial Protection, (5) chairperson of the SEC, (6) chairperson of the FDIC, (7) chairperson of the CFTC, (8) director of the Federal Housing Finance Agency, (9) the chairman of the National Credit Union Administration Board, and (10) an independent member (with insurance expertise), appointed by the president for a term of six years.
164. "FDIC Failed Bank List," <http://fdic.gov/bank/individual/failed/banklist.html>, accessed January 21, 2011.
165. Helen M. Burns, *The American Banking Community and New Deal Banking Reforms, 1933–1935* (Westport, CT: Greenwood Press, 1974), 9–27.
166. Letter from Ogden L. Mills to Guy Emerson, March 12, 1932, from Ogden L. Mills Papers, Container 110, Library of Congress.
167. US Senate, Banking and Currency Committee, *Hearings S.4115, I*, 160 as quoted by Helen M. Burns, *The American Banking Community and New Deal Banking Reforms, 1933–1935* (Westport, CT: Greenwood Press, 1974), 27.
168. Mason, 93.
169. The law was called the Competitive Equality Banking Act of 1987 (CEBA).
170. "FDIC shifts cost burden to big banks," CNNMoney.com, "Business News," May 22, 2009, <http://money.cnn.com/2009/05/22/news/companies/fdic_banks.reut/index.htm?postversion=2009052214>, accessed December 2010.
171. Office of Inspector General Semiannual Report to the Congress, April 1, 2008–September 30, 2008.
172. The two women got off easy compared to the two men. The judge (a white woman, if

that matters) ruled more harshly on the men because they were still on probation for prior convictions, and the women were facing their first offenses. Some people have questioned why the white women got the more favorable media attention (nobody called the men handsome or referred to them as "Ken"). They also wondered why the sentences were so radically different and were especially light for the women convicted of felony bank robbery.

173. The Emergency Farm Mortgage Act, 1933.
174. The Frazier-Lemke Farm Bankruptcy Act, 1934. It was renewed four times.
175. Enviornmental Working Group, Farm Subsidy Database, <http://farm.ewg.org/farm/progdetail.php?fips=00000&progcode=total&page=states>, accessed December 2010.
176. The poll was conducted by WorldPublicOpinion.org and used a nationwide sample of 765 from March 25 to April 6, 2009. The margin of error is plus or minus 3.7 percent. WorldPublicOpinion.org is a project managed by the Program on International Policy Attitudes at the University of Maryland. Funding for the research was provided by the Rockefeller Brothers Fund and the Calvert Foundation. We have a long history of giving cash subsidies and passing other laws in support of family farms. For example, in 1933 the Frazier-Lemke Farm Mortgage Act allowed the federal courts to write down a farmer's debt to the value of the land. If the farmer could then afford the reduced loan balance over six years at 1 percent interest, he wouldn't have to pay anything more. If he couldn't afford the new loan, he was then allowed to keep his land and be a paying tenant. The Supreme Court ruled the law unconstitutional because it allowed the farmer to take land from the mortgage holder without due process. So Congress passed another law, the Farm Mortgage Moratorium Act, in 1935, that allowed bankrupt farmers to stay on their land for three years if they paid a fair rent. This one passed legal muster and was renewed several times before it expired in 1947.
177. The law was called the Frazier-Lemke Farm Mortgage Act.
178. The law was called the Farm Mortgage Moratorium Act.
179. Kenneth C. Carraro, "The 1987 Agricultural Recovery: A District Perspective," Federal Reserve Bank of St. Louis, April 1988, <http://research.stlouisfed.org/publications/review/88/03/Agricultural_Mar_Apr1988.pdf>, accessed December 2010.
180. "History of the FCA and FCS," Farm Credit Administration, <http://www.fca.gov/about/history/historyFCA_FCS.html>, accessed December 2010.
181. Derived from their 2008 annual reports.
182. *Bert Ely's Farm Credit Watch*, July 2008 (No. 124).
183. Each individual institution must publish this information, and the Farm Credit Administration website provides a link to the reports. < http://www.fca.gov/exam/crs.html>, accessed December 2010. The law requiring this program is contained

in Section 4.19 of the Farm Credit Act of 1971, and by Section 614.4165 of the FCA regulations.

184. The FCA reports that in 2007, 37 percent of all Farm Credit System assets were tax exempt.

185. The FHLBs were originally headquartered in Cambridge, MA; Newark, NJ; Pittsburgh, PA; Winston-Salem, NC; Cincinnati, OH; Indianapolis, IN; Evanston, IL; Little Rock, AR; Topeka, KS; Des Moines, IA; Los Angeles, CA; and Portland, OR.

186. Moody's Investors Service, Moody's Global Banking—Federal Home Loan Banks, Credit Analysis, February 2009, <http://corp.fhlbatl.com/WorkArea/showcontent.aspx?id=2125>, accessed December 2010.

187. FHLBanks Office of Finance, as of December 31, 2006.

188. Ibid.

189. Brian K. Landsberg, ed., "Federal Home Loan Bank Act (1932)," *Major Acts of Congress,* (Macmillan-Thomson Gale, 2004). eNotes.com, 2006, April 1, 2009,<http://www.enotes.com/major-acts-congress/federal-home-loan-bank-act>, accessed December 2010.

190. David C. Wheelock, "The Federal Response to Home Mortgage Distress: Lessons from the Great Depression," *Federal Reserve Bank of St. Louis Review*, May/June 2008, (Part 1), 138–48.

191. The Housing and Economic Recovery Act of 2008 requires borrowers to pay in cash an amount at least 3.5 percent of the property's appraised value and any financed closing costs. The loan-to-value ratio cannot be more than 100 percent.

192. Peter G. Miller, "FHA Gives Up Billions to U.S. Treasury," RealtyTrac News and Trends Center, July 28, 2008, <http://www.realtytrac.com/ContentManagement/RealtyTracLibrary.aspx?a=b&ItemID=4898&accnt=64953> accessed January 2011.

193. Proceeds from the 20 percent tax are used to pay off the Resolution Funding Corporation (REFCORP) bonds, sold in six issues in 1989 with interest ranging from 8.125 percent to 9.375 percent and maturities ranging from October 2019 to April 2030. The FHLB Board anticipated paying these bonds off completely in 2011. The proceeds of the bonds helped fund the Resolution Trust Corporation (RTC), an independent agency whose sole purpose was to dispose of failed thrift assets. The RTC was dissolved in 1996.

194. The amount FHLBs are eligible to borrow depends on their collateral, which is approved by the Treasury Department. The debts of any one FHLB with the Treasury's "Government Sponsored Enterprise Credit Facility" become the obligation of all FHLBs. In other words, if the FHLB borrows from this Treasury program and can't satisfy the debt, all other FHLBs have to pony up (pay) the money.

195. SEC 10-K Filings and the FHL Banks Office of Finance. Total capital ratio for all

banks is regulatory capital stock plus retained earnings (Retained earnings are the earnings that a bank keeps rather than paying dividends) as a percentage of total assets except Chicago. Chicago's total capital ratio is regulatory capital and designated amount of subordinated notes divided by total assets. Chicago had not implemented a required regulatory capital plan and was placed under a cease-and-desist order on October 10, 2007. The C&D required a minimum capital ratio of 4.5 percent.

196. Matthew R. Feldman was named president and CEO effective May 5, 2008, and received $723,433 in compensation that year. J. Mikesell Thomas held that position until his "separation" from the bank effective April 13, 2008, which provided for a total compensation paid in 2008 of $1.48 million.
197. Seattle met the required total capital ratio but failed a second regulatory capital requirement, the risk-based capital requirement.
198. At year-end 2009, the US government debt totaled $12.3 trillion (US Treasury Bureau of Public Debt); Fannie Mae's debt totaled $884 billion (SEC 10-K, 262); and Freddie Mac's debt totaled $837 billion (SEC 10-K, 209).
199. "Iraq War Price Tag Nearing Cost of Vietnam," Associated Press, July 26, 2008, FoxNews.com, < http://www.foxnews.com/story/0,2933,391603,00.html>, accessed July 26, 2008.
200. As an example of the Great Society, both Medicare and Medicaid were enacted while Johnson was president. On another note entirely, The Great Society was also a rock band from 1965 featuring singer Grace Slick performing the song "Somebody to Love." "Somebody to Love" became a lot more famous when she left The Great Society to sing with the Jefferson Airplane band. This information is presented for the benefit of readers who are not too young to remember Jefferson Airplane or who know the difference between Grace Slick and Grace Potter.
201. William Poole, former president of the Federal Reserve Bank of St. Louis, gave the $300 billion estimate in his remarks to the Macroeconomic Advisors Conference, September 10, 2008.
202. The Secondary Mortgage Market Enhancement Act of 1984 also allowed states to pass their own laws overriding this federal law, and by 1991 about twenty-one states had done so, according to Fannie Mae's 1991 "Information Statement," published on March 30, 1992.
203. Bethany McLean, "The Fall of Fannie Mae," *Fortune Magazine* 151, no. 2 (January 24, 2005), <http://money.cnn.com/magazines/fortune/fortune_archive/2005/01/24/8234040/index.htm>, accessed October 10, 2010.
204. "Assessing the Public Costs and Benefits of Fannie Mae and Freddie Mae," Government Printing Office, Congressional Budget Office, Washington DC, May 1996.
205. Bethany McLean.
206. Wayne Passmore, "The GSE Implicit Subsidy and Value of Government

Ambiguity," Board of Governors of the Federal Reserve System, Finance and Economic Discussion Series, Dec. 19, 2003, <http://www.federalreserve.gov/pubs/feds/2003/200364/200364abs.html> accessed October 10, 2010.

207. Snigdha Prakash, "Housing agencies' regulator hints Freddie helped crimp staff plan," *American Banker*, October 13, 1993, <http://www.americanbanker.com/issues/158_108/-29416-1.html>, accessed December 2010.

208. Snigdha Prakash, "Regulator for Fannie and Freddie loses first round over staffing," *American Banker*, September 27, 1993, <http://www.americanbanker.com/issues/158_96/-28017-1.html>, accessed December 2010.

209. "The Largest Failure: J.P. Morgan Chase CEO Jamie Damon on the lessons of Fan and Fred," *Wall Street Journal*, "Review and Outlook," April 18, 2009, A12.

210. Bethany McLean.

211. Julie Kosterlitz, "Q&A With Rep. Richard Baker, R-La," *National Journal Magazine*, May 12, 2000, <http://www.nationaljournal.com/njmagazine/print_friendly.php?ID=nj_20080512_2948>, accessed September 15, 2009.

212. Raines graduated from Harvard University with honors, attended the prestigious Oxford University on a Rhodes Scholarship, and graduated from Harvard Law School with honors. His impressive resume included stints on the boards of Time Warner, PepsiCo, and Pfizer. He was a partner with Lazard Freres & Co., a New York investment banking firm. He served as an intern in the Nixon White House, was associate director of the Office of Management and Budget for Jimmy Carter and later as director of OMB for Bill Clinton. While at Harvard, he reportedly joined both the Young Democrats *and* the Young Republicans, and at one time he was respected by Republicans and Democrats alike.

213. Its board included William F. Aldinger, the chairman and CEO of Household International; Dennis Dammerman, the chairman and CEO of GE Capital Services; Maurice R. Greenberg, the chairman of American International Group; William B. Harrison Jr., the president and CEO of Chase Manhattan Corp.; Richard M. Kovacevich, the president and CEO of Wells Fargo & Co.; and Thomas H. O'Brien, the chairman and CEO of PNC Bank Corp.

214. Julie Kosterlitz ,"Siblings Fat and Sassy," *National Journal Magazine*, May 12, 2002, <http://www.nationaljournal.com/njmagazine/cs_20000512_3844.php>, accessed October 10, 2010.

215. The Center for Responsive Politics, <opensecrets.org>. The data the center presents was obtained from quarterly lobbying disclosure reports filed with the secretary of the Senate's Office of Public Records. The data on Fannie Mae can be found at <http://www.opensecrets.org/lobby/clientsum.php?year=2005&lname=Fannie+Mae&id=.>, accessed October 10, 2010.

216. Broderick Perkins, "New Alliance Confronts FM Watch, Champions Existing Housing Finance System," at realtytimes.com, October 5, 2000.

217. David D. Kirkpatrick and Charles Duhigg, "Loan Titans Paid McCain Adviser Nearly

$2 Million," *New York Times*, September 21, 2008, A16, <http://www.nytimes.com/2008/09/22/us/politics/22mccain.html#>, accessed October 10, 2010.
218. Rob Garver and Rob Blackwell,"Anti-GSE Lobbying Group in Disarray," *American Banker*, March 9, 2001.
219. Eric Winig, "Fannie, Freddie top charts in biz mortgage lending," *Washington Business Journal*, August 31, 2001, <http://www.bizjournals.com/washington/stories/2001/09/03/newscolumn2.html>, accessed October 10, 2010.
220. Anne Christenson, "Fannie Mae: Article a reader 'disservice'," *Washington Business Journal*, Monday, April 23, 2001, <www.bizjournals.com/washington/stories/2001/04/23/editorial3.html>, accessed August 2009.
221. "Fannie Mae Enron," *Wall Street Journal, Review and Outlook*, February 20, 2002, <http://online.wsj.com/article/SB1014169323358510560.html>, accessed August 21, 2008.
222. Paul A. Gigot, "The Fannie Mae Gang," *Wall Street Journal,* "Opinion," July 23, 2008, A17, <http://kensey.com/articles/WSJ-0807-The%20Fannie%20Mae%20Gang.htm>, accessed August 1, 2008.
223. Mclean, loc cit.
224. Erick Bergquist and Marc Hochstein, "Issues at Freddie Costing Fannie Money, CEO Says," *American Banker*, July 31, 2003.
225. Mclean, loc cit.
226. "Report of Findings to Date; Special Examination of Fannie Mae," Office of Compliance, Office of Federal Housing Enterprise Oversight, September 17, 2004, i, <http://ofheo.gov/webfiles/2286/92204StatementFNMAcctgReview.pdf>, September 20, 2008.
227. The New York-headquartered firm they hired was Paul, Weiss, Rifkind, Wharton & Garrison LLP.
228. "The OFHEO Report: Allegations of Accounting and Management Failure at Fannie Mae," hearing before the Subcommittee on Capital Markets, Insurance and Government Sponsored Enterprises of the Committee on Financial Services, US House of Representatives, One Hundred Eight Congress, Second Session, October 6, 2004, Serial No. 108-115, US Government Printing Office, 97-754 PDF Washington, D.C., 2004.
229. Ibid.
230. Henry Blodget, "Fannie Mae CEO Franklin Raines: Don't blame him for the mortgage giant's scandal... yet," *Slate Magazine*, October 7, 2004, <www.slate.com>, accessed September 11, 2009.
231. Darlene Superville, "Raines' Fall Is a Surprise to Many Who Knew Him," Associated Press, *Los Angeles Times*, January 5, 2005, <http://articles.latimes.com/2005/jan/05/business/fi-raines5>, accessed October 2010.
232. Matt Cover, "Former Fannie Mae, Freddie Mac CEO's: 'It was the Market's Fault,'" December 9, 2008, <CNSNews.com>, accessed March 11, 2009.

233. In his testimony before the House Committee on Oversight and Government Reform on December 9, 2008, Frank Raines reported that the Rudman Report, as it became known, cost $80 million.
234. "A Report to the Special Review Committee of the Board of Directors of Fannie Mae: Executive Summary," February 23, 2006, 5. Known as the Rudman Report, its authors included Warren B. Rudman, Robert P. Parker, Alex Young K. Oh, Daniel Kramer from Paul, Weiss, Rifkind, Wharton & Garrison LLP, and George E. Massaro and Jeffrey H. Ellis from Huron Consulting Group Inc.
235. "Raines pays in Fannie Mae scandal," Associated Press, *Los Angeles Times*, April 19, 2008, <http://articles.latimes.com/2008/apr/19/business/fi-raines19>, accessed October 2010.
236. "OFHEO ISSUES CONSENT ORDERS REGARDING FORMER FANNIE MAE EXECUTIVES," Office of Federal Housing Enterprise Oversight Board (OFHEO) news release, April 18, 2008, <http://www.fhfa.gov/webfiles/1542/41808OFHEOconsentordersFNMexecs.pdf>, accessed October 18, 2010.
237. "Too Political to Fail," *Wall Street Journal*, "Review and Outlook," April 21, 2008, <http://online.wsj.com/article/SB120873813171529991.html>, accessed October 10, 2010.
238. Charles Duhigg, "Pressured to Take More Risk, Fannie Reached Tipping Point," *New York Times*, October 4, 2008, A1, <http://www.nytimes.com/2008/10/05/business/05fannie.html>, accessed October 10, 2010.
239. Robert Stowe England, "The Rise of Private Label," *Mortgage Banking Magazine*, October 1, 2006, and *Inside Mortgage Finance* database, <http://www.robertstoweengland.com/images/stories/mbm.10-06%20england%20private%20label%201.pdf>, accessed October 10, 2010.
240. House of Representatives, Committee on Oversight and Government Reform, October 22, 2008, hearings on "Credit Rating Agencies and the Financial Crisis." In the same hearings, Rep. Chris Shays (R-CT) said, "[W]hen the referee is being paid by the players, no one should be surprised when the game spins out of control. This is what happened on Wall Street when credit rating agencies followed the delirious mob making millions on mortgage-backed securities and sold their independence to the highest bidder."
241. SEC Form 10-K, Table 24, Fannie Mae, December 31, 2008.
242. The private-label securities market had seen their market share fall from 56 percent in 2006 to only 4 percent in 2008.
243. Ben S. Bernanke, Federal Reserve chairman, "The Future of Mortgage Finance in the United States" speech given at the UC Berkeley/UCLA Symposium: The Mortgage Meltdown, the Economy, and Public Policy, Berkeley, California, October 31, 2008. The historical reference he made was obtained from Kenneth Snowden (1995), "Mortgage Securitization in the United States: Twentieth Century Developments in Historical Perspective," in *Anglo-American Financial Systems: Institutions and*

Markets in the Twentieth Century (New York: McGraw-Hill), Michael D. Bordo and Richard Sylla, eds.

244. "Housing's Contribution to Gross Domestic Product (GDP)," National Association of Homebuilders database. < http://www.nahb.org/page.aspx/landing/sectionID=113>, accessed October 10, 2010. GDP is the total value of all goods and services produced in the United States. Housing figures include construction of new single-family and multi-family structures, residential remodeling, production of manufactured homes, brokers' fees, rent paid by tenants, the imputed value (estimated) of housing services to homeowners, and the amount paid to hotels by households for housing services.

245. The September 2008 takeover was allowed by the Federal Housing Finance Regulatory Reform Act (signed into law July 30, 2008) and by the Federal Housing Enterprises Financial Safety and Soundness Act of 1992.

246. Fannie Mae, December 31, 2008, 10-K report filed with the SEC.

247. Lenders today offer discount points as a means to lower interest rates on loans. It can serve as a way to lower the annual interest rate in return for paying a fee upfront. The more points a borrower pays can sometimes result in larger reductions on interest rates.

248. Peter M. Carrozzo, "Marketing the American Mortgage: The Emergency Home Finance Act of 1970, Standardization and the Secondary Market Revolution," *Real Property, Probate, and Trust Journal*, January 1, 2005, <http://www.allbusiness.com/operations/facilities-commercial-real-estate/990652-1.html>, accessed October 10, 2010.

249. *A Guide to the Federal Home Loan Bank System*, FHLB System Publication Corporation, Washington DC, March 1987, 57.

250. The divestiture was required by the Financial Institution Reform, Recovery, and Enforcement Act.

251. Ross Guberman, "Balancing Act: Fannie Mae Projects a Happy Image. But as Its Debt Grows Bigger and Its Executives Get Richer, Should Taxpayers Start to Worry?" *The Washingtonian*, August 2002.

252. PricewaterhouseCoopers restated financial results (November 21, 2003) reported net income of $3.66 billion in 2000 compared to the $2.55 billion previously reported, $3.16 billion in 2001compared to the $4.15 billion previously reported, and $10.09 in 2002 compared to the $5.76 billion previously reported. That means they *understated* earnings by $1.19 billion in 2000, *overstated* them by $989 million in 2001, and *understated* them again by $4.3 billion in 2002. In all, the mistakes resulted in understating earnings by $4.45 billion over three years! The details are contained in Freddie Mac's 2002 annual report, 28.

253. Armando Falcon Jr., testimony before the House Financial Services Subcommittee on Capital Markets, Insurance, and Government Sponsored Enterprises on the OFHEOs December Report of the Special Examination of Freddie Mac, January

21, 2004, reported by Christine Dugas, Del Jones, and Elliot Blair Smith, "Freddie Mac report accuses former execs; Probe reveals pattern of profit manipulation," *USA Today*, July 24, 2003, B01.

254. Armando Falcon Jr., director of OFHEO, testimony before the US Senate Committee on Banking, Housing and Urban Affairs, July 17, 2003.

255. John Tierney, "Privileged Life in Peril for 2 Mortgage Giants," *New York Times*, June 17, 2003, <http://query.nytimes.com/gst/fullpage.html?res=9E05E2DC1238F934A25755C0A9659C8B63&sec=&spon=&pagewanted=1>, accessed October 10, 2010.

256. "What They Said About Fan and Fred, *Wall Street Journal*, Oct. 2, 2008, <http://online.wsj.com/article/SB122290574391296381.html>, accessed October 10, 2010.

257. "FEDERAL HOME LOAN MORTGAGE CORPORATION ("FREDDIE MAC") PAYS LARGEST FINE IN FEC HISTORY," press release by the Federal Elections Commission, April 18, 2006.

258. Pete Yost, "Freddie Mac lobbyist staged 50 GOP fundraisers as Congress let legislation die," Associated Press Newswires, July 18, 2003.

259. Mary Jacoby, "Critics question Fannie Mae's influence," *St. Petersburg Times*, July 17, 2000, 1A.

260. Ibid.

261. Center for Responsive Politics <OpenSecrets.org>, accessed October 10, 2010.

262. Joseph Rosta, "Thank Goodness for Uncle Sam," *U.S. Banker Magazine*, August 2008, <http://www.americanbanker.com/usb_issues/118_8/-359369-1.html>, accessed October 10, 2010.

263. David S. Hilzenrath, "Freddie Mac Problems Led to Tougher OFHEO," *Washington Post*, November 20, 2004, E01, < http://www.washingtonpost.com/ac2/wp-dyn/A63950-2004Nov19>, accessed October 10, 2010.

264. The Center for Responsive Politics <OpenSecrets.org>.

265. The Keating Five was the name given to five US Senators who improperly intervened to disrupt an investigation of Lincoln Savings and Loan in 1987. Charles H. Keating was chairman of the thrift and a major donor to the politicians. Lincoln failed two years later. The five senators were Alan Cranston (D-CA), Dennis DeConcini (D-AZ), John Glenn (D–OH), John McCain (R-AZ), and Donald W. Riegle Jr. (D- MI).

266. Rob Blackwell, "In HUD IG Report, Allegations of an OFHEO Vendetta," *American Banker*, November 22, 2004.

267. David S. Hilzenrath, "Mortgage Regulator To Keep Agency Job," *Washington Post*, September 16, 2004, E04, <http://www.washingtonpost.com/wp-dyn/articles/A24484-2004Sep15.html>, accessed October 10, 2010.

268. Terence O'Hara and Kathleen Day, "Legislators To Take Up Replacing OFHEO; Previous Attempts To Change Regulator Have Been Stymied," *Washington Post*,

April 6, 2005, E01, <http://www.washingtonpost.com/wp-dyn/articles/A28498-2005Apr5.html>, accessed October 10, 2010.

269. Eric Lipton, "Man Who Toppled Chief of Fannie Mae Is Seen as a David Who Beat Goliath," *New York Times*, December 23, 2004, <http://www.nytimes.com/2004/12/23/business/23regs.html>, accessed October 10, 2010.

270. In their amended filings with the SEC on Form 10-K as of December 31, 2008, Freddie Mac reported a lower net income and lower total assets than was shown in the 2004 annual report. The more recent 10-K showed net income of $2.6 billion versus $2.9 billion in the annual report. Form 10-K also showed total assets of $780 billion vs. $795 billion in the annual report.

271. "Rebuilding confidence. Leading responsibly. Freddie Mac 2004 Annual Report," *A message from the Chairman*, p. 2.

272. Quotes in parentheses were from Dick Syron's prepared congressional testimony, "The Role of Fannie Mae and Freddie Mac in the Financial Crisis," Hearing Before the Committee on Oversight and Government Reform, House of Representatives, December 9, 2008, Serial No. 110-180, US Government Printing Office, Washington DC, 2009, 17–19.

273. Ibid.

274. Matt Cover, "Former Fannie Mae, Freddie Mac CEO's: 'It was the Market's Fault,'" December 10, 2008 , CNSNews.com>, accessed September 9, 2009.

275. Joanna Chung, "Fannie and Freddie chiefs accused of ignoring warnings on 'reckless bets,'" *Financial Times* newspaper, December 10, 2008, <http://www.ft.com/cms/s/0/6e6e1aac-c65c-11dd-a741-000077b07658.html>, accessed October 10, 2010.

276. President Obama's comments were broadcast live from an appearance before politicians and reporters in the Roosevelt Room of the White House on March 16, 2009.

277. Congressman Frank's comments were obtained from his letter to Director Lockhart, dated March 19, 2009, and contained in a press release entitled "Frank Calls on Lockhart to Cancel Fannie and Freddie Bonuses," issued by his office on March 20, 2009, <http://www.house.gov/apps/list/press/financialsvcs_dem/press032009.shtml>, accessed October 10, 2010.

278. Patrick Rucker, "Lawmaker sees Fannie, Freddie bonus 'insult'," *Reuters News, UK Edition*, April 4, 2009, < http://uk.reuters.com/article/2009/04/03/usa-fannie-bonus-idUKN0335729620090403>, accessed Decenber 2010.

279. Foon Rhee, "Grassley: Suicide call was 'rhetoric'," *Boston Globe*, March 17, 2009, <http://www.boston.com/news/politics/politicalintelligence/2009/03/grassley_suicid.html>, accessed December 2010.

280. "Iowa Senator Backs Off On AIG Suicide Remark," The Associated Press, March 17, 2009, published online at TBO.com, <http://www2.tbo.com/content/2009/mar/17/171321/senator-says-aig-execs-should-quit-or-commit-suici/>, accessed December 2010.

281. Charles Duhigg and Jack Healy, "Reported Suicide is Latest Shock at Freddie Mac," *New York Times*, April 22, 2009, <http://www.nytimes.com/2009/04/23/business/23freddie.html>, accessed October 10, 2010.

282. Poole is a Senior Fellow at the Cato Institute, a nonprofit organization that promotes the ideals of market liberalism, which they describe as one that "combines an appreciation for entrepreneurship, the market process, and lower taxes with strict respect for civil liberties and skepticism about the benefits of both the welfare state and foreign military adventurism."

283. William Poole, president, Federal Reserve Bank of St. Louis, "Housing in the Macroeconomy," speech at an Office of Federal Housing Enterprise Oversight Symposium, Ronald Reagan Building and International Trade Center, Washington DC, March 10, 2003, <http://bodurtha.georgetown.edu/enron/Poole_housing_in_the_macroeconomy_2003_03_10.htm>, accessed December 2010.

284. John T. Woolley and Gerhard Peters, *The American Presidency Project* [online]. Santa Barbara, California: <http://www.presidency.ucsb.edu/ws/?pid=13246>. Italics added by this author.

285. Yuliya Demyanyk, "Ten Myths about Subprime Mortgages," *Federal Reserve Bank of Cleveland Economic Commentary*, <http://www.clevelandfed.org/research/commentary/2009/0509.cfm> and Yuliya Demyanyk and Otto Van Hemert, "Understanding the Subprime Mortgage Crisis," *Social Science Research Network, Review of Financial Studies*, 2008, <http://ssrn.com/abstract=1020396>, accessed December 2010.

286. "*Expanded Guidance for Subprime Lending Programs*," OCC, Federal Reserve Board, FDIC, and OTS Interagency press release, January 31, 2001.

287. Ibid.

288. "The State of the Nation's Housing 2006," Joint Center for Housing Studies of Harvard University, Graduate School of Design, John F. Kennedy School of Government.

289. Danielle DiMartino and John V. Duca, "The Rise and Fall of Subprime Mortgages," *Economic Letter—Insights*, Federal Reserve Bank of Dallas, vol. 2, no. 11, November 2007.

290. Neil Cavuto, interview with Congressman Xavier Becerra on "Your World With Neil Cavuto," FOX News, September 18, 2008.

291. Orson Scott Card, "Would the Last Honest Reporter Please Turn On the Lights?" *Rhinoceros Times* newspaper, October 9, 2008, < http://greensboro.rhinotimes.com/orson.10.09.08.html>, accessed December 2010. Card became an English professor at Southern Virginia University in the fall of 2005.

292. Maurice Jourdain-Earl, "The Demographic Impact of the Subprime Mortgage Meltdown," *ComplianceTech*, Arlington, VA, 2006, <http://www.mortgagebankers.org/files/Conferences/2008/RegulatoryComplianceConference08/

RC08SEPT24HMDAMauriceJordain.pdf>, accessed December 2010. The report used HMDA data from 2004 to 2006.

293. Robert R. Callis, "Moving to America, Moving to Homeownership: 1994–2002," *US Census Bureau Current Housing Reports*, September 2003, < http://www.census.gov/prod/2003pubs/h121-03-1.pdf>, accessed December 2010. National average is the median income.

294. US Department of Housing and Urban Development Notice PDR-2002-01, issued January 31, 2002, and US Department of Commerce Census Bureau reports on Residential Vacancies and Homeownership Report, Table 8, October 25, 2004.

295. US Census Bureau, American Community Survey, 2005–2009, Table S1903: Median Income in the Past 12 Months, American Community Survey 5-Year Estimates Data Set, <http://factfinder.census.gov/servlet/STTable?_bm=y&-context=st&-qr_name=ACS_2009_5YR_G00_S1903&-ds_name=ACS_2009_5YR_G00_&-CONTEXT=st&-tree_id=5309&-redoLog=false&-_caller=geoselect&-geo_id=01000US&-format=&-_lang=en>, accessed December 2010.

296. Alfred O. Gottschalck, "Net Worth and the Assets of Households: 2002," U.S. Census Bureau, Current Population Reports, Household Economic Studies P70-115, April 2008.

297. "Report to the 79th Legislature: Use of Credit Information by Insurers in Texas," Texas Department of Insurance, December 30, 2004.

298. "Report to the Congress on Credit Scoring and Its Effects on the Availability and Affordability of Credit," Board of Governors of the Federal Reserve System, submitted to the Congress pursuant to section 215 of the Fair and Accurate Credit Transactions Act of 2003, August 2007, <http://www.federalreserve.gov/boarddocs/rptcongress/creditscore/creditscore.pdf>, accessed December 2010. This report showed that "blacks, Hispanics, single individuals, those younger than age 30, and individuals residing in low-income or predominantly minority census tracts have lower credit scores than other subpopulations defined by race or ethnicity, marital status, age, or location."

299. Maurice Jourdain-Earl, "The Demographic Impact of the Subprime Mortgage Meltdown," *ComplianceTech*, Arlington, VA, 2006, <http://www.mortgagebankers.org/files/Conferences/2008/RegulatoryComplianceConference08/RC08SEPT24HMDAMauriceJordain.pdf>, accessed December 2010.

300. Ibid.

301. Debbie Gruenstein Bocian,, Keith S. Ernst, and Li Wei, "Unfair Lending: The Effect of Race and Ethnicity on the Price of Subprime Mortgages," Center for Responsible Lending, May 31, 2006, <http://www.responsiblelending.org/mortgage-lending/research-analysis/rr011-Unfair_Lending-0506.pdf.>, accessed December 2010.

302. Shown on television's *Comedy Central* network, August 5, 2007, <http://www.thedailyshow.com/watch/wed-august-1-2007/subprime-loans>, accessed March 2010.

303. Alfred O. Gottschalck, "Net Worth and the Assets of Households: 2002," U.S. Census Bureau, *Current Population Reports*, Household Economic Studies P70–115, April 2008.
304. Tierney Plumb, "Most subprime loans didn't go to low-income borrowers," *Washington Business Journal*, July 31, 2008, <http://www.bizjournals.com/washington/stories/2008/07/28/daily54.html>, accessed December 2010.
305. *National Mortgage News* QDR, Inside Mortgage Finance and testimony of Brendan McDonagh, CEO, HSBC Finance Corporation to the Senate Committee on Banking, Housing, and Urban Affairs, March 22, 2007, <http://banking.senate.gov/public/index.cfm?FuseAction=Files.View&FileStore_id=6091edf4-21b6-42f7-a900-127b670a16e3>, accessed December 2010.
306. Roger T. Cole, director, Division of Banking Supervision and Regulation testimony before the US Senate Committee on Banking, Housing, and Urban Affairs, March 22, 2007, <http://www.federalreserve.gov/newsevents/testimony/cole20070322a.htm#f3>, accessed December 2010.
307. "Predatory Lending Practices," National Association of Consumer Advocates, September 2, 2009, <http://www.naca.net/predatory-lending-practices/>, accessed December 2010.
308. Yuliya Demyanyk, "Ten Myths about Subprime Mortgages," *Federal Reserve Bank of Cleveland Economic Commentary*, <http://www.clevelandfed.org/research/commentary/2009/0509.cfm>, accessed December 2010.
309. For those of you unfamiliar with the term rip-off, please consult somebody over forty for a definition.
310. David Greenlaw, Jan Hatzius, Anil K. Kashyap, and Hyun Song Shin, "Leveraged Losses: Lessons Learned from the Mortgage Meltdown," *U.S. Monetary Policy Forum Report No. 2*, Rosenberg Institute, Brandeis International Business School and Initiative on Global Markets, University of Chicago Graduate School of Business, 2008.
311. Based on dollar volume of loan originations in the fourth quarter of 2006.
312. "Subprime Spillover: Foreclosures Cost Neighbors $202 billion; 40.6 million homes lose $5,000 on Average," *CRL Issue Paper*, Center for Responsible Lending, January 18, 2008.
313. Ronald Campbell, "Subprime's dearly departed," *Orange County Register*, October 1, 2008, <http://mortgage.freedomblogging.com/category/company-watch/option-one/>, accessed December 2010.
314. Chris Arnold, "Former Ameriquest Workers Tell of Deception," *NPR Business News*, May 14, 2007, <http://www.npr.org/templates/story/story.php?storyId=10165859>, accessed December 2010.
315. Erin Conroy, "Green jobs, subprime confessions," AP business editor, *USA Today*, August 5, 2008.
316. Ellen Schloemer, Wei Li, Keith Ernst, and Kathleen Keest, "Losing Ground:

Foreclosures in the Subprime Market and Their Cost to Homeowners," Center for Responsible Lending, December 2006, <http://www.responsiblelending.org/mortgage-lending/research-analysis/losing-ground-foreclosures-in-the-subprime-market-and-their-cost-to-homeowners.html>, accessed December 2010.

317. Georgia Department of Banking and Finance, as of September 30, 2009, <http://dbf.georgia.gov/00/article/0,2086,43414745_46389324_67825643,00.html >, accessed December 2010.

318. HSBC Finance Corporation, SEC Form 10-K, filed with the SEC for the years ending on December 31, 2006, 2007, and 2008.

319. Patrick Hosking, "Dismissed HSBC executives had received $40m in bonuses," banking and finance editor, *The London Times*, February 23, 2007.

320. According to page 6 of their December 31, 2008, annual report (Form 10-K) filed with the SEC, consumers residing in California accounted for 11 percent of domestic consumer receivables, Florida 7 percent, New York 6 percent, Texas 5 percent, Pennsylvania 5 percent, and Ohio 5 percent.

321. The top tier holding company is HSBC Holdings plc, London, England. Financial data was obtained from its June 2009 Interim Report, <http://www.hsbc.com/1/PA_1_1_S5/content/assets/investor_relations/hsbc2009ir0.pdf >, accessed December 2010.

322. GE 2007 annual report, 51, <http://www.ge.com/ar2007/pdf/ge_ar2007_full_book.pdf>, accessed December 2010.

323. Merrill Lynch 2007 annual report, 38, <http://sec.gov/Archives/edgar/data/65100/000095012308002050/y46644e10vk.htm>, accessed December 2010.

324. Wells Fargo 2007 annual report, 6, <https://www.wellsfargo.com/downloads/pdf/invest_relations/wf2007annualreport.pdf >, accessed December 2010.

325. H&R Block 2007 annual report.

326. June 30, 2008, Uniform Bank Performance Report (UBPR).

327. Ginnie Mae is restricted to purchasing certain mortgage products, primarily FHA and VA loans and in 2008 had a relatively small market share.

328. Bear Stearns securitizations included $21.8 billion of agency mortgage-backed securities and $99.3 billion of other mortgage- and asset-backed securities.

329. UBS annual report 2007, *Annual Review*, Global Asset Management, http://www.ubs.com/1/e/investors/annual_reporting2007/ar2007/0006.html, accessed December 2010.

330. Julie Creswell, "After Losses, UBS Ousts Its Chief," *New York Times*, July 6, 2007, C1, <http://www.nytimes.com/2007/07/06/business/06ubs.html>, accessed December 2010.

331. The hedge funds were the Bear Stearns High-Grade Structured Credit Strategies Fund and the Bear Stearns High-Grade Structured Credit Strategies Enhanced Leveraged Fund.

332. Roger Lowenstein, *When Genius Failed: The Rise and Fall of Long-Term Capital Management* (Random House Publishing Group, January 2001).
333. "George W. Bush, The President's News Conference" transcripts, August 9, 2007, published by The American Presidency Project, <http://www.presidency.ucsb.edu/ws/index.php?pid=75649>, accessed December 2010.
334. Sebastian Boyd, "BNP Paribas Freezes Funds as Loan Losses Roil Markets," *Bloomberg News*, August 9, 2009, <http://www.bloomberg.com/apps/news?pid=20601087&refer=home&sid=aNIJ.UO9Pzxw>, accessed December 2010.
335. Federal Reserve Board press release, August 17, 2007, <http://www.federalreserve.gov/newsevents/press/monetary/20070817b.htm>, accessed December 2010.
336. *Merrill Lynch Definitive Proxy Statement*, Schedule 14A, filed with the SEC on March 14, 2008, 33.
337. Eric Dash and Andrew Ross Sorkin, "Citigroup Sells Abu Dhabi Fund $7.5 billion Stake," *New York Times*, November 27, 2007, <http://www.nytimes.com/2007/11/27/business/27citi.html?pagewanted=1&_r=1>, accessed December 2010.
338. *Citigroup Inc. Definitive Proxy Statement*, Schedule 14A, 74, filed with the SEC on March 13, 2008.
339. TAF results and Fed press releases announcing discount rate changes are available at the Board of Governors of the Federal Reserve System website, <http://www.federalreserve.gov/monetarypolicy/default.htm>, accessed December 2010.
340. In addition, the Federal Reserve also authorized "temporary reciprocal currency arrangements," often called swap lines, with the European Central Bank (ECB) and the Swiss National Bank (SNB), where they swapped up to $24 billion of US currency for foreign currency. The central banks of these foreign countries guaranteed repayment to the Federal Reserve themselves (privately owned foreign banks cannot borrow directly from the Fed), and they could use the money to help jump-start their economies by providing more liquidity to European banks. The swaps were good for six months.
341. Congressional Budget Office Cost Estimate on HR 5140, the Economic Stimulus Act of 2008 as cleared by the Congress on February 7, 2008, <http://www.govtrack.us/congress/billreport.xpd?bill=h110-5140&type=cbo >, accessed December 2010.
342. "Did the 2008 Tax Rebates Stimulate Short-term Growth?" June 10, 2009, *Congressional Budget Office Economic and Budget Issue Brief*, <http://www.cbo.gov/ftpdocs/96xx/doc9617/06-10-2008Stimulus.pdf>, accessed December 2010.
343. Leno told the joke in his opening monologue on *The Tonight Show with Jay Leno*, NBC, July 16, 2008.
344. Ibid.
345. Patrice Hill, "McCain advisor talks of 'mental recession'," *Washington Times*,

July 9, 2008, < http://www.washingtontimes.com/news/2008/jul/09/mccain-adviser-addresses-mental-recession/>, accessed March 2010.

346. Kevin Hamlin, "Freddie, Fannie Failure Could Be World 'Catastrophe,' Yu Says," Bloomberg.com, August 22, 2009, <http://www.bloomberg.com/apps/news?pid=20601080&sid=aslo2E01QVFI >, accessed September 2010.

347. Joe Nocera, "Lehman Had to Die So Global Finance Could Live," September 11, 2009, *New York Times*, <http://www.nytimes.com/2009/09/12/business/12nocera.html>, accessed December 2010.

348. Francesco Guerrera, "BofA to buy Merrill Lynch for $50 bn," *Financial Times*, London, September 14, 2008.

349. Hugh Son and Erik Holm, "Fed Takes Control of AIG With $85 Billion Bailout," September 17, 2008, Bloomberg.com, < http://www.bloomberg.com/apps/news?pid=20601082&sid=a1lyqdbt6HGY >, accessed December 2010.

350. Carol J. Loomis, "AIG's $150B bailout (cont.)," *Fortune,* December 29, 2008, <http://money.cnn.com/2008/12/23/news/companies/AIG_150bailout_Loomis.fortune/index3.htm>, accessed December 2010.

351. "Factors Affecting Efforts to Limit Payments to AIG Counterparties," a study by the Office of the Special Inspector General for the Troubled Asset Relief Program, November 17, 2009, <http://www.sigtarp.gov/reports/audit/2009/Factors_Affecting_Efforts_to_Limit_Payments_to_AIG_Counterparties.pdf >, accessed October 2010.

352. The bailout package will undoubtedly change several times as debts are reduced, collateral obtained or released, and capital needs dictate. The package in effect as of March 2009 was comprised of a $60 billion Fed line of credit, a $22.5 billion Fed loan to fund Maiden Lane II (a company setup to buy back AIGs mortgage-backed securities used as repos), a $30 billion Fed loan to fund Maiden Lane III, a company set up to allow AIG to repurchase securities from those who were holding it as part of their credit default swap collateral obligations, a $40 billion investment from Treasury in the sale of preferred stock, and a $30 billion line of credit that when drawn requires AIG to issue the Treasury additional preferred stock. The name Maiden Lane comes from the New York Fed's address in lower Manhattan.

353. Michael Mackenzie and Paul J. Davies, "Money markets fund sector shocked," *Financial Times*, September 17, 2008, <http://www.ft.com/cms/s/0/8bcf03ac-84e1-11dd-b148-0000779fd18c.html>, accessed December 2010.

354. Christopher Condon and Bryan Keogh, "Funds Flight From Commercial Paper Forced Fed Move (Update 1)," *Bloomberg News*, October 7, 2008, <http://www.bloomberg.com/apps/news?pid=20601103&sid=a5hvnKFCC_pQ >, accessed October 2010.

355. For details on this program, see the Fed's press release dated October 21, 2008, <http://www.federalreserve.gov/newsevents/press/monetary/20081021a.htm >, accessed December 2010. For a summary of the Federal Reserve's response to

the crisis, go to their website, <http://www.federalreserve.gov/monetarypolicy/bst_crisisresponse.htm>, accessed December 2010.

356. Tami Luhby, "New World on Wall Street," CNNMoney.com, September 22, 2008, <http://money.cnn.com/2008/09/21/news/companies/goldman_morgan/index.htm>, accessed December 2010.

357. Drew DeSilver, "Feds seize WaMu in nation's largest bank failure," *Seattle Times*, September 26, 2008, <http://seattletimes.nwsource.com/html/businesstechnology/2008204758_wamu26.html>, accessed December 2010.

358. On October 3, 2008, a different merger agreement was in place when Wells Fargo made a more generous offer of $6.50 a share for the entire company and without any specific FDIC guarantees. After some legal maneuvering by all three banks, the deal with Wells closed at year-end 2008.

359. Eric Weiner, "Stan O'Neal: The Rise and Fall of a Numbers Guy," October 29, 2007, NPR Business News <http://www.npr.org/templates/story/story.php?storyId=15739285&ps=rs>, accessed December 2010.

360. Landon Thomas, Jr., and Jenny Anderson, "Risk-Taker's Reign at Merrill Ends With Swift Fall," October 29, 2007, *New York Times*, <http://www.nytimes.com/2007/10/29/business/29merrill.html?_r=1>, accessed December 2010.

361. John Cassidy, "Anatomy of a Meltdown," *New Yorker*, December 1, 2008, <http://www.newyorker.com/reporting/2008/12/01/081201fa_fact_cassidy#ixzz0bm2MbP8F>, accessed December 2010.

362. **TAF** was the **T**erm **A**uction **F**acility, where depository institutions could bid on loans. The final auction was conducted in March 2010.

TSLF was the **T**erm **S**ecurities **L**ending **F**acility, where, for a fee, the New York Fed's Primary Dealers (the broker-dealers they use to buy and sell securities as part of their Federal Open Market Committee operations) could exchange less liquid Fannie Mae-, Freddie Mac-, and Ginnie Mae-backed securities for more liquid Treasury securities. The program was opened in March 2008 and closed on February 1, 2010.

PDCF was the **P**rimary **D**ealer **C**redit **F**acility, where Primary Dealers (and others) could get overnight loans from the New York Fed (with help from the Atlanta and Chicago Feds) in order to reduce the severe strains these dealers had in managing securities repurchase agreements (repos). The program was opened in March 2008 and closed on February 1, 2010.

AMLF is an **A**sset-backed commercial paper and **M**oney market mutual fund **L**iquidity **F**acility, and the **CPFF** is a **C**ommercial **P**aper **F**unding **F**acility. Both lending facilities were provided by the Federal Reserve to increase liquidity to the commercial and investment banks so they could continue to invest in "commercial paper." When the Primary Fund (a private company) "broke the buck," suddenly everybody wanted out of their own money market mutual funds. These funds were the main buyers of commercial paper, which meant they were using people's investments in their fund to provide the short-term loans needed by large US companies. When people wanted out of their money market mutual funds, the fund managers had to sell the commercial paper to get cash. In a crisis like this, there were few folks wanting to buy the commercial paper. The Fed stepped up to loan these money market mutual fund managers the money they needed to meet their investors' withdrawal demands. The program was opened on September 19, 2008 (two days after the Primary Fund "broke the buck"), and was closed on February 1, 2010.

The Federal Reserve System had no losses under any of these programs (and actually generated fees and interest income with them). Program details can be found at the Board of Governors website and in particular at <http://www.federalreserve.gov/monetarypolicy/bst.htm>, accessed December 2010.

363. Sudeep Reddy, "Bernanke Feared a Second Great Depression," *Wall Street Journal*, July 27, 2009.
364. Many agencies and individuals were working long, hard hours to develop sound solutions to the financial debacle, and it is with some regret that time and space considerations do not allow a more in-depth review of their programs and people.
365. FDIC Statistics on Depository Institutions for all Institutions Nationwide, June 30, 2008 and June 30, 2007. The number of bank and thrift loans secured by business properties, described in part as "mom and pop" loans here, is more accurately defined by the FDIC as "number of loans secured by nonfarm nonresidential properties."
366. $2 billion in 1933 is roughly equal to about $33 billion in 2009.
367. Chris Isidore, "Bailout plan rejected—supporters scramble," September 29, 2008, CNNMoney.com, <http://money.cnn.com/2008/09/29/news/economy/bailout/index.htm >, accessed December 2010.
368. Carl Huse and David Herszenhorn, "House Rejects Bailout Package, 228–205; Stocks Plunge," *New York Times*, September 29, 2008, <http://www.nytimes.com/2008/09/30/business/30bailout.html>, accessed December 2010.
369. The amended bill was the Paul Wellstone Mental Health and Addiction Equity Act, which addressed physician referrals to treatment centers where they had a financial interest.
370. The conversion rate of GBP to US dollars at that time was about 1.73 to 1.
371. The nine institutions were represented at the meeting by Ken Lewis of Bank of America, Vikram Pandit of Citigroup, Jamie Dimon of JPMorgan, Richard Kovacevich of Wells Fargo, John Thain of Merrill Lynch, John Mack of Morgan Stanley, Lloyd Blankfein of Goldman Sachs, Robert Kelly of Bank of New York Mellon, and Ronald Logue of State Street Bank.
372. The "CEO Talking Points" document was obtained by Judicial Watch, a conservative

advocacy group, under the Freedom of Information Act and can be found at their website, <http://www.judicialwatch.org/news/2009/may/judicial-watch-forces-release-bank-bailout-documents >, accessed October 2010.

373. Mark Landler and Eric Dash, "Drama Behind a $250 Billion Banking Deal," *New York Times*, October 14, 2008, <http://www.nytimes.com/2008/10/15/business/economy/15bailout.html >, accessed December 2010.

374. "Troubled Asset Relief Program, Monthly 105(a) Report," Department of the U.S. Treasury, October 2009, <http://www.financialstability.gov/docs/105CongressionalReports/October%20105(a)_11.10.2009.pdf >, accessed December 2010.

375. For more information on the value of these warrants, see "TARP Warrants Valuation Methods," by Robert A. Jarrow, September 22, 2009, which can be found at the Treasury's website, < http://www.treasury.gov/initiatives/financial-stability/investment-programs/cpp/Documents/Jarrow%20TARP%20Warrants%20Valuation%20Method.pdf >, accessed March 12, 2011.

376. A copy of this letter can be found at scribd.com, < http://www.scribd.com/doc/14341747/American-Bankers-Association-Letter-to-Treasury-Secretary-Timothy-Geithner>, accessed December 2010.

377. The American Research Group Inc. poll had a margin of error + or – 3 percentage points. The poll results can be found at <http://americanresearchgroup.com/economy>, accessed December 2010.

378. US Department of Labor, Bureau of Labor Statistics. The previous highest unemployment rate was 7.3 percent in January 1993.

379. Joe Adler, "Bair Calls Tarp Capital an Error," *American Banker*, November 16, 2009.

380. Average household income is more technically called Median Household Income. For a comprehensive report, see Carmen DeNavas-Walt, Bernadette D. Proctor, and Jessica Smith, "Income, Poverty, and Health Insurance Coverage in the United States: 2008," U.S. Department of Commerce, September 2009, <http://www.census.gov/prod/2009pubs/p60-236.pdf > accessed December 2010.

381. Michael Daly, "Pin AIG woes on Brooklyn boy: Joseph Cassano walked away with $315 million while company staggered," *NY Daily News*, March 17, 2009, <http://www.nydailynews.com/money/2009/03/17/2009-03-17_pin_aig_woes_on_brooklyn_boy_joseph_cass-1.html>, accessed December 2010.

382. Matt Taibbi, "The Big Takeover," *Rolling Stone*, March 19, 2009.

383. Brian Ross and Tom Shine, "After Bailout, AIG Execs Head to California Resort," ABC News, October 7, 2008, < http://abcnews.go.com/Blotter/story?id=5973452&page=1 >, accessed December 2010.

384. Corky Siemaszko, "AIG executives cancel planned California spa retreat," *NY Daily News*, Oct. 9, 2008, <http://www.nydailynews.com/

money/2008/10/09/2008-10-09_aig_executives_cancel_planned_california.html, accessed December 2010.

385. Linda Shen and Hugh Son, "AIG Retention Bonus Plan Dates From December 2007: Timeline," *Bloomberg News*, March 19, 2009, <http://www.bloomberg.com/apps/news?pid=newsarchive&sid=aklO4CAzLvmc>, accessed December 2010.

386. Summers made those comments in his appearance on *This Week with George Stephanopoulos*, ABC news broadcast, March 19, 2009.

387. Matt Taibbi "AIG Exec Whines about Public Anger, and Now We're Supposed to Pity Him? Yeah, Right," March 27, 2009, whose blog is posted on The Smoking Chimp website, <http://www.smirkingchimp.com/thread/20988>, accessed December 2010.

388. The deductibility of performance-based compensation is addressed under Section 162(m) of the IRS code. This particular "private letter ruling" applied to only one company but caused an uproar because it opened the door to more restrictive interpretations.

389. The "Shareholder Vote on Executive Compensation Act" (HR 1257) passed the House on April 20, 2007, by a 269–134 vote, but it died in the Senate. Other compensation bills under consideration included Senate Bills 1074, 1006, and 3675.

390. The Congressional Budget Office estimates the cost of the bill to be $787 billion over ten years. The act requires an Accountability and Transparency Board to monitor all expenditures under the program, and they have developed a very good website, Recovery.gov, which contains substantial information about the program, and specific details on expenditures throughout the country.

391. The stock provision only applies to the most highly paid employee of an institution that received less than $25 million of TARP funds, to the five most highly paid at an institution that received between $25 million and $250 million, to the senior executive officers and ten most highly paid at an institution that received between $250 million and $500 million, and to the senior executive officers and twenty most highly paid at an institution that received over $500 million.

392. "Pay Czar's Move to Cut Salaries Raises Questions About Limits of Authority," by FOXNews.com, October 22, 2009, <http://www.foxnews.com/politics/2009/10/22/pay-czars-cut-salaries-raises-questions-limits-authority/?loomia_ow=t0:s0:a16:g2:r2:c0.047359:b28469789:z0 >, accessed October 2010.

393. "Testimony of Kenneth R. Feinberg" before the House Committee on Oversight and Government Reform, October 28, 2009, < http://oversight.house.gov/images/stories/TESTIMONY-Feinberg.pdf >, accessed October 2010.

394. Federal Reserve Board press release, October 22, 2009, <http://www.federalreserve.gov/newsevents/press/bcreg/20091022a.htm>, accessed December 2010.

395. Matt Taibbi, "The Great American Bubble Machine," *Rolling Stone* 1082/1083, July 9–23, 2009, 52.

396. Susanne Craig, "Goldman's Soft Sell: Its Warm, Fuzzy Side," *Wall Street Journal*, October 15, 2009, <http://online.wsj.com/article/SB125556536458586219.html>, accessed December 2010.

397. John Arlidge, "I'm doing 'God's work'. Meet Mr Goldman Sachs," *Sunday Times*, London, November 8, 2009, <http://www.timesonline.co.uk/tol/news/world/us_and_americas/article6907681.ece>, accessed December 2010.

398. The Colbert Report, *Comedy Central*, November 11, 2009, <http://www.colbertnation.com/the-colbert-report-videos/255237/november-11-2009/goldman-sachs-does-god-s-work>, accessed December 2010.

399. Ian Katz and Jesse Westbrook, "Mark-to-Market Lobby Buoys Bank Profits 20% as FASB May Say Yes," Bloomberg.com, March 29, 2009. <http://www.bloomberg.com/apps/news?pid=20601109&sid=awSxPMGzDW38&refer=home>, accessed December 2010. The authors attribute the information to Richard Dietrich, Ohio State University accounting professor.

400. "Instant View: U.S. eases mark-to-market accounting," Thomson Reuters news service, April 2, 2009, <http://www.reuters.com/article/newsOne/idUKTRE5314PX20090402?pageNumber=1&virtualBrandChannel=0>, accessed December 2010. See also Kara Scannell, "FASB Eases Mark-to-Market Rules," *Wall Street Journal*, April 3, 2009, <http://online.wsj.com/article/SB123867739560682309.html >, accessed December 2010.

401. The KBX Index is comprised of twenty-four geographically diverse bank stocks.

402. Quotes obtained from "Instant View: U.S. eases mark-to-market accounting," Thomson Reuters news service, April 2, 2009, <http://www.reuters.com/article/newsOne/idUKTRE5314PX20090402?pageNumber=3&virtualBrandChannel=0>, accessed December 2010, except Toby's quote, which was heard firsthand over a cold beer at Alli and Rob's house.

403. Gwen Robinson, "Further reading, all about the Geithner PPIP plan," *Financial Times* blog, March 24, 2009, <http://ftalphaville.ft.com/blog/2009/03/24/53929/further-reading-all-about-the-geithner-ppip-plan/>, accessed October 2010.

404. "FDIC Statement on the Status of the Legacy Loans Program," FDIC press release June 3, 2009, <http://www.fdic.gov/news/news/press/2009/pr09084.html>, accessed December 2010.

405. Daniel Indiviglio, "The Greatest Program That Never Occurred," the *Atlantic*, June 29, 2009, http://www.theatlantic.com/business/archive/2009/06/-the-greatest-program-that-never-occurred/20260/, accessed December 2010.

406. The Keating Five senators were Alan Cranston (D-CA), Dennis DeConcini (D-AZ), John Glenn (D-OH), John McCain (R-AZ), and Donald W. Riegle Jr. (D-MI). These men intervened on behalf of Charles H. Keating Jr., chairman of the Lincoln Savings and Loan Association, a $5.5 billion thrift in Irvine, California, to stop an investigation by the FHLB of San Francisco in 1987. The thrift failed two years later. In 1993, Keating was convicted of seventy-three counts of wire and

bankruptcy fraud, and sentenced to twelve years and seven months in prison. He served fifty months.

407. Bair's quote was from her testimony before the Financial Crisis Inquiry Commission, January 2010. Greenspan's quote was from testimony before the House Committee of Government Oversight and Reform, October 23, 2008. Mack's quote was from a widely reported *Vanity Fair*- and *Bloomberg*- hosted event in New York covering the financial crisis, on November 18, 2009. Cox's quote was from an SEC press release on September 26, 2008, entitled "Statement of Chairman Cox on IG Reports Regarding CSE Program."

408. "Investigation of Failure of the SEC to Uncover Bernard Madoff's Ponzi Scheme—Public Version," U.S. Securities and Exchange Commission, Office of Investigations, August 31, 2009, Report No. OIG-509.

409. "Kozlowski's colors," the *Economist* magazine, January 24, 2002, <http://www.economist.com/businessfinance/displaystory.cfm?story_id=E1_JVPRPG>, accessed December 2010.

410. Matthew Jaffe, "Obama Bank Tax: Wall St. Mulls Court Challenge," ABC News, January 18, 2010, <http://abcnews.go.com/Business/obama-bank-tax-wall-street-banks-mull-legal/story?id=9593507&page=1>, accessed December 2010.

411. The liquidity ratio was defined as cash plus the borrowing value of unencumbered collateral as a percentage of total unsecured debt maturing over the next twelve months.

412. David Reilly, "Bankers Craving Bonuses Fudge Loan-Loss Reality," *Bloomberg News,* August 21, 2009, <http://www.bloomberg.com/apps/news?pid=20601039&sid=a4LNv_COFnzY>, accessed December 2010.

413. Jaime Peters, "Wachovia Corporation Analyst Report," Morningstar.com, Jan. 1, 2008.

414. Nomi Prins, "Worse Than Enron," the *Daily Beast*, December 1, 2009, <http://www.thedailybeast.com/blogs-and-stories/2009-12-01/worse-than-enron/full>, accessed December 2010. Prins is also the author of It Takes a Pillage: Behind the Bonuses, Bailouts, and Backroom Deals from Washington to Wall Street (Wiley, September 2009). Before becoming a journalist, she worked on Wall Street as a managing director at Goldman Sachs and ran the international analytics group at Bear Stearns in London.

415. Nichael McKee and Scott Lanman, "Greenspan Says U.S. Should Consider Breaking Up Large Banks," *Bloomberg News*, October 15, 2009, <http://www.bloomberg.com/apps/news?pid=newsarchive&sid=aJ8HPmNUfchg> accessed February 2011.

416. Information on the Southeast failure was obtained from *Managing the Crisis: The FDIC and RTC Experience 1980–1994*, Federal Deposit Insurance Corporation, Washington, DC, August 1998, Part II, chapter 9, 653–664.

417. *History of the Eighties—Lessons for the Future, Volume 1: An Examination of the*

Banking Crisis of the 1980s and Early 1990s, prepared by the FDIC's Division of Research and Statistics, 1997, <http://www.fdic.gov/bank/historical/history/index.html>, accessed February 2011.

418. FDIC Statistics on Depository Institutions.
419. Leonard Sloan, "Savings Depositors to Be Paid More Interest (and Attention)," *New York Times,* January 11, 1992, 148.
420. Kate Kelly, "Bear CEO's Handling Of Crisis Raises Issues," *Wall Street Journal,* November 1, 2007, A1, <http://online.wsj.com/article/SB119387369474078336.html>, accessed March 12, 2011.

Bibliography

Adams, J. R. *The Big Fix: Inside the S&L Scandal.* New York: John Wiley & Sons Inc., 1990.

Baumol, W. J., and A. S. Blinder. *Economics: Principals and Policy.* New York: Harcourt Brace Jovanovich Inc., 1979.

Bowers, Q. D. *Obsolete Paper Money, Issued by Banks in the United States, 1782–1866.* Atlanta: Whitman Publishing LLC, 2006.

Butkiewicz, J. L. "The Reconstruction Finance Corporation, the Gold Standard and the Banking Panic of 1933." *Southern Economic Journal* 66, no. 2 (1999): 271+.

Burns, H. M. *The American Banking Community and New Deal Banking Reforms 1933–1935.* Westport, CT: Greenwood Press, 1974.

Cox, J. D., R. S. Thomas, and D. Kiku. "SEC Enforcement Heuristics: An Empirical Inquiry. " *Duke Law Journal* 53, no. 2 (2003): 737+.

Dowd, K., ed. *The Experience of Free Banking.* New York: Routledge, 1992.

Ferguson, E. J. *The Power of the Purse: A History of American Public Finance, 1776–1790.* Chapel Hill, NC: University of North Carolina Press, 1961.

Geisst, C. R. *Wall Street: A History.* New York: Oxford University Press, 1999.

Greider, W. *Secrets of the Temple: How the Federal Reserve Runs the Country.* New York: A Touchstone Book, Simon & Schuster Inc., 1989.

Hasan, I., and G. P. Dwyer, G. P. "Bank Runs in the Free Banking Period. " *Journal of Money, Credit & Banking* 26, no. 2 (1994): 271+.

Haupert, M. J. "New York Free Banks and the Role of Reputations." *American Economist* 38, no. 2 (1994): 66+.

Hoffmann, S., and M. Cassell. "What Are the Federal Home Loan Banks Up to? Emerging Views of Purpose among Institutional Leadership." *Public Administration Review* 62, no. 4 (2002): 461+.

Horne, H. O. *A History of Savings Banks.* London: Geoffrey Cumberledge, Oxford University Press, 1947.

Jacobs, B. G. *HDR Handbook of Housing Development Law 2008–2009.* New York: Thomson Reuters/West, 2008.

Kamensky, J. *The Exchange Artist: A Tale of High-Flying Speculation and America's First Banking Collapse.* New York: Viking Penguin, a member of Penguin Group (USA), 2008.

Klein, J. J. *Money and the Economy.* New York: Harcourt Brace Jovanovich Inc., 1978.

Konx, J. J., B. Rhodes and E. H. Youngman. *A History of Banking in the United States.* New York: Bradford Rhodes & Company, 1903.

Lowy, M. *High Rollers: Inside the Savings and Loan Debacle.* New York: Praeger Publishers, 1991.

Lubetkin, M. J. *Jay Coole's Gamble: The Northern Pacific Railroad, the Sioux, and the Panic of 1873.* Norman: University of Oklahoma Press, 2006.

Lynch, G. P. "U.S. Presidential Elections in the Nineteenth Century: Why Culture and the Economy Both Mattered." *Polity* 35, no. 1: 29+.

Mason, D. L. *From Buildings and Loans to Bailouts: A History of the American Savings and Loan Industry 1831–1995.* New York: Cambridge University Press, 2004.

Mihm, S. *A Nation of Counterfeiters: Capitalists, Con Men, and the Making of the United States.* Cambridge, MA: Harvard University Press, 2007.

Myers, M. G. *A Financial History of the United States.* New York: Columbia University Press, 1970.

Payne, P. L. and L. E. Davis. (1956). *The Savings Bank of Baltimore, 1818–1866: A Historical and Analytical Study.* Baltimore: The Johns Hopkins Press.

Roberts, F. D. *The Social Conscience of the Early Victorians.* Stanford, CA: Stanford University Press, 2002.

Roberts, J. M. *History of the World.* New York: Oxford University Press, 1993.

Saunders, A., and M. M. Cornett. *Financial Institutions Management: A Risk Management Approach, 6th ed.* New York: McGraw-Hill Higher Education, a Division of McGraw-Hill Companies, 2008.

Sharp, J. R. *The Jacksonians Versus the Banks: Politics in the States after the Panic of 1837.* New York: Columbia University Press, 1970.

Taylor, G. R., ed. *Jackson Versus Biddle: The Struggle over the Second Bank of the United States.* Boston: D. C. Heath, 1949.

Tett, G. *Fool's Gold: How the Bolod Dream of a Small Tribe at J.P. Morgan was Corrupted by Greed and Unleased a Catastrophe.* New York: Free Press, a Division of Simon & Schuster Inc., 2009.

Tucker, D. M. *The Decline of Thrift in America: Our Cultural Shift from Saving to Spending.* New York: Praeger Publishers, 1991.

Velde, F. R. "Following the Yellow Brick Road: How the United States Adopted the Gold Standard." *Economic Perspectives* 26, no. 2 (2002): 42+.

Whalen, C. "New House Rules: How the Feds Are Seeking to Make the World Safe for Derivatives." *The International Economy* 18 (Summer 2004): 54+.

Whalen, C. "The Cox Revolution: How the Former U.S. Lawmaker Is Changing the SEC." *The International Economy* 20 (Winter 2006): 40+.

Woelfel, C. J., G. G. Munn and F. L. Garcia. *Encyclopedia of Banking & Finance, 10th ed.* Chicago: Probus Publishing Company, 1994.

Wright, R. E. *The First Wall Street: Chestnut Street, Philadelphia, & The Birth of American Finance.* Chicago: The University of Chicago Press, 2005.

Index